University of East London

Settler Colonialism
Transformation of Anth

Writing Past Colonialism Series

Series editors: Phillip Darby, Margaret Thornton and Patrick Wolfe, Institute of Postcolonial Studies, Melbourne

The leitmotiv of the series is the idea of difference – differences between cultures and politics, as well as differences in ways of seeing and the sources that can be drawn upon. In this sense, it is postcolonial. Yet the space we hope to open up is one resistant to new orthodoxies, one that allows for alternative and contesting formulations. Though grounded in studies relating to the formerly colonized world, the series seeks to extend contemporary global analyses.

Also published in the series

Phillip Darby, *The Fiction of Imperialism: Reading Between International Relations and Postcolonialism*

SETTLER COLONIALISM AND THE TRANSFORMATION OF ANTHROPOLOGY

The Politics and Poetics of an Ethnographic Event

Patrick Wolfe

CASSELL
London and New York

Cassell

Wellington House, 125 Strand, London WC2R 0BB

370 Lexington Avenue, New York, NY 10017-6550

First published 1999

© Patrick Wolfe 1999

All rights reserved. No part of this publication may be reproduced or transmitted in any form or by any means, electronic or mechanical, including photocopying, recording or any information storage or retrieval system, without permission in writing from the publishers.

British Library Cataloguing-in-Publication Data

A catalogue record for this book is available from the British Library.

ISBN   0-304-70339-7 Hardback
       0-304-70340-0 Paperback

Typeset by Ben Cracknell Studios

Printed and bound in Great Britain by Biddles Ltd, Guildford and King's Lynn

Contents

	Illustrations	vi
	Acknowledgements	vii
	Credits	viii
	Note on Terminology	ix
INTRODUCTION	**Text and Context** ANTHROPOLOGY AND SETTLER COLONIALISM	1
CHAPTER 1	**White Man's Flour** VIRGIN BIRTH IN ANTHROPOLOGY AND IN AUSTRALIAN SETTLER DISCOURSE	9
CHAPTER 2	**Science, Colonialism and Anthropology** THE LOGIC OF A GLOBAL TRANSFORMATION	43
CHAPTER 3	**Mother-Right** SEX AND PROPERTY IN VICTORIAN ANTHROPOLOGY	69
CHAPTER 4	**Totemism Yesterday, Today and Tomorrow** VICTORIAN ANTHROPOLOGY'S ETERNAL DICHOTOMY	106
CHAPTER 5	**Survival in a Paradigm Shift** E.B. TYLOR AND THE PROBLEM OF THE TEXT	129
CHAPTER 6	**Repressive Authenticity**	163
	References	215
	Index	242

Illustrations

Figure 1　From Spencer and Gillen's *The Native Tribes of Central Australia* (1899)

Figure 2　From Carl Strehlow's *Die Aranda- und Loritja- Stämme in Zentral-Australien* (1907) and from Spencer and Gillen's *Across Australia* (1912)

Figure 3　From Radcliffe-Browne's 'The Social Organization of Australian Tribes'

Figure 4　Artist Unknown, *The Dangers of the Palmer – A Native Attack*. From *The Illustrated Sydney News*, 22 July 1876

Figure 5　W. H. Fernyhough, *Natives of New South Wales Drinking 'Bull'*, and Charles Rodius, *Scene in the Streets of Sydney*

Figure 6　Eugène von Guerard, *Natives Chasing Game* (1854)

Figure 7　Two-Dollar Coin

Figure 8　From A. O. Neville's *Australia's Coloured Minority* (1947)

Acknowledgements

Linda Williams combined intellectual scepticism with emotional encouragement in a way that somehow cohered. Thank you, Linda.

Substantial portions of this book originated as a PhD thesis which, even allowing for distractions such as employment and parenting, I took far too long to write. At different times and in different places, I had three supervisors, Maurice Bloch, Greg Dening and Dipesh Chakrabarty. I would have been lucky to have had any one. Thank you all. Dipesh, the last in line, read and commented on the whole draft. Thanks again, *bandhuji*.

Significant other readers at that stage were my two examiners, Talal Asad and George W. Stocking, Jr. Both were as gracious as they were acute. Had they been less gracious, I would probably be driving taxis. Had they been less acute, I might have published the PhD rather than written a book – which is to say, I might have taken a less direct route to taxi-driving. Despite illness and overwork, George Stocking has stayed in touch, encouraging, advising and inspiring. I lack the words to do any sort of justice to such a debt, but I shall never forget and I shall always try to follow the example.

Once I had finally rewritten it as a book, I gained further from the insightful and learned response of Cassell's anonymous reviewer. At an even later stage, my friends and colleagues Phillip Darby and Michele Grossman read the whole and said hard things in a soft way.

Different parts have benefited from the comments of Jeremy Beckett, Tony Birch, Gary Foley, Richard Handler, John Hutnyk, Roger Just, Roni Linser, Stuart Macintyre, Peter McPhee, John Morton, Michael Muetzelfeldt, Peter Pels, Tim Rowse, Deborah Bird Rose, Lynette Russell, Oscar Salemink, Julie Stephens and Mary Wolfe. Thanks to each of you.

I would also like to thank Mike Wolfe, who vacated his study to let me write Chapter 6.

An Australian Research Council Postdoctoral Fellowship, which I held in the History Department at the University of Melbourne, provided the time, resources and collegial good times that I needed to write this book.

Throughout the process of publication, Janet Joyce at Cassell Academic has been the kind of editor you hope for.

Credits

An earlier version of Chapter 1 was previously published as '"White Man's Flour": Doctrines of Virgin Birth in Evolutionist Ethnogenetics and Australian State-Formation', *History and Anthropology*, vol. 8, nos. 1–4, 1994: 165–205.

An earlier version of Chapter 6 was previously published as 'Nation and MiscegeNation: Discursive Continuity in the Post-Mabo Era', *Social Analysis*, no. 36, 1994: 93–152.

The opening paragraphs of the Introduction are similar to the opening to 'Should the Subaltern Dream? "Australian Aborigines" and the Problem of Ethnographic Ventriloquism', in S. C. Humphreys (ed.), *Cultures of Scholarship* (Michigan University Press/*Comparative Studies in Society and History*, 1997: 57–96), pp. 57–60.

Permission to republish is gratefully acknowledged.

I would like to thank the Royal Australian Mint for permission to print an image of the two-dollar coin (Figure 7) and for generously supplying me with the transparency.

I am also grateful to the National Library of Australia, Rex Nan Kivell Collection, for permission to reproduce Figure 5 (Rodius) and Figure 6 and to the Mitchell Library, State Library of New South Wales, for permission to reproduce Figure 4 and Figure 5 (Fernyhough).

Note on Terminology

This book's object of analysis is anthropological discourse. Accordingly, 'Aborigines', 'aborigines', 'Arunta', 'Aranda', 'savage', 'native', 'Black', 'black', 'blackfellow', 'Australian', etc., are figures of discourse, here reproduced as they appear in the primary textual data. I generally spell and capitalize these terms in accordance with the usage of the text or the author(s) under discussion. To avoid offence, however – and bearing in mind that others can legitimately quote from what follows without reference to this note – I use a capital 'A' for Aborigine/Aboriginal except in the case of direct quotations. Where I intend reference to indigenous people in Australia themselves rather than to others' representations about them, I use the term Indigenous.

Since the terms 'Arunta' and 'Aranda' recur throughout the book, it should be noted that the descendants of Spencer and Gillen's original informants are the Arrernte people of central Australia.

*For Margaret and Edward Wolfe
of Harrogate, Yorkshire
My Mother and Father*

INTRODUCTION

Text and Context

ANTHROPOLOGY AND SETTLER COLONIALISM

This book is a history not so much of anthropology itself as of its ideological entanglements. It charts historically shifting ways in which an evolving tradition of metropolitan anthropology was turned to local ends at different stages in the development of Australian settler colonialism. The specificity is important. For all the homage paid to heterogeneity and difference, the bulk of 'post'-colonial theorizing is disabled by an oddly monolithic, and surprisingly unexamined, notion of colonialism. This would seem to spring from two distinct sources. The first is a pervasive Eurocentrism – or, as we might better term it, Occidocentrism – on the part of academic theorists, for whom colonialism figures, narcissistically, as a projection (the Western will to power, etc.). The second consists in the historical accident (or is it?) that the native founders of the postcolonial canon came from franchise or dependent – as opposed to settler or creole – colonies. This gave these guerrilla theoreticians the advantage of speaking to an oppressed majority on the supply of whose labour a colonizing minority was vulnerably dependent. For Amil Cabral (1973: 40), for instance, genocide of the natives could only be counterproductive, creating 'a void which empties foreign domination of its content and its object: the dominated people'. Analogously, (in this regard at least), when Frantz Fanon asserted (1967: 47) that 'colonization and decolonization are simply a question of relative strength', he was referring to relative capacities for violence, on which basis the colonizer was ultimately superfluous. Given certain African contexts, especially in the 1960s, the material grounds for such optimism can reasonably be credited. But what if the colonizers are not dependent on native labour? – indeed, what if the natives themselves have been reduced to a small minority whose survival can hardly be seen to furnish the colonizing society with more than a remission from ideological embarrassment?

In contrast to the kind of colonial formation that Cabral or Fanon confronted, settler colonies were not primarily established to extract surplus value from indigenous labour.[1] Rather, they are premised on displacing indigenes from (or *re*placing them on) the land; as Deborah Bird Rose points out (1991: 46), to get in the way all the native has to do is stay at home. The relationship between Native and African Americans illustrates the distinction particularly well. In the main, Native (North) Americans were cleared from their land rather than exploited for their labour, their place being taken by

---

1 Since the situation of Indigenous people is the operative factor, this classification cuts across Richard Pares' cogent (1961: 56) distinction between 'colonies of exploitation' and 'colonies of settlement'.

displaced Africans who provided the labour to be mixed with the expropriated land, their own homelands having yet to become objects of colonial desire. The ramifications of this distinction flow through, particularly in so far as they affect the different constructions of 'miscegenation' that have been applied to the two communities. Briefly, whilst the one-drop rule has meant that the category 'black' can withstand unlimited admixture,[2] the category 'red' has been highly vulnerable to dilution. This is consistent with a situation in which, whilst black labour was commodified (so that white plantation owners fathered black children), red labour was not even acknowledged (so that white fathers generated so-called 'half-breeds' whose indigeneity was compromised). In Australia the structural counterparts to African slaves were white convicts, which has meant that racial coding and questions of emancipation have operated quite differently between the two countries. Where the respective Indigenous populations have been concerned, however, there are substantial similarities between the racial calculations on which official policies have been premised.[3]

In the Indigenous case, it is difficult to speak of an articulation between colonizer and native since the determinate articulation is not to a society but directly to the land, a precondition of social organization. Since it is incoherent to talk of an articulation between humans and things, this social relationship can be conceived of as a negative articulation. Settler colonies were (are) premised on the elimination of native societies. The split tensing reflects a determinate feature of settler colonization. The colonizers come to stay – invasion is a structure not an event. In contrast, for all the hollow formality of decolonization, at least the legislators generally change colour. Such distinctions ramify throughout the different colonial formations concerned.[4] They are particularly apparent at the level of ideology – the romance of extinction, for instance (the dying race, the last of his tribe, etc.), encodes a settler-colonial imperative that would be confounded by the hyperfecundity, natural sense of rhythm, etc. that are typically attributed to slave races.

If we are to take the heterogeneity of different colonial formations seriously, we cannot use morphological generalizations such as 'the level of ideology' without qualification. Since any given colonial formation at any given time constitutes a specific configuration of elements and relations, we should expect that distinctions as to the workings of different ideologies will not be confined to their representational contents. Rather, the mechanics, location and relative efficacy of ideology itself – regardless of its specific contents – will vary between different colonial formations whose 'levels' will not necessarily be commensurable.[5] In this respect, settler colonies' relative immunity to the withdrawal of native labour is highly significant. As noted,

2 The most comprehensive and systematic account of the one-drop rule is Davis (1991). See also Dominguez (1994), Haney Lopez (1996), Higginbotham (1978), Williamson (1984), Wright (1994). Charles Mangum's classic (1940) account remains instructive.

3 For official classifications of Native Americans, see Jaimes 1992, Forbes 1988, Native American Consultants Inc. 1980. For a remarkable example of the contingencies of such classifications in juridico-bureaucratic practice, see Clifford 1988: 277–346, cf. Torres and Milun 1990. For Australia, see Chapter 6 below. For official constructions of Aboriginality more generally, see Chesterman and Galligan 1997: 84–120, Clarke and Galligan 1995, Beckett 1988.

4 A notable exception to the general tendency is Thomas 1994, which stresses and exemplifies the heterogeneity of colonialism.

this immunity contrasts sharply with the master–slave structuring of Fanon's schema, in which the colonist 'owes the fact of his very existence, that is to say his property, to the colonial system' (1967: 28). In the settler-colonial economy, it is not the colonist but the native who is superfluous. This means that the sanctions practically available to the native are ideological ones. In settler-colonial formations, in other words, ideology has a higher systemic weighting – it looms larger, as it were – than in other colonial formations. In the most extreme cases, this means that for the native ideology is all there is: the zero-sum conflict with the settler is constituted at the level of ideology and is waged around the issue of assimilation.

Where survival is a matter of not being assimilated, positionality is not just central to the issue – it *is* the issue. In a settler-colonial context, the question of who speaks goes far beyond liberal concerns with equity, dialogue or access to the academy. Claims to authority over indigenous discourse made from within the settler-colonial academy necessarily participate in the continuing usurpation of indigenous space (invasion is a structure not an event). This theoretical conclusion is abundantly borne out by the Australian academy's deep involvement in successive modalities of settler-colonial discourse. Whether by accident or design, whether by measuring, quantifying, pathologizing, expunging or essentializing, a comprehensive range of authorities – anthropologists in particular, but also historians, biologists, archaeologists, psychologists, criminologists, the whole Foucauldian line-up – have produced an incessant flow of knowledge about Aborigines that has become available for selective appropriation to warrant, to rationalize and to authenticate official definitions, policies and programmes for dealing with 'the Aboriginal problem'.

In tracing anthropology's ideological entanglements, I am concerned with the discipline's public impact rather than with the private contingencies (the unpublished letters, etc.) that participated in its production. My tribe is the anthropologists. I am trying to explore some of the cultural relations of anthropological practice, especially in so far as they continue to affect the present. Since this means that (*pace* George Stocking) I am doing Whig history, I should explain that, rather than reordering the past in the light of the present, I am hoping to do the reverse – to trace the genealogies of certain classic anthropological narratives whose ideological half-lives continue into the present. My ultimate concern is with the present as it selects out of the past.

Anthropology is analysed here, in a manner adapted from Marcel Mauss, as a total discursive practice: in this case one that encodes and reproduces the hegemonic process of colonial settlement.[6] Anthropological debates are, therefore, my primary data rather than a means to a shared end. I neither attempt to answer the questions that anthropologists have asked themselves nor arbitrate in their disputes, since to do so would be to analyse Indigenous, as opposed to anthropological, discourse – a practice which, as will become

---

5 '[T]here *cannot* be a general theory of ideology, a theory which will specify the universal preconditions, significances and effects of discourse' (Asad 1979: 620).

6 'In these *total* social phenomena, as we propose to call them, all kinds of institutions find simultaneous expression: religious, legal, moral, and economic. In addition, the phenomena have their aesthetic aspect and they reveal morphological types' (Mauss 1925 [1970]:1).

clear, is inescapably invasive in the Australian context, a context in which there can be no innocent discourses on Aboriginality. The object of analysis is an anthropological construct and not any presumptive Indigenous precedent. Indigenous discourses only intrude into the analysis when they submit to anthropological language, at which point they acquire significance in relation to oppositions and associations that have developed within the colonizing culture. As we follow these associations through, anthropology begins to emerge as a kind of soliloquy – as Western discourse talking to itself. This is not to suggest that there was no dialogue, that nothing transpired between natives and anthropologists in the field. That would be absurd. The point is that there is little if any evidence of these dialogues having had any impact on anthropological theory. Not only are they insufficient to account for the theory's development but, even as a partial explanation, they are redundant. Anthropology's distinctive theoretical features are already overdetermined by its own internal conversation.[7]

Hence there are both political and methodological reasons for stressing that the object of analysis is an anthropological construction. Moreover, the two converge. Any attempt on my part to recuperate a pristine Indigenous trace from behind the surface of the anthropological text – any slippage, as Gayatri Spivak (1988: 288) put it, 'from rendering visible the mechanism to rendering vocal the individual' – would not only be invasive. It would also be empirically self-defeating – the soliloquy is self-sufficient and endlessly recursive; interrogating it only leads to more of the same. Thus the insistence on discourse analysis is not merely some moral or political scruple that can be distinguished from scholarly investigation. Whilst it may be such a thing, it is also a necessary outcome of methodological rigour.

In preference to ventriloquizing the native, then, this book seeks to unpick the fabric of anthropological theory. Thus texts – more specifically, the propositional structuring of anthropological arguments – are central. This is not to divorce the analysis from the realms of the practical, the historical or the socioeconomic. On the contrary, the opposition between the discursive and the practical – including such variants as the ideal versus the material, the cultural versus the instrumental and so on – is a false one. Representations dialectically inform the understandings that permeate practical activity, and vice versa. In the wake of Clifford and Marcus' (1986) *Writing Culture*, a distinctive mode of analysis has become so caught up in (con)textual pragmatics that it seems to forget that anthropological practice is substantially determined by the fact that anthropologists think, write and represent through and against theoretical formations that have specific propositional genealogies. To say this is not to lapse into the reactionary mysticism that sees texts as immaculately conceived. It is rather to insist on the centrality of logical and epistemological considerations to the practical historical conditions that inform the conduct of anthropology. Whilst observing the observers in the field, we should not lose sight of them in the library.

---

7 This is quite apart from the fact that such dialogue as did take place was hopelessly imbalanced – that, as Marx might have put it, the natives had their own points of view but not under conditions of their own choosing.

The development of anthropological theory was conditioned by a range of factors, some external and some (assuming the appropriate caveats) 'internal' – i.e. that arose from necessities that were axiomatic to individual theories. In some instances, the contorted logic of colonialism can be tracked through the minutiae of individual texts, where authors grapple to contain the contradictions that it generates. To the extent that such texts are influential, they ground, authorize and culturally reproduce the logic in question. The external determination of anthropological theory has, however, been well and truly treated by others. Moreover, stressing external influences at the expense of the logical pressures that gave theories their particular characteristics conduces to the sterile notion that anthropological texts were inert reflectors or vehicles of the ideologies of their day. Rather than this, anthropology is treated here as integrally and inseparably participating in the production, maintenance and transformation of its context. Text *is* context – at once both produced by and productive of the whole social world. Hence I would reverse Dominick La Capra's (1983: 95) 'The context itself is a text of sorts'. Rather than reducing history to textuality, we should be restoring the historical dynamism to texts that prompt human activity. Text is characteristically a context, and not merely 'of sorts'.[8]

The quest for factors that originated in the internal dynamics of anthropological theory-construction but fed out into the wider world of colonial power-relations takes us to the logical and epistemological properties of particular theories. Ideological pressures that arose from within the theoretical process are exemplified in the concept of debating-effect, which is explored in the three chapters (3, 4 and 5) that are devoted to close readings of key anthropological texts. Since the focus is logical and strategic (rather than figurative or descriptive), the analysis might be described as a procedural one. It is intended to discern logics that bind together social practices that otherwise appear – or ideologically present as – unrelated.

Though any number of debating-effects might be generated in the production of a given anthropological theory, there is nothing necessary or foreordained about their ideological impact. Nor need theorists' intentions be involved. Ideologies are selected or appropriated, elective affinities crop up, ideas have different lives in different times. Thus we need not detain ourselves with talk of colonial handmaidens or with trying to decide whether particular anthropologists were good guys or bad guys. More often than not, the contexts within which their theories were appropriated into colonial practice were remote from the problems that the theories had been intended to resolve. The significant issue is not, therefore, the moral or political credentials of individual anthropologists but the social effects of the publicizing of their theories. In this connection, the key question is the conditions under which particular theories became suitable for appropriation to political ends. To encompass these conditions, the analysis moves between global institutions and the fine points of anthropological debating, a kind of geopolitics of detail. Here again, the approach is as much indebted to anthropology as critical of it. To a greater extent than any other discipline,

---

8 In this connection, see also Thornton (1983: 513–14).

anthropology has developed techniques for tracking the subtle mediations whereby ostensibly separate social institutions and practices ultimately interact with each other within the all-enveloping ether of culture. It seems unlikely that another discipline could be better equipped to account for the cultural conditions of its own possibility, or to trace through the wider implications and consequences of its own practice.

The wider context of analysis is the heterogeneous phenomenon of colonialism. Within this world-historical framework, we will focus on the selections, intersections and contingencies whereby the global scope of anthropological theory came to be whittled down for local appropriation to Australian settler-colonial ends. The observation that colonial formations promote contextually specific ideologies entails that different modes of anthropology have taken hold in different colonial contexts.[9] This applies both spatially and historically – ideological regimes vary not only between colonial sites but across time within the same site. A complex picture begins to emerge in which, alongside the political and socioeconomic changes that transformed global and local contexts alike from around the turn of the twentieth century, anthropological theory underwent a major paradigm shift, in which evolutionism gave way to a range of relativistic methodologies. As we shall see, this shift occurred partly as a result of the precipitation of contradictions that were internal to the evolutionary paradigm and partly in response to the series of global transformations that were reconstituting modernity as a whole. Thus we will be tracing a shifting and often indirect set of connections between, on the one hand, a developing and substantially autonomous anthropological tradition and, on the other hand, the wider scientific and sociopolitical processes in which this tradition participated at both local and global levels.

Chapter 1 opens with the ethnographic event that serves to organize the analysis as a whole. Spencer and Gillen's assertion that the Arunta of Central Australia were unaware of the physiological cause of conception brought together a wide range of evolutionary-anthropological themes at the same time as it inaugurated what was to become one of the great debates of twentieth-century relativism. On the local level, Spencer was not only an anthropologist but an adviser to the Australian government on Aboriginal affairs, in which capacity he made recommendations that were to have fateful implications for the assimilation policy, under which, for most of the twentieth century, Australian officials sought to break up Indigenous families. The chapter retraces the theoretical genealogy that framed the anthropological discovery and the political genealogy that produced the assimilation policy in order to characterize the mutuality between them. With this mutuality established in a preliminary way, Chapter 2 situates it in the widest of global contexts, emphasizing the changes that independently transformed both Western science and Western imperialism as the nineteenth century gave way to the twentieth, and relating these two sets of changes to the paradigm shift that reordered Western anthropology in the same period. Within this wider context, the following three chapters retrace the fabrication

---

9 Comparably, Bruce Trigger (1984) argues that archaeology is strongly influenced by the position that the society in which it is practised occupies within the capitalist world-system.

of evolutionary-anthropological theory. Chapter 3 reconstructs the theoretical career of the doctrine of mother-right, which, though dominating evolutionary anthropology, was not to survive the paradigm shift. Unsurprisingly, the chapter finds that mother-right owed its hegemony over late nineteenth-century anthropology to the gender politics of the day. Yet it also emerges that this was not all that was going on, since developments in the struggle for women's rights combined with theoretical contradictions that were purely internal to evolutionary anthropology in a way that presaged the collapse of that paradigm. Chapter 4, which traces the theoretical origins of the concept of totemism, plumbs the opposite extreme to Chapter 2. In this chapter, rather than geopolitics, the text is all there is. Totemism emerges as the most internal of anthropological conversations, a pure soliloquy that reveals most clearly how text is also context, with specific effects of its own. Chapter 5 analyses both the academic politics and the logical structure of E.B. Tylor's concept of survivals, an evolutionary byword that was destined to succumb to the paradigm shift. In its failure to persist into twentieth-century anthropology, the concept has much to tell us about the differences between the successive paradigms and their respective engagements with colonized people. In Chapter 6, we return full-circle to Australia, charting the historically shifting ways in which the anthropological constructs whose theoretical production we have been studying came to be selectively incorporated into local settler-colonial discourse.

By the time we return to Australia at the beginning of Chapter 6, anthropology's theoretical development will have emerged as autonomous to the extent that no necessary or foreordained connection can be said to have linked it to Australian politics. None the less, the two have always been crucially linked, to the extent that Australian Aboriginal policies have consistently been informed by anthropological representations of Aboriginal society. Thus the relative independence of the chapters on anthropology from those on Australian history is a function of the contingent relations between the two – their linkage is a product of history rather than of necessity. To make them seem naturally or intrinsically connected would be misleading. In stressing both the theoretical autonomy and the practical interweaving of anthropology and colonialism, what follows is an argument against determinacy and in favour of context and of selection. To that extent, this book itself aspires to a kind of Darwinism.

CHAPTER 1

White Man's Flour

VIRGIN BIRTH IN ANTHROPOLOGY AND IN AUSTRALIAN SETTLER DISCOURSE

Late in 1896, on an Aboriginal ceremonial ground in Central Australia, Spencer and Gillen made an extraordinary discovery. They were observing the last great *Intichiuma* ritual, a swansong to savagery staged for their benefit[10] by the men of the Arunta tribe. In the course of the proceedings, the two ethnographers came across 'the idea firmly held that the child is not the direct result of intercourse, that it may come without this' (Spencer and Gillen 1899: 265).

At that moment – though not for long afterwards – such astounding ignorance was without parallel in the ethnographic record. Bespeaking, as it seemed to, the deepest recesses of prehistory, it rounded off the Arunta's status as the ultimate in living savagery.[11] A century later, however, Spencer and Gillen's ethnographic coup points more to the history of anthropology than to any credible version of prehistory. Thus it was not only the fruit of a well-organized venture into ethnographic fieldwork, but it inaugurated one of the most resilient controversies in twentieth-century anthropology, one that was to constitute something of a shibboleth for proponents of relativism – what, after all, could be more injurious to the alleged universality of causal concepts than heterodoxy in regard to the efficient cause of human life itself? (to which others would respond that the very question was evidence of relativist ethnographers being taken in by their informants' own ideological dogma[12]). From an external perspective, however, both epistemologically and politically, the curious ethnogenetics of Spencer and Gillen's

---

10 Gillen, a Justice of the Peace, had had a local mounted constable named W.H. Willshire arraigned for the murder of a number of Indigenous people. Though Willshire was acquitted by the Adelaide court, he was not reassigned to the Centre, so Gillen's action had effectively terminated his homicidal reign there (Mulvaney 1989: 127–30). As T.G.H. Strehlow (1969: 48–9) takes up the story, 'Gillen's courage was never forgotten by the Aranda; and some years later their gratitude found its expression in the ceremonial festival held at Alice Springs in 1896, where the secret totemic cycle of Imanda was revealed for the first time before the eyes of white men – to Gillen and to his friend, Baldwin Spencer.'

11 As Freud would observe in *Totem and Taboo* (1912: 115), 'People who had not yet discovered that conception is the result of sexual intercourse might surely be regarded as the most backward and primitive of living men'.

12 Some of the more well-known contributions to this controversy include Lévy-Bruhl 1910, Read 1918, Warner 1937: 23–24, Leach 1969, Ashley-Montagu 1937, Spiro 1968, Kaberry 1936; 1968, R. Tonkinson 1978, Barnes 1973, Scheffler 1976, Yengoyan 1978, Malinowski 1916; 1929, Mountford 1981, Delaney 1986. It shows little sign of abating, cf. Hodge and Mishra 1991: 60, Trigger 1993. For a concise and authoritative account of the debate, see Hiatt 1996: 120–41, though the paragraph on pp. 140–41 is probably best passed over in silence.

Arunta pointed as much to anthropology's evolutionist past as it did to its relativist future. In Hegelian terms, as we shall see, it represents an ingestion of evolutionist anthropology, a dense summation of the historical determinations that had combined to produce the paradigm. Through a reconstruction of its deeper genealogy, therefore, we can move towards a relativization of relativism.

This is not merely playing with words, doubling up on the relativist's own game. Rather, through recovering the conditions that produced Spencer and Gillen's announcement as an ethnographic event, we can map out key relationships between anthropological theory and colonial power. These relationships are at once both local and global. By stressing the former at the expense of the latter, relativism has disguised the systematicity of colonial domination – in universalizing particularity, it has hidden its own. To counter this effect, we can return relativism to the geopolitical conditions that have nurtured and sustained it. We can begin this by retrieving what relativism suppresses: the homogeneous, the global, the unitary – which is to say, pre-eminently, the economic.

Relativism has often been criticized for privileging the non-economic, the ideational, the superstructural.[13] This is particularly true of those versions of the literary turn that reduce social processes to a set of textual strategies. These two features of relativism – the particularism and the idealism – converge as commonly obscuring the unified economics of global imperialism. In what follows, therefore, I intend to situate one of relativism's most celebrated examples in this wider context.

For convenience, the allegation that Spencer and Gillen's Arunta did not realize that conception was the result of sexual intercourse will be termed 'nescience'. This term not only reflects *fin de siècle* usage.[14] It also has the advantage of emphasizing how diametrically the Arunta were discursively counterposed to the scientific ideals with which their ethnographers identified. This polarity provides an initial convergence of ethnography and imperialism since it replicates the opposing territorial interests at stake in the context of settler colonialism. Thus we can consider whether or not it was merely coincidental that the one bifurcation should obtain in both the scientific and the geopolitical domains. In this regard, the career of Baldwin Spencer is exemplary since, as well as marking a high point in evolutionist ethnography, Spencer was centrally involved in constructing a policy with which Australian governments sought to eliminate the Aboriginal race.

His and Gillen's ethnographies attained such international renown that, in Australia, Spencer acquired a virtually unrivalled authority on Aboriginal matters. In 1911, after Australia's Northern Territory had been placed under the jurisdiction of the federal government, Spencer was appointed Chief Protector of Aborigines, with a brief to report on the Aboriginal situation in

---

13 The most explicit such critique is probably Maurice Bloch's (1977) 'ritual discourse', although W.E.H. Stanner's (1967) critique of Durkheim is analogous. More recent examples include David Lloyd's (1990) 'aesthetic culture' and Jeremy Beckett's (1988) 'homo religiosus', with which my own *homo superorganicus* (below) is clearly cognate.

14 'The proof of Arunta primitiveness, the only proof, has been their nescience of the facts of generation' (Lang 1905a: 193).

the Territory (Mulvaney and Calaby 1985: 264–304). In his report, Spencer distinguished between 'half-castes' and 'quadroons who may be regarded as belonging to the white population'. The procedures that he recommended for dealing with 'half-castes' were simple but effective:

> No half-caste children should be allowed to remain in any native camp, but they should all be withdrawn and placed on stations. So far as is practicable, this plan is now being adopted. In some cases, when the child is very young, it must of necessity be accompanied by its mother, but in other cases, even though it may seem cruel to separate the mother and child, it is better to do so, when the mother is living, as is usually the case, in a native camp. (Spencer 1913: 21)

Spencer made this recommendation at a time when the abduction of Aboriginal children was becoming central to the state-forming strategy of the fledgling Commonwealth of Australia, a national amalgam of previously distinct colonies that had only been constituted in 1901. Such abductions, which were carried out until the late 1960s, were a key element in what came to be known as the assimilation policy. This policy, which, as will be seen, was standardized for all the states of mainland Australia in 1937, sought to eliminate Aborigines through the eugenic expedient of 'breeding them white'.

As it relates to Baldwin Spencer, therefore, the question of the relationship between ethnography and imperialism becomes the question of whether it was merely by chance that the same man should have come to promulgate both nescience and the assimilation policy. I contend that the coincidence was neither random nor particular to Spencer. Rather, it was symptomatic of a determinate logic that was common to the ostensibly separate projects of ethnography and ethnocide.[15] To substantiate this, I shall first establish the two genealogies involved – an epistemological series running through evolutionary anthropology and a politico-economic series involving the establishment and consolidation of Australian settler-colonization – and then show that nescience precipitated the cultural logic that bound these two genealogies together. This cultural logic rendered ethnography organic to the settler-colonial project in a manner at once more subtle and more thoroughgoing than can be expressed by 'handmaiden of colonialism'-style analyses in which anthropology figures as inertly determined by colonizing imperatives. In the 1990s, there can hardly be any remaining need to demonstrate that evolutionist ethnography, presupposing as it did the extreme inferiority of colonized indigenes, legitimated their oppression. Though undoubtedly true, this is both too obvious and too general to repay proving again. If we remain satisfied with catch-all descriptive congruencies such as 'epistemic violence', we miss the specific connections whereby hegemony is realized in local practice. This can be appreciated once the relevant contexts have been fleshed out. Thus we turn first to the epistemological series, situating nescience in the context of evolutionary-anthropological theory.

---

15 I use this term in this context because, as opposed to genocide, which suggests physical extermination, ethnocide is directed against collective identity, which does not preclude leaving individuals alive (cf. Clastres 1988). See also Orlando Patterson's 'social death', in particular the element of natal alienation (Patterson 1982: 5). For a general discussion of the concept and definitions of genocide (which is Raphael Lemkin's term) see Legters 1988.

The Circumstantial and the Cognitive

Nescience conjoined two originary narratives in evolutionary anthropology – a social-organizational one deriving matrilineal kinship systems from primal promiscuity and a cognitive or ideographic one which attributed beliefs in supernatural impregnation to the doctrine of animism. The former, which came to be known as 'mother-right', was of considerable cultural depth, dating back at least as far as classical antiquity.[16] For our purposes, however, it is sufficient to locate it in John Millar's (1771) *Observations Concerning the Distinction of Ranks in Society*, which, being published as Cook returned to England after his first landing in Australia (at the time New Holland), made no reference to the land or its inhabitants and shows no sign of being influenced by earlier reports or speculations about them. Thus it is safe to take Millar's narrative as a European – or, at least, wholly non-Indigenous – invention. Indeed, as might be gathered from his title, Millar's discussion was directed towards his own society, his purpose being a liberal argument for the emancipation of slaves, women and Scottish miners. Where he could, Millar supplemented his conjectural history of human society with travellers' reports culled from sources ranging from classical antiquity through to his own day. Though contending that society developed out of despotically patriarchal families in which women were chattels without rights, he also noted that Herodotus and other classical writers had suggested an even more barbarous arrangement, which could 'in some countries' have preceded any form of marriage whatsoever:

> To a people in this situation it will appear that children have much more connection with their mother than with their father. If a woman has no notion of attachment and fidelity to any particular person, if notwithstanding her occasional intercourse with different individuals she continues to live by herself, or with her own relations, the child which she has born, and which she maintains under her own inspection, is regarded as a member of her own family, and the father, who lives at a distance, has no opportunity of establishing an authority over it. In short, the same ideas which obtain among us, with regards to bastards, will, in those primitive times, be extended to all, or the greater part of the children produced in the country. (Millar 1771: 30)

In the next century, as a result of the writings of McLennan and Morgan, this scenario of primitive promiscuity precluding the possibility of nominating fathers came to dominate evolutionary anthropology, constituting the central premise behind the theory of mother-right. Moreover, Australian natives were held to be living embodiments of the theory.

Though predicated on amorality and confusion, mother-right acquired its name from a book in which the female principle figured as sublimely virtuous. In his famous and convoluted (1861) treatise on the subject, Johann Jakob Bachofen took issue with Herodotus' dismissal of the Lycian custom of reckoning descent through the mother as an isolated non-Hellenic

---

16 There is much to be said in this regard – though I do not say it here – about Western and Christian discourses on Judaic matrilineality, especially in the context of the campaign for Jewish emancipation, which did not occur in Britain until 1871.

aberration. 'Closer observation', contended Bachofen (1967a: 70), 'must lead to a deeper view. We find not disorder but system. Not fancy but necessity'. *Das Mutterrecht* was devoted to chronicling the historical unfolding of this necessity. The chaste vision that Bachofen detailed was not, however, reflected in the consensus that came to dominate evolutionary anthropology. Rather, for McLennan, Morgan, Lubbock, Wilken and others,[17] 'mother-right' consisted in a matrilineality that resulted from a generalized uncertainty of paternity along precisely the lines suggested by Millar (whom no one acknowledged), which situation was held to be the evolutionary precursor to a patrilineal patriarchy more consistently termed 'father-right'.

The initial statement of the evolutionary-anthropological version of mother-right came in John Ferguson McLennan's (1865) *Primitive Marriage*. Though McLennan later conceded to Bachofen the distinction of first proposing a stage of descent through women, he maintained that his theory had been conceived independently of Bachofen's, which he deemed a descriptive and inferior account on the grounds that Bachofen had merely seen 'the *fact* that kinship was anciently traced through women only but not why it was the fact' (McLennan 1876: 323). McLennan's own theory explicitly focused on kinship (understood as perceptions of consanguinity) to which the scenario that Millar had envisaged was central:

> The connection between these two things – uncertain paternity and kinship through females only, seems so necessary – that of cause and effect – that we may confidently infer the one where we find the other. (McLennan 1865: 161)

Citing contemporary Welsh and Bedouin marriage rites in which mock captures of the bride were enacted by men of the groom's party, McLennan's theory of the origins of kinship linked marriage with violence with all the system of that catch-phrase of a later anthropology, 'we marry our enemies'. He invented the terms 'endogamy' and 'exogamy' to denote, respectively, in-marrying and out-marrying tribes (McLennan 1865: 48–49), out-marrying operating by virtue of a 'rule which declares the union of persons of the same blood to be incest'. Though according a fundamental role in the origin of society to the avoidance of incest, McLennan's theory is notable for the lengths to which he went to exclude psychological or instinctual motives from the emergence of incest regulations. His developmental engine was a Malthusian one, 'the early struggle for food and security', whereby warring hordes engaged in a constant and ruthless battle for survival against other groups and surrounding nature. It followed from this that, whereas men would have been at a premium, the relative weakness of women would have rendered them unwelcome additions to a horde (or 'stock'), so that female infanticide would have arisen as a general practice.[18] The ensuing shortage of women meant that they had to be captured from outside and shared around. This ecologically-motivated need to obtain women from other

---

17 E.g. Morgan 1866; 1871; 1877, Lubbock 1870; 1885, Wilken 1884; 1921, Tylor 1885; 1889; 1896.

18 In *The Descent of Man*, Darwin (1871: i, 132–5) took up McLennan's theory, approvingly citing infanticide as a mechanism for the selection of human varieties that would be favourable enough to secure humanity's break with the lower primates.

groups formed the basis of McLennan's theory of the development of exogamous tribes:

> If it can be shown, firstly, that exogamous tribes exist or have existed; and secondly, that in rude times the relations of separate tribes are uniformly, or almost uniformly, hostile, we have found a set of circumstances in which men could get wives only by capturing them. (McLennan 1865: 54)

Citing George Grey's journal of exploration, McLennan could confidently assume that Australian savages would be recognized as fitting the bill:

> That the practice of getting wives by capture de facto prevails among the natives of Australia, is a fact familiar to most readers ... The reader may imagine the extent to which, among the myriad hordes of savages, the women are being knocked about, and the men accustomed to associate the acquisition of a wife with acts of violence and rapine. (McLennan 1865: 73; 77–8)

Thus evolutionary anthropology had been capitalizing on the possibilities of ignorance of paternity long before Spencer and Gillen were to record nescience in the 1890s. But there are considerable differences between the ignorance entailed in mother-right and the ignorance that Spencer and Gillen were to allege. In particular, McLennan's untraceable paternity did not involve the cognitive deficiency that was to be inherent in the failure to appreciate the principle of insemination as Spencer and Gillen were to report it. In fact, quite the reverse was the case – as Millar's reference to bastards in his own eighteenth-century Scottish society indicates – the whole point of an uncertainty arising from promiscuity was that it was only too consistent with civilized logic. Indeed, the critical bite of McLennan's theory came precisely from its uncomfortable bearing on the sexual double standard which maintained a thriving Victorian underlife of prostitution and 'illegitimacy' (it was a wise Victorian who knew his own father).[19] At least in so far as the British evolutionists are concerned, the theory of mother-right had immediate links to domestic sexual politics. Gripped by a post-Malthusian obsession with population growth, the British state, notably by means of a series of Contagious Diseases Acts that were introduced in the 1860s, intervened crudely and repeatedly into the sexuality (ostensibly the fertility) of, in the main, working-class women (Harrison and Mort 1980, Jeffreys 1985, Lynd 1945, McHugh 1980, Smith 1971, Weeks 1981). So far as more respectable women were concerned, a long-running battle over women's rights (or lack of them) to hereditary marital property was to result in the landmark Married Women's Property Act of 1882, which curtailed the automatic passing of a daughter's property to her husband on marriage (Holcombe 1983). In cases of divorce, women did not have rights to their children. All in all, it requires little interpretive licence to recognize the distinctive themes of the mother-right narrative – primal promiscuity, uncertain paternity, the subordination of maternal descent, the primacy of patriarchal property, and so on – as refractions of Victorian sexual politics (cf. Coward 1983). In the case of

---

19 As McLennan (1865: 167) put it: 'Savages are unrestrained by any sense of delicacy from a copartnery in sexual enjoyments; and, indeed, in the civilised state, the sin of great cities shows that there are no natural restraints sufficient to hold back man from grosser copartneries.'

mother-right, the motive for ignorance of paternity was, clearly, circumstantial confusion rather than cognitive deficiency.

Yet we cannot simply say that there were two different kinds of nescience: one circumstantial and merely concerned with fathers' identities, the other cognitive and concerned with the principle of insemination itself. This is because, as was to be made explicit by Spencer and Gillen amongst others, the full nescience of the principle of insemination could also result from circumstantial causes. Assuming the kind of sexual chaos that sprang so readily to the repressed Victorian imagination, a chaos in which young girls and old women were alike involved, sexual intercourse would be a constant rather than a variable. As a result, there would be no call to correlate it either with the onset of menstruation or with the menopause – on the basis of the available evidence, sex need have no more to do with conception than had eating or sleeping.

For clarity, therefore, we need to distinguish two kinds of nescience and two kinds of motive, noting that the distinctions are not coterminal. So far as the motives are concerned, the distinction between cognitive and circumstantial seems straightforward enough. The two types of nescience can be distinguished as nescience of agent (paternity uncertain) and nescience of principle (insemination unknown).[20] Nescience of agent, the inability to nominate fathers because of a surfeit of candidates, was exclusively circumstantial. As Shouten, in 1757, seems to have been the first to state in so many words (which later authorities never tired of repeating), 'maternity is a matter of fact; paternity one of inference'. Since nescience of agent was a discourse on immorality, it was taken for granted that Aborigines would be prime exemplars, an expectation that their ethnographers did not disappoint. Thus, as Lorimer Fison, one of the founding fathers of Australian ethnography, famously put it in relation to the Kamilaroi of New South Wales:

> when a woman is married to a thousand miles of husbands, then paternity must be, to say the least of it, somewhat doubtful. (Fison and Howitt 1880: 73)

Though nescience of principle, the failure to link intercourse to impregnation, could spring from the same promiscuous factors as those underlying mother-right, it added a cognitive narrative which was separate from the moral discourse underlying the circumstantial version. This cognitive narrative was Edward Burnett Tylor's theory of animism, which Spencer and Gillen's announcement empirically confirmed.

Tylor, a Quaker and a rationalist, was a prominent advocate of the principle of the psychic unity of mankind.[21] This principle sustained the side of Reform in relation to two recurrent nineteenth-century issues. Despite the 1833 banning of slavery throughout the British empire, the issue of slavery had periodically resurfaced (especially, of course, in the USA) in the controversy between monogenists and polygenists, since different Adams could have generated offspring of an order of difference profound enough to warrant

---

20 Were it not so confusing, the two forms could be more precisely expressed as being nescience of 'principal' and of 'principle' respectively.

21 Given the connotations that attach to the term 'psychic' today, this principle is probably better conceived as 'psychological' or 'cognitive' unity.

separate standards of moral treatment. In this regard, the psychic unity of mankind represented a comprehensive negation of polygenesis (cf. Stocking 1987: 159, 270). Secondly, where the question of progress versus degeneration was concerned, the same principle made it impossible for the whole of mankind to have started out on an equal footing from which an unequal distribution of innate endowment must have caused some races to progress while others fell into decay (Stocking 1987: 161).

In keeping with his emphasis on psychic unity, Tylor was an intellectualist, seeking cognitive explanations for social phenomena. Hence he attributed a whole range of obsolescent customs to a savage mental propensity that he termed 'the association of ideas'. This distinguished his theories from those of McLennan, who, as noted, went to considerable lengths to avoid resorting to psychological or instinctual explanations for social phenomena. To this extent, therefore, the difference between cognitive and circumstantial expresses the difference between Tylor and McLennan. Thus the two forms of nescience encompassed perhaps the deepest anthropological dichotomy of all – that between the concrete mechanics of social organization (the umbilical binding of matrilineal stocks) and the genesis of abstract ideas (spirit conception). Tylor's theory of animism exemplifies his intellectualism. In common with other evolutionary anthropologists, Tylor aspired for his new discipline to solve the great human questions, in particular those concerning the origins of religion and abstract thought. It is important to recognize that this goal was common. For, though McLennan and his successors – in particular, William Robertson Smith (1889) and Emile Durkheim (1912) – attempted to start their explanations from morphological or social-organizational bases, their *explananda* were no less ideational than Tylor's. This meant that critical moments arose in their theories at points where they tried to switch from social morphology to ideational levels of explanation. By contrast, Tylor's problem was to disguise the fact that, though he was offering an account of the genesis of ideas, there was nothing social about it.

To achieve his end, Tylor simply substituted universal for social, attributing abstract concepts to reflections on the experience of dreaming that could theoretically occur to anyone (or, at least, to any savage). He coined the term 'animism' for a theory which, once elaborated in his epochal (1871) *Primitive Culture*, exercised enormous influence on late nineteenth-century thought. For evolutionary anthropologists, metaphysics defined humanity, in that the problem of the origins of human consciousness was conceived as a requirement to account for the way in which people had first come to populate the material world with invisible entities residing in or behind concrete objects. Divinities being abstractions *par excellence*, theology and epistemology coincided around this problem, whose principal props were fetishism and totemism. In this context, Tylor's theory of animism proposed that the idea of a spiritual double connected to bodies or to other physical objects initially arose from the memory of moving about in dreams and trances despite others' reports that one's body had remained still. Herbert

Spencer's (1870a: 537) 'ghost theory', which was also influential, displaced the same idea from sleeping bodies to dead ones. Either way, it was the initial duality that mattered; animism having accounted for the attribution of vitality to one inert body, it could readily be generalized to others. Once conceived, abstract vitalities, whether as invisible spirits residing in things or as the ghosts of dead ancestors, were invested with powers. This was the beginning of religion.

In keeping with the conventional evolutionist conflation of phylogeny and ontogeny, or species and individual developments, Tylor (1871: *i*, 431) dubbed animism a childish doctrine, 'the infant philosophy of mankind', which was no different to the nursery belief that sticks or toys were alive. Twenty years on, this was precisely the basis on which the English solicitor and folklorist Edwin Sydney Hartland commenced his series of investigations into 'the savage philosophy of things', a faithfully Tylorean concept which he described as:

> that infantine state of mind which regards not only our fellow men and women, but all objects animate and inanimate around us, as instinct with a consciousness, a personality akin to our own. (Hartland 1891: 25)

The savage philosophy of things proceeded from three premises: animism, transformationism and witchcraft (understood as the power to cause transformations) (1891: 334–7). Hartland's 1891 book ended with the observation that, if there were a human state more primitive than the savagery whose mental echoes were preserved in fairy tales, then work would have to be done to ascertain it. The questions that such work would raise would be avowedly cognitive, taking the investigator 'across the border of folklore into pure psychology' (1891: 352).

On the basis of the savage philosophy of things, people could enter into transactions with animals and objects in the surrounding world on just the same terms as they could with other humans. This possibility would even extend to marriage, 'wherein one party may be human and the other an animal of a different species, or even a tree or plant' (1891: 27). Since it was possible to marry such an entity, one could also have one for an ancestor. This was Hartland's explanation for totemism, which he understood as the worship of mythic ancestors of material or animal form. A direct offshoot of this construction, appearing two years later, was Hartland's notion of 'substitution', by which he meant the doctrine that a person's vital principle could be extended to an object, so that action on the object would have a corresponding effect upon the person (he instanced [1893: 466] the 'learned chirurgeon' of three centuries earlier anointing and dressing the weapon rather than the wound which it had caused). This version of action at a distance lent itself to the derived idea that, rather than a person's life merely spreading to an object by sympathy or contagion, it might be transferred *in toto* for storage or safe-keeping in the object. From this, two years later, sprang the theory of external souls, or 'life-tokens' (Hartland 1895), which were material entities whose fate was tied to a person's life, as with Dorian Gray's picture or the knife that went rusty when someone died. (There was, of course, an immediate link between these ideas and the bond which, in Frazer's *Golden Bough*, tied the mistletoe in the sacred grove at Nemi to the life of its distractedly vigilant priestly guardian.)

The possibility in animism that interested Hartland was thus the idea of a sharing or exchanging of vitality between people and things. Hence he ascribed (1895: 53–4; 442) the origin of the concept of property to shared identifications. He was interested in exchange since, if a person transferred the whole of their life to an object, it followed that they would actually become transformed into that object. His account of such a belief was pure animism:

> Starting from his personal consciousness, the savage attributes the like consciousness to everything he sees or feels around him. And holding that outward form is by no means of the essence of existence or of individuality, he looks upon the transformation as an ordinary incident, happening to all men at death, happening to many men and other creatures whensoever they will. (Hartland 1895: 441)

The idea that death could furnish a hinge for transformation amplified an equivalence between transformation and transmigration that Hartland had established in a book published the previous year (1894: 226–7). Transmigration, understood as a transformation mediated by death, thus derived from the same elaboration of animism as the life-token. For our purposes, the crucial feature of transmigration is that, since it provides for people's pre-existence, it only involves a short step to pregnancy without procreation (it constitutes, as it were, precreation). Nevertheless, even if individual lives do not need to be started, there still has to be some conduit whereby they transmigrate or transform themselves into the foetus in the womb. This recalls Hartland's understanding of totemism. Transactions between women and non-human entities would furnish the requisite mechanism. This was precisely the form that Hartland's thinking of the previous year had taken.[22]

Correlating stories of transformations, a collection of magical fertility practices and a body of myths involving supernatural births (or births resulting from metaphysical visitations upon women), Hartland had argued (1894: v) that the concept of life that underlay them was a sacramental one (the rhetorical implications for Christianity were overt). Though conceding (1894: 180) that magical practices such as the carrying of fertility dolls, as well as the superstitions justifying them, often augmented rather than replaced natural processes, Hartland had asserted that the parthenogenetic explanation preceded the natural one. He had claimed that myths involving supernatural births were to be found universally distributed, and that, rather than survivals of an era in which the bizarre or bestial unions recounted might actually have been practised, these myths were evidence of an evolutionary stage in which the principle of insemination had not been recognized. In other words, in what must surely count as an ethnographic

---

[22] I have overshot the actual introduction of nescience in order to show how it was integral to the trajectory of Hartland's thinking.

equivalent of the discovery of Pluto, barely two years before Spencer and Gillen were to announce the Arunta's nescience, Hartland had theorized its prehistoric occurrence in the course of a conjectural reconstruction that led from animism to transmigration. The actual 'prophecy' (retrodiction?) came about as follows:

Hartland (1894: 1–3) took the legend of Perseus as his key myth. After an oracle pronounced that he would be killed by the son of his daughter Danae, Acrisius locked her up in a brass tower to ensure her celibacy, a plan which Jupiter frustrated by visiting Danae in a shower of gold, after which she gave birth to Perseus.[23] Hartland's statement of this myth's significance juxtaposes the different themes which it brings together so clearly that one could draw lines through the text to divide them up. Thus our two types of nescience are distinguished, with the first reflecting circumstantial causes and the second implying these as well as an 'attitude of mind'.[24] Furthermore, though this attitude of mind is suggested by antiquarian evidence, Hartland makes an ethnographic reference to native Australians at the very point where he hypothesizes nescience of principle. In this regard, it is, however, noteworthy that mother-right was seen as a surviving trace of a long-superseded nescience, and that he does not suggest that contemporary native Australians might still persist in such ignorance:

> The researches of the last five-and-twenty years have established that among many savage races the father was held to be no relation to his children. Even where he exercised, as among the native Australians, despotic power over his wife and children, the latter were held to be his rather as owner than as begetter; and the ownership of both wife and children passed at his death to his brothers, while at the same time the relationships of the children were reckoned exclusively with their mother's kin. This system of relationships, known scientifically as Mother-right, traces whereof are almost everywhere found, can only have sprung either from a kind of promiscuity wherein the true father could not have been ascertained, or from an imperfect recognition of the great natural fact of fatherhood. Both causes, perhaps, played their part. But at least we may say that the attitude of mind which favours the practices and beliefs we have been discussing is one which would be consistent, and consistent alone, with the imperfect recognition of paternity. And it is unquestionable that the superstitions, once rooted, would be likely to survive long after paternity had become an accepted fact, and tenacious of their existence, would seek new grounds of justification. (Hartland 1894: 180–1)

23 Needless to state, Acrisius' precaution presupposes physiological awareness on his part. The point is the content, rather than the persuasiveness, of Hartland's theory.

24 As in the case of other implications of his theory, the wily McLennan had anticipated the circumstantial possibility of nescience of principle, only he had not developed it: 'blood-ties through fathers could not find a place in a system of kinship, unless circumstances usually allowed of some degree of certainty as to who the father of a child was, or of certainty as to the father's blood. A system of relationship through fathers could only be formed – as we have seen that a system of relationships through mothers would be formed – after a good deal of reflection upon the fact of paternity. And fathers must usually be known before men will think of relationship through fathers – indeed, before the idea of a father could be formed' (1865: 158). For all his perspicacity, though, McLennan could not think beyond *men* thinking of relationship through fathers. Indeed, for all the ingenuity – and it was considerable – that two generations of evolutionists devoted to this issue, not one of them ever entertained the prospect of the polyandrous mothers sharing a secret smile across the inexhaustible throng of unwitting suitors.

Such a restrained formulation may not seem much like prophecy. At this stage, however, it is not prophecy. It only becomes so retrospectively, in the light of Spencer and Gillen's Australian ethnography. The clearest symptom of this process is Hartland's tensing. In 1894, the illustrative allusion to Australia notwithstanding, his savagery is empirically a thing of the past ('the father *was* held to be no relation to his children'). In this regard, it contrasts strikingly with the robustly ethnographic presentism (and, it might be noted, increasingly cognitive emphasis) of his remarks once Spencer and Gillen's verification of his hypothesis had been established as the realization of an anthropological prediction:

> Ignorance of the real cause of birth, it might be thought . . . would not long survive the habitual commerce of men and women and the continual reproduction of the species. It would not, in our stage of civilisation and with our social regulations . . . [but] the savage who has not been thus favoured is still by comparison underdeveloped . . . His attention, not habitually directed to the problems of the universe, is easily tired. His knowledge is severely limited; his range of ideas is small. Credulous as a child, he is put off from the solution of a merely speculative question by a tale which chimes with his previous ideas, though it may transcend his actual experience. Hence many a deduction, many an induction, to us plain and obvious, has been retarded, or never reached at all; he is still a savage. (Hartland 1909: 255; 256)

Between Hartland's two statements, Spencer and Gillen's discovery had transformed his genteel literary speculation into a scientific prediction experimentally confirmed in the ethnographic laboratory. That the initial postulate had been framed in the context of a different milieu is suggested by his having perceived it necessary to paraphrase the concept which was 'known scientifically as Mother-right'. Thus it is revealing to retrace his first steps from letters to science.

Hartland's initial reaction to Spencer and Gillen's confirmation of his suggestion was one of bemusement. In fact, in his review of their 1899 book, which established Arunta nescience as a *cause célèbre*, he made no mention of *The Legend of Perseus*, confining nescience to a few understated remarks manifestly overshadowed by his preceding discussion of bilateral kinship:

> Besides all this we are given to understand [citing the pages] that paternity is not understood. It is distinctly held not to be the direct result of conjugal relations, but, if I rightly apprehend the author's [*sic* – he clearly meant Spencer's] meaning, because some spirit from the Alcheringa ['dream-times'] seizes an opportunity of reincarnation, or is induced by magical practices to seek such an opportunity. (Hartland 1899: 236)

It was not until the following year, in the course of his presidential address to the Folk-Lore Society, that Hartland acknowledged the substantiation of his conjecture. Even here, however, he displayed a distinct hesitance to accept the idea that his suggestion should have met with such literal confirmation:

> Some years ago I ventured to suggest that certain archaic beliefs and practices found almost all over the world were consistent only with, and must have arisen from, imperfect recognition of fatherhood. I hardly expected, however, that a people would be found still existing in that hypothetical condition of ignorance. Yet, if we may trust the evidence before us, it is precisely the condition of the Arunta. They hold the cause of birth to be simply the desire of some Arunta of earlier days to be reincarnated. (Hartland 1900: 65)

In both passages, Hartland seems unsure of Spencer and Gillen's evidence. This is understandable, since their 1899 testimony fell appreciably short of unambiguous clarity. On the same page (Spencer and Gillen 1899: 265) as the statement that children were not the direct result of intercourse, they had suggested that intercourse could prepare the way for spirit children. Hartland even cited this page in relation to a statement by Frazer that the Arunta believed that immaculate conception was the sole cause of human birth, adding the remark 'But it looks as though they "had their suspicions"' (Hartland 1900: 66, n.1.).

As we have seen, though, Hartland was to come round. In so doing, however, he only endorsed a construction that others were putting on the sequence of events. Thus, when Arnold van Gennep (1906b: *LXVII*) chided Andrew Lang for not conceding to Frazer that Arunta nescience was neither isolated nor aberrant, his question was rhetorical: 'Doesn't he know Mr. Sydney Hartland's study of the topic of supernatural births?' Van Gennep's question is central to the development of nescience, since it emphasizes the generality implicit in Hartland's hypothesis. As an evolutionary stage through which all must pass, nescience was unlikely to remain an idiosyncracy of the Arunta, but could be expected to surface wherever there were people whose status was deemed commensurable.

This implication had been anticipated from the very first response that Spencer and Gillen's book had received, from the influential pen of Frazer, who had been in consultation with Spencer through all the stages of its preparation. Unlike Hartland himself, Frazer unhesitatingly proclaimed a direct link between the Arunta and *The Legend of Perseus*. The way in which this link was expressed is illuminating, since it presaged a subsequent chain. For Frazer, the Arunta did not merely exemplify an extraordinary belief; they were 'the first' – a term which not only suggested that Spencer and Gillen had won a race, but assumed that others would follow them in:

> Students of folk-lore have long been familiar with notions of this sort occurring in the stories of the birth of miraculous personages [here he cites *The Legend of Perseus*], but this is the first case on record of a tribe who believe in immaculate conception as the sole cause of the birth of every human being who comes into the world. (Frazer 1899: 649)

The issue is not the accuracy of Frazer's claim (Spencer and Gillen had merely reported that the Arunta believed themselves to be thus conceived) but the pre-existence of a theoretical space which drew Spencer and Gillen's report into its implicational economy. Thus anthropological theory has been discussed before the account of Spencer and Gillen's fieldwork because that is the order which best reflects the empirical chronology. This body of theory was there before Spencer and Gillen. Whilst he was still in England, Spencer had worked with Tylor on the reinstallation of the Pitt Rivers anthropological museum (Mulvaney and Calaby 1985: 59–61). While preparing for his fieldwork, he had been in correspondence with both Tylor and Frazer (Marett and Penniman 1932). In establishing a theoretical context before proceeding to the ethnography, therefore, we are repeating Spencer's own historical experience. More generally, this procedure illuminates the projection onto Aborigines of European fantasies about Europe's own prehistory, fantasies whose origins were demonstrably independent of empirical Indigenous data.

Walter Baldwin Spencer, who had studied anatomy under Maudsley at Oxford (where Tylor had recruited him for the museological work), had gone to Australia to take up the foundation chair in biology at the University of Melbourne. In 1894, the year of *The Legend of Perseus*, he went to Central Australia as the biologist on a scientific expedition financed and led by an Adelaide businessman, William Horn. The expedition's anthropologist was Edward Charles Stirling, professor of medicine at the University of Adelaide and director of the South Australian Museum (Mulvaney 1996). In Alice Springs, which was the end of the overland telegraph line, Spencer met Frank (Francis James) Gillen, postmaster and Sub-Protector of Aborigines, who had local knowledge and established relations with Indigenous people in the area. The ethnographic possibilities offered by the combination of Gillen's local knowledge and Spencer's scientific competence appealed to both men, eventually leading to the publication of their two great works (Spencer and Gillen 1899, 1904). The first of these, *The Native Tribes of Central Australia*, sprang from the *Engwura* ceremonial ground, whilst the second, *The Northern Tribes of Central Australia*, resulted from an expedition which they mounted from Alice Springs up to the Gulf of Carpentaria in 1901–02.[25]

Following nescience through Spencer and Gillen's publications, it is asserted with a steadily growing confidence that strikingly mirrors the development of Hartland's responses to their discovery.

The report of the Horn Expedition, edited by Spencer, appeared in 1896. In the course of Stirling's anthropological contribution, nescience of principle was to all intents and purposes asserted, only by means of some negative phrasing which, whilst unequivocally cognitive, was almost perversely inconclusive. In response to the suggestion that the operation of urethral subincision might be intended as a contraceptive measure, Stirling objected that such an explanation would imply

> a knowledge of physiological processes, which, it appears to me, we are not justified in attributing to people of the mental status of Australians any more than we should attribute circumcision to the knowledge of the hygienic or pathological disadvantage of a long prepuce. (Stirling 1896: 34)

25 For compendious details concerning Spencer and his partnership with Gillen, see Mulvaney and Calaby's (1985) biography.

After the Horn Expedition, Spencer and Gillen's partnership was consolidated in fieldwork undertaken together from 1896 to 1897, which resulted in their classic 1899 book. In this book, the Arunta's nescience was explicitly asserted in the course of their own denial that subincision was an attempt at contraception:

> Time after time we have questioned them on this point, and always received the reply that the child was not the direct result of intercourse, that it may come without this, which merely, as it were, prepares the mother for the reception and birth also of an already-formed spirit child who inhabits one of the local totem centres. Time after time we have questioned them on this point, and always received the reply that the child was not the direct result of intercourse. (Spencer and Gillen 1899: 265)

Early in the new century, Spencer and Gillen mounted the expedition from Arunta country up to the shores of the Gulf of Carpentaria from which, in 1904, their second major ethnography resulted. The 1904 version of nescience was stronger than the previous one on two counts. Firstly, the idea that conception could occur without intercourse even taking place was strengthened by the omission of any suggestion that intercourse might constitute some kind of preparation for childbirth. Secondly, the belief was now alleged of all natives living between Alice Springs and the Gulf of Carpentaria:

> the natives, one and all in these tribes, believe that the child is the direct result of the entrance into the mother of an ancestral spirit individual. They have no idea of procreation as being directly associated with sexual intercourse, and firmly believe that children can be born without this taking place . . . In every one of the tribes dealt with by us there is fundamentally the same belief with regard to conception as we have previously described in connection with the Arunta. Every individual is regarded as the reincarnation of an ancestor. (Spencer and Gillen 1904: 330, 606)

In view of this level of certainty, it is instructive to observe how, in an article published while their 1899 work was still in preparation, nescience had been alleged with much more circumspection. Indeed, following a year after Stirling's Horn Expedition report, Spencer's prose is only marginally more affirmative:

> When a woman conceives it is supposed that it is one of such a group of spirits who goes inside her and thus it naturally follows, granting the premises firmly believed in by the natives, that the totem of the child is determined solely by the spot at which the mother conceived, or, what is the same thing, believes that she conceived, the child. (Spencer and Gillen 1897a: 25)

Like Hartland, therefore, Spencer and Gillen grew in confidence. In Hartland's case, there are all sorts of possible reasons. He may just not have been convinced (the ethnography left plenty of room for doubt); he may not have liked Frazer's appropriation of the topic; or he might have resisted the idea that his antiquarian achievement of penetrating further back in time than history or philology could go might still be emulated by ethnography. Such possibilities do not, however, apply to Spencer and Gillen. Indeed, it is hard to see why an open-and-shut question like nescience should be expressed with differing degrees of equivocation. In this regard, it is difficult to ignore the presence, over in Queensland, of Walter Roth, who had been a co-member with Spencer of Maudsley's Oxford anatomy group (Mulvaney and Caluby 1985: plate 11). As is well known, in 1903 (in other words, a year before Spencer and Gillen's second book), Roth was to allege nescience of principle of the Tully River blacks (Roth 1903, cf. Leach 1969). More intriguingly, however, back in 1897 – the year after Stirling's Horn Expedition report and the year in which Spencer's first circumspect formulation appeared – Roth too had made a statement on the relationship between urethral operations and contraception, one whose not-quite-conclusiveness was, if anything, even more tantalizing than Stirling's:

> In this connection it is interesting to note that even the possibility of taking artificial measures to prevent fertilisation, &c. (I am not speaking of abortion), is apparently beyond their comprehension: thus I have reports from station-managers who assure me that only with great difficulty could their 'boys' be made to understand, if ever they did, the object of spaying cattle. (Roth 1897: 179)

All in all, it is as if Spencer and Gillen were engaged with Roth in a race to fulfil Hartland's prophecy. In their 1899 book, Spencer and Gillen (1899: ix, 265) noted the correspondence between Roth's 1897 data and theirs. Roth's fifth bulletin of 1903 was then somewhat less equivocal about Tully River beliefs than Spencer and Gillen had been about the Arunta's, whereupon their 1904 book presented the strongest statement of all (cf. Spencer and Gillen 1904: 145, n.). It was at this juncture that Hartland himself seems to have given up resisting the prophetic momentum (although in a way which avoided subscription to the Frazer camp), observing of Spencer and Gillen's 1904 book that:

> Its special value is that it supplies in great measure the links which unite the beliefs and practices of the Arunta with those described by Mr. Walter Roth. (Hartland 1904: 474)

But if there was a race, why did Roth (and, for that matter, Stirling) hold back? Why did they not come out and proclaim their discovery of a people who did not connect copulation to pregnancy? Whilst it is, of course, hard to say, it is worth noting that neither Stirling nor Roth, both physiologists by training, would have had any particular call to be aware of Hartland's book until the reaction to Spencer and Gillen's revelations gave it a wider than folkloric significance.[26] Spencer, on the other hand, was in constant contact with Frazer, who was not only well aware of Hartland's conjecture but, like Hartland, was endeavouring to devise a theory that could account for the data of totemism. Frazer had already pinned his hopes on two separate

---

26 Thus an earlier claim about the Arunta (Aranda) escaped such attention, presumably because it was made outside British scientific discourse – in German, in a relatively obscure periodical, by one of the first of the German Lutheran missionaries to the Aranda at Hermannsburg Mission – who reported the Aranda to believe that God gave them children: *'Die Kinder, sagen sie, schenkt Altjira (Gott)'* (Kempe 1883: 53).

theories of totemism, neither of which had worked. Nescience of principle was to provide him with a third and final explanation, 'conceptional totemism', according to which totemism originated spontaneously as an animistic account of pregnancy. The satisfaction that this explanation afforded Frazer (1905: 457–8) was palpable: 'after years of sounding, our plummets seem to touch bottom at last'.

With Spencer and Gillen's Arunta nescience, the displacement from a Eurocentric antiquarianism to (settler-)colonial ethnography was consummated in two major respects. Cognitively, it gave animism an empirical foundation (cf. Stocking 1987: 236–7) which, being independent of dreaming, did not derive its plausibility from individualist introspection. Thus savage ignorance no longer needed to be something that we all shared. As a result (and secondly), the moral implications could also be categorically externalized in a way that had been precluded by the nescience of agent that had sustained mother-right. As a cognitive condition, nescience need no longer be of a piece with Millar's Scottish bastards or the contradictions of Victorian sexual practice. Though potentially continuous with mother-right so far as the circumstantial narrative was concerned, Spencer and Gillen's Arunta nescience of principle actually produced a thoroughgoing cognitive separation.

So far as the epistemological series is concerned, then, it is clear that nescience was anticipated to the point of overdetermination by the antecedent context of evolutionary-anthropological theory.[27] Thus it remains to situate Spencer and Gillen's text in the context of Australian settler-colonization. Here, there is no doubt about the empirical complicity whereby ethnography and politics converged – Spencer was chosen to be Protector of Aborigines and commissioned to prepare his report on account of his ethnographic credentials. On its own, however, this convergence does not explain very much. To appreciate its systemic nature, we need to explore the cultural logic whereby Spencer's combination of the two roles symptomatized rather than brought about their commonality. Thus we turn now to the political series, situating Spencer's text in the context of Australian state-formation.

Nation and MiscegeNation

In its broad context, Australian settler-(or creole-)colonization is part of the Western European project of global colonization that stems from the fifteenth

---

[27] I do not understand why Morphy (1997) should be at such pains to question Spencer's manifest and consistent subscription to evolutionism, especially when it involves him (Morphy) in such palpable inconsistencies. Consider, for instance, the following consecutive sentences: 'Spencer and Gillen have been labelled too easily as evolutionary theorists when evolutionism informed little of their arguments ... [section heading] ... Spencer and Gillen were both strongly influenced by Darwinian evolutionary theory' (Morphy 1997: 30). Morphy's intention is to argue that there is more to Spencer and Gillen's ethnography than evolutionary theory. In particular, their empirical findings impacted significantly on evolutionary theory, whilst their dual role as theorists-cum-fieldworkers anticipated the participant observership of twentieth-century professional anthropology. As this chapter and Chapter 5 should make clear, however, neither of these considerations are inconsistent with Spencer's deep and abiding commitment to evolutionism, a commitment which stands out with particular clarity when his writings of the 1920s are put alongside those of Malinowski and Radcliffe-Brown. Morphy's difficulty would seem to stem from his willingness to take Spencer at his own word in preference to analysing his texts in depth, a preference that appears to be at odds with Morphy's approach to Aboriginal utterances.

century. Thus it is consistent that the first detachment of British invaders, made up of convicts and their custodians under the command of Captain Arthur Phillip, should have been commissioned in the wake of the American colonies' attainment of independence from Britain, a development which, amongst other things, closed off an outlet for convict shipment. When the First Fleet first set foot on Gamaraigal land, on 26 January 1788, their enterprise was already horizoned with precedents, conventions and expectations. Moreover, the new land was by no means completely new, having already been mapped and named by Cook and Banks, whose reports had suggested New Holland (*Terra Australis*, The Great South Land or the Antipodes to earlier navigators and speculators) as a suitable place for settlement (Carter 1987, Frost 1990). Though instructed to engage in friendly commerce with the natives, Phillips' party very soon resorted to shooting them (Stanner 1977), establishing a pattern that was to be repeated across the face of the continent over the next century and a half. For, regardless of instructions to the contrary, the invaders entertained few practical doubts as to their entitlement to settle the land, an entitlement whereby indigenous self-defence was itself seen as invasion.

Phillips' instructions (and, for that matter, the Mabo judgement[28]) notwithstanding, Australian settler-colonization was phrased in terms of the doctrine of *terra nullius* rather than of any acknowledgement of native title. As it had been elaborated by eighteenth-century European jurists such as Wolff, Vattel, Pufendorf and Blackstone, land had to become property for rights of ownership to apply to it. Property entailed a twofold criterion, one material or technical and the other political or regulative. In the first instance, the land should have been improved – which is to say, rendered a more efficient provider of human subsistence than the natural state – through labour being mixed with it. Practically, this meant that the land should have been cultivated, irrigated, built on and enclosed. Secondly, a system of legitimate sanctions had to operate whereby those who had improved the land should have the right to unfettered enjoyment of the fruits of their labour – or, in other words, to private property in it. Practically, this meant centralized governance, formal laws, policing and, again, enclosure (or acknowledged boundaries). Unless these two criteria were met, the inhabitants were not a society but legally transparent entities, so that, for ownership purposes, the land was no one's (a bourgeois elaboration of the Roman *vacuum domicilium*). A third, pragmatic criterion, which was generally derived from the first two, reflected the growth of urbanizing Europe's concern over population densities. It held that, if an area was being so inefficiently used that it was only supporting a fraction of the population that it otherwise might, then more efficient societies were entitled to export their surplus population to realize its potential (the convicts being a paradigm case).[29]

Though ostensibly codifying indigenous rights (or the absence of them), *terra nullius* was primarily a systematization of the mutual rights and obligations of rival European powers. It specified the conditions under which

---

28 In this judgment, in 1992, the Australian High Court negated the doctrine of *terra nullius*.

one such power could lay claim to a foreign territory as against all the others. Its obvious relation to bourgeois society is confirmed by the fact that it only began to take hold from the seventeenth century on, displacing the earlier formula for laying claim to a colony, which (asserted for longest by feudal and Catholic Spain) had been based on the Pope's authority over islands (Frost 1990: 65).

As progressively encoded into Australian law,[30] *terra nullius* was, of course, a rationalization rather than a motive for colonial invasion. The motive was greed – specifically, greed for land. The specification is necessary because it expresses the particular nature of settler-colonialism. As observed in the introduction, settler-colonialism consists in a negative articulation between invaders and the land.[31] The cultural logic which is organic to a negative articulation is one of elimination. In its purest form, as in the case of the Guanches (indigenous Canary Islanders), Tainos, Caribs, etc., the logic of elimination strives to replace indigenous society with that imported by the colonizers. In local Australian practice, this cultural logic was actualized by virtue of the fact that the economic use to which the colonized land was principally turned was that of pastoral settlement, whose requirement for territory was inherently exclusive. This is because the introduced cattle and sheep competed with indigenous fauna for subsistence, consuming the tubers, shoots and seeds whereby the indigenous fauna reproduced itself and rapidly reducing waterholes to mud. In a relatively short time, little subsistence remained available to Indigenous humans apart from the introduced fauna whose protection was basic to the pastoral project (McGrath 1987: 1–23, Reynolds 1981: 128–30). Hence pastoral settlement became a zero-sum conflict. Thus the pattern of violence established by the First Fleet was neither gratuitous nor random but systemic to settler-colonization.

Since frontiers moved across Australia from coastal beachheads variously established over the century following the landing of the First Fleet, it is not possible to date the development of Australian settler-colonization as a whole. Thus it is convenient to organize its establishment and consolidation into a typology of phases, a heuristic which is enabled by the consistency of the general pattern.[32] The initial phase, in which the land was first seized, is principally characterized by indigenous mortality, attributable to four main (and mutually supportive) agencies – homicide, sexual abuse, disease and

29 For analyses and discussions of the primary formulations of *terra nullius* (Blackstone 1783, Vattel 1758, Wolff 1764, Grotius 1609; 1625, Locke 1690, Pufendorf 1688) see, e.g. Frost 1990, Hulme 1990, Reynolds 1992.

30 As the British Privy Council declared in the case of Cooper v. Stuart (1889.14. Appeal Cases, 286), 'There is a great difference between the case of a colony acquired by conquest or cession, in which case there is an established system of law, and that of a colony which consisted of a tract of territory practically unoccupied, without settled inhabitants or settled law, at the time it was peacefully annexed to the British dominions. The colony of New South Wales belongs to the latter class.'

31 A significance of the negative articulation is that, since it provides for the elimination of Indigenous groups, Indigenous/invader relations cannot be specified in terms of class (cf. Hartwig 1972), i.e., in terms of groups' respective relations to the means of production. This is because, in the rigorous sense in which such relations are specified, Indigenous groups are outside the mode (forces plus relations) of production (which is to say, ideally they do not exist). This is not to say that class relations do not empirically occur (since some Indigenous people survived the initial invasions, their labour naturally became exploitable). It is rather the case that, in a strict analytical/definitional sense (i.e. in terms of the settler-colonial social formation), settler exploitation of indigenous labour represents a contradiction, rather than an inherent component, of the system.

starvation.[33] Though conditioned by ecological factors, this phase was very short. As the settler, anthropologist and Victorian government official Edward Curr put it,

> In the first place the meeting of the Aboriginal tribes of Australia and the White pioneer, results as a rule in war, which lasts from six months to ten years, according to the nature of the country, the amount of settlement which takes place in a neighbourhood, and the proclivities of the individuals concerned. When several squatters settle in proximity, and the country they occupy is easy of access and without fastnesses to which the Blacks can retreat, the period of warfare is usually short and the bloodshed not excessive. On the other hand, in districts which are not easily traversed on horseback, in which the Whites are few in number and food is procurable by the Blacks in fastnesses, the term is usually prolonged and the slaughter more considerable . . .
>
> The tribe, being threatened with war by the White stranger, if it attempts to get food in its own country, and with the same consequences if it intrudes on the lands of a neighbouring tribe, finds itself reduced to make choice of certain death from starvation and probable death from the rifle, and naturally chooses the latter. (Curr 1886: 100–101; 103–4)

In addition to the differences in firepower, Indigenous resistance to settler-colonization, though universally offered (Broome 1982, Lippmann 1981, McGrath 1995, Miller 1985, Morris 1989, Read 1988, Reynolds 1981), was hampered by a number of factors. Chief among these were the ravages of introduced diseases – smallpox, syphilis, typhoid, whooping cough, diphtheria, tuberculosis, dysentery, influenza and the rest – against which they had not developed immunities (Butlin 1983, Campbell 1983: 198, cf. Crosby 1986); the activities of native police or troopers recruited and armed by settler authorities to put down their tribal enemies (Rosser 1991, cf. Fels 1988); and other intranecine conflicts resulting from refugee crises occasioned by the invasion (Rowley 1978: 36–7).[34] In the event, the standard pattern was one of decimated but largely pacified survivors improvising a variety of livelihoods in the pores of the now-established settler society, which generally regarded them with distaste. The varied subsistence which tribal territory had previously provided was now replaced by the ubiquitous ration of tea, sugar and 'white man's flour', which thus condensed and potently signified the historical process of expropriation. To this day, flour laced with strychnine still stands for genocide in Australian parlance. In the second phase, the

32 For alternative typologies for this process, see Beckett 1989, Broome 1982, Drakakis-Smith 1984, Read 1988.

33 See, e.g. Butlin 1983, Christie 1979, Critchett 1990, Elder 1988, Goodall 1996, Green 1984, Jenkin 1979, Loos 1982, Markus 1974, Milliss 1992, Pepper and Araugo 1985, Plomley 1991, Reece 1974, Reid 1982; 1990, Reynolds 1981; 1995, Rowley 1970, Turnbull 1949, and others.

34 Insofar as it constitutes an apology for the invasion, the claim that more Aborigines died at the hands of other Aborigines than at the hands of whites (Blainey 1975: 108–9; Nance 1981) betrays a depressing paucity of historical reflection. It should surely be unnecessary to point out that the invasion could not but have produced refugee crises in regions where resources were already subjected to unprecedented strain. There are no *prima facie* grounds for imagining that the consequences should have differed greatly from ones which have characterized comparable situations in Europe. The causal chain required to attribute such consequences to the invasion is hardly too long to tax a normal historical intelligence.

survivors were generally gathered at fixed locations, either by the lure of rations or by coercive measures,[35] a procedure which, whilst no longer directly homicidal, continued the effect, consistent with the logic of elimination, of vacating Indigenous country and rendering it available for pastoral settlement. In keeping with both evolutionist premises and the tangible evidence of their decimation, these people's sojourn on the missions, stations and reservations where they had been gathered was seen as a temporary expedient, since they were a dying race (the evolutionist rationale for this being that, unstiffened by selection as they were, they would be entirely unfit to survive in the presence of their immeasurably distant future). Though couched in philanthropic rhetoric which contrasted strongly with the homicidal sentiments of the first phase (the missionary role was held out as 'smoothing the dying pillow'), the premise of the dying race was no less consistent with the logic of elimination.

During both these phases, the colonists exploited native labour. The example of the Native Mounted Police, who were used extensively in Queensland and the Port Phillip District (later to become Victoria) has already been cited. Beyond this, though, settler-colonization relied upon Indigenous labour at every stage and in every site of its development. Indigenous people guided, interpreted for and protected explorers. They cut bark, built fences, dug, planted, maintained, shepherded, stock-rode, mined, pearl-dived, sealed and performed every conceivable settler-colonial task except governance.[36] On cattle stations, they typically kept house and provided sexual services, whereby pastoralists 'bred their own labour' (Bleakley 1961: 317, McGrath 1987: 68–94, Huggins 1988). Thus it is not the case that, in practice, settler-colonization *only* eliminated the natives. It is rather the case that the exploitation of native labour was subordinate to the primary project of territorial acquisition. Settler-colonists went to stay. In the main, they did not send their children back to British schools or retire 'home' before old age could spoil the illusion of their superhumanity. National independence did not entail their departure. Thus even though, being established too late and too far north for convicts to be available, the northern Australian cattle industry relied very heavily indeed on Aboriginal labour, it is an exception that does not alter the rule. It merely slowed down its operation somewhat – for instance, no sooner had equal wages for Aborigines been introduced in the 1960s and 1970s than Aboriginal labour was dispensed with and relegated to container-settlements at a revealingly rapid rate (Berndt and Berndt 1987, Drakakis-Smith 1984: 100, Rowse 1993a).

This notwithstanding, one element in the foregoing stands out as particularly contrary to the logic of elimination. White men's sexual exploitation of Indigenous women produced offspring who, growing up (as they almost invariably did) with their maternal kin, could be accounted native rather than settler. Moreover, far from dying out, this section of the

---

35 See, e.g. Attwood 1989, Brock and Kartinyeri 1989, Brook and Kohen 1991, Chesterman and Galligan 1997: 121–155, Christie 1979, Critchett 1980, Gunson 1974, Haebich 1989, Rosser 1978; 1985.

36 See, e.g. Beckett 1977, Christie 1979, Curthoys 1982, Evans 1984, Goodall 1996, Haebich 1989, May 1983; 1986, McGrath 1978; 1987, Pope 1988, Reynolds 1990, Ryan 1981, M. Tonkinson 1988.

native population threatened to expand exponentially. Crucially, in other words, the sexual element of the invasion contradicted the logic of elimination (to put it another way, the behaviour of individual colonizers was bound to negate the interest of colonization). In other colonial situations, where native (as opposed to imported) labour is at a premium, people with combined ancestry can be accounted settler-become-native (as in the case of Latin American *mestizaje* [Bartra 1992, Canny and Pagden 1987, Mörner 1967; 1970]) or something separate from either native or settler (as in Colette Guillaumin's sharp specification [1988: 27] of South African 'coloreds' as a 'class formed by people belonging in fact to one *and* the other group [which] is declared to belong to neither one nor the other but to itself'). In Australia, by contrast, as the logic of elimination would indicate, the only category whose expansion was tolerable was the settler one. In other words – and in stark distinction to situations in which a metropolitan society depicts itself as being contaminated from within, as in the case of Nazi Germany – the answer to the problem of 'miscegenation' could only be absorption into the settler category.[37]

As the nineteenth century progressed, the romance of the dying race steadily gave way to the spectre of 'the half-caste menace'. Towards the end of the century, a movement for the federation of the separate Australian colonies gathered momentum. As envisaged by its predominantly entrepreneurial promoters, federation would dismantle barriers hindering free trade between the separate Australian colonies, a development that would prepare the ground for separate nationhood (with dominion status). At the turn of the twentieth century, this goal was achieved. The Commonwealth of Australia was constituted by an act of the British parliament that took effect from the first of January 1901. At this moment, 'Australia' became a national as well as a geographic entity. This was not a natural convergence. Despite Australia's insular geography, New Zealand was at one stage to be included in the federation, whilst at another, Western Australia was not. Nationalist rhetoric aside, therefore, before 1901 'Australia' was a natural rather than a cultural category. Hence Edward Curr's above-cited book, *The Australian Race* published in 1886, was about Aborigines, who were part of the natural features of the land mass on which the several colonial polities were constituted. Accordingly, at a single stroke (the last one of 1900) settlers became, and Aborigines ceased to be, Australians – an inversion which was formalized by Aboriginal natives' exclusion from the terms of the new constitution. As if in anticipation of structuralism, therefore, the 'half-caste menace' straddled the boundary between nature and culture, threatening the basis on which the citizenship and geography of the new imperialist nation-state were predicated.

The official response to 'the half-caste menace' was the assimilation policy, whereby people of mixed descent were not to be accounted Aboriginal – which is to say, they were to be accounted settler. As

---

37 Here and elsewhere (e.g. Wolfe 1994), I stress the specificity of constructions of 'miscegenation' to the structural particularities of the different colonial relationships that produce them. Inclusive discourses (assimilation, etc.) harmonize with the eliminatory character of settler-colonial social formations once they have reached a point at which the natives are multiply outnumbered (which need not take long at all). In this respect, my analysis differs from the general stress on exclusion that is a feature of Ann Stoler's stimulating analyses (Stoler 1989; 1995: 50–52; 133; 1997).

administratively implemented, this meant the separation of people of 'mixed race' from their natal kin. This strategy constitutes the third phase of Australian settler-colonization. The first instance of such legislation occurred in Spencer's colony, Victoria, in 1886 (the year of Curr's book), when an act was passed which provided for the expulsion of 'half-castes' from Aboriginal reserves (Attwood 1989: 81–103, Christie 1979: 178–204, Critchett 1980, Wilkinson 1987). As federation approached, other colonies began to follow suit. This process was effectively completed by the outbreak of World War One, the conflict which, in nationalist mythology, constitutes the national baptism.

For Indigenous people, however, the baptism of blood depended on whether or not their particular portion of it was 'full'. As the new nation and the twentieth century unfolded, official policy progressively turned from a negative strategy of expelling 'half-castes' from reserves (which, so far as it worked at all, only produced 'fringe-camps' and a rural landscape punctuated by destitute Indigenous people shuffling between the margins of more or less hostile country towns) to a positive strategy whereby the products of 'miscegenation' were taken from their kin and incorporated into the settler domain.[38] This strategy was applied to children, whose natal links could more readily be obliterated. Assuming continued 'miscegenation', the policy of leaving behind a 'full-blood' population as the only officially recognized Aboriginal category would ensure that this category became an ever-dwindling one. In other words, the legislation was intended to reinstate the dying of the dying race – or, as it was put by J.A. Carrodus, secretary of the Australian Department of the Interior, at the national conference which formulated a version of assimilationism for uniform implementation across all states:

> It would be desirable for us to deal first with the people of mixed blood. Ultimately, if history is repeated, the full bloods will become half-castes. (Commonwealth of Australia 1937: 21)

In its ideological genealogy, the assimilation policy combined historical discourses with both metropolitan and colonial applications. As the eighteenth century drew to a close and the invasion of Australia was set in motion, offering a new outlet for relieving some of the pressing excess of urban poor now that North America was closed off, few if any British officials had seen anything to fear from savage sexuality. Indeed, it had often been conceived in romantic, even Edenic, terms. On the other hand, the sexuality of the metropolitan dispossessed was rapidly becoming *the* overriding social concern of the day (Weeks 1981: 19–20). This, after all, was what was responsible for producing the excess – one which, even after furnishing the energy to pacify the antipodean wilds, would still pose a constant threat to domestic stability.

In 1798, this concern had been momentously encapsulated in Thomas Malthus' *An Essay on the Principle of Population*.[39] A conservative, reacting against the French Revolution, Malthus had sought to expose the fearful consequences to which progress logically tended. The twin motors of his

---

38 See, e.g. Beckett 1988, Edwards and Read 1989, Hasluck 1988, Jacobs 1990, Mulvaney 1989: 199–205, Neville 1947, Read 1983a; 1983b; 1984, Wilkinson 1987.

Hobbesian vision were hunger and sex. Hunger (and, consequently, merciless terminal struggle) was the natural result of finite resources being outstripped by a population explosion which, once enabled by scientific advances, was produced by unbridled sexual activity. Throughout the following century, the British state – which, on the basis of Malthusian logic, had become preoccupied with birth statistics – intervened increasingly (and mainly by way of women) in the sexuality and family organization of the urban poor (Weeks 1981: 19–20, Coward 1983: 50–2). As is well known, Malthus' logic of struggle also inspired (independently, it seems) the thinking of Herbert Spencer, Charles Darwin and Alfred Russell Wallace, whose theories, as glossed and (at least, in Darwin and Wallace's case) teleologized, were combined to make up the rough Lamarckian amalgam that came to be known as Social Darwinism.[40]

In such roundabout ways, Aborigines and the white proletariat (or, more particularly, *lumpenproletariat*) both became subject to Malthusian discourse, with Aborigines ironically coming to replicate the very threat that had previously sent whites to Australia. With a new state to build, white Australia came to realize that it had on its hands not so much a dying race as, immeasurably more threatening, an exploding population which, though not black, was neither white nor dying out. Once within the boundaries of colonial settlement, the contradiction in white men's sexual exploitation of Aboriginal women became active. This was especially the case in the south-eastern centre of white settlement, where Aborigines were seen not as sources of labour but, like proletarians in the strict sense, as producers of nothing but offspring. Thus did the fledgling Australian state come to find itself with a dilemma comparable to that which had confronted the fledgling industrial power of a hundred or so years earlier.

The assimilation policy, a eugenic *realpolitik* that would have been worthy of Malthus himself, continued the logic of elimination by rendering Aborigines the pure term of a descending opposition whereby 'part-aboriginal' came to mean 'non-aboriginal'. Hence it was not merely an expression of some unspecified racial prejudice but continued the cultural logic subtending Australian settler-colonization in a manner consistent with the homicidal activities of the first phase. That this continuity obtains in cultural logic does not mean it is merely an analytical abstraction. On the contrary, the overlap between frontier homicide and the social death attending 'miscegenation' was constant. Indeed, Gillen's nemesis, mounted constable Willshire, did not scruple to publicize his homicidal exploits in the outback. In one passage, for instance, he clarified an account of a massacre that he had directed with the material qualification that '[i]t's no use mincing matters – the Martin-Henry carbines at this critical moment were talking English in the silent majesty of those great eternal rocks' (Willshire 1896: 41).

---

39 Eight years later, this concern was buttressed with more explicit policy implications, Malthus entitling the third (1806) edition *An Essay on the Principle of Population: Or, a view of its past and present effects on human happiness with an inquiry into our prospects respecting the future removal or mitigation of the evils which it occasions*. For the eighteenth-century background, see Whelan 1991.

40 Whether Social Darwinism was Darwinian or Lamarckian (cf. Stocking 1968f: 238–9; 1987: 145–6) probably depends upon the Darwin that is selected. As radically context-specific, in the pure reading advocated by Greenwood (1984), Darwinian thought was hostile to any suggestion of teleology or guidedness (cf. Cope 1887: 225, Hawkins 1997: 39–44, Jones 1980: 6–7).

Yet Willshire saw no tension between this account and a comparison that he had ventured a few pages earlier, in which the 'full-blood' had been sentimentally accommodated:

> I do not object to them; they are the pure aborigine, who are gradually going to extinction. But I certainly do object to the mongrel half-caste, who inherits only the vices of civilization. If it is a male he is born for the gallows or to be shot; if a female, she becomes a wanton devoid of shame, and despair she knows not. (Willshire 1896: 35)

The context in which Spencer recommended to the Commonwealth government that 'half-caste children . . . should all be withdrawn and placed on stations' was, in sum, one in which an emergent nation-state was implementing a post-frontier version of a cultural logic that was generic to settler-colonization. Spencer was neither the first nor the only official to recommend such measures.[41] Rather, he was integral to a wider process that cannot be reduced to individual design. The policy that Spencer helped to construct stayed in place until 1967, when a national referendum overwhelmingly authorized the removal of the constitutional exclusions to which Aborigines had been subject (Attwood and Markus 1997). More recently, the Indigenous community organization Link-Up, established to reunite families that were officially broken up under the policy, estimated the number of people directly affected to remain in excess of 100,000 (Edwards and Read 1989: xvii).

Though assimilation and homicide conduced to a common settler-colonial end, they belong to different phases in the formation of a satellite state. As Benedict Anderson has influentially argued in his classic work *Imagined Communities* (1983), nationalism promulgates shared memories whereby historical happenstance becomes converted into collective destiny. In the Australian case, though there is no shortage of appropriate memories (pioneers, gold-diggers, bushrangers, etc.), the project of national memorization was above all one of forgetting the criminal legacy of genocidal theft upon which, in the absence of any form of treaty or mutual resolution, the settler-colonial state continued (as it continues) to be established.[42] As nationalist ideology, in other words, the Australian state was proclaiming its own virgin birth. Thus the recalcitrant presence of Aborigines within the pores of the body politic embodied a decisive refutation of the legitimatory narrative whereby the national community (comprising the normative

---

41 Here again, Roth and Spencer were in accord, though, in this regard at least, there was no doubt as to Roth's priority, his recommendation having been made to the Western Australian Government in 1904 (Commonwealth of Australia 1997: 103–4). For the development and spread of the policy across all the Australian states and territories, see Commonwealth of Australia 1997: 27–146. For further background and analysis, see Chapter 6 below.

42 Thus the frankness in relation to the violence visited upon Indigenous people which characterized many nineteenth-century accounts of settlement was generally suppressed in twentieth-century Australian history-writing, resurfacing in the radical tradition of frontier historiography which is conventionally traced back – with some injustice to Bill Beatty (1962: 168–84) – to the work of Charles Rowley in the late 1960s (Biskup 1982: 12). Outside history, however, even in the case of Aboriginal administrators, this was not always the case (see, e.g. Bleakley 1961: 68–75). Though Clive Turnbull's *Black War* is undoubtedly exceptional in this regard, the ideological consequences of a bounded narrative, the alleged fulfilment of the Van Diemen's Land (Tasmanian) genocide, are very different from historical evidence of incomplete genocides. The difference, of which present-day Palawas (Indigenous Tasmanians) must be only too well aware, is between the acknowledged existence and alleged absence of survivors whose descendants may one day be entitled to compensation. For background, see Ryan (1981) and Steve Thomas' film 'Black Man's Houses' (1992). On collective forgetting, see Freud (1917).

citizenship regulating non-Aborigines) was officially imagined. Throughout the twentieth century, the anxiety produced by this primal flaw in Australian nationhood has rendered Aborigines a legislative preoccupation to an extent entirely disproportionate to the demographic numbers involved.

In contrast to the invasive frontier strategy of outright homicide, assimilation was not simply more 'benign'. It also consummated the shift from satellite colony to nation-state. Constructing an autochthonous citizenship within finite national boundaries requires an ideological regime altogether different from one appropriate to the process of territorial expansion. Assimilation provided for Aborigines' civic invisibility, an ideological rather than a material elimination. Though the ultimate aim was 'breeding them white', the threat that Aborigines posed to the nation-state was not primarily physical (they could no longer materially impede the state's development of the continent's economic possibilities). Rather, Aborigines signified a differently grounded rival memory which contradicted the national narrative upon which a homogeneous citizenship was predicated. Assimilation sought to detach Aborigines from that memory. So long as they could be grafted onto the new history imagined by the nation-state, their physical characteristics were relatively unproblematic. In taking the children away, therefore, the Australian state sought to remove a primary obstacle to its own legitimation.

It remains, therefore, to characterize the logic of assimilationism in order to correlate it with that of evolutionary anthropology. Now that the respective genealogies of the two series have been shown to be distinct, this will enable us to focus on the cultural priorities that precipitated their mutuality.

As observed above, the essential feature of assimilationism, the principle that 'part-aboriginal' meant 'non-aboriginal', can be described as a descending opposition. This consists of a rigorous identity criterion whereby anything that does not embody all and only all the features of a given category is not merely outside that category but is, rather, positively categorized in opposition to it. Thus a single homogeneous category collectively denominates the rest of the world. To put it more formally, appropriating Wittgenstein (1955: 73), 'The propositions "p" and "not p" have opposite senses, but to them corresponds one and the same reality'.[43] For our purposes, the salient characteristic of such a category is that it has no tolerance for contamination. Rather, contamination means conversion into the other (i.e. from the Australian state's point of view, into self), which is to say, contamination assimilates. To begin to relativize the virgin birth narrative, therefore, we will turn now to the question of how this logical structure of descending opposition also animated evolutionist ethnography. To this end, we can begin by noting that, for evidenciary purposes, 'miscegenation', the key term of the assimilation policy, was also central to nescience – if there was any doubt as to whether or not the Arunta really 'knew', the surest test would be the grounds on which they accounted for light-skinned babies. Thus we move now to the direct interface between the ethnographic and the political logics.

---

43 Thanks to Graeme Marshall for bringing this formulation to my attention.

Textual Symptoms

A key premise of evolutionary anthropology was the collapse of time and space whereby ethnography recapitulated prehistory – to leave Europe was to travel back in time.[44] Hence the equivalence asserted between contemporary Aborigines and Europeans' primal forebears was not just a projection onto colonized people of European fantasies of self. It also furnished an evidenciary supplement. The nineteenth century was obsessed with origins. The prehistoric record, restricted as it was to material traces, was necessarily incomplete, a condition that could be alleviated by ethnography. In this there lies one of the possible motives for Hartland's resistance to Spencer and Gillen's realization of his evolutionary conjecture. Social evolutionists were methodological rivals, competing over whose theoretical vehicle could penetrate furthest back into prehistory. In Bachofen's case, the vehicle had been texts; in McLennan's, marriage rites; in Morgan's, kinship systems; in Tylor's, cultural survivals, and so on. Hartland's vehicle, suggesting a German inspiration, was folklore.

Methodologically, therefore, ethnography could represent a rival as well as a supplement. Hartland's personal motivation aside, this consideration underscores the symmetry between ethnography and prehistory. Both were originary narratives which strove to recover the primal, defined in terms of distance from the modern. For prehistory, this distance was constituted temporally within the space of Europe, its ethnographic reflex being present cultural and geographic distance beyond that space. The problem posed by prehistoric data was that they were materially fragmentary and semantically blunt. Conversely, the problem with ethnographic evidence was that, though theoretically complete, it decayed on contact, which instantaneously condensed all the time it had taken to reduce European prehistory to fragments. Hence all anthropology was salvage anthropology (cf. Clifford 1987, Gruber 1970).[45] Societies were significant not in themselves but for the light that they could shed on Europe's past. This varied to the extent that societies retained their original purity, which meant the extent to which they remained uncontacted. Thus ethnography was inherently contradictory, its data being jeopardized in the gathering. The irony of salvage anthropology is that the anthropologists' mere presence substantiates their sense of urgency. Spencer and Gillen's Arunta were already not there.

This much is, of course, not new. The point, however, is not the contradiction in the logic of evolutionist ethnography but its identity with the logic of assimilationism. As explained, the operative logic of assimilationism was a descending opposition that produced a radically unstable otherness that constantly converted into self. The crucial factor is the extreme instability of otherness, whereby 'part-aborigine' automatically meant 'non-aborigine'. This instability is the point at which the logic of

---

44 Anne McClintock (1995: 40) neatly quotes J.-M. Degerando to this effect: 'The philosophical traveller, sailing to the ends of the earth, is in fact travelling in time; he is exploring the past.' (cf. Fabian 1983: 25)

45 As Malinowski (1922: xv) was to put it, 'Ethnology is in the sadly ludicrous, not to say tragic position, that at the very moment when it begins to put its workshop in order, to forge its proper tools, to start ready for work on its appointed task, the material of its study melts away with hopeless rapidity.' (cf. Lévi-Strauss 1973)

assimilationism fused with that of evolutionist ethnography. For either discourse, contact with Europeans despatialized savagery, displacing it out of the present and into a different time-frame.[46] In crossing the frontier (or in being crossed over by the frontier) the native crossed into history. The point is that this was not a spatial progression. It could be done whilst standing still (as noted, merely by staying at home, the native gets in the way of settler colonization). Rather than spatial, the movement into history was a purely discursive progression, one that undid the evolutionist conflation of time and space. Bereft of its spatial dimension, savagery was left as a thing of the past. This spatio-temporal split produced a hyper-susceptibility to contact that was asserted by evolutionist ethnography and the Australian state alike. Both specified minimally inclusive, prehistoric criteria for authentic Aboriginality, a coincidence which, given the prestige attaching to scientific validation, powerfully naturalized assimilationism. On this basis, it is not hard to see why evolutionist ethnography was so well adapted for appropriation into Australian state discourse – or, accordingly, why an ethnographer should be entrusted with recommending an appropriate policy on Aborigines.

Put thus, the logical symmetry between the two series is clear, but it lacks historical realization. Just as any number of geometries could construct spatial relations as well as the Euclidean, so can various logical designations be imposed on complex historical phenomena. How can we know that this logical structure, common to ethnography and colonialism, is not simply an analytical imposition of my own making but that it was active in the minds of historical actors? To know this, we need an example or examples of its entry into practice. In presenting Spencer and Gillen with an evidenciary dilemma that precipitated the logical linkage between their ethnography and settler-colonization, nescience prompted such an example. For, if the Arunta failed to distinguish the paternity of 'half-caste' children, then Spencer and Gillen would have proof positive of their extraordinary discovery.[47] But the cost of such proof would be high – if the Arunta were so uncontaminatedly savage, how was it that the women were producing white men's offspring? Thus Spencer and Gillen's dilemma was that the very 'miscegenation' that could have corroborated nescience simultaneously undermined their ethnography in relation to the general project of salvage anthropology, which nescience otherwise pre-eminently validated (as observed, such astounding ignorance was unparallelledly savage). Hence categorical purity subverted itself – as well it might in a situation where, whatever black men may have said about paternity, white men were definitely denying it.

In response to this dilemma, Spencer adopted a textual strategy that revealingly encodes the threat posed by 'miscegenation'. Cultural brokership, the fruit of long-term local residence, was Gillen's contribution to the partnership. As a result, to the ethnographic testament of Spencer's peerless photography, they could add the qualification of being accepted as initiated

---

46 This aspect of my analysis is consistent with Johannes Fabian's (1983) 'denial of coevalness'.

47 'In a society where children are believed to have been reincarnated from totemic ancestors, there are no parents in our sense of the term. The ancestor himself, or something that once belonged to him, has entered the baby of a married woman in order to be reborn as a human being; and there can be no question of illegitimacy even when a half-caste infant is born to a full-blooded aboriginal couple' (T. Strehlow 1947: 21).

Arunta (though there was no mention of subincision). A further element in their claim to have gained access to an otherwise intact savage world was Gillen's linguistic expertise – their 1899 book was liberally strewn with italicized Arunta words (Figure 1). Having thus established their credentials, it was presumably immaterial that their subsequent expedition took them outside Gillen's territory and, despite the offices of their Arunta assistants, necessitated an exclusive reliance on pidgin. In any event, in their 1904 book, Aboriginal discourse continued to be rendered in italicized Aboriginal idioms.

Since, by 1911, Gillen was dead, Spencer undertook on his own the expedition from which his recommendations to government resulted (Mulvaney and Calaby 1985: 265). In addition to the recommendations, he produced another ethnography, of which italicized Aboriginal words remained a feature. There was, however, a conspicuous exception, when the bastard pidgin was not merely acknowledged but actually reproduced in a manner which, had it appeared in other contexts, could only have undermined ethnographic credibility. The exceptional topic was 'miscegenation', addressed in relation to nescience (which Spencer was asserting of a more westerly portion of northern Australia than had been encompassed in his and Gillen's earlier works). The difference between the newly fledged settler-colonial administrator and the descriptive ethnographer of fifteen years earlier is striking. For, where nescience was concerned, not only were 'miscegenation' and pidgin now acknowledged but, in a manner reminiscent of Stirling's Horn Expedition report (a model that Spencer had not adopted at the time) genetic hybridity acquired a linguistic correlate. But note how, at the moment of contradiction, Spencer cordons it off by means of the crucial 'for some time' which lasts long enough for nescience, 'miscegenation' and Spencer to coincide, but surely no longer:

> There is one very interesting and suggestive point in this connection [nescience], and that is the common explanation of the existence of half-castes given universally by their mothers, speaking in pidgin English, viz., 'Too much me been eat em white man's flour'. The chief difference that they recognised between their life before and after they came into contact with white men was, not the fact that they had intercourse with white men, instead of or side by side with, blacks, but that they ate white flour and that this naturally affected the colour of their offspring. I have seen old natives in Central Australia accept, without question, their wives' half-caste children, making no difference whatever between them and the pure bred ones. On the other hand, it is, of course, naturally, a belief that is one of the first to become modified when the natives have been *for some time* in contact with white men. (Spencer 1914: 25–6, my emphasis)

The loaded 'for some time' enables an ethnographic corridor to be inserted into history, so that precontact culture might survive for long enough for Spencer to salvage it. After this, despite the physical persistence of some of its erstwhile inhabitants, the lost world only survives in his record, to which subsequent information must conform if it is to be admissible. Thus the

with the idea of achieving a result which can be obtained otherwise without pain or trouble to themselves, and when also they know perfectly well that the desired result is not obtained by the performance of the operation. Added to this we have amongst the Arunta, Luritcha, and Ilpirra tribes, and probably also amongst others such as the Warramunga, the idea firmly held that the child is not the direct result of intercourse, that it may come without this, which merely, as it were, prepares the mother for the reception and birth also of an already-formed spirit child who inhabits one of the local totem centres. Time after time we have questioned them on this point, and always received the reply that the child was not the direct result of intercourse; so that in these tribes, equally with those dealt with by Mr. Roth, the practice of sub-incision cannot be attributed to the desire to check procreation by this means.

In the south of the Arunta tribe the ceremonies again are somewhat different from these, both in the west and in the east. At Charlotte Waters, for example, the following is an account, in outline, of what takes place.

When the time arrives for a boy to be initiated, his *Okilia* talks to men who are *Umbirna* to the boy and arranges with two of them to carry out the first part of the proceedings. Towards evening the two *Umbirna* go to the boy, who has no idea of what has been arranged, and one of them takes hold of him while the other comes up from behind, carrying a special small white stone called *aperta irrkurra*, which he puts under the armpit of the boy. Then taking hold of him, one by each arm, they take him along with them to the camp of his mother and father. Here, by previous arrangement, the different members of the camp are assembled. All the men sit in a roughly semi-circular group, and together with them are women who stand in the relationship of *Mia* and *Uwinna* to the boy. The latter, with an *Umbirna* man on either side of him, is then told to lie down in front of the group, and behind him again are gathered together the women who are *Ungaraitcha*, *Itia*, *Unawa* and *Unkulla* to him. These women commence to dance to the singing of the men, and when this has gone on for some little time they retire

Figure 1. From Spencer and Gillen's *The Native Tribes of Central Australia* (1899)

salvage paradigm makes Aboriginal society a textual construct that evaporates on contact.

Spencer's tell-tale resort to pidgin is a textual symptom of the primary linkage between his ethnography and the politics of assimilation, which consisted in their common production of a time-bound Aboriginality that was thereby maximally 'pure'. In this regard, the contradictory relationship between nescience and 'miscegenation' worked both ways, for, to maintain its purity, the Aboriginal category should have mirrored white society's aversion to 'half-castes' (hence the ideological significance of the reports of 'half-caste' children being killed at birth [Beckett 1988: 198, n.10]).[48] Ignorance of paternity would have frustrated this occurrence. Thus not only could 'miscegenation' corroborate nescience but, reciprocally, nescience could sustain 'miscegenation'. Either way, therefore, both the salvage paradigm and assimilationism would be subverted.

As a symptom, Spencer's pidgin text is intrinsically empty. A form of historical parapraxis, it signifies extrinsically – its content is its context. This does not mean that nescience made Spencer's policy happen or even, more generally, that ethnography produced assimilationism. Clearly, assimilationism was produced by settler-colonization. To specify a positive determination, therefore, it would be necessary to account for the settler-colonizing impulse, an agency which is conventionally derived from Western Christendom's fifteenth-century struggle to break Muslim trade-monopolies. But even this could only furnish a why, rather than a how. To reconstruct the weighted play of unintended consequences whereby global determinations unfold through definite relations that are, as Marx put it, indispensable and independent of people's will, we have to try to decipher the mediations and affinities around and through which prevailing tendencies are socially sustained. To suggest the complexity of the definite relations that brought together ethnography and Australian state-formation, it is important to retain the relative independence or self-containedness of the two series, which is why they have been recounted separately. But complexity is not indeterminacy. Thus, though it is not the case that the salvage paradigm was simply produced in the interests of genocide, it nonetheless is the case that, given the salvage paradigm, a scientific warrant was available for the social elimination of those whose expropriation was prerequisite to settler-colonization. Thus it is necessary to distinguish between determinacy and necessity.

The qualified (or, perhaps, elective) determinacy of Spencer's dual role takes us back to the statement that it was not an individual coincidence. In so far as he was an anthropologist, Spencer's policy expressed sentiments that had been and would be shared by other anthropologists (e.g. the support for a nationwide implementation of the assimilation policy that was to be voiced half a century later by a subsequent doyen of Australian Aboriginal anthropology, A.P. Elkin [1947, cf. Wise 1985: 200; 202]). Nor was Spencer alone so far as the specific link to nescience was concerned. As we have seen,

---

48 '[I]t has been asserted that the native women of Australia and Tasmania rarely produce children to European men; the evidence, however, on this head has now been shown to be almost valueless. The half-castes are killed by the pure blacks' (Darwin 1871: 220).

Stirling's contribution to the Horn Expedition's report had contained an offhand remark that seemed to prefigure Spencer and Gillen's discovery. Eighteen years later, the correspondence was no less striking. Two months after Spencer's recommendations to the Australian government, Stirling was suggesting to a South Australian royal commission on Aborigines a plan which, whilst like Spencer's in acknowledging maternal bonding, was more developed in terms of specific implementation. Stirling was of the opinion that the more 'half-caste' children who could be absorbed into white families the better, proposing that the 'attractiveness of infancy' rendered it desirable to remove them early, since whites who were 'disinclined to take them when they were older' might nonetheless be prepared to take them young. By 'young', however, he meant two or three years, since, in the case of absolute infants,

> then you would have the burden of them that all children are at such a young age. When they are a couple of years of age they do not require so much attention and they are young enough to be attractive. (Stirling 1913: 125)

Thus the coincidence of nescience and assimilationism was not an individual idiosyncrasy on Spencer's part. On the other hand, nor was it simply a predictable reflex of, say, the doctrine of progress. Rather, its determinacy lay in a cultural logic that Australian settler-colonization (but not necessarily other forms of imperialism) shared with an ethnography which, as Frazer's distinctive rhetoric was to illustrate, epitomized the salvage paradigm:

> we may conjecture that in many other parts of the world a similar ignorance of physical paternity may have led to the institution of similar totemism, wherever that institution has been found. If that is so, we may say that the secret of the totem has been longest kept by the isolated tribes of Central Australia – till at last they revealed it to Spencer and Gillen, who snatched it from them just before that final decadence of the tribes set in, which otherwise would have rendered the revelation for ever impossible. (Frazer 1938: viii)

But the decadence had already set in, even back on the Horn Expedition. For that matter, so had the use of pidgin as a marker for 'miscegenation'. So, too, had the special context of white man's flour, densely signifying the expropriation on which Australia was founded. Here again, Stirling's contribution is revealing. For, in the following passage, it is hard not to see a model for his editor Spencer's packaging of ethnographic contradiction. Unlike Stirling, however, Spencer would not have admitted the damaging possibility of an Aboriginal husband being 'perfectly satisfied of his own paternity':

> the little accident of the birth of a suspiciously light-coloured offspring of a full blooded lubra was thus explained by the mother in full belief that the statement of cause and effect was perfectly rational, and indeed the legitimate husband, also a full-blooded black, was perfectly satisfied of his own paternity – 'sposen lubra

eat 'um flour picaninny long a pompey eat 'um too, then him jump up close up whitefellow; flour all day, like it, that make 'um'. Suppose the woman eats flour the child in the belly eats it too, and then the child is born closely resembling a white. (Stirling 1896: 129, n.)

As historical parapraxis, this pidgin becomes impossible to contemplate in isolation from the colonial context in which it is entangled, which it presupposes and reproduces. Though the context is epochal and global, the entanglement is quite particular. Beginning to trace this entanglement is beginning to relativize the text, which is – or should be – to precipitate history.

— * —

We should look twice at anything taking place in the 1890s, when the whole world was beginning to shift. The age of capitalist imperialism was dawning, with trusts being formed in America and colonial monopolies emerging as the primary mode of contest between the European powers. Colonial nationalists were turning to militancy, trade unionism was burgeoning and Western women were on the march. Modernism was beginning to transform the arts. The horseless carriage, aeroplanes, moving pictures and quantum physics were being born. Freud was connecting dreams to wishes. Within anthropological writing, though evolutionism was at its zenith, cracks were developing that, with hindsight, would turn out to be fateful. In America, Boas was doing fieldwork and beginning to think relatively whilst, in France, Durkheim was extracting from the works of Comte, Herbert Spencer, Robertson Smith and others a concept of function that, before long, would revolutionize British anthropology. The Torres Strait Expedition was soon to set off from Cambridge. In Switzerland, Saussure was about to start lecturing. And much more besides.

To put it summarily, anthropology was poised before a paradigm shift that was itself part and parcel of the wholesale transformation that ushered in the twentieth century. Nescience gathers together – enables us to see – the complex intersections that bound anthropology's theoretical shift into this global transformation. In so far as the method is synecdochic, it recalls that of Mauss in *The Gift* – nescience is a strategic analytical site, a point of convergence for the multitude of narratives that were circulating in a discursive regime. Where Mauss' methodology was inherently synchronic, though, with 'all kinds of institutions' finding 'simultaneous expression' (1925: 1), I hope to show that nescience enables a double mediation, one that links sequential paradigms as well as coexistent discourses.

In the twentieth century, nescience was to become involved in very different anthropologies and very different politics. As noted, rather than clinching the Arunta's evolutionary abasement, it was to function as a test case in an ongoing debate over cultural relativism. Whatever the theoretical differences at stake, the participants in this debate have been united in affirming a liberal respect for the natives whose heterodoxy has been at issue. In the political realm, the transformation has been even more striking, with the emergence of an official neoromanticism in Australian politics seeing nescience included among the grounds for Aboriginal land rights.

Neither the paradigm shift in anthropology nor the development of Australian government policy took place in a vacuum. Both participated in a global arena that was characterized by the emergence of new colonialisms and new modes of thought. We turn now to this wider arena. In the following chapter, the great paradigm shift that began to transform anthropology from around the beginning of the twentieth century will be situated in the widest of scientific and geopolitical contexts. Within this most general of contexts, we will then move, in the following three chapters, to fine-grained textual analyses of the development of anthropological theory. Finally, in Chapter 6, the analysis turns full-circle, coming back to Australia to chart the selective appropriation of certain aspects of that developing body of theory into official policies on Aborigines. First, though, the wider global context.

CHAPTER 2

Science, Colonialism and Anthropology

THE LOGIC OF A GLOBAL TRANSFORMATION

For our purposes, two significant paradigms ground to a halt in the course of the first quarter of the twentieth century. Geographically, Western colonialism stopped expanding whilst, epistemologically, Western anthropology turned away from sociocultural evolutionism. Given the intimacy of colonialism and anthropology, it is hardly possible that the two developments can be separated. Moreover, the new paradigms that came to the fore in the two domains bore a striking resemblance to each other. From the wholesale triumphalism of the expanding frontier, colonialism shifted to a diffident posture, offering indirect rule and fostering local autonomy. Analogously, the anthropological narrative shifted from an all-encompassing developmental hierarchy to a plurality of relativized and self-sustaining sociocultural isolates.

It is a 'post'-colonial truism that anthropology and colonialism have tightly interlacing histories. So far as I am aware, though, the epistemological grounds for their mutuality have not been specified – at least, not across time in a way that might keep track of the cultural logic within which the ties between anthropology and colonialism have developed as both colonial social formations and anthropology's theoretical formations have changed shape. This is distinct from the utilitarian approach that illustrates how anthropology came in handy for colonial purposes. Rather, by identifying the logical and epistemological structures that commonly denominated the two projects, we can begin to get behind the mere fact of their relationship to the conditions of its possibility. To the extent that we can achieve this, we can move beyond accidental affinities (the two happened both to coexist and to harmonize) towards a more positive explanatory relationship, but one that does not involve the crudeness of intentionality (the anthropologist as villain, as puppet, etc.).

As a first step in this direction, I shall try in this chapter to specify logical structures that span the full extent of anthropology's politicization – i.e. that characterize a discursive field whose limits extend from the practice of pure science on the one hand to that of colonial domination on the other. I shall try to do this across the two paradigm shifts that coincided in the first quarter of the twentieth century. Thus the analysis will have four main components, with science and colonialism each being divided into two modalities that roughly correspond to the two centuries. This will provide us with the wider discursive parameters, extended across time, within which anthropology's simultaneous integration into both the political and the scientific domains can be mapped.

Before moving on to the analysis proper, it will be helpful to set out the distinctive features of the transformation that reordered Western sociocultural anthropology in the early part of the twentieth century (between, let us say, 1890 and 1930 – i.e. over an extended academic generation). Though the detailed sequence of this shift is probably unchartable, we can state, in before-and-after mode, that a stadial, sequential and monolithic evolutionism went in at one end of the process, whilst a set of relativized, atomistic and synchronic models emerged at the other. I will gloss these latter models under the common heading of 'synchronic relativism', which encompasses three principal national variants: French structuralism, British structural-functionalism and American cultural relativism. Whatever their mutual distinctions (which, to their practitioners at least, were considerable), these national variants shared in three distinctive movements vis-à-vis their common evolutionist inheritance. Each comprised a coordinated movement from, first, armchair to field (in relation to the anthropologist's acquisition of data); second, teleology to stasis (in terms of the paradigm's temporality), and, third, universalism to particularity (where the framing of individual studies was concerned).[49] In addition to these three defining movements – and more impressionistically – synchronic relativism represented a shift from a comprehensive sociology explicitly correlated with physical data to a focused preoccupation with ritual and metaphysical (Herbert Spencer's 'superorganic') phenomena. There is nothing particularly controversial about this list, which probably accords fairly well with synchronic anthropologists' own understandings of the change, apart perhaps from the additional characteristic (the ritual/metaphysical bias), which a number of prominent anthropologists have already noted (Beckett 1988, Bloch 1977, Leach 1969, Stanner 1967). The question is not the components of the shift but its political significance.

Though synchronic relativism took hold in these three major national anthropological traditions, I shall concentrate on the British case. Britain is, of course, a prime site for analysing science, colonialism and anthropology, whether separately or in concert. Nonetheless, it should be borne in mind that, give or take adjustments for local particularities, the analysis presented here is intended to have applications that go beyond structural-functionalism and British imperialism. To this end, we will start with evolutionism.

Evolution, Otherness and the European Self

The distinctive trait of the evolutionist narrative was not its hierarchical structure, a feature that had also characterized the Great Chain of Being (Lovejoy 1960, Bynum 1975). Nor was it the comprehensive organization of its classifications, which Enlightenment taxonomies had already evinced (Boorstin

---

49 Though adding little (apart perhaps from the third feature) to Stocking's (1990: 722) 'synchronic functionalism', I stress the relativism rather than the functionalism because, whilst structural-functionalism was clearly also relativist (as a corollary of its stress on systemic containedness), cultural relativism was not necessarily also functionalist (in the integrated, holistic sense).

1984: 420–464, Foucault 1970: 125–165). What distinguishes the evolutionist narrative is, rather, that it *was* a narrative, in the strict sense. It had a temporal syntax; it was sequential, cumulative and end-driven. The four-stage theory of the Scottish Enlightenment was not new in holding pastoralism superior to nomadism, agricultural settlement superior to both and urban commerce the highest of all. Neither the ancient Greeks nor the biblical Hebrews would have disagreed. The novelty that the Scottish Enlightenment unveiled was not this hierarchical ordering but its cumulative temporality – pastoralists were not merely superior to nomads; they were so because they *had once been* nomads but were so no longer.[50] True, elements of this formula had been there previously (in John Locke's beginning, for instance, all the world had been America). But its systematization into the cumulative narrative that global imperialism presupposes was new. It was not until the late eighteenth century – in full cry, well into the nineteenth – that the doctrine took hold that subordinate modes of life were not lesser coexistences (Vico's 'gentiles') but *residues*, with all the ominous redundancy that this entailed.

Evolutionism did not simply provide that 'their' present was 'our' past, as in the case of Locke's Americans. It consigned each of them to a particular moment from that past, which is to say that it constructed each as embodying its own specific quantum of redundancy. This temporalized commonality meant that statements made about 'them' also referred to 'us' and vice versa. It rendered complex an instability between us and them which predated evolutionism (we see it clearly in Caliban, for instance). This instability, which had found its rhetorical apotheosis in the Noble Savage, exploited the ambiguous possibilities of simultaneously stressing and erasing difference.

The Noble Savage was inherently imported. A literary variation on a well-established and ongoing physical practice (Columbus' Arawaks at the Spanish court, Montaigne's cannibals, the 'Hottentot Venus', Ota, etc. [Bradford and Blume 1992, Feest 1987]), it had an inseparable obverse. This was not simply the ignoble or depraved concomitant that is conventionally noted. Rather, in its importedness, the Noble Savage was but one half of a single movement which simultaneously projected out, which ascribed to colonized indigenes all those internal anomalies and contradictions that beset European society and that, prior to acquiring a convenient empirical topos in the colonies (initially, with the assimilation of Europe's anthropophagi to the Caribs/cannibals [Hulme 1986]), had been located in heterotopic spaces within (e.g. the Wild Man) or fabulous spaces without (e.g. the Antipodes) (Boas 1948, Burke 1972, Friedman 1981, Husband 1980, White 1972, Wittkower 1942). The reverse also applies. For instance, as Charles Zika (1994; 1997: 87–89) has shown, for a crucial interlude in the sixteenth century, European witches and Amerindians had come to share an iconography. Even physically, imported cannibals had their counterparts in exported convicts (not to mention religious freaks), whilst African slaves embodied both aspects

---

50 Meek (1976: 22–3) isolates the germ of this perspective in Locke's *Two Treatises on Government* (1690), wherein 'hunting, pasturage, and agriculture did *not* in fact coexist in the "first ages" of Asia and Europe, as Genesis had led so many to believe. The way was thus for the first time really laid open for the emergence of the idea of an orderly sequence or succession of different modes of subsistence through which societies could be conceived as progressing over time.' This is not, of course, full-blown nineteenth-century-style unilinear evolutionism. Rather, as Meek concedes in relation to the four-stages theory, one can find stray anticipations, but they are neither complete nor systematic nor established.

of the movement. In the previous chapter, we saw how Malthus' theory of population growth had both metropolitan and colonial applications. This is but one instance of an extremely important general phenomenon, one that we will encounter repeatedly throughout this book. Recognizing it enables us to approach evolutionary anthropology as simultaneously both an inwardly-directed discourse on the European self and an outwardly-directed one on colonized others. We can also examine the interplay between the two aspects of this single characteristic.

Though most evolutionary-anthropological discourse evinced a balance (of varying proportions) between internal and external reference, the two can be picked out and their separate implications clearly discerned. I term the two modes 'autography' and 'xenography' respectively, a distinction that the existing, highly porous boundaries between anthropology, ethnology and ethnography are incapable of expressing. The autographic/xenographic distinction has a particular efficacy when it is inverted, when the civilized become savages or, conversely, when speculations about prehistoric Europe become objectified in (or projected onto) the colonized. For instance, the study of antiquities, being devoted to uncovering European prehistory, was an autographic discourse, whilst a concept such as fetishism was pre-eminently xenographic. Yet Marx, as is well known, gave fetishism an incisively autographic reference. Analogously, the discourse of psychoanalysis imported evolutionary anthropology's phylogenetic taxonomy of ethnographic differences into the ontogenetic development of the modern European individual.[51]

A key instance of the relations between autography and xenography is provided by the practice of craniometry. This practice mediates between the modern disciplines of anthropology and psychology. That their distinction is a historical contingency is evident from the most casual reading of Kant's (1798) anthropology, which is clearly a precursor to modern psychology (Verwey 1985: 1; 41–52). This does not mean that the autographic/xenographic distinction simply expresses the usual alternations between the individual and the collective or between the somatic and the conventional. Whilst such dualities undoubtedly relate to the distinction, they are categorically secondary to the principal opposition – colonizing European/colonized native – that it expresses. As embryonic in Kant's anthropology and as explicated in the phrenology developed in Vienna by Gall and Spurzheim, divergence from the high-European norm was not only pathological but was craniomorphologically registered. Thus it is no accident that not only natives but Europe's own psychopathological exemplars had their heads measured throughout the nineteenth century. Hence, in keeping with Ernst Haeckel's dictum that ontogeny recapitulated phylogeny, 'their' smaller brains indicated that they were like our children. Correspondingly, as the renowned Italian criminologist Cesar Lambroso was to assert later in the century (Gould 1977b: 120–5; 1981: 122–42, Ellis 1890: 133–4), our criminals were simply atavistic throwbacks to their contemporary state of savagery (hence the 'whitened primitive' comic

---

51 The sub-title of *Totem and Taboo* (Freud 1912) says it all: *Some Points of Agreement between the Mental Lives of Savages and Neurotics.*

stereotype of the heavy-browed, flat-nosed, brawny burglar with swag and mask).

The point is, therefore, that, in Kant's as much as in these subsequent anthropologies, the European referent was not innocent. It was, rather, the unstated subject at the apex of evolutionism's global hierarchy, that transparent paragon in relation to which all difference was default. Accordingly, though Kant's anthropology (or, for that matter, Gall and Spurzheim's clinical phrenology) may look like purely Eurocentric narratives, they have to be understood in the context of the globally subdivided category of man that the Enlightenment had produced.

To note that Kant's anthropology looks like modern psychology is to note that anthropology has lost something – specifically, that which today we grant to psychology. The same applies to what today we call sociology. In terms of our distinction, therefore, we can say that, through losing psychology and sociology, anthropology lost its autography – i.e. it became restricted to finding its objects from among the colonized alone. Needless to state, this was only an appearance: just as anthropology in the modern sense retains continuities with Kant's cerebral speculations, so has it continued to construct the Western subject in a number of crucial ways. Nonetheless, so far as twentieth-century sociocultural anthropology's avowed area of professional competence is concerned, we can say that the paradigm shift removed the autographic element from ethnography, thus effecting a rupture between 'us' and 'them' which, for all the claims to have morally improved on evolutionism that were to be advanced by certain practitioners of synchronic relativism, ironically recapitulated the doctrine of polygenesis.

Of this, more below. For the time being, the significance of anthropology's twentieth-century confinement to a xenographic purview (its self-distancing, for instance, from Hartland- or van Gennep-style folklorism)[52] is that it highlights the single overwhelming feature of the paradigm shift's global context, which is that the nineteenth-century consolidation of bourgeois power culminated, at the end of the century, in the completion of the initial expansionary phase of Europe's colonizing project. This completion constitutes the first, geopolitical dimension of the global context in which I wish to situate anthropology's paradigm shift. Anthropology's loss of autography was a function (or, perhaps, a consequence) of the three defining movements of that shift, those from armchair to field (and back), from evolution to synchrony and from universalism to particularity. The shift to synchrony detached anthropology's objects from a history in which they were being incorporated into European colonial structures (which is to say, it kept their distance). This effect was compounded by a shift away from an explicitly universal framework to an epistemological fragmentation that spatio-temporally isolated the societies that it analysed. As Johannes Fabian (1983) has argued, both space and time were essential to this isolation, whose breaching was preliminary to fieldwork. Thus Europe (the armchair) became the scene of reading, and returning to write, the scene of universal history against which the remaining two movements – the timelessness and the

---

[52] For the failure of the Ethnographic Survey of the United Kingdom in the 1890s, see Urry 1993: 95–6.

fragmentary particularity of the field – were constructed. In the combination of their effects, therefore, the three distinctive features of synchronic relativism constructed the most thoroughgoing of ethnographic alterities. So far as context is concerned, therefore, we are concerned with factors that conduce to a shift out of chronology (or teleology), universality and system and into timelessness, particularity and autonomy.

Geopolitics

To start with the globalizers themselves: one of the great ironies of nescience is that, if anyone was troubled by uncertainty over origins, it was the nineteenth-century bourgeoisie. Evolutionary theory evinced a preoccupation with descent that betrayed a usurper's desire to formulate a pedigree that might measure up to the ancestral legitimacy sustaining the landed order that the bourgeoisie had so rudely displaced.[53] As Douglas Lorimer put it (1978: 159), 'lacking an aristocratic lineage and yet seeking the trappings of gentility, pride of race formed one substitute'.

The opposition between autographic and xenographic discourse is bound up with the nineteenth-century development of the bourgeois world-order, a process whose outer limits can be expressed in terms of the generalized transformation that took place between the French and the Russian revolutions. In other words, our geopolitical context consists in the nineteenth-century consolidation and global extension of bourgeois hegemony. Ideologically, the century began with the suppression, within Europe, of the Noble Savage, a disruptive other whose strategic value had been for an emergent, recruiting bourgeoisie still engaged in mobilizing opposition to the dominance of a landed order. Between the two revolutions, the universalist rhetoric of bourgeois liberalism was contradicted by the reality of domination by the minority capitalist class. In the course of the century, this contradiction unfolded in the form of oppositional groupings that insisted on taking liberal rhetoric seriously. To adapt Raymond Williams' (1977: 121–127; 1980: 40–45) terminology, liberal universalism had been the recruiting rhetoric of an emergent order seeking to secure allies in its struggle against the aristocracy. Once the bourgeoisie had become established in power, however, it became susceptible to the very universalist rhetoric that had enabled it to supplant the now residual aristocracy. Hence discourses that fragmented or subdivided universal categories had considerable hegemonic value. On this basis, as has often been pointed out (Engels 1954: 307–8, Gould 1977a, Sahlins 1977, Williams 1980: 86–103), Social Darwinism legitimated colonizing laissez-faire capitalism in that, though uniting the species, it simultaneously redivided it phylogenetically, making progress its own reward.

As a global hierarchy, evolutionism was inherently autographic in that colonized others figured as superseded antecedents of the bourgeois self.

---

53 It could be said that the Glorious Revolution had produced an alliance between the bourgeoisie and the aristocracy in England. Whilst I happen to think that the sense of usurpation still permeated Victorian bourgeois discourse, the preoccupation to which I am referring here could find expression either way. Consider, for instance, Perry Anderson's (1987: 23) paraphrase of Marx: 'Fearful of the working-class beneath it, the English bourgeoisie imitated and tried to link itself to the aristocracy.'

Thus the theory constituted the bourgeoisie in relation to each subordinate category at once. Whatever their articulation – whether they were externally or internally colonized, whether they were natives, Irish, proletarians, women, Jews, lunatics or criminals – there was an evolutionary niche for each of them, and it was always below the apex. Unity, in this single world narrative, was made up of differences (Burrow 1966: 98).

Around the turn of the twentieth century, however, a whole range of geopolitical developments conspired to test this calibrated evolutionary scheme. Though there is dispute as to whether the New Imperialism (Eldridge 1978: 122–148) that suddenly took off in the last quarter of the nineteenth century coincided with a period of economic decline (Cell 1979: 205), for our purposes the actual extent of Britain's post-1872 reversal is immaterial. What matters is the universal perception of decline, in which connection imperialism was widely seen to offer compensation for domestic adversity (Eldridge 1978: 149–214, Hyam 1976: 70–102, Madden 1959, Porter 1987: 33–81, Roberts 1989: 82–127, Shannon 1974: 349–363). This assessment could unite anti-imperial militants in the colonies and senior parliamentarians at Westminster. Thus M.N. Roy and Joseph Chamberlain agreed (despite attaching very different values to the conclusion) that unrest on the part of the metropolitan proletariat could be assuaged by means of the wealth that accrued from colonization (Wolfe 1997a: 392). For the argument to come, two aspects of the turn-of-the-century milieu are salient. First, so far as perceptions were concerned, the pervasive sense of decline was associated with widespread subaltern revolt both at home and abroad which intensified as the fledgling century progressed. Second, between the high point of evolutionism and the establishment of structural-functionalism (i.e., during the first three decades of the twentieth century), a complex interplay of global pressures produced a shifting set of conceptualizations of empire – from notions of uplift and the white man's burden through trusteeship and Lugard's dual mandate to Indirect Rule and even the first hints of partnership – a tactical shift whose overall tendency was towards a relatively apologetic (albeit no less determined) mode of imperialism (Hyam 1976: 377–79, Kennedy 1983, Porter 1968: 239–329, Robinson 1965, Thornton 1965; 1966).[54] These years were marked by what Michael Bentley has termed (1984: 278) a 'sense of life mounted on wheels'. This sense was associated with a number of signal developments that got the new century off to a tumultuous start. The overall pattern, as Hobsbawm (1987: 10) described it, was one of 'the society and world of bourgeois liberalism advancing towards what has been called its "strange death" as it reaches its apogee, victim of the very contradictions inherent in its advance'. Briefly, the principal constituents of this pattern were as follows:

Despite the 1886 defeat of the Home Rule bill – followed by the disgrace and, in 1891, subsequent death of Parnell – there was no end to the Irish Question (Boyce 1988: 34–43, Loughlin 1986, Lyons 1977: 476–603, Mansergh 1991, O'Brien 1968: 277–356, Shannon 1988: 33–135), a demand whose echoes

---

54 '[T]he options and latitude for proconsular adventuring and even independent action were already beginning to close off, at differing times for different regions, before the Great War imposed another and more final discontinuity. While the longevity of the empire after that cataclysm remains a puzzle, its more vital energies were probably sapped' (Benyon 1991: 168).

were gathering some momentum (and 'terrorist' backing) in India (Gordon 1974: 135–60, Haithcox 1971: 25–30, Ker 1918) even as the Japanese pulled off the unthinkable in the form of an Asian military victory over a European power. A relative handful of ill-equipped Boer farmers (like the Irish in being both European and denied self-government) had succeeded in embarrassing the full might of empire for far longer than had ever been thought possible. Moreover, as revelations of systematic crop destruction, massacre and appalling death rates in the concentration camps that had been set up to hold Boer women and children began to filter back from the Transvaal, the imperial idea, as A.P. Thornton put it (1966: 109), 'suffered a contraction, a loss of moral content, from which it never completely recovered'. Nor was Japan the only non-European threat. Apart from the efflorescence of nationalism in the colonies of settlement (Jebb 1905), producing forms of independence for Canada, Australia and New Zealand that came, in 1907, to be generalized as dominion status, the ascendancy of the United States was emphatic. The emergence of the self-styled democratic and republican USA as an industrial economy which exceeded the most powerful in Europe had contributed, in the 1890s, to a capital outflow from Britain which, in stimulating a sharp rise in British interest rates, encouraged the world's main lenders of capital to keep their money at home, thus obliging debtor economies to repay and occasioning a generalized contraction of world economic activity (Kindleberger 1984). Within Europe itself, burgeoning imperial rivalries, heightened by the dramatic industrial and military expansion of Bismarck's Germany, had not been forestalled by the division of Africa that had been agreed at the Berlin Conference of 1885 (Crowe 1970). The German build-up pushed Britain into the era of the Dreadnought (Hinsley 1959: 554), a period of massive defence spending which, as Offer notes (1985: 205), amounted to a sectoral transfer that benefited the shipbuilding and weapons industries at the expense of agriculture. British agriculture hardly needed further problems. In 1893, the price of wheat had dipped below the one-pound level for the first time in over one hundred years (Ensor 1936: 283). By the end of the century, agriculture's share of the net national income, which had stood at twenty per cent in the 1850s, had fallen to six per cent (Saul 1969: 35–6). In 1897, a royal commission reported that 'over a very considerable part of this country true rent has entirely vanished, since the owners are not receiving the ordinary interest on the sum which it would cost to erect buildings, fences, etc., as good as those now existing' (Ensor 1936: 283). Many of these factors were mutually compounding – for instance, the need for a strong navy was closely linked to Britain's inability to feed herself. This combination of domestic and foreign adversity found expression in Chamberlain's 'social imperialism' (Semmel 1960), a radical departure from Victorian Britain's unflinching commitment to laissez-faire in favour of a combination of tariffs and colonial trade arrangements intended to strengthen the empire whilst simultaneously assuaging unrest at home, a formula that rendered the weary imperial Titan ingloriously dependent on the goodwill of its dominions (cf. Eddy and Schreuder 1988: 19–20). Moreover, in concert with the structural reverses, unrest at home was intensifying on all fronts. After the great 1889 London dock strike had forced the concession of a half-a-crown a day, trade unionism had grown at an unprecedented rate (K. D. Brown 1982, H. Brown 1983, Lovell 1982). Feminists were in the forefront of political agitation, developing new organizational bases, particularly around the issue of suffrage. In Europe, revolutionary communism was not only gaining strength (despite German revisionism) but, at the early twentieth-century cominterns, non-European delegates were to push the line, ironically mirroring Chamberlain's, that there could be no metropolitan revolutions before the colonies had been liberated, since exploiting the colonies enabled the bourgeoisie to buy time from the European working class (Carrère d'Encausse and Schram 1969: 15–16; 26–31). Almost as one, in short, the subalterns were becoming unmanageable. As Robert Ensor saw it, writing from memory:

> The years 1906–14 in Great Britain witnessed a crescendo of rule-breaking ... by labour strikers and their Syndicalists, by the house of lords and its Die-hards, by the Ulster Volunteers, by the Irish Volunteers, and by many others; until the fabric of democracy came into real danger. In that direction the W.[omen's] S.[ocial and] P.[olitical] U.[nion] set the earliest and not the least strident example; sawing, by a strange irony, at the very bough, on which its members were demanding the right to sit. (Ensor 1936: 398–9)

There is nothing new in this thumbnail recitation. The point is not to contribute to historical knowledge but to indicate the overall tendency in which the anthropological paradigm shift participated. At the level of the most general of cultural logics, it can be seen that, compared to the beginning of the nineteenth century, factors such as the foregoing mark the bourgeoisie's transition from newly established (or post-emergent) dominance to a settled hegemony which no longer looked over its shoulder at its residual predecessor. Far from posing a threat, most British aristocrats had, in the course of the nineteenth century, simply become bourgeois too, having sold off portions of their estates to arriviste industrialists to buy strategic footholds in the ever-expanding capitalist order (Anderson 1987: 22–30, Hobsbawm 1987: 40). The new threats, calling for new ideological deployments, came from below or abroad rather than from behind. Not that such threats somehow created a new theory. All the same, they certainly constituted a set of social conditions that were amenable to the success of such subtler legitimatory narratives as should appear.

In the more complex ideological climates of internal colonization, trusteeship and dual mandates, the great value of a fragmented, relativized perspective was its ideological versatility. In the African case, for example, as Talal Asad and his colleagues argued (Asad 1973), structural-functionalism demographically complemented the exercise of colonial administration, providing for an ascending hierarchy of nested social segments that subtended the suzerainty of an apical master-segment based in London.[55] Thus structural-functionalism retained enough from evolutionism to allow

---

[55] As one of Asad's contributors, Stephen Feuchtwang, summarized it, this entailed 'an evolution towards more complex and higher-order systems. They are systems of integration. Change is reduced to integration[.] The more encompassing level is that imposed by "western administration" in the imperial experiment' (Feuchtwang 1973: 90).

for the hierarchical integration of its modular societies, a feature that was congenial to a centralized system of franchise-colonial labour exploitation. In the settler-colonial case, by contrast, what was stressed was not the aggregability of the modules but their very modularity, their mutual discreteness. The difference is crucial. In settler-colonial formations, it was not so much that structural-functionalism organized colonial power as that it hid it. Hence it is not surprising that structural-functionalism should resemble American cultural relativism. In both cases, an atomized representational paradigm masked the practical expropriation of settler-colonized indigenes, an ideological effect that relied on a synchronic mode of representation. Accordingly, though there are clear differences between a franchise-colonial representational practice that regimented the natives and an Australian one that essentialized them, the two comprise a single paradigm as it was differently inflected within different colonial formations.

If the end of globalization is unexceptioned incorporation (with production redirected to consumption), this is a process that culminates unevenly. Settler-colonization represents the limit of this trend, a containment that anticipates, even exaggerates, the global internment that has proceeded since the beginning of the colonial era. In regard to twentieth-century settler-colonialism, synchronic relativism's principal ideological significance is as a suppressor of consequences. It has this effect because it constructs indigenous societies as self-generating entities. Thus they figure as neither transformed by nor dependent on the society of the European invaders. The paradigm's stress upon systemic equilibrium, which underwrote the tidy co-ordination of its parts, precluded the disruptions and incongruities involved in historical change. For instance, in keeping with the logic of a synchronic theoretical perspective, one of the founding giants of structural-functionalism, Radcliffe-Brown, regularly (e.g. 1929: 53) disparaged Enlightenment-style conjectural history. But this was a ploy, since structural-functionalism's commitment to stasis precluded *all* history, not just the evolutionism that, by the 1920s, was becoming an increasingly soft target.

As one of his staunchest supporters had to admit, Radcliffe-Brown's model dealt in informants' prescriptive models of their societies: 'One obvious difficulty with this position is that the stated norms and customary usages are not necessarily a good guide to what people actually do . . . It is surely always best to distinguish a normative form, the sum of various conventions, and a statistical form, the sum of observed actions of various kinds' (Kuper 1977: 4). In this sense, Radcliffe-Brown's approach was ideal as opposed to real; it simply endorsed the ideologies of its informants. By the same token, however, it was also ideal as opposed to material, inscribing abstract schemes rather than concrete practices – a preference which appreciably facilitated fieldwork. These two aspects of the approach's idealism had complementary implications for colonization. Represented as prescriptive ideals – as they were 'meant to be' rather than as they were – societies unproblematically emerged as coherent, regular and self-sustaining. Moreover, this effect was compounded by an abstractedness that belied the material impact of colonization. An outcome was our fourth, supplementary characteristic of the paradigm, its metaphysical bias, a propensity to dwell on prescriptive abstractions (religious beliefs, classificatory kinship nomenclatures, etc.) which, in an ironically unDurkheimian manner, transcended social processes. This is not to say that the paradigm makes no reference to traditional subsistence practices. Rather, traditional subsistence practices are the *only* ones that it refers to. The outback safari stereotype of the hunter returning to camp with a wallaby draped over one shoulder[56] blandly disguises the wholesale ecological and economic transformation engendered by pastoral grazing (it would be a different story indeed if the hunter had a sheep over his shoulder).

Compounding the effect of its prescriptiveness, by virtue of its stress on particularity, synchronic relativism was description but not taxonomy – none of the parts named the whole. As in Russell's (1910) problem of types – another sign of the times – there was no provision for the catalogue of individualized units to include itself, the containing and organizing principle. As rendering hegemony transparent, relativism should be seen not as a retreat from imperialism but as its consolidation. Thus evolutionism emerges as an expansive or conquering narrative and synchronic relativism as a containing or consolidating one, as a symptom of the completion of Europe's global expansion.

Though the final scramble for Africa had left scattered areas of the globe still unpacified, outside the Far East, parts of central Asia and Abyssinia at least, almost everywhere was effectively dominated by one and/or another of the Western powers. A consequence of this consummation of the colonial centrifuge was the internalization of savagery, a consequence whose ethnographic reflex was the spectre of the vanishing primitive underlying the salvage paradigm (cf. Clifford 1987, Gruber 1970).

In settler colonies, both evolutionism and synchronic relativism were specifically modulated. Though classic twentieth-century Australian and New Zealand anthropology was largely conducted by British or British trained anthropologists, the completion of the colonial invasions brought about a comprehensively internal mode of colonization that was not so much analogous to the situation imposed on the bulk of other British colonial subjects as to that of indigenous peoples in other settler colonies such as the USA, even though that state was behaving like a European one in the Caribbean and the Philippines (one of the ironies of twentieth-century geo-politics is that American shamefacedness about imperialism was a symptom of mastery rather than of decline). Where internal colonization is involved, the representational import of the autographic/xenographic distinction can hardly be overemphasized. For, in relocating internally colonized indigenes into some unspecified heterotopia, the xenographic mode of anthropological representation not only denies their expropriation. It also compounds it, by discrediting the ethnic integrity of those natives who survive incorporation (Wolfe 1997b: 75–8). In this ideological regime, savages' nobility is a function of distance – once inside the frontier, they become like lumpenproletarians.

---

56 The prevalence of this stereotype was drawn to my attention by Lynette Russell, who was struck by it in the course of doing a content analysis of the journal *Walkabout*.

An irony of the movement from autography to xenography is, therefore, that empirical colonized subjects were moving the other way, increasingly being subsumed into colonial structures. This, above all, is why post-paradigm-shift ethnography – a discourse whose natives were categorically externalized – had the effect of disguising settler-colonial incorporation.

There are definite limits to how much of precontact social life can be maintained, reproduced, adapted or recreated by invaded indigenous people – less so by their ethnographers – after incorporation. As Radcliffe-Brown demonstrated, it is possible to construct whole kinship systems from the sole testimonies of individuals from an assortment of decimated tribes who have been placed together on an island leper colony.[57] Indeed, a fair portion of the kinship data from Aboriginal Australia – the *locus classicus* of kinship studies – has been elicited in gaols or police lock-ups. Myths can also be collected in such circumstances, whilst ritual performances often require a number of members of a given social group to be together at one time and, in some cases, at a particular place. When this last requirement applies, rituals may not survive relocation. Otherwise, though – and assuming ethnographic preconditions such as the penetration of secrecy – rituals can be observed in situations that are considerably distant from the social context of their precontact analogues. By contrast, spear skills tend not to survive more than one or two generations of shotguns and rations, whilst the celebrated example of the steel axe (Sharp 1952) is but one fragmentary instance of the wholesale reordering of production, use and exchange that was an immediate consequence of invasion.

In other words, the issue is one of articulation. Since capitalist colonization is a primarily economic articulation, economic aspects of Indigenous life are either replaced or reconstituted in accordance with the overriding requirements of capitalism. This is not simply to say that certain institutions are economic, so they vanish, whilst others are not, so they persist. Rather, to adapt Edmund Leach (1954), if different institutions can be seen to have a communicative *aspect* (in his case, comprised in ritual), then it follows that they should also have an economic aspect, constituting different proportions of different institutions. Thus institutions in which the economic aspect

---

[57] The 'lock-hospital' on Bernier Island, where Radcliffe-Brown, accompanied by Grant Watson, collected the data which produced his formative analysis of the Kariera system, was principally given over to the confinement of victims of syphilis, though most such institutions were also for the confinement of Aboriginal people suffering from leprosy. As Grant Watson (1968: 64) described the technique for recruiting inmates for the Bernier Island hospital: 'A man, unqualified except by ruthlessness and daring and helped by one or two kindred spirits, toured the countryside, raided native camps, and by brute force 'examined' the natives. Any that were obviously diseased or were suspected of disease were seized upon. Their hands, which were so small that they could slip through any handcuffs, did not offer sufficient means of control, so their necks were chained together [see cover illustration]. They were marched through the bush in further search for syphilitics. When a sufficient number had been collected, the prisoners were marched to the coast, and there embarked on an ancient lugger to make the last stage of their sad journey. These journeys, from start to finish, often took weeks, and many prisoners died by the way. Flies in clouds buzzed about suppurating sores. The chains were never removed, for if they had been the natives would have been quick to escape. Men and women were mingled, and it was not surprising that all the survivors were thoroughly infected by a variety of ailments by the time they arrived at their destination.' I am not suggesting that Radcliffe-Brown was either a willing or an insouciant participant in such activities. On the contrary, he is recorded as courageously saving fugitive Aborigines from armed police parties by hiding them in his tent (Grant Watson 1946: 109–10) and as being unfailingly respectful in personal interaction with his informants (Grant Watson 1946: 58). The point, rather, is the radical disjuncture between the equilibrium of the formal kinship systems and the empirical circumstances from which they were constructed.

predominates will be more effectively constrained or reconstructed than those with a lesser economic ratio. To put it another way, the proportion of retainably non-economic residue varies between institutions.

The purest example of a non-economic residue is perhaps an abstract kinship diagram constructed from the testimony of an informant, dependent on the invaders' rations, who is the sole survivor of a people who used to live in a different location. On the whole, however, whereas myth, ritual and (at least, as a conceptual pattern) kinship do not stand in the way of capitalism, hunting and gathering do (once sheep and cattle have taken over the waterholes and vegetational substrates of the indigenous ecology, they become all that there is to hunt). Increasingly, therefore, the Indigenous institutions which persisted as material for salvage anthropologists' synchronic cameos were lacking an economic dimension (though attaining its zenith in synchronic relativism, this tendency had been emerging in evolutionist ethnography).[58]

Upon internalization, then, the native became a kind of de-economized *homo superorganicus* (Wolfe 1994: 108–18) lacking any perceptible means of material support. Prior to this, evolutionism had entailed a geographical implication – to travel in space was to go back in time. Hence the demise of evolutionism corresponded with the emergence of the time machine (Wells 1895), a vehicle that had not been required by fantasy travellers from Gulliver to the assorted dimension-stretchers whom Jules Verne had thought up.[59] Evolutionism's spatial dimension had compensated for the inconsistent juggling of species, varieties, races and types whereby the discourse sought simultaneously to inscribe both unity and diversity. Given geographical substance, otherness could concur with the psychic unity of mankind.

Ideologically, therefore, the great breakthrough achieved by *homo superorganicus* was an otherness within, something that was there but not there. In this regard, the fantasy which marks the beginning of the end of the unknown world is not the time machine but Samuel Butler's (1872) *Erewhon*, a nowhere existing somewhere which ironically confounded the utopianism of the other end of the colonizing process. Australian anthropology's supreme *Erewhon* is the Dreamtime (Wolfe 1991), a heterotopia that made its appearance at the same time as psychoanalysis. Citing Australian ethnography, the German anthropologist Hans Peter Duerr was still intoning in 1981 that 'the "dream-time" is always and never. You might say that the term "dream place" does not refer to any particular place and the way to get to it is to get *nowhere*' (Duerr 1985: 121).

In constructing a timeless, ritually constituted native world, synchronic relativism effected an ideological insulation that was impervious to spatial internalization. Kinship, myth and ritual became the authenticating signs of a rarefied native realm that hovered in a mythical space which did not conflict with the exigencies of colonial settlement. As such, it ceased to be nineteenth-century savagery – a violent Hobbesian (or, more specifically, Malthusian) scenario of sex, death and scarcity – and became once more a Rousseauesque

---

58 Hubert and Mauss (1899: 210) had complained of it in Spencer and Gillen's work, whilst it is apparent as early as 1880 in Fison and Howitt's landmark reports from the more thoroughly colonized south east of Australia.

59 Verne (1887) was an Australian travelogue.

primitivism, displacing the Hobbesian mantle onto the empirical dispossessed. The shift from the Noble Savage to professional ethnography was, therefore, a shift from a fiction which brought savagery in to one which projected it out. In between, the world was incorporated.[60]

Thus synchronic relativism's insulated superorganic realm was symptomatic of the forces that brought about World War One, when the fully expanded universe of imperialism turned back in on itself. This is not to claim a one-to-one causal relationship between any given 'external' factor and the paradigm shift in anthropology – or, for that matter, the converse. On the contrary, as we shall see, evolutionism had more than enough internal contradictions to collapse from their own weight alone. Nonetheless, the contribution of enabling and permissive factors, of conditions, catalysts and affinities, needs to be theoretically enunciated. Tracing the collapse of the evolutionary paradigm is not the same as explaining the emergence of synchronic relativism. Anthropologists did not suddenly, late in the 1890s, cease to practise evolutionism. Most evolutionists continued to be so, whilst the young Turks of synchronic relativism were to start off with evolutionist problematics which, to a greater or lesser extent (or in varying degrees of transformation) they retained through their later careers. But evolutionism could no longer produce anything new. Being defunct, the paradigm became incapable of resisting the installation of a new paradigm that derived support from external factors. The capacity to resist – paradigms are resistant so long as they have not used up their epistemological slack – is important, since it underlines the requirement, for an idea to be successful, that its time should have come. It would have been to no avail to postulate structural-functionalism in the 1870s (much of it was at least implicit in Herbert Spencer's utilitarianism anyway), since no one would have felt the need for new questions whilst existing ones remained unanswered.

On the one hand, then, there needs to be internal space for a new theory – paradigm morbidity, or a lack of new problematics within a given theoretical field. On the other hand, there also needs to be a wider elective affinity whereby particular narratives find favour as candidates for filling the vacuum. The point is, however, that these two conditions need not be met simultaneously. Though structural-functionalism is generally, and not unreasonably, dated from the year 1922, in which the death of Rivers coincided with the appearance of Radcliffe-Brown's and Malinowski's first ethnographic books (Stocking 1995: 367), evolutionism, as argued, had been effectively moribund since the 1890s. Moreover, if there was a central watershed through which the whole age turned, this would clearly be found in the years which encompassed the Great War and the Russian Revolution.

It is not, therefore, a question of paradigm breakdown signalling long live the paradigm, but a question of spaces and potentialities. For instance, structural-functionalism was not the only candidate to succeed evolutionism in British anthropology. Indeed, as promoted by Rivers and Elliott-Smith, diffusionism looked for some time as though it might fill the gap (Kuklick 1991: 129). Yet, in that it was neither particularistic nor metahistorical,

---

60 As Anthony Brewer put it (1990: 7), 'The natural resources of the whole planet were opened up for exploitation.'

diffusionism was not as ideologically opportune as structural-functionalism. Nonetheless, it was not summarily excluded, as if by some mechanical principle of historical censorship. It simply found the going harder, so that the whole would-be paradigm, rather than just the individual miscreant, became vulnerable to the discredit arising from Perry's (1923) heliolithic excesses (Elliott Smith, Malinowski, Spinder and Goldenweiser 1928, Kuklick 1991: 126–133; 211–212, Langham 1981: 162–163; 182–189). This is not, however, a statement about diffusionism itself. First, though Perry would seem to have been seriously wrong to detect Egyptian cultural influence in the south Pacific, it is not as if structural-functionalism can be shown to have been empirically 'right'. Second, diffusionism became much better established and had a much longer career in Germany, where the legitimation of empire was not, of course, a comparable ideological requirement.[61]

In contextualizing the failure of evolutionism, then, the intention is to account for one of synchronic relativism's preconditions, rather than to explain its genesis. Nonetheless, as indicated at the outset, we can go somewhat further than the full free-market (or Darwinian) capitulation to unexplained forces (which would operate here to produce a kind of spontaneous theoretical mutation) by considering the logical and epistemological structuring of anthropology's colonial involvement. But this is to reach over from the domain of geopolitics into that of scientific theory-formation. Before doing so, therefore, we might summarize synchronic relativism's ideological value for colonialism in geopolitical terms by recalling that, as a detemporalized epistemology stressing fragmentation and self-containedness, it harmonized with the completion of the initial conquering phase of the bourgeois world-project. With this in mind, we turn now to the realm of science.

Particles and Particularism

The commonality between science, colonialism and nineteenth-century anthropology was so complete that it has a name, albeit a misleading one. Though clearly formative, however, the diffuse Lamarckism that generally substituted for Darwinism, especially in its social version (cf. Stocking 1968f: 236–69[62]; 1987: 145–46, Hawkins 1997: 39–44), originated in a relatively unspecialized field. Moreover, being directly inspired by Malthus and, therefore, by the principle of market competition, Darwinism evinced a prior, and patently ideological, template. For the purpose of a critique of the politics of scientism, in other words, evolutionary biology is a soft (albeit a well-worn) target. This is not to discount the salience of the biological metaphor in anthropology – indeed, this metaphor was one of the few traits to come through the paradigm shift with renewed vigour. Whether as homeostatic equilibrium (Radcliffe-Brown) or as the satisfaction of needs (Malinowski),

---

61 That is, of course, after World War One. Previously, German anthropology – in particular, ethnographic museology (Urry 1993: 26; 106) – had reflected Bismarckian colonial ambitions.

62 Though presented as 'a careful study of the enormous secondary literature on the subject' (cover note), Hawkins' (1997) account of Social Darwinism fails to mention Stocking's influential analysis. Stocking is not the only inconvenient (for the purposes of Hawkins' argument) authority to be omitted. For instance, there is no mention of Greenwood's cogent (1984) elaboration of a perspective that directly conflicts with Hawkins'.

however, biologism was explicitly affirmed by the proponents of structural-functionalism themselves (Mandelbaum 1969: 310–13, Urry 1993: 123). Accordingly, pointing out their biologism merely endorses their own self-representations. For analytical purposes, it is more revealing to reverse Hans Reichenbach's (1938: 6–7) insistence on the context of justification and concentrate instead on the wider cultural logics that informed the context of discovery. What were the diffuse, perhaps tacit paradigms that structured anthropological theory at a deeper level than its practitioners' self-conscious invocations of biology?

Whilst the biological analogue can do justice to structural-functionalism's co-ordinated, systemic properties, it fails to express other determinate features of the discourse, features that its practitioners did not necessarily acknowledge or promote. In the realm of temporality, for instance, biology remained strongly aetiological and developmental – whether ontogenetically/embryologically or phylogenetically/genealogically, it continued to chart the progressive realization of potentialities (Richards 1983: 76–7). Moreover, a mechanistic paradigm fails to account for the atomistic plurality of synchronic relativism's global overview, which replaced evolutionism's monolithic world-picture with a decentred, granular one. In these and other regards, the model of biology fails to capture the full extent of the revolution that undid the categorical imperative for the twentieth century, transforming concepts of time, space, causality, system, structure and perspective across a much wider field than anthropology alone. To appreciate this fuller picture, we should turn to the series of breakthroughs that were transforming physics and inaugurating the nuclear age. Here, at least, there is no question as to the specialized nature of the knowledge involved. Moreover, even if, at some level, this knowledge could be shown to have had ideological motivation, this could hardly be attributed as readily as in the case of Darwinism.[63]

It is not hard to find terminological borrowings from twentieth-century physics in synchronic relativism (consider, for instance, Evans Pritchard's [1940: 94–138] 'fission' and 'fusion' or Lévi-Strauss' [1973] 'atom' of kinship). Tempting though it might be to dwell on such metaphors, however, I wish to go beyond formal or rhetorical details of these theories to their basic epistemological architecture. Accordingly, though it is superficially noticeable that the physics developed by Einstein shared nomenclature with the type of anthropology developed by Boas, Benedict, Mead, Malinowski and others, we should be cautious about this coincidence since, in contrast to the fragmentary structure of anthropological relativism, Einstein's theory rested on an ultimate invariance (the speed of light, in relation to which, and only in relation to which, the momentous collapse of the Newtonian opposition of time and space was effected).[64] Moreover, it is hard to see Einstein's theory as having had much influence outside the more specialist reaches of theoretical physics before at least 1919, when photographs of an eclipse of

---

63 Physics' methodological prestige is not just a twentieth-century phenomenon. Darwin's influence notwithstanding, it was 'the laws of physics rather than biology that provided the exemplification of scientific method to which other sciences ought to aspire' (Jones 1980: 3).

64 'Einstein's great contribution was to demonstrate that the constancy of the speed of light brought with it a new picture of space and time in which the two are fused into a single continuum with the space and time parts having different aspects for different observers' (Boorse et al. 1989: 149).

the sun, taken on Eddington's expedition to Principe Island in the Gulf of Guinea, showed that, as it passed close to the rim of the sun, light from a remote star curved in towards the sun's gravitational field (Eddington 1920: 114–16). It could just as well be said that Max Planck's theory of quanta – which appeared five years prior to, and remained naggingly at odds with, Einstein's theory – provided a template for fragmentary epistemologies in so far as it reduced the most wave-like of phenomena (action, light) to pellets.[65] Without questioning the diffuse influence of such breakthroughs, however, both were intimately related to a much more tangible (and experimental rather than theoretical) genealogy, that of the nucleus.

It is possible to talk of an originary moment in relation to the nucleus because, though emerging from a routine and well-established set of scientific practices whose production had been the discursive labour of many centuries, the crucial developments occurred by chance. Indeed – though to say so risks falling for popular scientific apocrypha – the discovery of the nucleus can be seen to have resulted from a series of (two, at any rate) accidents. The first of these was Wilhelm Röntgen's discovery of X-rays (initially also called Röntgen rays) which he can reasonably be said to have stumbled on in 1895, at about the same time as Spencer and Gillen were discovering nescience. Having noticed, to his surprise, that some emanations from a discharge tube passed through black cardboard which was opaque to ordinary light, he found that, if a barium platino-cyanide coating was applied to paper, it would 'fluoresce' in darkness when the tube was turned on. The process whereby fluorescence occurred being unknown, Röntgen's report inspired Henri Becquerel, in Paris, to investigate the relationship between fluorescence and X-rays. As is well known, the upshot of his research was that it was not, after all, fluorescence that produced X-rays. This, however, came about as a consequence of a second accident. After a number of experiments, Becquerel believed that he had shown that sunlight could trigger an X-ray-producing fluorescence in a uranium compound even through several sheets of black paper. (When placed in sunlight, crystals of the compound registered on a photographic plate even though both were wrapped in the black paper.) That was, until he found that other crystals of the compound, which he had left in a dark drawer, had had precisely the same effect on other photographic plates which (in anticipation of one of his intentional experiments) he had happened to leave in the same drawer. This meant that the sunlight could not have occasioned the emanation that affected the photographic plate.

Becquerel's 'experiment' having ruled out a process of light conversion, it was left to the Curies to develop its implications. For her doctoral thesis, Marie Curie investigated the nature of the radiation that Becquerel had observed (which she was to term 'radioactivity'). Pursuing the source of radiation in pitchblende, a uranium compound which, had it been

---

65 Motz and Weaver 1989: 201–12. The reduction of light to corpuscular units, or quanta, was initially conceived by Planck as a means of expressing its mode of emission and absorption. The subsequent concept of the photon (or light-quantum) was a development resulting from a gedanken- (thought-) experiment of Einstein's ('Light not only comes in quanta, Einstein argued, it *is* quanta' – Crease and Mann 1986: 25). Though initially discounted, Einstein's insight was experimentally confirmed by Robert Millikan in 1915 (see, e.g. Boorse, Motz and Weaver 1989: 143, Crease and Mann 1986: 23–5, Gamow 1966: 22–7, Motz and Weaver 1988: 386–91; 1989: 201–15).

homogeneous, could not have been able to generate as much radiation as it actually did, Curie first isolated polonium, which, though hundreds of times more powerful than the pitchblende aggregate, still could not account for the quantity of radiation that was in fact emitted. In 1898, she finally isolated radium.[66]

To isolate a few grams of polonium and even less of radium had required the processing of tons of pitchblende.[67] In this sense, we could represent the exploration of radiation as a quest inwards, since the pursuit of more from less leads logically to the extraction of the most powerful objects from within more complex (and otherwise less potent) structures. Logically, therefore, the quest would progressively transform the smallest of simple objects into complex structures containing a new set of smallest known objects, and so on. This would be consistent with Ernest Rutherford's demonstration, in 1910, that atoms, previously the smallest of known objects, were not even dense.[68] To see the process this way is, however, to miss the point – it is to see it as chemistry rather than as physics. Clearly, there was nothing new about the eliminatory procedures whereby elements were isolated. The development of these procedures had been the stock-in-trade of experimental chemistry for centuries. What was revolutionary about the work of Becquerel, the Curies and Rutherford was not the isolations that it involved but the radically new physicists' grail that autonomous generators of energy represented. This was all so strange that it was difficult even for sophisticated outsiders to comprehend. Hence, though Rutherford himself was bemused at the time (Eve 1939: 183), it is not hard to see why he should have been awarded the 1908 Nobel Prize for chemistry rather than for physics.

The manifest potency of the elements that the Curies had isolated did not in itself dispel the assumption that the radiation that these elements emitted had been acquired from an external source and stored up. This assumption was reinforced by a general preoccupation with matter as a whole rather than with its constituent atoms. In any event, as Motz and Weaver (1989: 239) succinctly point out, attention to the atom would not necessarily have made a difference since 'the atomic concept means indivisibility, contrary to radioactivity, which implies that the radioactive atom is not indivisible because it emits a particle'. For subatomic insights, it is necessary to turn to Rutherford's work.

In collaboration with Frederick Soddy, Rutherford not only noticed but measured changes (specifically, decline) in the radiation that atoms produced, an observation that inspired him to propose the half-life, a chronological concept premised on the revelation that some atoms are unstable – through

---

66 For this celebrated series of developments (including J.J. Thomson's contribution, which Rutherford's work renders unnecessary for the purposes of my argument) see, e.g. Boorse et al. 1989: 103–8; 114–18, Motz and Weaver 1989: 224–31, Romer 1982: 15–29, Shamos 1959: 213–20, Thomson 1964: 38–125.

67 'Radium was fantastically rare; the Curies processed tons of uranium to get microscopic amounts of radium, and by 1916 the total world supply was less than half an ounce, parceled out in minute doses among the score of laboratories investigating its properties' (Crease and Mann 1986: 16).

68. Strictly, the demonstration was provided by Hans Geiger, Rutherford's assistant. Geiger was, however, acting under the direction of Rutherford, who had deduced the necessity for the nucleus (Boorse, Motz and Weaver 1989: 179–182, Feather 1940: 130–139). Though Hantara Nagaoka had earlier (in 1904) suggested a similar model, his work did not produce consequences and has not attracted much attention – as Campbell (1923: *vi*) assessed the status of Nagaoka's model in relation to that of Rutherford, 'for the purposes of science, the author of an idea is he who first uses it to explain facts'.

the emission of radioactive (alpha, beta or gamma) rays, they become transformed into different elements. Measuring the rate of 'decay' (i.e. transformation into another element) enables a calculation of how long it has taken a given compound to arrive at the proportions in which it is found in the natural state. Following up his destabilization of the atom, in 1917 Rutherford led the charge into the nucleus when, by bombarding nitrogen atoms with alpha particles, he was able to knock away a part of each nucleus, leaving oxygen – rather than nitrogen – nuclei behind. In so doing, he was not only the first to realize the alchemist's dream of changing one element into another, but, more fatefully, he showed that there was a way into the nucleus – and, therefore, into the unimaginable store of energy which it had to contain, a radium of radiums.[69] The rest, as it were, is history.

The figure of the nucleus animates synchronic relativism in a number of ways. Most obviously, the X-ray presented a charismatically vivid image which it is hard not to see influencing a methodology that aimed to uncover enduring anatomical structures that held societies together below the level of surface appearances, whilst the quest for autonomous sources of energy is reflected in the fragmentary perspective whereby societies were seen as self-contained isolates. Moreover, in nuclear physics and in synchronic relativism alike, a granular cosmology was above all characterized by endless internal complexity on the part of each individual grain. But our analysis should not be confined to discerning symmetries. Unless we can point to some of the wider contextual factors that precipitated the mutuality of physics and anthropology, it remains a mere potentiality. Moreover, to chart the epistemological scope of the paradigm shift, it is necessary to appreciate the *change* that the new physics represented. We shall turn to this first.

To understand the change that the pursuit of autonomous generators brought about, we need to abandon present-day canons of relevance (on which basis the destructive applications of the project obviously loom large) in favour of concentrating on what was important to evolutionist intellectuals in the late nineteenth century. Going backwards rather than forwards from the discovery of radiation, we encounter an epistemologically quite distant theory whose consignment into oblivion was a by-product of the discovery. Consequently, hindsight has made it easy to underestimate the significance of William Thomson's theory of the age of the earth, which, though vanishing without trace, had earlier been prestigious enough to get him into the House of Lords.

Like most Victorian science, Thomson's theory intermeshed with biblical theology. After all, it had only been with James Hutton's (1788, 1795) geology (which, though revolutionary, had attracted little attention until Playfair popularized it in 1802 [Hutton 1973]) that there had emerged a serious challenge to Archbishop Ussher's seventeenth-century Mosaic chronology, which, by dating Jesus at about four thousand years after Adam, had arrived at an age of just under six thousand years for the world (or, as John Lightfoot, Vice-Chancellor of the University of Cambridge, was impishly to refine

---

69 These results were published in 1919. For the developments leading up to them (for the purposes of my argument, it has not been necessary to include the crucial contribution of Niels Bohr) see, e.g. Boorse, Motz and Weaver 1989: 103–8; 114–18, Crease and Mann 1986: 15–19, Evans 1939: 42–129, Eve 1939: 211–66, Feather 1940: 77–153, Gamow 1966: 32–6, Howorth 1958: 77–85, Motz and Weaver 1989: 234–40, Thomson 1964: 38–53.

Ussher's calculation: 'heaven and earth, centre and circumference, were created together in the same instant and clouds full of water . . . this took place and man was created by the Trinity on October 23rd, 4004 BC at nine o'clock in the morning').[70] On the basis of Hutton's landmark dictum that 'the present is the key to the past', the history of the earth could be read synchronically from the patterns on its surface, where strata spoke like the rings of a tree. By 1830, Charles Lyell had added the principle of uniformitarianism (Whewell's word), which provided that, throughout all time, change had occurred on the basis of constant principles and, therefore, at an even rate. Thus the changes discernible across strata should be dated on the basis of the time that such changes would take under presently existing conditions (Albritton 1980: 139, Eicher 1968: 8, Gieke 1905: 299).[71] This made the earth fantastically, incalculably old, a consequence whose theological implications can hardly be overstated.[72] Today it is impossible to imagine how it must have felt to have the floor of time whipped away. In any event, the issue caused a furore as unsettling as that which Darwin was to provoke in the second half of the century.

Thomson's achievement was to question the principle of uniformitarianism on scientific grounds. He did so on the basis of vulcanist notions that were at least as old as Buffon's attempts to gauge the age of the earth by timing how long it took heated metal balls to cool down and then extrapolating back up to the estimated mass of the earth (Albritton 1980: 84–5). Thomson agreed that, assuming uniformitarianism, the earth could be as old as Lyell and the other geologists claimed. But, he argued, the earth cools down at irregular rates, depending on the frequency of volcanoes, which let out extra heat. Since it could not be proved that volcanoes had never been more common than they were in the nineteenth century, there was no basis to uniformitarianism. In fact – and here the impact that radiation was to have becomes clear – it was overwhelmingly likely that, in the past, there had been many more volcanoes, but that the rate had slowed down in keeping with the dissipation of the earth's store of heat (Thomson 1864: 159). In other words, the rate of change increased exponentially as one went backwards (Albritton 1980: 180–204, Burchfield 1975, Gray 1908, Thompson 1910: i, 535–51).

Thomson's theory was, therefore, based on the assumption that the earth's energy was a fixed stock. To appreciate how this assumption would be swept away by the developments succeeding the discovery of radiation, we have only to recall how Becquerel initially took it for granted that fluorescence had to be stored-up sunlight. Radiation's novelty lay in its providing an autochthonous source of energy. As such, it was impervious to volcanoes. Thus we can imagine the satisfaction with which Rutherford, in 1904, used his half-life methodology finally to vindicate Hutton and Lyell, demonstrating

---

[70] Though Daniel (1962: 11) misses Lightfoot's humour (or, perhaps, suppresses it in the interest of dramatizing the Huttonian breakthrough), his account is otherwise reliable. Burnet's (1681) *Sacred Theory of the Earth*, although considerably more scientific than Ussher's estimate, accorded with it chronologically (see Albritton 1980: 58–64).

[71] Though Lyell's status – in particular, the credit for enunciating uniformitarianism – is controversial (Bartholomew 1979, Gould 1987: 102–12, Greene 1982, Porter 1976, Rupke 1983, but cf. Wilson 1972; 1980), it is at least the case that the uniformitarianism associated with his name provoked a theological furore.

[72] For philological adjustments to biblical chronology, see Trautmann 1987: 211–20. For the pre-eighteenth century background, see Rossi 1984.

to the Royal Society that the earth had to be hundreds of times older than Thomson had claimed (Eve 1939: 107). Nonetheless, before the discovery of radium, Thomson's theory had been difficult to disprove, so geologists, palaeontologists, biologists, archaeologists and anthropologists had been subjected to the discomfort of having to live with it whilst Thomson produced a series of global timetables whose shallowness on occasion threatened to approach that of Archbishop Ussher's. Accordingly, though Thomson's theory tends to be overlooked today, this merely reflects the fact that he lost in the end, and is not a measure of his significance before the issue was settled. Prior to the quite unexpected entry of radiation onto the scientific stage, Thomson (or Lord Kelvin, as he had by then become) represented the still viable possibility that a floor of time might be reinstalled for the twentieth century to stand on, with all the theological, geological, anthropological and other comprehensively transforming implications that this would have entailed. Things would truly have been different.

Science, Colonialism and Anthropology

Physics' epistemological structuring effect only becomes apparent in this fuller historical light. For more is involved than the retrospective set of priorities whereby anything associated with the splitting of the atom must have been significant, even if it occurred before later implications of that research could have been foreseen. In unveiling autonomous generation, radiation provided the template for a transformed historical consciousness, in which the coordinated temporal sequence proceeding mechanistically from a determinate point of origin was not merely challenged (in a limited and inconsequential way, polygenesis had done that). Rather, in the most prestigiously inorganic realm of the natural sciences, such mechanicism was being emphatically abandoned in favour of a plural universe of discrete complex units. Accordingly, to cite radiation and the nuclear physics that it ushered in as formative is not simply to assert congruencies between, say, the X-ray and synchronic relativism in anthropology, linked though these do seem to be. Rather, what was formative – what jumped out at modernist intellectuals as they scanned their collective mentality – was a reconfiguration of reality itself.

Nuclear physics burst the bounds of hard science, charismatically inspiring imitation across the whole gamut of Western intellectual practice between the two world wars.[73] At the risk of Hegel, but in a demystified manner, we have to entertain some species of *zeitgeist* – or, rather, *zeitgeisten*[74]: discontinuous, coexistent, diffusely influential conceptual fashions (or, to put

---

[73] As Thomas Cowles observed at the time (1936: 341), 'The years of the present century . . . have seen the use of concepts originally developed in physics applied to history and the other social sciences more or less generally'. For a wide-ranging early response to this phenomenon, see Rueff 1929. With particular reference to history, see Cole 1933, Flewelling 1934. Much more recently, Wilkes (1988: 268) could still observe of the discipline of psychology that 'The analogical application of ontologies, concepts, models, principles, norms and methods of popular physical theories has continued unabated.'

[74] I use the plural advisedly. Even within the realm of physics, the nucleus was not the only breakthrough in the early twentieth century. Relativity has been mentioned above. The career of the wave was as revolutionary as that of the particle, and their union (I have in mind Heisenberg's uncertainty relations and Borg's principle of complementarity) perhaps even more so. But the two dimensions – or, more carefully, perspectives –

it phenomenologically, horizons). Reviewing the 'prejudices' that guided the development of his philosophy from the 1920s to the 1940s, for instance, Bertrand Russell (1959: 24) cited one 'in favour of explanations in terms of physics wherever possible'. Even in the creative arts, a field often taken to be antithetical to science, Vasily Kandinsky proclaimed that the end of the old atom was the end of the existing world order, an end that made a new beginning possible (Holton 1991: 180). In this connection, we should not forget that Foucault's 'microphysics of power', which today speaks so strongly of the 1970s, was taken from his teacher Gaston Bachelard's work in the 1930s (Bachelard 1934: 72–9; 138–40). One could multiply such examples indefinitely. The point is not their number, however, but their system – which, as noted, takes us beyond practitioners' self-representations.

Anthropology's epistemological shift from a monolithic evolutionism to an atomized set of synchronic perspectives echoed the emergence of a nuclear physics that had shifted from a mechanistic Newtonian purview to a concern with the energy generated within complex individual components of matter, and it did so with an intertextuality that cannot be reduced to the individual choices of particular anthropologists. This shift was a propositional phenomenon – anthropology's representational contours changed shape. To miss this is to leave the prince out of Hamlet. Especially in the wake of Foucault but, more generally, in understandable aversion to the kind of idealism that divorced the logical structuring of discourse from its material and practical conditions, postcolonial critiques of anthropology have tended to overlook its formal properties. For instance, it has been pointed out by Henrika Kuklick (1991: 184–93, cf. Urry 1993: 110–17) that British anthropology held itself out as providing a practical scientific methodology for understanding – and, accordingly, for efficiently managing – the social dynamics of colonized peoples. Yet the distinctive features of the scientism involved have either been left unexplored or, more often, been limited to general allusions to a laboratory-like systematizing of fieldwork methodology. Thus the rhetoric of science becomes reduced to a funding strategy. No doubt it was, but there is more to be said on the matter. Similarly, whilst it is no doubt the case that scientists routinely 'fulfilled a role as agents of imperial design' (Pyenson 1990: 923), this kind of instrumentalism does not address the specific notational protocols of the discourses that these scientists reproduced. Thus it cannot distinguish generically between the sociopolitical effects of different paradigms (text is also context). Subtler voluntaristic accounts can have similar limitations. For instance, Paul Cocks (1995) argues that the rhetoric of science (the term is his) was astutely turned to anticolonial ends by Malinowski and other functionalist anthropologists. Yet Cocks' anxiety to stress the agency of his anthropologists leads him to discount the determinacy of functionalist logic in a way that ironically detracts from their achievement.

Approaches such as these are not so much wrong as incomplete. For instance, given anthropology's scientific pretensions, it is only to be

remained separable (Einstein did not succeed in unifying the field). I am not claiming any monopoly of discursive authority for particle physics. Indeed, had I been concentrating primarily on American cultural relativism rather than on British structural-functionalism, I would have laid greater emphasis on relativity and uncertainty. In my experience, it is still not uncommon to hear Werner Heisenberg's name dropped at seminars, often in tandem with Chaos Theory, in defence of relativism, reflexivity and postmodernist positionality. This is not, of course, Heisenberg's fault.

expected that a model emanating from the most prestigious zone of the hard sciences should impact more directly on anthropological than on artistic or literary discourse. On this basis, the structural convergence of anthropology and nuclear physics is not inconsistent with the argument relating to funding – rather, it expands and supplements it. Without discounting analyses such as the foregoing, therefore, we should note that they approach the relationship between science and colonialism externally or pragmatically, which is to say that they do not engage with the (cosmo)logical structuring of scientific discourse. This seems a strange omission. It is as if the price of avoiding idealism is the exclusion of epistemology from the episteme. To invoke science in a general way, as if all that it entailed was a transcendent commitment to methodological rigour, is to ignore one of science's foundational characteristics, which is the fact that it is constantly changing. At any given moment, certain patterns of scientific thought are epistemically formative. We need to delineate these patterns and trace their distribution.

The sea-change in early twentieth-century physics stands out as central to and emblematic of a modernist cast of mind that went way beyond paradigm shifts in particular disciplines. Synchronic relativism bore its conceptual imprint. This commonality was, however, formal rather than sociopolitical. There is no necessary link between the logical form of nuclear physics and the practical exigencies of empire. In this regard, anthropology was uniquely positioned in a space that encompassed both these otherwise independent spheres. Other sciences were not definitively xenographic; colonialism's primary object of control did not constitute their primary objects of investigation.[75] It is apparent, first, that anthropology, in common with other Western discourses, participated in a science-driven epistemological shift and, second, that this shift took place in the context of the emergence of new forms of colonialism. In the case of the other discourses, however, this coincidence was no more than that. Only anthropology mediated these developments. Methodologically, therefore, the significant factor is not simply symmetry *per se* but motivated or selective symmetry, which traverses the full extent of a cultural field.

The rise of anthropological particularism conformed to ideological reorientations whereby a strategically adaptive colonialism conceded indirect rule and limited autonomy on a local (or, as in the case of India, local and communal) basis. Alternative anthropological paradigms, in particular diffusionism, were less well adapted to these ideological conditions. As stated, this is not meant to explain how synchronic relativism came to be thought up. Nonetheless, selective symmetry takes us beyond the merely permissive determinism of spontaneous developments. The ultimate context in which I have sought to situate professional anthropology's first great paradigm shift is in the dichotomy between hard science and political ideology. As a soft science, falling somewhere between the two poles of this dichotomy, anthropology is easy enough to claim for either. It can be seen as disinterested science or as servile ideology – neither alternative is hard to

---

75 The qualification 'primary' is important. Needless to say, innumerable other disciplines were involved in colonialism (consider, e.g. cartography, psychology, epidemiology, etc.), but their fields were not coterminous with that of colonialism.

find. Clearly, there is nothing new about this. What I have tried to sketch out is not the dichotomy itself but a mediation of it.

I have tried to delineate features that unite the ideologically quarantined realms of geopolitical ideology and natural science, and to do so in a way that goes beyond idiom and metaphor to the propositional architecture of discourse. For different reasons, capitalist imperialism and nuclear physics were both beginning to replace integrated mechanistic perspectives with decentred plural ones from around the turn of the twentieth century. Sociocultural anthropology mediated the two transformations. Accordingly, without claiming that there was any necessary connection between the discovery of radiation and ideological shifts on the part of a threatened bourgeoisie, we can see that anthropology not only mediated between science and politics in the sense of being a 'soft' science. Systemically, in realizing a logical structure that was shared by capitalist imperialism and nuclear physics alike, anthropology articulated the two within an integrated modernist episteme.

— * —

We turn now from the global processes in which anthropology participated to the fine details of anthropological theory-formation, a process in which, as will become increasingly clear, nescience figured centrally. To use Cornel West's deft phrase, nescience provides a methodological moment – in this case, one that enables us to take stock of evolutionism's constituent narratives, tracing those that survived on into the succeeding paradigm and identifying those that did not. I shall contend that paradigm survival or failure is a consequence of the end-related, competitive nature of scholarly debating. This is a crucial part of the argument, since it is the point at which logic most clearly emerges as an active social determinant rather than a formal abstraction, the point at which the logical is most visibly sociological. The principles involved will be exemplified in the following three chapters. Pending this substantiation, they can be stated programmatically:

Working within a theoretical paradigm, powerful minds, competing for immortality, open up the paradigm's logical potential, pushing it to its theoretical limits. A consequence of this competition is that no possibility is left unturned, so that the paradigm's full theoretical repertoire becomes activated, exhausting the epistemological slack available for the shifting or postponing of its immanent contradictions, necessities, redundancies, etc. Terminal contradictions, hitherto obviated or contained, are simultaneously precipitated, and the paradigm breaks down. This is the explanatory principle. Nescience enables us to see it working in the case of evolutionary anthropology.

To put it another way, whereas in myth or dream narrative traverses the limits of a mentality's potential, so does the dialectical crossfire of competitive theorizing scour out the far corners of a theoretical paradigm. Hence the key moment when the whole life of evolutionary anthropology flashes before our eyes at once. Thus the methodology, whose Marxist–Hegelian provenance hardly needs elaborating, stresses the containment of tensions. Foundational tensions, together with the strategies for containing them, constitute the determinate characteristics of a given theory, which is thus defined in terms of 'internal' properties. It then becomes possible to pick out the articulations whereby it dialectically interacts (producing and being produced) with 'external' discourses, institutions and practices.

To bring out some of the tension-containing strategies employed in theoretical competition, I shall use the concept of debating-effect.

It is easy enough to point, descriptively, to imagery – to impressions such as the promiscuity, brutality, childishness, etc. that were characteristic of evolutionism's savage stereotypes. Such images are ideographic equivalents of features on a map. To illuminate the general forces that form and keep in place these representations, we also need a kind of ideographic geology, one that can show, for example, how evolutionism's hierarchical ordering legitimated colonial domination, patriarchy, private property and so on – one that can show, in short, why evolutionism was so fit for social selection as an ideological support for patriarchal–bourgeois society. Yet, whilst such explanations clearly represent an advance on the descriptive landscape, the great workings of macro-level determinations are not always enough. We also need to be able to catch the small-scale dynamics – local-level deflections, refractions and combinations that can have surprisingly far-reaching consequences. Debating-effects are such dynamics and they operate in the domain of theory-formation.

Debating-effects are not free choices on the part of individual theorists, nor are they social or historical structures. Rather, they spring from the risks that theorists take in order for their theories to exist – from the frustrated antitheses, alternatives or objections that theories ignore at the moment they are postulated. Like the irritant that prompts the formation of a pearl, these disregarded objections provoke defensive elaborations designed to cover them over. In this way, the objection has its revenge, determining the substantive form that a theory takes. Having its roots in an anticipatory or defensive strategy, a debating-effect is born of the dialogical cut-and-thrust. Though (il)logical in structure, however, debating-effects are not purely abstract or formal, since the risks that prompt them are ideologically motivated (otherwise, they would make no sense).

This programmatic assertion stands or falls on empirical analysis. The following three chapters will elaborate and substantiate it. Each is devoted to one of evolutionary anthropology's three defining narratives – to the theories of mother-right, totemism and survivals. In combination with the doctrine of animism, which has already been introduced, these three open up evolutionary anthropology's whole propositional gamut. As explained, there is no necessary link between anthropological theory and Australian history, deep and systematic though their relationship has been in practice. Thus the following three chapters take us far from Australia. Once the anthropological theory has been analysed, however, and some of its social and theoretical articulations described, we will be in a position to return to the Australian context for a fuller appreciation of what it was that made anthropology so amenable to the contingent ideological uses to which it came to be put in that particular colonial context. We will start with mother-right. As indicated, this takes us directly to the Woman Question in Victorian Britain.

CHAPTER 3

Mother-Right

SEX AND PROPERTY IN VICTORIAN ANTHROPOLOGY

Formulated in the thick of the mid-Victorian battle over married women's property, the doctrine of mother-right acquired instant hegemony in British anthropological thought. In this battle, however, feminist appearances could be deceptive, since liberals who stood for women's rights often did so on grounds that actually served to reinforce patriarchy. This chapter will attempt to show that the mother-right narrative had just this effect in that, though it excavated a maternal principle out from under the Mosaic moorings of the Victorian bourgeois family, it simultaneously reconfirmed the patriarchal basis to property ownership by associating the emergence of legitimate property rights with the suppression of matrilineal succession. At first sight, this may seem contrary. After all, as Hobsbawm wrily noted (1987: 202), 'a greater degree of equal rights and opportunities for women was implicit in the ideology of the liberal bourgeoisie, however inconvenient and inopportune it might appear to patriarchs in their private lives'. But class and gender interests do not necessarily converge – indeed, they are notorious for conflicting with one another. Thus it need not follow that liberal rhetoric should reflect bourgeois practice any more reliably in the case of women than it did in the case of other subordinate groupings.

Despite the undoubted feminist sympathies of the Thomas Erskine Perrys, John Stuart Mills or Richard Pankhursts of the world of Victorian liberal men, the campaign over married women's property does not make historical sense if it is read, at face value, as a gender issue. For, if women's causes were as advanced as the final[76] passing of the Married Women's Property Act in 1882 might suggest, why did aristocratic and bourgeois women have to wait until 1918 to acquire a suffrage comparable to that which working-class men had acquired in 1868? Such anomalies do not arise if the Married Women's Property Act is read as addressing a class issue, especially when it is recognized that the rights that it granted to married women as a whole had been available to wealthy women all along. In this light, there is nothing inconsistent in the fact that the mother-right narrative – which, in subverting the historical foundations of the Victorian bourgeois family, had unmistakably radical implications – should simultaneously have been deeply conservative in its patriarchalism. To elaborate these points, we will first survey the political context of the Victorian struggle over married women's property and then examine the textual encoding of that struggle in mother-right theory.

---

[76] 'Final' in that it was the eighteenth married women's property bill to have been introduced into Parliament in the previous twenty-five years (Holcombe 1977: 26).

Married Women's Property

1865, the year in which McLennan's *Primitive Marriage* was published, was also the year of Palmerston's death. As such, it has often been seen as the year that marks the onset of the great mid-Victorian era of reform that climaxed in the flood of liberal changes introduced by the first Gladstone government (1868–74). Yet it was also the year after the passing of the first of the Contagious Diseases Acts in 1864. By 1869, two more of these Acts would be passed. Ostensibly framed to check the spread of venereal disease, they provided for women to be arrested and subjected to intimate medical examinations on grounds no stronger than a police affirmation that they were suspected of being prostitutes. The campaign to have these Acts repealed, led by Josephine Butler (Caine 1992 : 169–72), provided a major mobilizing point for feminist agitation, as did the developing movement for women's suffrage, which acquired considerable impetus from a House of Commons speech made by J.S. Mill in 1867 (and, later, from the much delayed publication of his *The Subjection of Women* in 1869) (Holcombe 1977: 13, Rendall 1985: 285–91). Towards the end of the 1860s, a number of British feminists began to address public meetings held to further the cause of women's suffrage, a breakthrough into the public realm that prompted Queen Victoria to remark that one of them (Lady Amberley, later to become mother to Bertrand Russell) should be whipped (Holcombe 1983: 133). As Mill's conspicuous contribution illustrates, however, the various but related campaigns to widen women's 'proper sphere' were largely a matter of the winning-over by middle- and upper-class women of influential men to their cause. Nonetheless, they were ultimately effective (even though, in the case of suffrage, this would require the intensification of activism that was to characterize campaigning in the Edwardian era). The campaign over married women's property[77] was centrally bound up with the other major feminist issues of the day. In 1869, for instance, the radical MP Richard Pankhurst – later to become husband to Emmeline and father to Christabel, Sylvia and Adela – nearly succeeded in securing municipal votes for some women on the basis of their meeting the householder's property qualification.[78] As will become clear, property and marriage were central elements in the doctrine of mother-right. Since the doctrine unequivocally linked legitimate property ownership to patriarchal and patrilineal social organization – indeed, since, as will be shown, it explicitly separated property rights from the realm of matrilineal transmission – it would be perverse to try to separate the anthropological career of mother-right from the campaign over married women's property with which it was contemporaneous.[79]

At common law, a married woman's identity was submerged in that of her husband. Stealing something from the person of a married woman was an offence not against her but against her husband (by the same token, a

---

[77] The following account of the campaign to reform the married women's property law relies heavily on the definitive work of Lee Holcombe (1977; 1983).

[78] Pankhurst's initiative – an amendment to a municipal franchise bill – was subsequently frustrated by the judiciary in the case of R. v. Harrald (Holcombe 1983: 128).

[79] 'That these years were also very nearly the exact period of the anthropological debate over the evolutionary priority of "matriarchal" marriage seems scarcely an historical coincidence' (Stocking 1987: 201).

husband could not steal from, or even fail in his duty to support, a wife). The dire consequences of this provision were dramatized in a number of cases that fortuitously came to prominence as the campaign over married women's property rights got under way. Lee Holcombe describes one of the most notorious of these cases, that of Susannah Palmer:

> Her husband had treated her brutally for many years, beating her, turning her and their children out of the house into the streets at night and bringing in other women, and at last showing an incestuous interest in his own daughter. Susannah Palmer had finally left her husband in order to establish a new home and support herself and her children by her own efforts. But then her husband appeared and seized all her possessions, as he had every legal right to do, and at last she struck back [stabbing him]. The facts of the case, detailed in court and publicized by Frances Power Cobbe in *The Echo* and by other writers, aroused such interest that a public subscription was raised to provide for Susannah Palmer and her children. Fortunately she had only wounded and not killed her husband, and when she was released from prison after a few months a post was found for her where she would be safe from him. But, a final irony, the money and articles of furniture could not be given to her legally, for then they would have been her husband's property, so that everything had to be put into the name of the sheriffs of London as the legal owners. (Holcombe 1983: 144)

Despite appearances, however, the question at issue was not simply one of gender, since women of means (in practice, their fathers) routinely avoided the provisions of the common law by establishing trusts which, though available at Equity, involved considerable expense. In championing reform in the House of Commons, Robert Lowe asserted that the common law stood condemned by every such equitable trust: 'No Member of Parliament would allow his own daughter to marry without a settlement, and Parliament should stand *in loco parentis* for all women, granting them that protection of their property now available only to women of the wealthier classes'.[80] Thus the campaign over married women's property rights was intended to extend to all married women the rights that unmarried ones enjoyed at common law and, for all practical purposes, wealthier married ones enjoyed at Equity. Though the principal agitators were women,[81] as noted, parliament being barred to them, they could only succeed in so far as they were able to persuade influential men to promote legislative reform. Thus the prominent Liberal Sir Thomas Erskine Perry had been persuaded by a petition organized by Bessie Parkes and Susan Rye to introduce a Married Women's Property Bill into parliament as early as 1857, but this bill had been frustrated by the simultaneous passage of the Divorce Act, which provided for much less significant adjustments to women's property rights. A decade later, another petition, this time organized by The Married Women's Property Committee, was presented to Lord Brougham's Social Science Association, as a result of which George Lefevre introduced a new Married Women's Property Bill, which closely resembled Perry's ill-fated 1857 version, into the House of

---

80 Quoted in Holcombe (1977: 16).

81 Caroline Norton, Barbara Leigh Smith (Bodichon), Bessie Parkes, Frances Cobbe, Millicent Fawcett, Maria Rye, Ursula Bright, Elizabeth Wolstenholme and others.

Commons in 1868. After heated and recurrent debate over the succeeding year and a half, the Commons finally passed the bill in 1870, only to see its central provisions deleted or distorted by the Lords. In 1874, a Tory government was returned, so progress slowed down considerably, though the issue continued to surface periodically (in 1877, for instance, such property rights as married women did enjoy were extended to Scotland). After Gladstone's new Liberal government had been returned in 1880, things took an anticlimactic turn – Lord Chancellor Selbourne, previously a bulwark to progress, was persuaded to support reform, whereupon the Married Women's Property Act of 1882 was passed with little serious opposition. More with a whimper than with a bang, it was all over.

Viewed in terms of gender alone, the decline in opposition to the Married Women's Property Bill makes little sense. As observed, it was not accompanied by any commensurate development so far as suffrage was concerned, whilst even the Contagious Diseases Acts, which were to remain in place a further four years, were a measure that had affected poor women rather than women as a whole (Rubinstein 1986: 51, Walkowitz 1980). As a class-based extension to poorer women of rights already enjoyed by wealthy ones, however, the Act was a rational measure in keeping with the spirit of the juridical and other major reforms of the Liberal Party. In this context, the Act was quite consistent. Indeed, in the very year that it was passed, another legislative innovation, the Settled Land Act of 1882, provided that settled estates could be sold or let, a provision that crucially enabled the landed aristocracy to cash in hereditary holdings in order to invest in the industrial economy. The Married Women's Property Act was not, therefore, an exception to the patriarchal rule so much as a measure that was part and parcel of an economically motivated liberal drive to deregulate the property market.[82] Hence Ensor (1936: 87) cited these two Acts as commonly 'illustrat[ing] and promot[ing] the passing of the English governing class from a landowning to a commercial basis'.[83] On this basis, it makes sense that proponents of married women's property reform should generally have framed their arguments in economic terms whilst, from the outset, opponents had characterized the issue as one of gender.[84]

Though the doctrine of mother-right was clearly right for its times, motivating circumstances are only part of the story. For, in addition to encoding the sexual politics of the day, the theory generated its own internal necessities, and these had their own specific effects. In turning now to the textual production of the theory, therefore, we are not simply pursuing external determinations, as if the text were a kind of political incubator.

82 M.J.D. Roberts (1995: 88–9; 107–8) argues persuasively that Victorian feminism from the 1860s to the mid 1880s was not so much a gender-based campaign as one designed to ensure that women were not excluded from the universalist logic of libertarian individualism.

83 On the other hand, it would also be misleading to deny that gender-based reforms were taking place. As Carol Smart (1984: 31) points out, the Summary Jurisdiction (Married Women) Act of 1895 consolidated previous legislation, which had been passed in 1878 and 1886, under which wives acquired relief from domestic violence and became potentially eligible for both custody and maintenance. My intention is not to suggest that such advances should not be read as feminist victories. It is rather that the Married Women's Property Act was neither only nor even necessarily one of them.

84 For instance, the 1857 Divorce Act's limited property reforms, which were enough to frustrate Perry's bill, had been deliberately inserted by Lord St. Leonards with a view to sabotaging a 'most mischievous' bill which could have given a wife 'all the distinct rights of citizenship' (Holcombe 1977: 12).

Dialectically, we are also tracing pressures that arose as a result of the particular form that the theory took.

From Horde to House in McLennan

In evolutionist anthropology, patriarchal property played a transcendent role as the factor whose emergence transformed naturally given collectivities into human societies. As the bridge between nature and culture, the moment of the social contract, patriarchal property was conducive to the rationalist project of replacing religious accounts of human consciousness with material ones. In this respect too, therefore, science and ideology converged.

As observed in Chapter one, an intellectualist account of the origin of abstract concepts acquired influence in evolutionary anthropology through its formulation in Tylor's theory of animism. A rival school, represented by McLennan, Robertson Smith and others, attempted to derive the capacity for such concepts from material social processes (i.e. in our earlier terminology, from circumstantial rather than from cognitive factors). Mother-right provided the key to this attempt. As will be seen, the mother-right narrative explained society's transcendence of natural determination as resulting from (or as originating in) a fusion of two naturally-given determinants of collectivity, blood and land,[85] which fusion was consequent upon the fulfilment of patriarchy, a situation itself occasioned by the rise of patrilineal succession. The transcendent status of patriarchal property was a premise that united matriarchalists who were otherwise conspicuously opposed. Thus it was a point on which, for all their other differences, Bachofen, McLennan and Morgan could agree. We will start with McLennan.

The idea of incest is central to McLennan's theory, his account of its emergence being marked by a rigorous refusal of psychological or metaphysical explanations (McLennan 1865: 45).[86] He attributed its emergence to the combined effect of two social practices, exogamy and marriage by capture, which had both developed out of mundane material conditions. These conditions were distinctly Malthusian, the 'early struggle for food and security' (1865: 165) which resulted from the strain imposed on static resources by a growing population. As explained above, responses to this ecological pressure included female infanticide, which necessitated the capture of brides from other hordes. This scenario was meant to account for the rise of exogamy and, accordingly, of its converse, the ban on incest. In fact, McLennan's narrative did no such thing – rather than explaining the origin of the idea of incest, it merely provided a motive for men to require more women than they already had. Nonetheless, the arresting scenario of erotic violence effectively disguised a weak appeal to habit[87] at the frontier between nature and culture:

---

85 I have avoided Kuper's (1988) 'blood and soil' because I find its Nazi connotations inappropriate.

86 Though he did once allude, in what his brother Donald deemed a 'slip of the pen', to 'the primitive instinct of the race against marriages between members of the same stock' (1886b: 63).

87 In keeping with bourgeois hostility to the inherited and the irrational, this was a common theme. Thus Herbert Spencer (1876 [1904]: 69–70) associated the 'fixity of habit' with early maturation, itself a symptom of primitiveness. This also distinguished classes in the same society (where lack of development sustained conservatism), but was most marked where the 'uncivilized man' was concerned, whose 'simpler nervous system, sooner losing its plasticity, is still less able to take on a modified mode of action'.

the cruel custom which, leaving the primitive human hordes with very few young women of their own . . . forced them to prey upon one another for wives. Usage, induced by necessity, would in time establish a prejudice among the tribes observing it – a prejudice strong as a principle of religion, as every prejudice relating to marriage is apt to be – against marrying women of their own stock . . . The scarcity of women within the group led to a practice of stealing the women of other groups, and in time it came to be considered improper, because it was unusual, for a man to marry a woman of his own group. (McLennan 1865: 140; 289)

Thus McLennan's theory ultimately hinged on the claim that an aversion to doing something unusual could develop to the point of withstanding sexual inclinations. Since inertia was a negative quantity that did not require explanation, however, it also enabled the exclusion of psychological explanations for humanity's progression from nature into culture. Thus, after asserting the religious intensity of usage induced by necessity, McLennan continued (1865: 140): 'A survey of the facts of primitive life, and the breakdown of exogamy in advancing communities, exclude the notion that the law originated in any innate or primary feeling against marriage with kinsfolk'.

Since exogamy and the notion of kinship (understood as representations of consanguinity) entailed each other, McLennan's task not only involved accounting for their emergence. He also had to demonstrate how it might be that they had *not* existed previously. So far as paternity was concerned, as has already been explained, primal promiscuity provided sufficient ground for the appropriate nescience. An absence of maternal kinship was, however, another matter. Nonetheless, such were the thoroughgoing lengths to which McLennan pursued his wild scenario of marriage by capture that nescience could even apply to maternity as well.

He started with a locally-bounded horde of men. This horde was homogeneous (i.e., it knew no internal divisions of kinship) and it killed off the bulk of its female infants. The ensuing shortage of women led to their being shared ('copartnery') and to dissension and fighting over them. Since an individual male could not hope to fend off all the rest, the fighting would have occurred between groups who shared their women in common rather than between individuals (1865: 168). These groups gave McLennan his first stage out of an undifferentiated promiscuity. They held their wives and children in common, as goods of the horde. The contrast between this early filiation to the horde, which consisted simply in coresidential ties ('contiguity'), and the later development of kinship was complete, since even children initially belonged to the men of the horde rather than to their mothers. The generality of this horde tie reveals the bizarrely frantic vision of marriage by capture that McLennan had in mind, since the incessant to-and-fro of capture and loss was so bewildering that the filiation of children to the group was a consequence of mothers' liability to be carried off at any time. Certainty of biological paternity – on so much as a horde basis, let alone that of individual fathers – was, obviously, equally impossible under conditions 'where mothers are stolen from their first lords, and liable to be restolen before the birth of children' (1865: 226).

Prior to the rise of kinship, therefore, male hordes were bound together by territorial co-residence, which was associated with a kindred affection that McLennan (1865: 151) was prepared to admit as naturally given. This co-residential sentiment was categorically presocial. Animals congregate. In kinship, McLennan isolated the beginnings of human sociability, and kinship originated (i.e. it 'became an object of thought' [1865: 151]) in ideas about shared blood that could only arise from observation and reflection.

How, therefore, did kinship begin? As we have seen, there was no doubt how it first came to be ordered: 'Promiscuity, producing uncertainty of fatherhood, led to the system of kinship through mothers only' (1865: 173). But a matrilineal – or any other – form of consanguineal kinship presupposes the prior emergence of concepts of consanguinity. Thus McLennan was not here demonstrating how kinship originated, merely how it came to take on a particular form. Moreover, when we follow him through the stages of his plan of social development, we find that he never did produce a satisfactory explanation. The point of such an exercise is not, of course, to catch McLennan out. It is, rather, to trace the positive effects of the rhetorical devices that he constructed to cover over the gaps in his scheme. For these devices became debating-effects, theoretical reaction-formations whose elaboration was to give evolutionary anthropology its propositional shape.

McLennan's account of the origins of kinship involved a matrilineal interruption to the otherwise male-determined sequence of principles of human grouping. Before this interruption, as we have just seen, the local group was a presocial one. After the interruption, however, the introduction of kinship, an 'object of thought', meant that the group had become able to represent itself to itself. It had become cultural. Thus the return to patriarchy was not simply a matter of returning to the local group, since it had been transformed – it had transcended nature – during the matrilineal interlude. Thus we need to examine this interlude more closely.

The copartneries that initially emerged from undifferentiated hostilities, fending off other takers for their shared women, would not have been very stable groupings. Nonetheless, their ability to keep their women to themselves would have allowed the offspring of each particular woman to come to form a recognizable unity within the copartnery once the idea of maternal kinship had developed:

> When, however, the system of kinship through females only had been firmly established, every group stood resolved into a number of small brotherhoods, each composed of sons of the same mother. And within these, the feeling of close kinship would simplify the constitution of the polyandrous arrangement. (1865: 170–1)

The rise of shared parentage is, of course, the rise of siblingship. If brothers share a wife exclusively, there is certainty as to the fact that her offspring are of the brothers' blood, even though the particular brother cannot be nominated. Thus the original maternal kinship that resulted from women being shared by an arrangement between males created brothers (1865: 170–1) who could then share wives and, consequently, share fatherhood. With this type of polyandry (adelphic or Tibetan), therefore, McLennan was in a position to move back into a male system, only one now transformed by the concept of consanguinity that the maternal era had introduced.

At this stage, therefore, he would seem to have found his way out of the copartnery of unrelated males through the polyandry of their wives' sons to a fusion of male kinship and the coresidential kindred tie.[88] The last women to be captured would have been the first mothers. In the next generation, the preconditions for patriliny would have been satisfied, since the common blood of the brothers produced by these first stably-maintained mothers would have been transmitted to the offspring of the brothers' exclusively-shared wives. It would only have been a question of the brothers taking to themselves the sisters whom other fraternities were obliged to disavow by virtue of the rule of incest/exogamy. In fact, McLennan would seem to have theoretically discovered sister-exchange. All it needed was a single generation of matrilineal kinship to create the siblingship necessary to forge the link between the initial copartnery compact and patrilineal virilocality.

Yet McLennan did not do this. Instead, from the original group of unrelated sharing males, he embarked on an elaborate and seemingly redundant excursus through a complex series of polyandrous stages that involved implausible shifts in residence arrangements and seemingly unnecessary strictures regarding property. The first of these stages, his 'ruder' or 'lower' (1865: 173) form of polyandry, which he associated with the Nairs (Nayars) – thus contributing to a distinguished anthropological pedigree[89] – involved the band of brothers not exchanging their sisters with other bands, but arranging for their own sisters to be visited by others:

> We must regard as the rudest case those in which the wife lives not with her husband, but with her mothers or brothers. In these cases a woman's children are born in and belong to *her* mother's house. (1865: 190–1)

This shift to the mother's house is crucial. McLennan is suddenly speaking from the point of view of the female line, rather than from that of the

---

88 I.e, for the anthropologically initiated, to patrilineal virilocality. For those who do not know the code, a little basic Latin is enough to get by. Patri- and matri- refer to fathers' and mothers' families respectively, whilst -local indicates residence and -line or -liny refers to descent (as opposed to -archy, which indicates authority). For practical purposes, viri- and uxori- (which refer to husbands and wives rather than to fathers and mothers) are exchangeable for patri- and matri- respectively. Hence patrilineal virilocality means descent through fathers and residence with husbands' families, matrilineal virilocality means descent through mothers and residence with fathers' families (McLennan's 'heterogeneous'), and so on.

89 Montesquieu, for instance, whose source was Pyrard de Laval, attributed Naire polyandry to the men's disinclination to be burdened with child-rearing and housekeeping, a motive which, as Chris Fuller (1976: 5) put it, involved 'a certain amount of climatological determinism as well'. Duarte Barbosa (1563: 35) attributed the system to class (or caste) factors – Nayre women slept with Nambudiri Brahmin younger brothers, whose oldest brothers maintained a strict monopoly on marriage with Nambudiri Brahmin women ('The brothers who remain bachelors sleep with the Nayre women, they hold it to be a great honour, and as they are Bramenes no woman refuses herself to them, yet they may not sleep with any woman older than themselves'). Two and a half centuries later, Buchanan (1807: ii, 412) asserted that 'In consequence of this strange manner of propagating the species, no *Nair* knows his father; and every man looks upon his sister's children as his heirs.'

erstwhile capturing males. This disguises the fact that, though the wives are the products of adelphic polyandry and live with their brothers, their visitors remain unrelated to each other. What, then, did he gain from this shift? The key factor is the ambiguity of the word 'house'. Exploiting this ambiguity enabled McLennan to slip from the metonymic sense in which 'house' conveys a social grouping to its other meaning as an object of property.

His move began with an unlikely stage that followed the Nair one (in which women had lived with their brothers and received unrelated male suitors). In this subsequent stage, the wife would no longer live with her own family ('house'), but she would not live with her husband's either. Rather, she would live 'in a house of her own' (1865: 191), and the visiting husbands would cohabit with her in it. The wife's offspring would still belong to her group, however, since, despite this further development into subsidiary property ownership on the part of her family, her sharing husbands continued not to be brothers:

> the want of a community of blood and interests among the husbands preventing the appropriation of the children to them. (1865: 191)

This improbable system would have been unstable in the extreme since, prior to the development of brotherhood among the husbands, they could have had no sisters either and would have died out. Yet McLennan required this stage since, by 'detaching the woman from her family', it 'prepared the way' for the system that he could have had in the first generation after the initial copartnery, 'a species of marriage still less rude',

> in which the woman passed from her family, not into a house of her own, but into the family of her husbands in which her children would be born, and to which they would belong. (1865: 191–2)

And the development which enabled this profound move? –

> This could only happen when the husbands were all of one blood, and had common rights of property – in short, when they were brothers. (1865: 192)

This sudden inclusion of a property criterion in the concept of brotherhood – which, as explained, had previously been defined in terms of locality and consanguinity alone – provides the key to McLennan's apparently unnecessary excursion through his complex stages of polyandry. For, though he betrayed no explicit awareness of the concept of sister-exchange, he was in fact alive to the implications that patrilocal matrilineal succession entailed for the exchange of other forms of property. When the wife finally moved in with the by-then propertied brothers:

> There being now a community of blood and interests in the husbands, there was nothing to prevent the appropriation to them of her children – an appropriation which would disqualify the children for being heirs to the property of her mother and brothers. To give effect now to the old [i.e., matrilineal] law of succession,

would be, not to keep property in families, but to introduce a system of exchanges of family estates. (1865: 192–3)[90]

By now, the strain imposed on the argument by the need for the husbands to own property becomes almost unbearable. Even prior to the rise of kinship, it will be recalled, women and children were affiliated to the local horde on the same terms as its other 'property'. In describing these ties, however, McLennan tellingly evaded the actual word. Nevertheless, his formula was palpably synonymous:[91]

> These groups would hold their women, like their other goods, in common. And the children, while attached to the mothers, would belong to the horde. (1865: 169)

McLennan could not have dispensed with these horde ties without losing his theory of exogamy. This is because, for the wife-capturing groups to renounce their own women – and thereby invent incest – there had to be some way for the principle of 'own women' to apply. As we have seen, the original proprietorial tie was not a legitimate social one, but needed to be replaced by kinship before social organization could develop. Hence the maternal interlude. But this interlude was only held out as producing kinship. How did it also convert the horde's possession of its territory into property? The answer lies in the fact that the shared maternal blood of the first generation of brothers was not enough for them to establish a patriline. They were not brothers until they had property in common. *But they had had property all along* – the horde's land and other 'goods' by analogy with which McLennan (1865: 247–8) depicted them as owning their wives and children. Thus the 'property' that made them brothers was different from the 'property' that they had owned all along. It was a property defined by the consanguinity of its owners.

In sum, therefore, McLennan's theory of kinship was not, after all, just a theory of ideas about blood. Nor, however, was it two theories – one of ideas about blood and another of ideas about property – whose development fortuitously coincided. Had it been two separate theories, the requirements of the argument distinguishing horde ties from property would not have had to disrupt the theory of kinship, requiring the redundant departure into polyandrous stages at the very point where McLennan could have satisfactorily accounted for patrilineal organization and dispensed with nescience. Rather, regulated proprietorial rights over women systematically coincided with the social organization of other forms of property. McLennan's was thus a unified patriarchal theory that co-constructed consanguinity and property.

It does not, of course, require all this reconstruction to sustain the conclusion that McLennan was an apologist for patriarchy. It would be easy enough simply to cite a few damning quotations (cf. Coward 1983, Fee 1974). Quite apart from the ahistoricism of assuming referential stability on the part

---

90 McLennan had earlier (1865: 51) equated such exchanges with the Roman Law system of *coemptio* (roughly, bridewealth).

91 As McLennan elsewhere put it in relation to Australians, who corresponded to this stage, 'as the tribes have little property, except their weapons and their women, the women are at once the cause of war, and the spoils of victory' (1865: 77).

of the relevant terms,[92] however, such a technique cannot address the question of just how this patriarchal ideology was produced and mediated through McLennan's texts. We can approach this question by returning to a major issue left outstanding from the previous discussion.

We have still not isolated quite where McLennan located the birth of the concept of kinship. It was not in the local horde, which required affiliation by the presocial ties of possession, yet it had emerged by the time of the polyandrous brotherhoods spawned by the ruder copartneries, since their brotherhood depended on it. Accordingly, kinship must have arisen during the stage in which compacts between unrelated sharing males superseded marriage by capture. This conclusion is strengthened by the fact that these compacts provided the first conditions under which motherhood could be stably reckoned, whilst they also continued to render fatherhood unascertainable by virtue of the lack of relationship between the husbands. These conditions enabled the concept of kinship to have mothers only for its original referent, which is what McLennan required.

Prior to the copartnery compact, both women and other goods were attached to the horde by simple possession. As we have seen, however, in the succeeding stage, women were bound to their families by ties of kinship, whilst their husbands remained unrelated by virtue of their lack of property. McLennan's subterfuge is clear. The reason why he swapped from the husbands' to the wife's perspective to characterize Nair polyandry, in which a wife is visited by unrelated husbands, is because he thereby avoided explaining how these husbands were ever going to get a 'house' of their own. If we stay with the husbands' perspective, nothing has changed; they still belong to the rudest of copartneries. Yet their wife suddenly appears in the midst of a functioning matriline, which they service without having any sisters to offer in exchange. Where did the wife's brothers get their wives from? We must therefore turn back to the critical transition from the unrelated copartnery to their related sons. As McLennan argued, these sons could become brothers by virtue of their shared maternal blood. But, as we have found him also arguing, shared blood alone does not make brothers. They also need collective property interests. They could not acquire these from their mother, who was no more than property herself. So could they acquire property from their fathers? Obviously they could, as their fathers, though unrelated by blood, shared their horde territory, which they possessed on the same terms as they possessed their wives. It therefore follows that, of McLennan's twin criteria for kinship – property and blood – the fathers possessed the former and the mothers the latter. In other words, the fathers were not in fact unrelated after all – rather, they had half the qualification for kinship – whilst the mothers alone could not pass on siblingship either, since they too had only half of its constituent elements to transmit. This in turn means that the whole argument from nescience, whereby maternal kinship was the first possible, was a ruse, since the fathers, related by their shared property, had just as much claim as the mothers to a unitary identity, which they could transmit to their sons in the form of their common land.

---

92 Hence I agree with Morphy (1997) that undue significance should not be attached to decontextualized words that subsequently acquired more specifically racist connotations.

Why, then, did McLennan not argue this? As we have seen, he could have avoided the whole vulnerable scheme of polyandrous stages by simply having the sons of the last captured wives take their own wives to live with them on their fathers' land. In this way, he would have been home and dry in the propertied patriline that was his propositional target. Had he done this, however, his concept of property would have been a presocial one, anterior to the rise of kinship and operating in parallel, rather than unison, with kinship. Thus the whole saga of matrilineal nescience was a detour designed to separate kinship from residence by representing them as successive, rather than as coexistent, aspects of social development. This separation meant that his scheme provided for a tripartite series of cardinal stages: the first was the presocial local horde, defined by common possession; the second was matrilineal kinship, defined exclusively in terms of consanguinity; whilst the third reintroduced residence, only now inseparably integrated with the kinship of the second stage, thus consolidating kinship and residence under a common social aegis.[93]

To find the moment at which McLennan smuggled in property, therefore, we should follow through his permutations of kinship and residence. In the ruder, Nair form of polyandry, the wife bore the offspring of the unrelated copartnery in her brothers' 'house', to which the offspring subsequently belonged. In the higher, Tibetan form of polyandry, on the other hand, wives moved in with the sharing brothers, and their offspring were of the brothers' blood. It thus emerges that there was only one point in McLennan's scheme where children did not belong to the horde in which they were born, and this was because they were not born in a horde at all, but in the improbable half-way house of the transitional stage of polyandry. It will be recalled that, though the husbands visited this house, it belonged to the wife's brothers. This anonymous stage is obviously preposterous, since it would have meant the men of the wife's stock visiting *their* wives in houses owned by yet other stocks, whose men in turn would also be absent, and so on, which would have meant that both men and women were away from home. What the nameless stage did, though, was effect a switch between two meanings of the word 'house': from the stock, or social group, of Nair polyandry to real estate (which is the difference between living 'with' and living 'in' a house).[94] Thus the actual breakthrough which occurred with Tibetan polyandry was not the shared blood of the brothers, which they could have achieved with much less trouble, but the confluence of their blood and their land.

Thus the matrilineal interruption to the continuity of male principles transformed the male horde's naturally given tie of locality, turning it into a social bond based on patrilineal landed property. It is worth looking at the tripartite structure of this transformation more carefully. The first stage, that of the local horde, involves territory but no kinship. Correspondingly – and

---

93 This became the general pattern. Though some exceptions to it (Darwin, Maine, Wake, Starcke, Cunow, Westermarck, *et al.*) are discussed below, no one, to my knowledge, questioned the priority of the land-based male horde except Letourneau (1892: 23): 'It is even allowable to suppose that certain numerically small and quite inferior human races, who have stopped at, or fallen back to, the humblest grade of social life, are strangers to the rude idea of hunting grounds, so common even amongst animals.'

94 'The order of social development, in our view, is then, that the tribe [i.e. a land-based category] stands first; the *gens or house* next; and last of all, the family' (McLennan 1865: 280, my emphasis).

this is the crux of McLennan's strategy – the second stage shifts the focus to the mothers' side, involving nescient matrilineal kinship *but no territorial tie*. The third stage then unites the previous two, territory and kinship, only it shifts back to the fathers' side, producing a landed patriarchy with patrilineal succession. Thus McLennan's strategy involved removing first maternity and then territoriality from nature and then separately reintroducing them in socialized form. This narrative structure concentrates the reader's attention on one aspect at a time so that the other, alternating aspect falls from view. The final move then reunites the two aspects. Once this structure is recognized, McLennan's debating-effect can be reconstructed. To do this, we will return to the still outstanding question of the origin of the idea of kinship.

Despite all his vaunting of its origin, McLennan's actual explanation for kinship was no stronger than the resort to habit with which he had accounted for the origin of exogamy:

> ideas of kinship must be regarded as growths – must have *grown* like all other ideas related to matters primarily cognizable only by the senses . . . the fact of consanguinity must have long remained unperceived as other facts, quite as obvious, have done. In other words, at the root of kinship is a physical fact, which could be discerned only through observation and reflection – a fact, therefore, which must for a time have been overlooked. No advocate of innate ideas, we should imagine, will maintain their existence on a subject so concrete as relationship by blood. (1865: 151–2)

In place of the psychologism of innate ideas, however, McLennan had no motive that could account for this highly consequential growth. When we look for the spur behind it, we find only repetition. Growth is its own explanation:

> The development of the idea of blood relationship into a system of kinship must have been a work of time. (1865: 154)

Thenceforth, the argument abandons the idea in favour of its forms:

> Once a man has perceived the fact of consanguinity in the simplest case – namely, that he has his mother's blood in his veins, he may quickly see that he is of the same blood with her other children. A little more reflection will enable him to see that he is of one blood with the brothers and sisters of his mother. On further thought he will perceive that he is of the same blood with the children of his mother's sister. (1865: 155)

Where did his mother get her brothers and sisters from? Kinship must have already been in operation. Without further labouring it, the point is that there was no maternal kinship to arise from observation before the stable motherhood which succeeded marriage by capture, and that situation rendered fatherhood stable too. In other words, McLennan's matrilineal interruption was a detour which prevented him from proposing a theory of the origin of kinship, requiring him to counterfeit one with a claim as to the initial forms which that concept took.

Yet a situation in which local hordes were constantly warring and hunting provided obvious opportunities for the development of a concept of cooperative unity based on ideas about blood. In fact, it was just such conditions that produced the 'brethren' whose idea of blood relationship was to develop into a system of kinship (1865: 153). But to derive the concept of consanguinity directly from naturally given territorial ties would have been to leave kinship as a presocial boys' club that provided no warrant for the subordination of the maternal principle. Thus the metaphor of common blood from which kinship continued could not be the original basis of stock unity. Rather, that unity had already produced the brethren before their comradeship came to be depicted in images of blood (1865: 152–3). Pushing McLennan back behind the brethren, we find him not only aware of the problem, but once more covering his tracks with a play on words. This time, rather than eliding two meanings under the cover of one morpheme (as in 'house'), he attempts the reverse, hiving off a non-existent distinction under the cover of a morphological variation that has no effect on the semantic nucleus ('kin'). He uses this distinction to claim that the feelings or affections associated with an idea might be innately endowed, even though the idea itself is not. This enables him blithely to claim that, before the emergence of any such concept as parenthood or brotherhood, feelings proper to the condition of being children or brothers could have been innately present:

> The earliest human groups can have had no idea of kinship. We do not mean to say that there ever was a time when men were not bound together by a feeling of kindred. The filial and fraternal affections may be instinctive. They are obviously independent of any theory of kinship, its origin or consequences; they are distinct from the perception of the unity of blood upon which kinship depends; and they may have existed long before kinship became an object of thought. (1865: 151)

The feeling of kindred is, of course, kinship under a (barely) different name. It predated the concept of shared blood because it had to be independent of that concept. Then kinship itself, though derived from the concept of shared blood, could express a notion of relatedness ('kindredness') that was independent of the metaphor of consanguinity which it inherited from the presocial brethren of the local horde. Here, too, therefore, we encounter a narrative structure in which the principles of blood and land are alternately permuted. We saw above how the tripartite sequence of principles of group organization suppressed territorial continuity in the interest of constructing a matrilineal phase during which consanguinity was the sole organizing principle, after which territorial organization was reintroduced. In precisely the same way, we now see that the kindred feeling was a way of suppressing kinship in favour of territoriality, one which was then supplanted by the local brethrens' attainment of consanguinity. Again, the final stage – kinship – was a compound of the first two, in this latter instance blending the kindredness of territoriality with consanguinity.

This consistency reveals more than a propositional manoeuvre that McLennan happened to favour. It takes us back to the unlikely prospect of horde ties existing without reference to motherhood. If the same tripartite narrative structure were to apply there too, then, at a stage earlier than the motherhood that was the first form of kinship, there should have been a prior form of motherhood, only the continuity between the two motherhoods would have been interrupted by some other factor. This reasoning gains force from the preceding demonstration that McLennan's whole basis for maternal kinship – uncertainty concerning fathers – was invalid on the grounds that motherhood could not become stable until the copartnery compact, which simultaneously stabilized fatherhood as well. Alerted by the recurrence of the same strategy, we therefore consider whether the absence of motherhood which preceded the origin of legitimate kinship was in fact an absence at all, or merely an interruption. If it were an interruption, then, as seems eminently reasonable, presocial motherhood – which is to say, a naturally given precedent for McLennan's nescient matrilineal kinship – would have been there all along. This would make the case of maternal kinship analogous to that of territorial association, whose natural continuity maternal kinship interrupted. What, then, could have interrupted the continuity of maternal filiation? By now, the answer hardly needs spelling out. Just as McLennan supplanted territorial ties with maternal kinship to legitimate a social mode of appropriating territory, so was the famously shocking saga of violent wife-capture a means of interrupting the continuity of a naturally given maternity. By filiating children to the horde on the ground that their mothers could vanish at any moment, McLennan made nescience of maternity underwrite the exclusively territorial basis of the wife-capturing primal horde. Having in turn suppressed both naturally given maternity and naturally given territoriality, he was able to reintroduce them on his own terms, terms which sanctified patriarchal property and subordinated the female principle in order to furnish the twin foundations of human society.

Considered as a debating-effect, McLennan's marriage by capture is multiply ironic. As the centrepiece for which *Primitive Marriage* became principally renowned, it not only institutionalized the cartoon caveman with a woman over one shoulder and a club over the other but also – to Engels' glee – kicked the biblical underpinnings out from beneath the Victorian bourgeois family. As such, it incurred a considerable measure of notoriety for McLennan, who never succeeded in securing an academic job. Yet when the shocking saga of marriage by capture is recognized as a debating-effect contrived to cover over a furtive switch between blood and land (the principles that would come to be polarized in twentieth-century British social anthropology as descent and residence), it emerges as a means for McLennan to craft an evolutionary narrative that would legitimate the institutions of a property-owning patriarchy. In other words, though his ideological agenda could hardly have been more congenial to Victorian patriarchal interests, the exigencies of reconciling the contradictory premises upon which those interests were predicated produced a narrative superstructure that was ironically subversive (cf. Stocking 1987: 206).

As a defence of patriarchal property, McLennan's theory constitutes a kind of gendered variant of *terra nullius*. The analogy is by no means gratuitous. To put it in the terms coined above, as far as rights to property are concerned, the subordination of women was to the subordination of the colonized as autographic to xenographic. Once a discourse that deprived women of property rights was displaced onto the colonies, savages became women and shared their dispossession. Thus primal promiscuity was not simply a fantasy that symptomatized Victorian sexual repression. More profoundly, it provided a warrant for the seizure of territory occupied by 'nomads'. In so far as the patriarchal narrative dispossessed both women and the colonized, therefore, Carol Pateman's (1988) sexual contract needs racializing. This could hardly be clearer than in the case of the tripartite structure of McLennan's narrative, in which the crucial median phase of matrilineal kinship categorically excluded territoriality. Since, prior to Spencer and Gillen's explorations in the centre in the 1890s, the great majority of ethnographic Aborigines were matrilineal, this structure perfectly harmonized with *terra nullius*. This is not, of course, to suggest that *terra nullius* thus became dependent on Aboriginal matrilineality. As will be seen, the consternation generated by Spencer and Gillen's discovery of the Arunta and other Central Australian patrilines was usually resolved by claiming that, rather than the evolutionary advance on matriliny that their patriliny might suggest them to have achieved, these tribes were actually less advanced than eastern-Australian matrilines, their status being not that of the post-nescience patrilines but that of the presocial local hordes. Thus the patriarchal (sexual/colonial) outcome remained constant. Either way, it found expression through a narrative structure whose enunciation was a debating-effect of McLennan's theory.

The discourse that gave common expression to colonial and sexual expropriation was one of transcendence. Savages, like women, were bound into the realm of the concrete, of nature, of the physical and so on (the list is a familiar one). As such, they were incomplete – in the Cartesian scheme of things, they were as matter awaiting the transcendent regulation of mind. Thus it was a completion that could only be achieved through subordination. McLennan's narrative expresses this perfectly. In it, the naturally given female principle (the uterine blood of kinship) provides the subjects of property – successors to inherit – whilst the naturally given male principle (horde territory) provides the object of property – what is to be inherited. In their fusion, nature is transcended and society results. In this fusion, however, the male principle retains a priority which, continuing into society, renders patriarchy transcendent. This transcendence is associated with others – the inferential capacity presupposed in reckoning consanguinity, for instance, that McLennan went to such lengths to distinguish from natural endowment. In this manner, patriarchy becomes responsible for humanity's transcendent representational capacities.

McLennan was not alone in this. Indeed, in enlisting the Ancient Greeks to the same end, Bachofen had underscored its genealogical depth. For Bachofen, in contrast to the concrete umbilical tie of maternity, the paternal principle was sublimely abstract, triumphing over the material connection required by sensory perception. Being mediated by the mother, the father appeared as a 'remoter potency'.[95] Since he was also the 'promoting cause', his immateriality contrasted with the 'nurturing and sheltering' Aeschylean mother's role as mere 'nurse', or vessel ('place and house of generation') for the male seed (Bachofen 1967a: 109). Fatherhood introduced a new radiant dimension, spiritual life, which alone constituted the transcendence of bestial existence:

> Maternity pertains to the physical side of man, the only thing he shares with the animals: the paternal-spiritual principle belongs to him alone ... Triumphant paternity partakes of the heavenly light, while childbearing motherhood is bound up with the earth that bears all things. (Bachofen 1967a: 109; 110)

the rise of fathers being thus a dawning:

> As long as religion recognises the seat of the generative principle in tellurian matter, the law of matter prevails: man is equated with unlamented lower creation and mother right governs the reproduction of man and beast. But once the creative principle is dissociated from earthly matter and joined with the sun, a higher state sets in. Mother right is left to the animals and the human family goes over to father right. At the same time mortality is restricted to matter, which returns to the womb whence it came, while the spirit, purified by fire from the slag of matter, rises up to the luminous heights of immortality and immateriality. (Bachofen 1967a: 129)

Father-right for Bachofen was therefore the era of Apollo and the sun – of abstraction, transcendence and individualism – over against the material regularity of the maternal earth-goddess Ceres or Demeter.

Though agreeing with Bachofen in assimilating patriarchy to human transcendence, McLennan's theory was crucially different from Bachofen's in that, unlike the idealist Bachofen, who derived the spur to social improvement from religion, McLennan, as observed, was at great pains to provide a material-social (what Robertson Smith, echoing Bachofen, would term a 'telluric') explanation. In this essential respect, McLennan's theory can be said to be anthropological where Bachofen's was merely antiquarian. As a first step to developing our provisional definition of evolutionary-anthropological theory, therefore, we can suggest that evolutionary anthropology was a discourse on transcendence that derived it from a sociogenic fusion of blood and land. This will be explored below. For the time being, it enables us to see more clearly the difference between Bachofen's theory and succeeding anthropological ones (McLennan's and Morgan's being paradigmatic) which, though sharing a name with Bachofen's theory, were strictly matrilineal and had no matriarchal component.[96]

---

95 This remoteness, which Bachofen optimistically proclaimed as strength, was, of course, the very weakness in monogamy which inspired the anxiety permeating the spectre of uncertain fatherhood on which nescience was premised. The same remoteness prompted Potter's (1902) contention that the theme of unintentional parricide – classically, where sons separated from their fathers in infancy come later to kill them in heroic combat, only then to realize what they have done, as in the case of Sohrab and Rustem – was a survival of mother-right (cf. Rivers 1915: 858).

96 In what we should presumably take to be another slip of the pen, McLennan himself once seemed to confuse matriliny with matriarchy (though he was here referring to Ancient Greece in a manner strikingly prefigurative of Mauss, Lévi-Strauss and alliance theory): 'A family system in which the mother was the family head, her children the heirs, and her daughters the continuers of the family and gens to which she belonged – her husband or husbands being strangers to the gens – would account for women attaining a considerable position, and also for their being reported to be, as they really were, the means of allying tribes to one another' (McLennan 1876: 287–8).

For Bachofen, mother-right had actually signified the exercise of power by women, who had revolted against the degradation to which male-imposed promiscuity ('hetaerism') had subjected them. Hetaerism, associated with the furious fertilization of a swamp, clashed with women's 'need for a higher life', an eternal dictate of feminine nature so imperious that, when resistance to promiscuity proved not to avail, women took up arms and exacted bloody revenge, imposing a pure and monogamous regime which constituted the triumph of ideal motherhood. This was the celebrated 'Amazonism', and it was from this revolution, rather than from subsequent patriarchates, that the Roman concept of having a nameable father dated (Bachofen 1967a: 98–105). Amazonism was, therefore, a far cry from a nescient world in which descent had to be traced through the female line as a consequence of male passions holding unfettered sway, although Bachofen recognized that condition as a prior stage:

> To be sure, the mother right which embodies only the child's matrilinear descent is *iuris naturalis*; it is as old as the human race and not incompatible with sexual promiscuity; but the matriarchy which gives the mother *domination* over family and state is of later origin and wholly positive in nature. It grows from the woman's reaction to unregulated sexuality, from which she is first to seek liberation. The initial determined resistance to the bestial state of universal promiscuity is woman's. It is the woman who artfully or forcefully puts an end to this degrading state. The staff is wrenched from the male, the woman becomes the master. This transition is inconceivable without individual marriage. (Bachofen 1967a: 142)

It follows that Aboriginal matrilines could hardly have recalled Bachofen's Amazonism.[97] Though sharing Bachofen's belief in an era of matrilineal descent preceding patrilineal patriarchy, the received anthropological scheme was simply Bachofen's *ius naturalis*, which gave way directly to father-right, dispensing with the virtuous Amazonian interlude. This interlude was not simply incompatible because it elevated the female principle. Rather, Bachofen's Amazonism was incompatible because it staggered rather than synchronized the respective origins of property and patriarchy. Amazonism was associated with agricultural settlement, the basis for the emergence of property. In Bachofen's scheme, therefore, settlement could occur – and virtue accordingly flourish – before patriarchy was inaugurated. Correspondingly, the rise of patriarchal-Apollonian abstract being could not have coincided with that of property, since property was already there, which meant that it had to have pre-existed in the concretely female realm of nature. By dividing the presocial realm into debased (hetaerism) and virtuous (Amazonism) stages, Bachofen precluded a unified shift from matrilineal chaos to propertied patriarchal regularity. Eliminate Amazonism from Bachofen's scheme and you are left with mother-right orthodoxy: a unified great transition from brutality to culture in which matrilineal chaos gave way to

---

[97] Fison and Howitt (1880: 127) invoked Lubbock to underline their Australian data's refutation of Bachofen: 'Bachofen supposes that descent through the mother arose out of a rebellion against communal marriage on the part of the women, who successfully established their rights against those of the men; and Sir John Lubbock, while dissenting from that view, on the ground that "savage women would be peculiarly unlikely to uphold their dignity in the manner supposed" says "It seems to me perfectly clear that the idea of marriage is founded on the rights, not of the woman, but of the man," and he quotes the "complete subjection" of the women among the Australian blacks in support of his opinion.'

patriarchal property, presupposing settlement (on this count too, therefore, nomads were excluded from human society).[98] Since Bachofen derived transcendence from an ideal source, his uncoordinated transition was not a problem. In eliminating Amazonism, therefore, the secular-materialist mother-right of anthropological orthodoxy eliminated the virtuous dictates of religion, leaving only mundane factors to account for the transition from the swamps of promiscuous hetaerism to the abstract Apollonian sunlight of patriarchal property.

In so doing, evolutionary-anthropological theory achieved the ideological breakthrough of linking the legitimation of patriarchy to the scientific-rationalist project of accounting for the higher faculties. It inserted patriarchy into the categorical imperative. In this regard, it is quite consistent that McLennan and his direct successor Robertson Smith should have been Scottish (cf. Burrow 1966: 233). In the best Humean tradition, they strove for mundane materialist explanations. Moreover, in making explicit the colonial/patriarchal foundations of that epistemology, they were unlikely to risk rousing another Kant from his dogmatic slumber (indeed, it might be that, with patriarchy vouchsafed, God loses His necessity and materialism its threat). In this context, the whole anthropological problematic of deriving consciousness from mundane social conditions is bound up in the mutually sustaining discourses of patriarchy and colonialism.

So far as this problematic is concerned, the 'matriarchalist' (as such theorists were termed) whose influence compared with that of McLennan was not the antiquarian Bachofen but the robustly anthropological 'father of kinship studies', Lewis Henry Morgan. Though devised in upstate New York, Morgan's theory was integral to British anthropology, whose development it profoundly influenced.

Morgan: From Communal Family to Private Property

As is well known, Morgan subscribed to an explicit teleology ('the plan of the Supreme Intelligence to develop a barbarian out of a savage, and a civilised man out of this barbarian' [1877: 563]). The means whereby this cosmic plan unfolded was, however, the mundane evolution of the arts of subsistence, a materialist dynamic that was to endear Morgan to Marx and Engels.

Morgan had encountered certain Iroquois, whose kinship terms ordered them into lateral groupings (that he called 'leagues' or 'gentes') rather than into the lineal descent groups that he took to be naturally given by consanguinity. Rather than calling one man 'father' and an indeterminate number of men 'uncle', an Iroquois called a number of men 'father'. Such a system was novel to Morgan and, at the time, he took it to be unique, using it to reconstruct a halcyon democratic idyll (*The League of the Iroquois*, 1851) reminiscent of the noble savagery whose career had waned in Europe.[99] He subsequently came to realize, however, that his Iroquois, like Bachofen's

---

98 '[M]ere hunting and fishing peoples lie outside the point where real development begins' (Marx 1973: 107).
99 But persisted in the United States (Berkhofer 1978: 77–81).

Lycians, were not alone. As evidence came in that Iroquois-style collateral relationship terminology was to be found all over North America, he began to think of the system as characterizing a whole cultural area; thinking that took on the proportions of a global theory of social origins when the same system surfaced in South India.[100]

Though Morgan's was a unified scheme of progress, in which physiological, technological, demographic, moral and other dimensions of social development were correlated, the whole theory stemmed from his interpretation of these collateral relationship nomenclatures, which became his 'classificatory' kinship systems. As the name implied, a classificatory system was one in which people were allocated identities according to their membership of classes of kin. The advanced alternative to this system was the civilized (Aryan, Semitic, Uralian) system, which Morgan termed 'descriptive'.

The descriptive system was a means of labelling the members of one's own family. It originated extremely early in human evolution, being 'one of the earliest acts of human speech' (1871: 470). With time and transmission (i.e. here too, with habit), the terminology became independent of its actual human referents, developing into 'an indurated system capable of resisting radical innovations' (1871: 471). The term 'descriptive' implies a direct correlation with reality, which is as Morgan intended, since what the system described was the true course of blood lines as they converged on the monogamous couple and uniquely specified individuals. In practice, therefore, classificatory systems were those that did not mark out a set of relationships that were indicative of monogamous pairing. The difference between the two systems was coterminal with that between the civilized and uncivilized nations, which, as Engels so appreciated, arose as a result of 'the development of a knowledge of property, of its uses, and of its transmission by inheritance' (1871: 470).

Though the descriptive system was more advanced than classificatory ones, its inauguration as one of the earliest speech acts resulted from the fact that the distinction between the two systems depended on how many relationships one had rather than on whether or not one chose to label them. Thus the excess of uncles (or, which was the same thing, the lack of fathers) testified to the familiar combination of primal promiscuity and nescience. A consequence was a system of collective, as opposed to individual, identities. In opposition to the individualism of the descriptive system, the classificatory system set up undifferentiated generational categories that were relatively independent of consanguinity, wildly exceeding it or arbitrarily cutting it off. With the rise of descriptive nomenclature, these categories gave way to specific individual ties – 'the *gradus* yields to the *nexus*' (1871: 470).

Like McLennan – only for different reasons – Morgan found himself embroiled in trying to explain how mothers as well as fathers might come to be unknown. Morgan's problem was the empirical symmetry of classificatory systems, which provided not just for a whole class of fathers (or uncles) but for a whole class of aunts/mothers as well. This problem variously reduced

---

100 For accounts of this celebrated progression see Trautmann 1987: 84–178, White 1957.

him to suggesting that sisters' common tribal status could lead to their also being standardized for kinship purposes (1871: 476); alternatively, since shared paternity made half-siblings brothers and sisters to each other, they could extend the logic to share mothers as well (1871: 478); or again – and even less convincingly – he simply asserted that the lack of distinction between lineal and collateral consanguinei would apply to maternity on the same grounds as it held for paternity (1871: 483, n. 10), this being in spite of his acknowledgement one page earlier that 'among the wives of these brothers they can distinguish their own mother' (1871: 482, n. 5) – an acknowledgement necessitated by the requirements of an era of matrilineal nescience.

Though matrilineal organization and the concomitant uncertainty of paternity were assuredly uncivilized, there was a series of even lower stages. Indeed, Morgan held kinship systems to be indices for the whole of human evolution (hence the biblical scope of his theory). The basis on which he held this was the structural similarity between the Dravidian (which he termed 'Turanian') kinship system and the Native American ones that he had studied (which he called the 'Ganowanian' – lit. 'bow and arrow' – system). To Morgan, this meant that Native Americans must be displaced South Indians. Accordingly, though he recognized (1871: 491) the difficulties entailed in the claim that their kinship system had been transmitted to America by physical migration (they would have to have become an Arctic people to cross the Bering Straits, only to have subsequently had to reacclimatize themselves to a hotter latitude), he nevertheless tolerated these problems in the interests of championing the historical longevity of kinship systems. This longevity resulted from the fact (to Morgan) that a kinship system actually ran in the blood, which gave it 'an instrument and a means for its transmission through periods of indefinite duration' (1871: 505). This arterial anchorage on the part of kinship systems rendered them historically more tenacious than even linguistic affinities, of which none had survived the epic transmigration. Mindful of the prestige of the historical reconstructions that Max Müller and, in the USA, ethnologists such as Stephen Du Ponceau and Albert Gallatin were achieving through comparative philology, Morgan sought to establish the superiority of his new science of comparative kinship, which had successfully determined the question 'whether an instrumentality could be found, in systems of consanguinity and affinity, which was able to take up the problem at the point where philology is now arrested' (1871: 506).[101] Even granting its octopodean ramifications, the entailments of Morgan's theory were so extensive that it could enable astonishing connections. For instance, in summing up the preceding argument, he concluded that Columbus had

---

[101] In his superb account of Morgan's 'invention' of kinship, Thomas R. Trautmann (1987: 73–83) distinguished originally and insightfully between three philological traditions that bore on Morgan's thinking. Müller's theory was unknown to Morgan at the time he wrote *The League of the Iroquois* (1851) and only became known to him at a stage when what Trautmann (1987: 75) calls 'the philological design' of his work (by which I take Trautmann to mean '*Systems*') was already established. Whilst such claims are inherently difficult to quantify, Trautmann's sketch of the development of these post-Jeffersonian theories is so true to the tenor of Morgan's thinking that I would not wish to quibble. None the less, there can be little doubt that what Trautmann elsewhere (1987: 216) terms the 'perceived success' of the Indo-Europeanist tradition associated with Müller gave it greater international prestige, a consideration that can hardly have failed to influence the ambitions of a scholar with as wide a network of international connections as Morgan. Trautmann is surely correct to attach lesser significance to the claims of the third tradition, Adam Smith's eighteenth-century conjectural philology.

actually been justified in calling Native Americans 'Indians' ('By a singular coincidence error was truth' – 1871: 508)!

Morgan's basis for asserting the historical durability of kinship systems was his famous lag-time between family organization and kinship nomenclature. He claimed that an 'indurated system' of kinship becomes so firmly entrenched that, even though a society may accede to the will of the Supreme Intelligence and institute progressive moral reforms to its family organization, the nomenclature lags behind, testifying to the unregenerate usage of the previous epoch. On this logic, therefore, the most primitive extant family organization would retain the terminological skeleton of its extinct predecessor. From an undifferentiated primal state of promiscuous intercourse, Morgan's schedule of development proceeded through the so-called Consanguine Family, which consisted in a sexual free-for-all between brothers and sisters (both classificatory and descriptive)[102] to Group Marriage, which consisted in either a group of sisters sharing a set of husbands or a group of brothers sharing a set of wives – 'In each case the group of men were conjointly married to the group of women' (1877: 393). Morgan saw the Turanian or Ganowanian kinship system of South India and North America as signifying Group Marriage. From the Turanian/Ganowanian system upwards, he had a continuous succession of systems culminating in Aryan monogamy. Thus all he needed to complete the whole series from Promiscuous Intercourse to monogamy was evidence of the Consanguine Family. On the basis of the lag-time, this evidence would survive in the kinship system of a society actually practising Group Marriage. Though Morgan claimed that the system that he interchangeably termed 'Hawaiian' or 'Malayan' bore witness to the Consanguine Family, contemporary Hawaiians did not actually practise Group Marriage. On the basis of the lag-time, therefore, what he really needed was a society in which Group Marriage actually took place. This would have a Malayan kinship system that would betray an earlier Consanguine Family.

This lag can, therefore, be seen to have been motivated by Morgan's moral imperative. All things being equal, his moral reformations would have caused previous family organizations to vanish without trace, leaving no possibility of reconstructing them. Thus the anachronistic nature of kinship systems was necessitated by the requirement to enquire behind the moral reformations. The converse – that the kinship system entailed the moral evolution – also applies. This is because the relationship between kinship systems was unidirectional. The Hawaiian/Malayan system could not have succeeded the Turanian/Ganowanian one, although that system could have been engrafted onto the Malayan, and 'it is not probable that the Turanian family could ever revert into the Malayan' (1871: 509). Again, the necessities ramified. Morgan needed this argument to eliminate Polynesia as a rival to South India's claim to be the source of the native Americans:

> It will follow, as a further consequence, that America was not peopled from the Polynesian Islands, the [Turanian/Ganowanian] system of relationship having

---

102 Morgan 1877: 403. How they acquired brothers and sisters was not made clear.

been completely developed in Asia after the Malayan migration [to Polynesia]. (1871: 509)

To get beneath the recursive complex of elements in Morgan's scheme to the primary principle binding them together, it is necessary, as in McLennan's case, to focus on the significance for his concept of consanguinity of the relationship between matrilineal kinship and property ownership. For, like McLennan, Morgan excluded territorial criteria from his notion of society until a point at which the evolution of a patriarchal system of kinship and marriage could enable property rights to be legitimated by means of an ideological fusion of blood and land.

Beneath the proliferation of types of kinship system, with their differently named but overlapping family counterparts, Morgan actually had only two basic stages of social organization (though he spliced on a prior one):

> the organisation of society upon the basis of sex, then upon the basis of kin, and finally upon the basis of territory. (1877: 7)

The fundamental division was that separating the final couple of this threesome, the political frontier between kinship and the state, which further coincided with the passage from the ancient to the modern era:

> The experience of mankind ... has developed but two plans of government ... The first and most ancient was a *social organization*, founded upon gentes, phratries and tribes. The second and latest in time was a *political organization*, founded upon territory and upon property. Under the first a gentile society was created, in which the government dealt with persons through their relations to a gens and a tribe. These relations were purely personal. Under the second a political society was instituted, in which the government dealt with persons through their relations to territory, e.g. – the township, the country and the state. These relations were purely territorial. The two plans were fundamentally different. One belongs to ancient society, and the other to modern. (1877: 61)

This great watershed variously involved technological developments leading to an increased level of moveable property (especially pastoral herds), which gave men a motive for wanting to ensure the legitimacy of their own heirs. Consequently, they needed to guarantee that their wives' children could not be of any other man's blood, which meant the institution of monogamy, which in turn enabled people to specify their relationships to each other accurately. As in the case of McLennan, from the propertied patrilocal patriline on, the modern state developed unproblematically. To proceed in a manner consistent with the treatment of McLennan, therefore, we have to ask what was happening to territory during the initial, person-based epoch extending from the origin of humanity to the Aryans' adoption of descriptive kinship.

Property must have existed before the transition to father-right or it could not have provided a reason for men to find mother-right irksome. Indeed, property for Morgan was one of the few 'germs of thought' whose development was directed by a natural logic that 'formed an essential attribute of the brain itself' (1877: 59–60). Though primally endowed, however, the property germ's effects lay dormant over the ages, since it was a motive lacking an object. Yet people obviously occupied territory. This can only mean that, as in the case of McLennan, the land-ownership which formed the basis of civilization was of an order different to earlier forms of territorial possession:

> Lands, as yet hardly a subject of property, were owned by the tribes in common. (1877: 538)

The key words here are 'in common'. Property, like marriage, was not legitimate until it was private. How, therefore, did the emergence of exclusive rights over women convert men's possession of their land into the institution of private property? As in the case of McLennan's horde 'goods', all possessions, not just the offspring whose legitimacy fathers wanted to ensure, passed from the female to the male line. This meant that the husband's occupancy of land became co-ordinated with his possession of grain and livestock. Just as McLennan suppressed the territorial dimension during the matrilineal interlude, in other words, Morgan used the moveability of grain and livestock to disguise the fact that men had occupied their land continuously. Though all fell under the common rubric of property, land (unlike women, grain and livestock) cannot be alienated while the owner stands still. This means that the property which a man was frustrated from transmitting to his son could not have included land, since the son would still have grown up on that land – even if we were to accept that he would eventually have had to use it to support alien livestock that his wife had brought with her. Indeed, Morgan's whole theory depended on the affections (McLennan's 'kindred sentiments') that grew from the cohabitation of fathers and sons. Without this affection, fathers had no motive for wanting to transmit property to their sons. Morgan provided no reason for either fathers or sons having to break this cohabitation by leaving their land. Thus the moment where Morgan smuggled land ownership into kinship was the point at which he conflated land and moveable possessions (which included women) under the common rubric of property that matriliny precluded a man from transmitting to his son. He even went as far as blandly representing the permanence of territorial subsistence as a subsidiary elaboration on the original property form which had arisen with pastoral herds – as if the herds had mystically bootstrapped their way into existence without the need for territorial subsistence. This new quality of permanence then became a significant contributor to the demise of mother-right:

> After domestic animals began to be reared in flocks and herds, becoming thereby a source of subsistence as well as objects of individual property, and after tillage had led to the ownership of individual houses and lands in severalty, an antagonism would be certain to arise against the prevailing form of gentile inheritance, because it excluded the owner's children, whose paternity was becoming more assured, and gave his property to his gentile kindred. A contest

for a new rule of inheritance, shared in by fathers and their children, would furnish a motive sufficiently powerful to effect the change. With property accumulating in masses and assuming permanent forms, and with an increased proportion of it held by individual ownership, descent in the female line was certain of overthrow, and the substitution of the male line equally assured. (1877: 355)

Accordingly, both Morgan and McLennan blessed the union of societies and their territory by expediently shifting between blood and land. In Morgan's case, however, the redeeming institution was not simply property *per se* (which, as he observed, could obtain in severalty) but private property. Why could land only be socialized when its ownership was private? We thus return to the key words 'in common'. Morgan's patrilocal patriline did not supplant mother-right until the advent of monogamy, which, despite the essential correspondence between their two schemes, contrasts in detail with the sharing of both wives and property practised by McLennan's Tibetan brothers. Yet an isomorphy whereby forms of marriage replicated forms of property was common to both – wives and land in each case being appropriated according to a single criterion, which had the effect of swathing real estate in the sacred aura of domestic morality. McLennan, however, retained a Hibernian identification with Scottish feudal institutions, so it is appropriate that he should have sanctioned land ownership at the point where it became instituted (and mother-right supplanted) on a family (or clan) rather than an individual basis. Morgan, on the other hand, was a Yankee individualist of the purest democratic temper. For him, though feudal institutions had been a historically necessary evil (since, though oppressive, they had consolidated the institution of property), their time had passed:

> Property and office were the foundations upon which aristocracy planted itself . . . Although several thousand years have passed without the overthrow of privileged classes, excepting in the United States, their burdensome character upon society has been demonstrated. (1877: 561)

To this difference between Morgan and McLennan should be added a further one concerning their respective critical referents. For, as noted above, McLennan's theory had autographic implications for the sexual politics of his own metropolitan society (i.e. as distinct from those of colonized nomads on the far side of the globe). By contrast, Morgan's Ganowanian tribes, whose marriage system did not constitute a qualification to own land, had been incorporated and internally colonized within his own settler society (indeed, it was his investment in railroads through their lands that had taken him among them [Resek 1960: 58–9; 85]). Thus it is hardly surprising that Morgan should have represented property as inhering in individuals rather than in collectivities.

In this regard, it is significant that Morgan's theory should have directly and formatively intervened into Australian Aboriginal anthropology. As mentioned, though the essential threshold in Morgan's theory of development was that separating social from territorial organization, he tacked on to the beginning a third term – sexual organization – which, being a form of social organization, would seem to have been superfluous. By sexual organization, he meant a division of society into exogamous classes. It did not figure in his first Herculean work, *Systems of Consanguinity and Affinity of the Human Family* (1871), but occupied a key position in his *Ancient Society* (1877), in which sexual organization was held to be the outcome of a rule banning brother and sister incest (by making them members of the same class). Such a rule would, of course, abolish the Consanguine Family, whose prior existence it thus confirmed (this was the first in a long line of analyses that tendered marriage classes as proof that Aborigines practised something that the classes rendered impossible). By *Ancient Society*, Aborigines were presented as contemporary instances of a society based on sexual organization, with Howitt's Australian co-writer Lorimer Fison being cited as Morgan's principal authority (Morgan 1877: 56; cf. 1872: 425).[103] Thus the Arunta were not the first Aborigines to fulfil theoretical prophecies. Whilst much has been (and, for that matter, remains to be) said about this, for present purposes it is enough to point out that, in common with McLennan's era of nescient matrilineal consanguinity, sexual organization suppressed territoriality as a basis for social organization.

With mention of Fison and Howitt, we begin to close the mother-right circle. For Spencer and Gillen dedicated their great 1899 book to Fison and Howitt, 'who laid the foundation of our knowledge of Australian anthropology'. Frazer was to assert that the evidence marshalled by Howitt, Spencer and Gillen made 'practically certain' the unmistakably Morganian conclusion that 'in Australia individual marriage has everywhere been preceded by group marriage, and that again by a still wider sexual communism' (Frazer 1905: 452, n.4). In McLennan's and Morgan's theories, we have encompassed the constituent features of the mother-right narrative, in particular the way it contrived a sociogenic combination of the principles of blood and land to account for the transcendence of natural determination. In 1882, in Britain, the Married Women's Property Act changed the outward form of the patriarchal order that the mother-right narrative had endorsed. Epistemologically (in anthropology at least) mother-right was not to survive the paradigm shift.[104] With this in mind, we turn now to the opposition that mother-right was to encounter.

103 In *Systems*, there had been no Australian data, so there had been no empirical support for the Consanguine (at that stage termed 'Communal') Family, which was the bridge that Morgan needed between Promiscuous Intercourse and the Group Marriage that he inferred from the Turanian/Ganowanian system. When Spencer and Gillen's Arunta had duly satisfied Morgan's classificatory requirements for the Consanguine Family (Spencer and Gillen 1899: 58), a finding that supported Frazer's view, in opposition to that of Andrew Lang, that the Arunta were maximally primitive, Lang (1908b: 6) turned the tables with characteristic zest: 'A Frenchman calls his wife his 'woman' (*femme*) and he calls every adult member of the fair sex 'a woman'. An Arunta calls his wife *unawa*, and all other women of her tribal status he terms *unawa*. *Ma fille* is 'my daughter'; *fille* is any girl in the world. Judging by language the lively Gaul has been more promiscuous than the Arunta.'

104 Though it did, of course, survive in psychoanalysis and in what today would be called New Age discourse (e.g. Briffault 1927), and could even recur in anthropology if the explanatory predicament was desperate enough, as in Donald Thomson's (1933: 510) 'The only possible explanation of this unusual totemism [Kawadji] that I am able to suggest is the one already advanced: that the personal totemism is a relic of a previous matrilineal condition.'

Mother-Right Under Challenge

The career of mother-right was central to that of evolutionary anthropology itself. Thus, though Theodor Waitz, eminence of the preceding generation, linked Aborigines to what was to become the distinctive premise of McLennan's theory, he did so with an innocence of nescience that is striking to hindsight:

> [Amongst Aborigines] Infanticide, especially of girls, is frequent: hence the proportionately small number of women. This proceeds partly from superstition, partly from the desire to escape the trouble of rearing them, and sometimes from revenge against the faithless father, especially if he be an European. (Waitz 1863: 164)

Over the following quarter-century, however, mother-right attained such theoretical hegemony that, by 1884, Bachofen's protegé Alexis Giraud-Telon (in a book jointly dedicated, believe it or not, to his mother and to Bachofen) pronounced himself in 'complete contradiction' not only with Morgan, McLennan, Fison and Howitt but, in relation to dual organization at least, with Bachofen himself. This notwithstanding, there was still 'an essential point on which we all agree':

> this is that the tribe [a territorial category] was the original grouping; that in this tribe was formed the matrilineal clan, and that finally, in the very last place, there appeared, in the bosom of the clan, the individual paternal family. (Giraud-Telon 1884: 135, n.1)

By this stage, Aborigines had become firmly located on the boundary between the first two stages. Thus Giraud-Telon also felt able to pronounce (1884: 80) Aboriginal social organization a rudimentary progression relative to the herd state of promiscuity, which, in turn, could simply be *'admis comme postulat'*. Such were the presuppositions of mother-right that it was long assumed that patriliny would not operate in Australia. Thus Giraud-Telon took Australian matrifiliation for granted as a 'general rule' (1884: 165), asserting that it only admitted 'rare exceptions'. Strictly, however, any exception, no matter how rare, should have put the cat amongst the pigeons. In *Primitive Marriage*, McLennan had claimed to have found 'the system of kinship through females only, universally prevailing among the Australian Blacks' (1865: 209), which hardly allowed for the fact that, by the 1880s, even given the number of Aborigines still unsurveyed, the exceptions amounted to some twenty per cent. Hence Frazer merely termed (1885: 473) Australian matrilines a 'large majority', explaining that 'the proportion of tribes with female to those with male descent is as four to one'. That this did not vitiate mother-right – even, for over fifteen years, in Frazer's own thinking – is a matter of record. In 1886, McLennan deemed the manifest holing of his universal worth no more than a cursory footnote ('This statement, however, requires qualification. It is now known that there are Australian tribes in which kinship is counted through males' (1886b: 115, n. 1)). Empirical confounding of mother-right actually made little difference. In any event, the presocial ties of McLennan's local horde provided an alternative to the advanced stage of father-right, so empirical Aboriginal patriliny merely set off a two-way loss. It is hard to divorce mother-right's theoretical resilience from its conformity with patriarchal ideology. This is not to say, however, that stray anthropological voices were not raised against it.

In the case of men of the stature of Darwin and Maine, the voices can hardly be considered stray. I wish to argue, however, that they were not anthropological either, and that this limited their critique. This may seem to be granting British anthropology a degree of definition or cohesion that is inappropriate to its status in the 1860s. Furthermore, it precludes a very tempting baseline date for evolutionary anthropology, one nicely different from but close to the epochal 1859 of Darwin's *Origin*. This date is 1861, the year which saw the publication of two books, Bachofen's *Das Mutterrecht* and Maine's patriarchalist *Ancient Law*, whose diametrical opposition would otherwise seem ideally to encompass the parameters of a discursive field. As stated above, Bachofen was an antiquarian rather than an anthropologist. Unlike McLennan and Morgan, he did not produce his Apollonian transcendence from a merger of blood and land. This merger was not to be found in Darwin or in Maine either.

Though Darwin lent his authority to patriarchalism, denying generalized promiscuity in favour of a picture of primordially Cyclopean families gathering about lone and jealous overlords in the manner of some of the great apes, most anthropologists simply ignored zoology where its details were inconvenient. Whilst unwilling to allow that human origins could have diverged so notably from the developmental pattern of other primates, Darwin nevertheless bowed to the dominance over anthropological thinking of the vision of primitive promiscuity, deferring to his next-door neighbour Lubbock, together with Bachofen, McLennan and Morgan, as 'all those who have most closely studied the subject, and whose judgment is worth much more than mine'. Darwin summarized these authorities' common belief as being 'that communal marriage was the original and universal form throughout the world, including the intermarriage of brothers and sisters', proceeding, despite his disagreement on this count, to concede that:

> It is evident in the case of communal marriages, or where the marriage-tie is very loose, that the relationship of the child to its father cannot be known. (Darwin 1871: 358–9)

Darwin might have added that the consensus was remarkable for the fact that its proponents were polemically and often bitterly divided on other points. Though Darwin felt obliged to dissent, it made little difference. Quite apart from its developing institutional bases (Burrow 1967: 118–26; Stocking 1987: 245–73) anthropology was beginning to acquire a sufficiently distinctive discursive orientation for zoological contributions, regardless of their prestige, to be extraneous (cf. Stocking 1987: 248–54). Even later on, after the strains in mother-right had begun to show, when Andrew Lang attempted to promote the Darwinian saga of primal parricide that had been thought up by his cousin, the Fijian tea-planter Jasper Atkinson, the (somewhat delayed) response came from psychoanalysis rather than from anthropology.[105] Freud himself recognized the anthropological implications of *Totem and Taboo*:

> I cannot suggest at what point in this process of development a place is to be found for the great mother-goddesses, who may perhaps in general have preceded the father-gods. (Freud 1912: 149)

In addition to the Cyclopean tradition inaugurated by Darwin, patriarchalism was championed by the jurist and legal historian Henry Maine. Moreover, unlike Darwin, Maine succeeded in drawing McLennan into debate, to which extent he was less marginal to anthropology. Maine's theory of the development of rational individualism, traced along the axis of legal systems and substantially based on Latin and Sanskrit texts, was rooted in the constitutional distinction between authority and power. The state developed out of the family as legitimate legal systems developed out of the unrestrained autocracy of the family head (*Patria Potestas*). Though Patria Potestas involved the metaphor of consanguinity, its ultimate basis was the power of the patriarch, which overrode biological affiliation. Thus kinship was a fact of power – adoptees could be kindred and emancipated consanguines could be aliens ('In truth, in the primitive view, Relationship is exactly limited by Patria Potestas. Where the Potestas begins, kinship begins' [Maine 1861: 149]).

The primacy of Patria Potestas was but one aspect of the contrast that Maine was drawing between contemporary and ancient institutions. For, just as the despotic power of the patriarch was taken over and legitimately exercised by the state, so the agnatic system, whereby one could only fall under the *potestas* of a single patriarch, gave way to bilineal kinship, whereby individual relationships were traced through both parents. Maine's opposition between agnation and cognation was, therefore, one between patrilineal and bilineal kinship. Hence the Roman maxim *mulier finis familiae est* (woman is the end-point of the family) meant that, whether or not a woman had children, she could not add to her family:

> If a woman died unmarried, she could have no legitimate descendants. If she married, her children fell under the Patria Potestas, not of her Father, but of her Husband, and were thus lost to her own family. It is obvious that the organisation of primitive societies would have been confounded if men had called themselves relatives of their mothers' relatives. (Maine 1861: 149)

In other words, there was simply no place – not even a word – for matrilines in Maine's theory. McLennan complained that ancient Rome was not very far back in human history. Indeed, some years before *Primitive Marriage*, McLennan had written an article on law for the *Encyclopædia Britannica* (McLennan 1859) in which he founded the state on the patriarchal family. Though some have taken this to indicate a rupture in McLennan's thinking (Burrow 1966: 233–4, Rivière 1970: xxx–xxxi, Trautmann 1987: 202–4),

---

[105] Though Malinowski may seem to be an exception so far as the demise of mother-right is concerned, his interest was clearly motivated by his regard for psychoanalysis rather than by his ethnography (see Malinowski 1924).

there is no conflict between *Primitive Marriage* and the notion that property originated in patriarchy. Indeed, *Primitive Marriage* fills in the prehistory of that origin.[106] From the point of view of my argument concerning Victorian sexual politics, this is a very significant point: the theoretical impasse between mother-right and patriarchalists such as Maine and Darwin was overridden by their agreement as to the patriarchal basis of property ownership. Thus McLennan did not challenge Maine's data.[107] He merely claimed that, in going back to a time when the family rather than the individual was the basic social unit, Maine had not gone far enough:

> at a yet older date we must conclude that neither the State, nor the family, properly speaking, existed. And at that earlier time the unnamed species of kinship – the counterpart and complement of agnation – was the chief determinant of social phenomena. (McLennan 1865: 229–30)

For McLennan, had Maine looked beyond his classical data to contemporary savagery, he would have found matrilineal societies holding together 'notwithstanding the conflict of laws in the domestic forum engendered by polygyny, exogamy and female kinship'. Kinship did not depend on convenience at all. The first kinship was the first possible, through mothers, a fact which operated 'to throw difficulties in the way of the rise of the patria potestas, and of the system of agnation' (McLennan 1865: 116).

A striking feature of the disagreement between McLennan and Maine is the incommensurability of their data. Whether constructed from historical or geographical ingredients, McLennan's primitives were entirely different from Maine's Romans or post-Vedic Hindus. The same can be said for Darwin's proto-(or pre-)human primates. If Maine's subjects were too late for anthropology, Darwin's were too early. But the most significant difference separating Maine and Darwin (or jurisprudence and biology) from anthropology was not their time-frame but their lack of sociology. Darwin's theory dealt in precisely the kind of hereditary endowment that McLennan was at such pains to avoid, whilst, in promoting the development of legal systems as a cause rather than effect of changing forms of social organization, Maine, like Bachofen, was an idealist. With transcendence secured by the apparently spontaneous evolution of Roman Law, Maine had no need to combine blood and land to produce it. Thus the *potestas* was independent of a consanguinity from which women, who continued to be male possessions, were anyway excluded. It was not, after all, their chronologies that separated Maine and Darwin from the anthropologists. Rather – and assuming for the moment the validity of our provisional definition of anthropology – it was the fact that neither of their theories problematized ideas about blood. McLennan's matrilineal

---

106 In this regard, Trautmann's (1987: 204) citation of McLennan [?] (1869) suggests that his view might not, after all, be inconsistent with mine. Since it has no bearing on my argument, I shall not dwell on the point here, but I would like to register my feeling that McLennan 1869 has been wrongly attributed to McLennan by *The Wellesley Index to Victorian Periodicals, 1824–1900*, vol. 1, the authority that Rivière (1970: xlix-l) cited for assigning the piece to McLennan. Though parts of this anonymous piece employ concepts clearly derived from *Primitive Marriage* (see, e.g. the discussion of grouping on p. 527), the book was already famous and influential by 1869. The marshalling of the argument, the choice of words and the rhetorical techniques employed in the 1869 article have little of McLennan's distinctive mordacity.

107 Nor, therefore, did he 'invert' Maine, as Adam Kuper (1988: 38) claims.

interruption of male organization, it should be recalled, was also the beginning of society having ideas with which it could represent itself to itself. Hence nescience, the primal science of maternal consanguinity, marked the birth of culture. Horde ties, periodic battles for ascendancy in the Cyclopean Family and the Patria Potestas were brute facts, reducible to a crude physics of power. Kinship, by contrast, was not externally discernible, nor was there only one form which it could take. In keeping with its critical orientation, therefore, the emergent science of anthropology was a metascience – the investigation of ideology. Since this investigation was framed as a narrative of transcendence to which matrilineal nescience was central, Maine and Darwin were external to it by virtue of their patriarchalism.

The extent of mother-right's acceptance within anthropology is apparent from its capacity to survive the most testing critiques of its outlying propositions.[108] McLennan's marriage by capture is a prime example, since it encountered considerable opposition. For instance, the respected Dutch matriarchalist G.A. Wilken argued (1884: 41–3) that McLennan's theory of female infanticide logically precluded the development of exogamy, since, if everyone had practised the infanticide, there would have been too few women left anywhere for the general shortage to be made up, even by capture (Wilken underestimated the strength, in precisely this regard, of McLennan's emphasis upon polyandry). One of the few opponents of McLennan's theory who did also question mother-right was a Yorkshire solicitor named C.S. Wake, who distinguished descent from other inheritances; matrilineal and patrilineal transmissions could coexist (Wake 1889: 386–7). But Wake's critique was not influential. Moreover, one of its most significant aspects was its date – almost a quarter-century after *Primitive Marriage*. The first major anthropological critic of mother-right (although he was not major beforehand) was the Finn Edvard Westermarck, whose (1891) *The History of Human Marriage* challenged a variety of anthropological stocks in trade, especially the hypothesis of primitive promiscuity. Westermarck insisted on the universality of the pairing family as a necessary concomitant to the pattern of infant development in humans:

> Marriage is nothing else than a more or less durable connection between male and female, lasting beyond the mere act of propagation till after the birth of the offspring. (Westermarck, 1891: 19–20)

The pace of infant development being such that parental co-operation was necessary for the species to survive, Westermarck saw the parental couple continuing to cohabit after the birth of their offspring. Though seemingly unremarkable, this observation struck at the root of the idea of the promiscuous primal horde, since it derived marriage from the family rather

---

108 For this reason too, therefore, my intention is to carry out an anthropology of anthropological theory rather than to arbitrate between theorists whose axioms and presuppositions were incommensurable with mine. Thus I am concerned not to refute the evolutionary anthropologists but to gauge the social implications of their practice. In this regard, my project is quite different from that of Les Hiatt, who, with enviable skill and authority, covers much of the same ground, only on the anthropologists' own terms: 'It is apparent from our review that the Australian data give no more support to Engels' assertion that women reigned supreme in early human history than to the associated hypothesis of communal marriage' (Hiatt 1996: 7).

than vice-versa: 'Marriage is therefore rooted in family, rather than family in marriage' (1891: 22).

Westermarck's rejection of the mother-right paradigm stemmed from its discursive linkage to the hypothesis of primitive promiscuity, which was his primary target. Though challenging the theory, Westermarck could hardly hope to overturn an established consensus by simply substituting one conjectural history for another. His eternal family provided no inducement for anyone else to jettison their own laboriously accumulated theoretical capital in favour of contributing to his.

The case of Heinrich Cunow was rather different. Though theoretically formidable, this ethnological correspondent to the German Socialist Party remained (with only the slightest exceptions, e.g. Lang 1903: 113; 117) unacknowledged in the British anthropological literature, whilst, when discussed by others (e.g. Durkheim 1898: 317–18) was generally treated in a disparaging fashion. In the course of an analysis undertaken because Australian Aborigines, as the lowest of human races, constituted the correct empirical starting point for a historical-materialist account of mother-right, Cunow rigorously distinguished residence, totemic affiliation and descent. The primary social form was a purely territorial promiscuous grouping with male descent, resembling McLennan's presocial horde. The second system to emerge, coterminal with the first, was not, however, a nescient matriliny but a male-transmitted local totemism, which arose as a result of increased association between hordes, which encouraged mutual distinctions of identity. Matrilineal totemism only arose in concert with developments in the incest taboo, which meant that people who could make no mistake as to their paternal affiliation (since it coincided with their residence) needed to ensure that they were not mating within prohibited degrees on the maternal side. This necessitated the maintenance of a record of maternal connections, the original function of matrilineal totemism, which was thus a relatively *late* development.

Compared to Cunow, even the Danish theorist C.N. Starcke was reasonably regularly cited, though he was not taken seriously by his contemporaries (except for Tylor [1896: 90], on a point that suited him). This was consistent with what Lang (1905a: 8) referred to as Starcke's 'eccentric opinion' (1889: 26) that female descent was not a universal stage and that, if it did occur, it was associated with totemism, being a development on patrilineal landed groupings (i.e., the reverse of the paradigm).

As is apparent from these sketches, though, on reading the would-be debunkers of mother-right, one is struck by the endless recurrence of a basic stock of themes which was common to the matriarchalists as well. Mere repermutation could not create anything new, so the consensus prevailed. But the demise of mother-right was at hand, so the proof of its resilience should not be taken too far. Storm clouds of one kind were gathering in North America, with Franz Boas (1897: 334–5) claiming to have discovered a northwestern transition from father-right to mother-right (i.e. in the opposite direction to that of the theory). As we have seen, though, mother-right could prove itself resistant to empirical refutation (Boas' father-right could, after all, have been dismissed as McLennan's presocial local horde). Certainly, the time was significant – by the 1890s, as observed, the sexual politics that mother-right had sustained was in the throes of a major shift. No doubt these factors played a part. But we have yet to look to internal factors – in particular, to the contradictions that mother-right contained. How were these precipitated? To establish this, we should return to the theory's elementary components, blood and land.

Negation

Bound up with the female and with nature, blood signified the realm of the concrete. It was transcended by the male principle, with its capacity for abstract culture (Bachofen's hyperumbilical 'remoter potency'). This formula recurred throughout evolutionary theory. Having assembled a standard schedule of motives (ecology, cohabitation, testamentary succession) for the transition to father-right, for instance, Hartland pictured the new system as an abstract legal construction in comparison to the materiality of its predecessor:

> It is submitted then that while motherright is founded upon blood, fatherright on the other hand had its origin in quite different considerations. Kindred with the father is first and foremost juridical – a social convention. (Hartland, vol. 2, 1909–10: 99)

Since individualism springs from unique and unrepeatable history, as opposed to cyclical natural becoming, consanguinity (Bachofen's universal motherhood) signified the antithesis of individualism. Nescience has an important consequence in this regard, since a shift in emphasis from conception to birth is conducive to collective identity. Robertson Smith (1907: 107–9; 275) had noted the effect of this emphasis in relation to the Semitic 'paternity of the bed', whereby the principle that 'the son is reckoned to the bed on which he is born' outweighed the significance of conception to the extent that men would solicit the impregnation of their wives by others whose seed would be an asset to the stock:

> Custom and feeling would not sanction so atrocious a proposal as that physical paternity should override the claims of a stock in which the child had been actually born and brought up. (Robertson Smith 1907: 115)

Presumptive fatherhood as a definition of group membership is not a matter of consanguinity. Accordingly, as Hartland himself pointed out, its moral implications are not necessarily an improvement on mother-right:

> father-right, far from being founded on certainty of paternity, positively fosters indifference, and if it does not promote fraud at least becomes a hotbed of legal fictions. It is a purely artificial system. (Hartland, vol. 2, 1909–10: 248)

A father-right independent of paternity could bring down the whole mother-right paradigm – if there could be nescient patrilines, then where was the importance of correct knowledge? Why not knowledgeable matrilines? Hence Hartland (vol. 1, 1909–10: 325) was led by the force of his own argument to the conclusion that mother-right was not based upon uncertainty of paternity.[109] The assumed identity of *genitor* and *pater* rendered mother-right vulnerable to the concept of social parenthood – though this, it may be remembered, had been a possibility at least since Morgan's attempts to get round the appearance of plural motherhood in his tables. Thus the mother-right narrative did not run into trouble because it had inner flaws – they had been there all along. Rather, the flaws came to fruition under particular circumstances. In fact, Ashley Montagu's compendious (1937) labouring of the assertion that social parenthood could apply to mothers as well as to fathers had long been prefigured, in a context of confusion in the mother-right paradigm, by van Gennep (1906b: LXIII): 'To the *is pater quem nuptiae demonstrant*, the Central Australians add an *ea mater quam nuptiae demonstrant*, where *nuptiae* signifies that the union between male (*pater*) and female (*mater*) has been publicly sanctioned ["*socialisée*"] by a ceremony'.[110]

A system of local group membership in the male line operating independently of consanguinity amounts to McLennan's original horde tie. To translate this into the idiom of nescience: to say that McLennan's horde tie operated before the development of the concept of kinship is to say that it operated in a context of nescience of principle (conception unknown) as opposed to the matrilineal nescience of agent (too many candidates for fatherhood) that succeeded it. This takes us back to Spencer and Gillen's Arunta. Once again, they were pivotal.

Spencer and Gillen's Arunta nescience fulfilled McLennan's theory at least as faithfully – if not as overtly – as it did that of Hartland. To recap, McLennan's first stage, preceding any notion of kinship, was the local horde, to which children 'belonged' on the same basis as the horde's 'other goods' (McLennan 1865: 92). For this theory to have applied to Aborigines, the most important of these 'other goods' would have been their land. Thus children would have had to belong to the 'horde' on the same basis as its territory did – a principle independent of consanguinity and procreation. Needless to say, Arunta spirit children satisfied this specification perfectly.

For the Arunta to be empirical manifestations of McLennan's first stage, they would have to have figured as evolutionarily lower, despite their patrilineal moieties, than matrilineal peoples, who, in turn, would be inferior to other patrilineal ones. This was precisely the status that Frazer, together with Spencer and Gillen, argued for the Arunta. Thus, contrary to Andrew Lang's claim that the complexities of Arunta marriage regulations, together with their patrilineal moieties, meant that they were relatively advanced, Frazer contended that Arunta patriliny was not an advance on a more primitive matriliny, but actually preceded any recognition of kinship

---

109 Hartland had been anticipated by Starcke, who had argued (1889: 37) that matriliny implied a lack of legal standing on the child's part rather than nescience: 'the female line does not sever the child from its father, but only from the father's clan'. This observation attracted no notice.

110 The first Latin phrase can be rendered as 'the father is he whom marriage certifies'; the second: 'the mother is she whom marriage certifies'.

whatsoever. The features that Frazer instanced in favour of his claim that the Arunta form of totemic spirit conception had 'all the appearance of extreme antiquity' readily translate into the horde ties of McLennan's first stage:

> It ignores altogether the intercourse of the sexes as the cause of offspring, and further, it ignores the tie of blood on the maternal as well as the paternal side, substituting for it a purely local bond. (Frazer 1905: 453)

His commitment to this theory, and to the Arunta's consequent primitiveness, presented Frazer with such grave problems that he was led, in 1905, to question the mother-right paradigm itself. His difficulty was that, having argued that the Arunta were the most primitive, he should have been able to find another tribe at the next level up – i.e. where local bonds were giving way to hereditary, matrilineal ones. As it transpired, he could only discover neighbouring systems (those of the Umbaia and the Gnanji) which mixed local spirits with patrilineal, rather than with the expected matrilineal, descent (spirits of husbands' totems were held to follow wives around, impregnating them in different totemic localities). After wrestling unsuccessfully with this dilemma, Frazer was obliged to concede that:

> if the present theory of the development of totemism is correct, the common assumption that inheritance of the totem through the mother always preceded inheritance of it through the father need not hold good. (Frazer 1905: 462)

Frazer had argued precisely the reverse only ten pages earlier. This had been necessitated because his theory not only required that the Arunta should be the most primitive; it also provided that Howitt and Fison's south-eastern tribes were the most advanced. These tribes were not only monogamous but unproblematically supported Morgan's theory by being patrilineal as well. Following Frazer's theoretical contortions through, the symptoms of terminal crisis are unmistakable. The paradigm has run out of slack, exhausted its capacity to defer internal contradictions – a situation exacerbated by the competitive forays of Andrew Lang.[111]

Frazer faced the problem that even the Arunta could not be made to conform to Morgan's Group Marriage which, like McLennan's local horde, involved men collectively owning their women. To get around this problem, Frazer simply individualized this ownership, as if oblivious to the tension between such a concept and the debased evolutionary level at which he wished to place the Arunta. His eventual formula betrayed his difficulty, investing private property with bestial connotations:

---

111 Lang had earlier (1903: 117) observed, in relation to Cunow's theory, 'The priority of male to female descent is not admitted, as a rule, by Mr. Tylor or any other English authorities'. Though Lang and Frazer were both Scottish, it is nonetheless the case that Frazer himself had previously stated, in relation to Howitt's recording a number of Aborigines 'wavering' between male and female descent, 'After the researches of Bachofen, McLennan, and Morgan, we may be sure that such a wavering marks a transition from female to male descent and not conversely' (Frazer 1910: I, 71). Frazer's recanting from maternal priority was, however, helpful to his argument, directed against Lang, that the Arunta were more primitive than other Aborigines. Given the mother-right paradigm, Arunta patriliny made this argument *prima facie* awkward – Frazer's interpreting Arunta patriliny as presocial rather than post-matrilineal was an attempt to obviate the problem. Lang reasonably took the retreat from maternal priority as a tactic to the same end, returning tirelessly to attack and ridicule the inconsistencies in Frazer's position (see, e.g., Lang 1905b: xii-xiii; 1907b: 88–9; 1910: 1108; 1911: 87–8).

> Denying, as they [Central Australian tribes] do explicitly, that the child is begotten by the father, they can only regard him as the consort, and, in a sense, the owner of the mother, and therefore, as the owner of her progeny, just as a man who owns a cow owns also the calf she brings forth. In short, it seems probable that a man's children were viewed as his property long before they were recognised as his offspring. (Frazer 1905: 462–3)

It is not easy to distinguish individual ownership of a wife from the individual marriage that Frazer could hardly dissociate from civility.

Frazer's difficulty was that any entertainment of the possibility that Arunta nescience might represent a positive metaphysics rather than a savage ignorance would be playing into the hands of his arch-rival Andrew Lang, who was asserting precisely this to sustain his claim that the Arunta were relatively advanced. This brings us back to the practical equivalence between McLennan's presocial horde tie and nescience of principle. Given nescience of principle, social organization could not be based on physiological procreation. But this only means that *it must have been based on something else*. Frazer's presentation of nescience was designed to encourage a negative reading. Viewed positively, however, just as nescience of agent signified the gaining of maternity, nescience of principle proclaimed the irrelevance, as opposed to the extent, of parenthood. In this light, the negation of mother-right can be seen to have been dialectically inherent in Spencer and Gillen's overstatement of its key element. For, though depending upon nescience of agent, mother-right was not strengthened but fatally invalidated by nescience of principle.

This invalidation occurred because, viewed positively, a move from nescience of agent to that of principle is not a deepening of ignorance at all – that would be merely the negative aspect. Rather, the difference between agent and principle is that between the gaining of maternity and the loss of consanguinity, which is to say *the gaining of territory*. In other words, Spencer and Gillen's move from agent to principle was a move from blood to land, which was not an extension but an antithesis. Yet they had not intended to subvert the established consensus. On the contrary, they had meant to augment it, by pushing nescience, its cardinal tenet, beyond a profounder frontier. Accordingly, whereas, say, Westermarck merely offered a divergent conjectural alternative from whose acceptance no one but Westermarck stood to gain, Spencer and Gillen's Arunta nescience was, as it were, hyperthetical, in that it perpetrated an unintended sin of excess. In this way, the seeds of the demise of the mother-right paradigm were internally sown. Moreover, as we have seen, with more than a decade having elapsed since the passing of the Married Women's Property Act, mother-right had substantially lost its compensatory ideological reinforcement from without.

— * —

In hindsight, Spencer and Gillen's revelation was like a worm within the evolutionist paradigm. It grew into social fatherhood. In the wake of evolutionism, sociocultural anthropology abandoned physiology – pater lost his genitals and became an institution. Following on from this oedipal shift, which was contemporaneous with Freud, structural-functionalism would distance itself from physical anthropology – and, with it, from human continuity (cultures differ more widely than bodies). Forsaking skulls, the salvage paradigm preoccupied itself with sociocultural phenomena (as Malinowski observed, the physical types would be available for centuries).[112] In twentieth-century sociocultural anthropology, difference came to be registered superorganically and synchronically. In such a climate, there was no room for an ancestral narrative that rested on a primal scene to which physiology was essential, and which was awkwardly continuous with Western mores. Mother-right faded from anthropological discourse. In retrospect, the theory encapsulates nineteenth-century anthropology, and, with it, the conquering progressivism of the expanding colonial frontier. In the demise of mother-right, therefore, we also see entailed the rise of new anthropologies and the changing colonial regimes of the twentieth century. As we shall see in Chapter 6, social fatherhood came to lie at the heart of Radcliffe-Brown's theory, a theory which was to shape twentieth-century Australian Aboriginal anthropology and land-rights legislation alike.

Compared to mother-right, which so clearly bore the marks of Victorian politics, the theory of totemism represents the most internal of anthropological conversations. As the purest of theoretical inventions, totemism provides us with a limiting case of textual determination. It lets us see how text is also context, with productive outcomes of its own. In turning to this theory, therefore, we now move deep into the internal workings of evolutionary-anthropological debating. In the chapter to come, the second of our three chapters on the fabrication of anthropological theory, the focus is not on anthropology's openness to its wider ideological context. It is, rather, on debating-effects as effects – as pressures that move out from texts into the rest of the social world, producing as well as being produced. Theories of totemism encompassed the tension between Tylor and McLennan, or between animism and sociology. Once we have examined these theories and ascertained the boundaries between the antagonistic traditions, we will be in a better position to specify a definition that can account for the whole field of evolutionary-anthropological theory. This, in turn, will lead us to a sharper appreciation of the qualities that rendered anthropology so conducive to settler-colonial ends.

112 Malinowski, who is quoted by Peterson (1990: 7) was, however, referring to a franchise-colonial context, where native extinction was not being foreshadowed. The skulls did not vanish from structural-functionalism overnight. Their disappearance was, however, a consistent trend. A limited exception was Australia, where native extinction was by no means being ruled out (see, e.g. Warner 1937: 518–19).

CHAPTER 4

Totemism Yesterday, Today and Tomorrow

VICTORIAN ANTHROPOLOGY'S ETERNAL DICHOTOMY

Theories of totemism represent a doubling-up of anthropology's preoccupation with otherness – a discourse on the Other's discourses on otherness. As accounts of how it might be that people should claim to be related to non-human entities, these theories all contain statements about the boundaries of humanity. In consequence, they have a mythic or transhistorical quality – as refractions of an absolute question, they endlessly recycle the same answers.

In contrast to other major anthropological topics, which had both savage and civilized variants (classificatory vs. descriptive, magical vs. scientific, promiscuous vs. monogamous, etc.), totemism had no immediate counterpart in civilized life. It was savagery *sui generis*, anthropology's final residue. Thus considerable critical or satirical mileage could be gained from equating civilized institutions with it. To one as given to iconoclasm as Andrew Lang, even evolutionary science itself provided an opportune target:

> The most common savage myth is of the Darwinian variety, each totem kin is descended from, or evolved out of, the plant or animal type which supplies its totem. (Lang 1903: 139)

As science's covert other, totemism becomes nescience – a conclusion that coincides with Frazer's (1905: 452–63) third theory of totemism.[113] This is not to say that Frazer himself betrayed any reflexive awareness. On the contrary, his horizons were firmly contained within evolutionism. Thus, in proposing that the earliest form of totemism was 'conceptional totemism', or the belief that women were impregnated by the entry into them of surrounding objects, Frazer was hoping to establish 'an intelligible starting-point for the evolution of totemism in general' (1905: 458).

From the point of view of the historical development of social anthropology as a whole, however, totemism's primary significance is as the means whereby anthropology's concrete induction, the discipline's distinctive fusion of the material and the ideational, was first accomplished. Once stated by McLennan and restated by Robertson Smith, this Cartesian conflation was to be definitively enunciated by Durkheim. Yet, despite its wide distribution, the formula that religion – even thought itself – was socially determined

[113] And discursively, of course, with Lévi-Strauss' humanist (1966) depiction of totemism as the 'science of the concrete'.

would continue to show signs of strain around the site of its original formulation. Hence Lévi-Strauss' intellectualist (1963) reclassification of totemism quickly met with the complaint that totems were not just for thinking with but, at least as importantly, for eating, territorializing and doing other material things with.

Frazer played this opposition both ways, his successive theories of totemism evincing a schizoid alternation between material and ideational explanations. His initial theory, first proposed in *The Golden Bough* (Frazer 1890: ii, 332–35), was, like Hartland's, a straightforward application of Tylor's theory of animism. It provided that people had a special relationship with their totems because they believed that their souls had been deposited in them for safe-keeping. In 1899, on the basis of Spencer and Gillen's early Arunta reports, Frazer abruptly dropped this explanation in favour of the strikingly materialist hypothesis that totems were intended to increase the tribe's food supply. Abandoning this theory in turn on the ground that its 'superficial resemblance to a modern industrial community organised on the sound economic principle of the division of labour' made it too rational a system for savages to have arrived at, he returned to the idealist concept of animism for his third and final theory (Frazer 1905: 456–8) whereby totemism originated as nescience – the external soul of his first theory being animistically transferred into the maternal womb from the nearby natural object in which it had been lodged.

Establishing a starting-point for totemism was no small ambition, since the riddle of the totem had come to signify that of the transition to culture itself. Conceptional totemism was, therefore, appropriately spontaneous, being so 'simple and obvious' (Frazer 1905: 457) that it could occur to the savage mind independently in different parts of the world. Independent invention was a methodological corollary to the psychic unity of mankind. It enabled the origin of a cultural trait to be accounted for without resort to the regressive argument from diffusion. Conceptional totemism was further spontaneous in that an infant's totem was determined by the accident of whatever surrounding object happened to engage its mother's attention when she first felt it stir in her womb. The absence of any requirement for a capacity to make long-range causal connections was also congenial to the idea's spontaneous occurrence in independent locations. Furthermore, the theory accorded with Spencer and Gillen's data. Thus it was that, in conceptional totemism, 'after years of sounding, our plummets seem to touch bottom at last' (Frazer 1905: 458).

For our purposes, the significance of Frazer's third theory lies not in its applicability to savage others but in the light that it casts on his own discourse. For the theory set the seal on logical and ideological relationships that held together the framework of debate within which he was thinking and which had been inherent in totemism from the outset, having motivated its emergence as an anthropological topic. Approached from the point of view of its relationship to nescience, the discourse of totemism appears in a fresh light.

This is not to suggest that a reflexive relationship between totemism and nescience has not been pointed out before. Indeed, in the benchmark twentieth-century account of totemism, Lévi-Strauss himself not only noted such a relationship but did so in the very context of Frazer's third theory:

> It was not by chance that Frazer amalgamated totemism and ignorance of physiological paternity: totemism assimilates men to animals, and the alleged ignorance of the role of the father in conception results in the replacement of the human genitor by spirits closer to natural forces. This naturalist view offered a touchstone which allowed the savage, within culture itself, to be isolated from civilized man. (Lévi-Strauss 1963: 2)

Though doubtless perceptive, Lévi-Strauss' assertion is hardly specific. It simply casts anthropology as the transparent vehicle of a general ideological imperative. Accordingly, without necessarily disagreeing with Lévi-Strauss – and, certainly, without denying anthropology's ideological utility – this chapter will focus on anthropology's empirical contingency, on the highly specific internal pressures which ultimately came to produce a set of postulates that were so suitable for ideological appropriation. The focus is, in short, procedural.

But can any specificity attach to an eternal question that recycles through the ages? Might it not be that histories that attempt to treat such questions merely become condemned – as, again, Lévi-Strauss would have it – to follow in anthropology's footsteps? As an absolute question that coincides with that of the boundaries of humanity, the problem of totemism becomes intractable, which is why it constantly recycles. Though this chapter focuses on Robertson Smith, therefore, the basic problem that his theory was intended to resolve is an eternal one.

It still might be that theories of totemism form a mythic discourse in the classic Lévi-Straussian mould, so that a history of them could not aspire beyond the reproduction of narratives that anthropology has already formulated. In an existential sense, this may indeed be the case, but a *procedural* history sidesteps this hall of mirrors in favour of distinguishing different historical and propositional strategies for reducing eternal questions to discourse. In this respect, Lévi-Strauss himself is available for history.

Lévi-Strauss contended that totemism constituted a category-error; it was not a discrete phenomenon in its own right but so many examples of a general human propensity to classify by means of systematic oppositions. Though he cited Tylor as a precedent (Lévi-Strauss 1963: 13–14), he could have added many others. For instance, in relation to hierarchically overlapping totem groups, Frazer (1885: 475) had claimed that 'In these totems superposed upon totems may perhaps be discerned a rudimentary classification of natural objects under heads which bear a certain resemblance to genera, species, etc.'. Across the Channel, van Gennep had analogously concluded that totemism was 'in origin, a simple system of classification' which initially referred to localities but subsequently developed into a portable abstraction (van Gennep 1906: xxxiv). Such examples are by no means confined to the evolutionist era. The earliest modern ethnographic instance of which I am aware, produced long before the synthetic concept of totemism had been developed, is that of Garcilaso de la Vega, writing at the beginning of the seventeenth century. Garcilaso (who, appropriately enough, was an Inca on his mother's side) attributed the large number of Andean folk cults involving plants and animals to a common interest in 'distinguishing themselves from one another, and each from all the rest . . . there was no beast too vile and filthy for them to worship as a god, merely in order to differ from one another in their choice of gods' (Garcilaso 1609: 31).

Though such predecessors can hardly be said to have pre-empted Lévi-Strauss' theory, they illustrate the recurrence of its elements. Moreover, in the case of Andrew Lang's account of the origin of totem names, it is harder to be sure that Lévi-Strauss had not indeed been anticipated:

> 'We' are 'The Men', but the nineteen other groups are also 'The Men' – in their own opinion. To us they are something else ('they' are not 'we'), and we are something else to them; *we* are not *they*, we all need differentiation, and we and they, by giving names to outsiders, differentiate each other. The names arose from a primitive necessity felt in everyday life. (Lang 1905a: 127–8)

Beneath the semblance of agreement, however, Lang's and Lévi-Strauss' theories represent opposing sides of a fundamental division over the basic issue of intellectualism. In contrast to the ideational endowment which motivated Lévi-Strauss' binary categorizations, Lang's 'primitive necessity felt in everyday life' was an eco-demographic phenomenon resulting from the increased level of intergroup contact that followed from a Malthusian combination of population increase and resource depletion. As we saw in the previous chapter, within a common theoretical arena, the two perspectives were bound to clash. Thus it is not surprising that Lang should have clashed with Frazer, who, at least so far as his intellectualism was concerned, was a precursor to Lévi-Strauss.

Here again, nescience figured centrally. If ever there was theoretical rivalry, it obtained between Frazer and Lang. Having both equated nescience with totemism and subscribed to an intellectualist view of totemism, Frazer had committed himself to what I have termed the cognitive version of nescience. Hence Lang's iconoclasm converged with his dialogic interests, since evidence of cognitive accomplishment on the Arunta's part would not only narrow the gap between civilized society and savagery; it would also damage Frazer's claim that the Arunta's intelligence was too limited for them to have made a connection between sex and conception.

With Lang patrolling the theoretical waters, Frazer was bound to an exacting standard of consistency. As will emerge in this chapter, a consequence of such demanding conditions was an abrupt about-turn on Frazer's part in relation to the controversial theory of the totem sacrament that had been proposed by his revered mentor Robertson Smith (to whom Frazer had dedicated *The Golden Bough*). This was despite the fact that Frazer had lauded his mentor's theory in characteristically fulsome terms and, when Spencer and Gillen found the Arunta enacting something that seemed to resemble the totem sacrament, had leaped at the opportunity to proclaim their fulfilment of a further ethnographic prophecy.

Spencer and Gillen had reported (1898: 278) that, in the Arunta *Intichiuma* ceremony, Arunta men ate freely of their own totem, which was something that they were otherwise forbidden to do. As will become clear, this report could have sounded remarkably like the totem sacrament. Certainly, it was more than enough for Frazer:

> Here, it is plain, we have at last the long-sought totem sacrament which Robertson Smith with the intuition of genius divined, and which it has been reserved for Messrs. Spencer and Gillen to discover as an actually existing institution among true totem tribes. (Frazer 1898: 284)[114]

In the wake of this triumph, however, the pattern of development was very different from the growing confidence that was characterizing successive accounts of the Arunta's nescience. In the first place, Spencer and Gillen themselves did not endorse the significance that Frazer had attached to the Arunta *Intichiuma* ceremony. Secondly, Frazer's own assertions became progressively more half-hearted until he finally came close to admitting to a back-down:

> Thus a totem sacrament of a sort has been discovered among the tribes of Central Australia and Robertson Smith's wonderful intuition – almost prevision – has been strikingly confirmed after the lapse of years. Yet what we have found is not precisely what he expected. (Frazer 1910: iv, 231)

This retreat was costly in terms of the theoretical rewards that the totem sacrament had held out for Frazer. Once the internal structure of his theoretical position is laid bare, however, a fundamental incompatibility between the totem sacrament and nescience becomes clear. As will emerge, this incompatibility lay in the fact that, despite their apparent differences, the two theories were attempting to explain the same phenomenon from opposing premises, Hartland's theory appealing to ideational causes and Robertson Smith's to social ones. In seeming to promise both nescience and the totem sacrament, therefore, Spencer and Gillen's Arunta actually forced a choice between them. Within the space of the same theory, it could be one or the other but not both. This dilemma was manifest in Frazer's first trying to have it both ways and then retreating over the totem sacrament.

This conclusion is, of course, arrived at from a distance of a century. At the time, committed as he was to nescience, all Frazer saw was that the addition of the totem sacrament produced anomalies and contradictions that his theoretical rivals were not slow to exploit. When we trace through the logic of Robertson Smith's theory, though, we see that it could not have been otherwise. The antagonism between nescience and the totem sacrament derived from an eternal opposition and, as such, was impervious to historical influences. Methodologically, therefore, it provides an opportunity to move away from the external articulations of anthropological theory and focus on its internal or specifically propositional dynamics. In particular, it exemplifies

---

114 Hubert and Mauss (1899: 208) were almost as prompt in accepting that the totem sacrament had found realization.

the progressive crowding of epistemological space that curtailed the further postponement of contradictions and signalled the morbidity of the evolutionist paradigm. In the process, text emerges as itself a productive context, generating specific necessities that determine ideological possibilities.

This chapter seeks to show that the totem sacrament intervened between McLennan's marriage by capture and Tylor's animism in a way that forced a choice between them. As explained above, these theories were both encompassed in nescience, McLennan's as the basis of the circumstantial version and Tylor's as the basis of the cognitive one. Thus nescience contained the most fundamental dichotomy in anthropology. Spanning this dichotomy was the theoretical achievement of – and, as we shall see, motivation for – the concept of totemism. This chapter will trace how it was that, given the catalyst of the totem sacrament, this containment was breached. We will also consider the choice that was made – what, when it could have been either nescience or the totem sacrament, was the significance of the Arunta's becoming physiological innocents rather than proto-Christian cannibals? To trace these and other questions through, we will follow the career of totemism from McLennan's texts through those of Robertson Smith and on to the theoretical corner into which Frazer ended up painting himself.

The Concrete, the Abstract and Totemism

The curious fact that a number of different peoples in various parts of the world had animal familiars, animal guardian spirits or animal family names was not the same thing as the master concept of totemism with all its distinctive ramifications. Rather, that concept was synthetic in two major respects. First, it retrospectively united a diverse range of earlier ethnographic reports. Second (though of primary importance for us), it brought together the spiritual and the social. In this doubly synthetic sense, the career of totemism commenced in the writings of Robertson Smith's mentor McLennan.

From early in his career, Robertson Smith had sought to provide concrete social genealogies for abstract spiritual concepts. This placed him on the telluric side of an ongoing controversy as to whether Semitic heathenism was purely astral or whether it also had telluric elements, a position which led him to challenge (1880: 76–7) the received Judaeo-Christian premise that the Semitic race was somehow blessed with 'a natural capacity for spiritual religion'. Robertson Smith's claim was not that there was nothing astral about Semitic gods; merely that their origins were traceable to totem stocks as these had been theorized by McLennan. The inspiration that Robertson Smith cited was not *Primitive Marriage* but a later series of articles entitled 'The Worship of Animals and Plants' (McLennan 1869–70).[115] In these articles, patrilineal

---

[115] Though McLennan's articles of 1869 and 1870 were clearly first in the field (containing material that had not been in his 1868 discussion of totemism) Lubbock was later to claim priority, a situation that McLennan (1886b: xiii) dealt with tersely: 'By a misprint, or slip of the pen no doubt, Sir John Lubbock is made to state in the third edition of his *Origin of Civilization* (f.n., p. 252) that the articles above mentioned appeared "since the last", i.e. the second, edition of that book. The words should have been "before the first". The first edition of the *Origin of Civilization* was published in 1870, some time after the *last* of the series of articles referred to had appeared. The preface to the first edn. of the *Origin of Civilization* bears date February 1870'. Herbert Spencer had also published an article (Spencer 1870) entitled 'The Origin of Animal Worship' in a *Fortnightly Review* of May 1870.

totem stocks were endowed with fictional ancestral figures who were well suited to provide a basis from which subsequent and more sublime theologies might develop. To follow the progression through from marriage by capture to spiritual concepts – which is to say, from social to ideational patterns, or from McLennan to Tylor respectively – we need, therefore, to follow through the stages whereby McLennan himself progressed from the social morphology of *Primitive Marriage* to the theogonic ancestral fiction that Robertson Smith was to lift out from the articles on animal and plant worship.

As might be expected of McLennan, however, the situation is not so simple. For what he offered in the later series of articles was 'not an hypothesis explanatory of the origin of *Totemism* be it remembered, but an hypothesis explanatory of the animal and plant worship of the ancient nations' (McLennan 1869–70: 213). Rather than explaining the prior existence of totemism, these articles presupposed it, contending that animal worship grew from 'the religious regard for the Totem' (1869–70: 213). When we go back to *Primitive Marriage*, however, we find that the only hint of religion consists in a passing characterization (1865: 263) of blood-feuds as a 'point of religion', the reference being to the sacrosanct status of the shared maternal blood binding together the band of brothers. Moreover, in *Primitive Marriage*, this blood bond had not required an external sign; matrilineal relationships had had names but not forms. Totems appeared incidental rather than necessary, the book making no claim to have explained their origins, but limiting itself to such vague formulations as 'the tendency to eponymy [sic]' (1865: 259).

Once again, therefore, what McLennan furnishes is not an answer but a strategy for covering over a lacuna – in this instance, the strategy being a staggering device whereby an explanation that appears to span separate publications actually gets relegated into the space between them. In that it purported to dispense with the eternal conundrum of transcendence, however, it was a highly productive strategy. Through its stationing of totemism on the dividing line between the ideal and the material, it made totemism into anthropology's great question (small wonder, then, that, forty years later, Frazer should still be searching for an intelligible starting-point for its evolution).

In McLennan's writings, totemism was already characterized by a referential ambivalence between religious ideas and social groupings. Though hardly mentioned in *Primitive Marriage*, totems played a critical covert role in the book's argument under the guise of 'family names', the rendering that McLennan provided for the word on the first occasion that he used it (1865: 122; cf. 142, 143, 144). To appreciate the fertile implications of this covert role, it is convenient to start with the co-residential kindred tie which, as explained in the previous chapter, was the territorial principle that united male hordes prior to the development of the concept of kinship, initially as matrilineal consanguinity.

Though the earliest male horde was held together by territorial contiguity, McLennan tacked on a martial solidarity that was to form the basis of the blood-feud: 'the *apparent* bond of fellowship between the members of such a group would be that they and theirs had always been companions in war or the chase' (1865: 152–3). As we saw, however, such companionship could not amount to brotherhood before any such concept existed. Brotherhood presupposed the rise of kinship, which enabled the male blood of the feud to be brought together with the female blood of motherhood. Thus McLennan's motive for tacking the element of martial solidarity onto the territorially-given kindred tie becomes clear: it provided him with a way of talking about land in terms of blood. Once this crucial move had been effected, it only remained to switch the gender of the blood.

Yet the blood-feud was fundamentally at odds with the co-residential companionship in war. For, far from consummating territorial contiguity, the blood-feud stood in opposition to it, setting coresidents against one another. When a cause for blood-feud arose within a horde which, though held together by ties of residence, was of heterogeneous matrilineal descent, 'the presence of so many *of the enemy* within the camp affords ready means of satisfying the call for vengeance; it being immaterial, according to the native code, by whose blood the blood-feud is satisfied, provided it be the blood of the offender's kindred' (1865: 114). The blood-feud therefore encouraged 'secession', or men's abandonment of heterogeneous territorial groupings in favour of the more secure option of homogeneity with their maternal kin.

The pivotal phrase in this account is 'blood of the offender's kindred'. As we saw above, 'blood' and 'kindred' were otherwise categorically opposed – kindred being the male, pre-kinship sentiment associated with coresidence. McLennan provided no motive for the disappearance of the local horde's kindred sentiment. He simply displaced it onto the emergent blood-bond of kinship, thus conflating the very two principles whose antagonism engendered secession. The totem afforded ideal cover for this move because, though denoting a relationship defined as consanguinity, totems were named after animals and plants that were distinctive of the horde's terrain. In other words, totems provided a bridge between blood and land.

At this point, a major contradiction in McLennan's argument emerges. For, despite the rhetoric of solidity in which it was depicted, the maternal blood tie was an abstraction lacking any material referent to compare with the concretely territorial determination that it was meant to supplant. Indeed, the tenuousness of the maternal tie could hardly be more graphically demonstrated than by McLennan's own trademark narrative, the to and fro of wife-capture whereby mothers were routinely separated from offspring who remained attached to the horde (1865: 169).[116] Moreover, a major consequence of the emergent bond of kinship was, as just observed, the heterogeneity whereby males had maternal relatives in other local hordes with whom they could take refuge in cases of secession. The point is that such relationships presupposed an overall record of maternal consanguinity, one that would be stable enough to survive all the vagaries of wife- (or mother-) capture. The necessity that totemism satisfied becomes clear when it is recognized as furnishing precisely such an overall record (given, that is,

---

[116] This tenuousness could also be inferred from another key feature of McLennan's narrative: 'It may be observed that the existence of infanticide, so wide-spread in itself, indicates how slight the strength of blood-ties was in primitive times' (1865: 141).

an appropriately permanent and portable textual basis – a consideration that was to lead Robertson Smith to his interest in tattoos).

In other words, totemism resolved a paradox at the heart of McLennan's Hobbesian scenario. On the one hand, the radical instability of marriage by capture rendered women – who possessed no land – transient and untraceable in the extreme, whilst, on the other, the emergent bond of kinship was predicated on the manifest solidity of maternal blood. The utility of totems was, therefore, indexical. They vouchsafed a maternal principle that would otherwise have been obliterated by the practice of capture.[117]

Yet none of this gets us – or, at least, McLennan – any nearer to switching the gender of the blood of kinship. Indeed, if anything, ensuring the indexical stability of maternal blood lines only compounded the paradoxes that he was trying to cram into an ostensibly straightforward narrative. For there was a systematic tension between two of *Primitive Marriage*'s most celebrated motifs, exogamy and marriage by capture. This is because the wives who had been captured from a variety of other hordes would transmit their respective kinship categories to their offspring, thus making the capturing horde internally heterogeneous. This, in turn, would mean that the principle of exogamy no longer necessitated the capture of wives from outside.[118] The crucial coefficiency of exogamy and wife-capture required homogeneity. The only way back to homogeneity was by means of patrilineal succession, the male membership of the horde being stable.

Though patrilineal succession – which, of course, united blood and land – was enough to produce the requisite homogeneity, McLennan nonetheless added a characteristically redundant supplement, the fictional ancestor. The pay-off on this redundancy could hardly have been higher. For, though introducing the fictional ancestor for the apparent purpose of resolving a problem of kinship, McLennan was, in fact, smuggling into kinship the ground from which divinities would subsequently develop. For all its mundanity, therefore, the entry of the fictional ancestor constitutes the precise point at which social anthropology's transcendental fusion of the relational and the ideational was first accomplished:

> with kinship through males would arise the habit of feigning common descent from some distinguished man – a fiction which would lead in many cases to the denial or neglect of such heterogeneity as existed. (McLennan 1865: 250–1)

117 In *Primitive Marriage*, indexicality had been secured by family names, the 'test whether persons are of the same stock or not', a proposition that McLennan illustrated by means of his favoured analogy of the Scottish clan: 'In the Aird district there were none but Frasers; about May there were none but McIntoshes' (1865: 106–7).

118 The possibility of an endogamous tribe comprising exogamous stocks reveals that the standard view (Rivière 1970: xl–xli) that McLennan failed to recognize that endogamy and exogamy were differences in scope rather than different types of tribe is in error. McLennan himself clearly revealed his appreciation of the complementarity of the two principles, e.g.: 'Under the combined influence of exogamy and the system of female kinship, a local tribe might attain a balance of persons regarded as being of different descent, and its members might thus be able to intermarry with one another, and wholly within the tribe, in consistency with the principle of exogamy' (1865: 254). Considered from the point of view of the necessities of his argument as a whole, it becomes apparent that McLennan was prepared to allow the superficial impression that he did not appreciate the mutuality of endogamy and exogamy in the interests of separating the two principles in time – and, with them, their concomitant homogeneous and heterogeneous forms of horde organization – in order to sustain the serial alternations necessary to fuse blood and land in the course of the transition to father-right.

If it is easy enough to see how one ancestor might have been the first god, it is perhaps more difficult to see why an earlier one should have been an animal. In the articles on animal and plant worship, McLennan accomplished this by transferring to the fictional ancestor not just the affectual content of the blood tie as it had been characterized in *Primitive Marriage* but, in addition, a concrete animal form to match the totem name. There had been no such form in *Primitive Marriage* (which, after all, had provided an explanation for matrilineal – rather than bestial – kinship). Staggered between separate publications, this jump from emotion to idea superadded *Primitive Marriage*'s group solidarity to animism, thus investing the metaphysical theory with moral compulsion. The concept which enabled this combination was fetishism, which, as variously depicted by de Brosses, Fontenelle, Lafitau, Hume, Long, Comte and others,[119] comprised an amalgam of vitalized objects (principally derived from Portuguese west Africa) and animal guardians (on the north-west-American model). As noted above, fetishism provided the basis for Tylor's theory of animism (or, as McLennan termed it, 'the animation hypothesis' [1869–70: 422]). McLennan asserted that Morgan's animal-named North American tribes and Grey's Australian *kobong* groups were both instances of a fetishism modified by the addition of three 'peculiarities'. The enlarged concept was totemism, its components being juxtaposed with a distinct lack of system or necessity:

> Fetichism thus resembles Totemism; which, indeed, is Fetichism *plus* certain peculiarities. These peculiarities are, (1) the appropriation of a special Fetich to the tribe, (2) its hereditary transmission through mothers, and (3) its connection with the *jus connubii* .[120] (McLennan 1869–70: 422)

The 'peculiarities' that totemism added to animism were, therefore, the principles of matrilineal social organization laid down in *Primitive Marriage*, only with the eponym being given the form of the fetish. Once thus charged with religious sentiment, however, the fetish could be detached from the enlarged concept, becoming an icon in its own right, without the social accompaniments. This reseparated, cathected fetish could then become the basis for the development of divinities that were both abstract and ethical (it was left to Durkheim to rescind the separation). By the end of McLennan's series of articles, the fetish – in this case, the North American *manitu* – had lost its three peculiarities without thereby ceasing to be a totem (McLennan was explaining how tribes could become devoted to unpleasant or threatening animals such as bears):

> It is quite intelligible that animal worship growing from the religious regard for the Totem or Kobong – the friend and protector – should, irrespective of the nature of the animal, be a religion of love. (McLennan 1869–70: 213)

If the empty (or, at least, formless) totem name was to the matriline what the fictional ancestor was to the patriline, the question arises of where the one gave way to the other. As noted, in *Primitive Marriage* the ancestor was

---

119 De Brosses 1760, Comte 1853, Fontenelle 1758, Hume 1757, Lafitau 1724, Long 1791. For potted histories, see Frazer 1910: i, 1, Reinach 1909: 11–13, Schmidt 1931: 55–9.
120 'The law of marriage'.

instrumental in the transition to patriliny. Understandably, however, McLennan did not dwell on the point, since, before that transition, the ancestor would have been female, and she need not have been fictional. In the later articles, the fictional ancestor was simply assimilated to the fetish and the two backdated into the matrilineal phase of social organization without any contradiction being acknowledged. The neuter gender served McLennan as a kind of stepping-stone to father-right:

> We have found that there are tribes of men (called primitive) now existing on the earth in the Totem stage, each named after some animal or plant, which is its symbol or ensign, and which by the tribesmen is religiously regarded; having kinship through mothers only, and exogamy as their marriage law. In several cases we have seen, the tribesmen believe themselves to be descended from the Totem, and in every case to be, nominally at least, of *its* breed or species. We have seen a relation existing between the tribesmen and their Totem, as in the case of the bear, that might well grow into that of worshipper and god, leading to the establishment of religious ceremonials to allay the Totem's just anger, or to secure *his* continued protection. (McLennan 1869–70: 427, my emphasis)

With the transition to patriliny, then, totemism's indexical function was discharged by the territorial boundary whilst its sacredness passed to the ancestor/fetish, who thus consummated the ideological union of blood and land as well as the theoretical union of society and cosmology. Totemism's resulting obsolescence sustained the inference that it was but a decadent survival in patrilineal societies, where, as Robertson Smith (1880: 75–6) was to put it, 'little by little the features of the original system may be obliterated till the connection between the animal gods and tribes bearing an animal name is no longer apparent'. In this second severance of name from form, the astral gods soared free of their social moorings and the bear became a constellation. Mediating between telluric matter and the astral ideal, totemism had provided McLennan with a theoretical chrysalis with which to swathe the passage from the material grub of social organization to the abstract butterfly of culture.

The appeal of starting, as McLennan tried to, from the externally observable data of material practices and social morphologies was that, as opposed to the intellectualist premises of animism,[121] at least such data were publicly verifiable. In this regard, though McLennan's attempt to switch from morphology to ideas may seem gauche, it should be noted that, in contrast to Tylor or Hartland, at least he made the effort. For, as an account of religion, Tylor's dream-based theory simply recapitulated its object, appealing to precisely the same individualist ground – introspective assent – as was invoked by advocates of prayer. The point is not, however, the respective merits of the two positions but their mutual exclusiveness. In this regard, Tylor's dismissal of McLennan's theory was predictable – totemism's importance was sociological rather than religious (he did not miss the strategic centrality of McLennan's bear):

---

[121] It follows from this (and, indeed, from the cognitive/circumstantial opposition generally) that I differ from Stocking (1987: 196) in so far as he categorizes McLennan among the British intellectualists.

From an angry bear in the backwoods to a supreme deity of the world is too long a course to be mapped out in merely ideal stages. (Tylor 1898: 141)

To appreciate how the opposition epitomized by McLennan and Tylor was precipitated once the theories of Robertson Smith, Hartland and Frazer intersected, we will start with Robertson Smith's concept of substitution, since it corresponds directly to Hartland's concept of transformation, which we encountered in Chapter 1.

Communion, Cannibalism and Transcendence

Substitution, for Robertson Smith, was central to the blood-feud. Indeed, the same idea had underlain the account of the break-up of heterogeneous hordes which had been presented by McLennan (1865: 114) in the passage quoted above: 'it being immaterial, according to the native code, by whose blood the blood feud is satisfied, provided it be the blood of the offender's kindred'. When this principle of human interchangeability is added to what Robertson Smith (1886: 137) called 'totem habits of thought', in which tribesmen, sacred animals and divine totem-ancestors share kinship, the blood-feud ceases to be a purely human affair, providing the basis for a rigorously materialist theogony: 'It cannot be too strongly insisted on that the idea of kinship between gods and men was originally taken in a purely physical sense' (Robertson Smith 1894: 49). Gods, people and animals become logically interchangeable, so that humans can offer animal substitutes for themselves to offended gods or, conversely, animals who share the nature of gods can die for their people (Robertson Smith 1885: 135–7). This does not explain the way in which the animistic element entered the principle of substitution – whence did the totem habits of thought derive the idea of invisible kinship between people, animals and shared abstractions if not from some Tyloresque psychologism involving dreams or related illusions? To combine the two elements whose merger McLennan had staggered over separate publications,[122] Robertson Smith developed the notion of shared male blood (i.e. the pre-kinship blood of battle and feud) which had been at the basis of McLennan's kindred tie. His concern was not, however, blood in itself but the literal, pre-metaphoric reality of shared substance that it represented.

In his *Encyclopædia Britannica* entry on sacrifice, Robertson Smith had cited an archetypical form of substitution, wolf-men, instancing the Greek figure of Lykaon, whose statue in wolf-form had stood in the Lyceum. By way of a legend in which first Lykaon then his sons were changed into wolves for offering human flesh to Zeus, Robertson Smith went on (1885: 135–6) to link lycanthropy to cannibalism. With cannibalism, it goes without saying, he had a realm in which the sharing of substance was more than merely metaphorical. Though relying extensively on the symbolism of blood, Robertson Smith did not follow McLennan in making blood irreducible (nor did he relegate it to the status of metaphor). Rather, whilst real enough, blood was not the full reality of physical unity but a 'synecdochic expression for this; strictly

---

[122] In the interval, McLennan had twice written briefly on totemism, but without making the social/religious linkage explicit (McLennan 1866 [1886a]: 588, n.; 1868).

speaking, the kindred are not only of one blood but of one flesh' (1894: 175). Thus the sharing of food (which converted into flesh) became a basis for kinship. The prototypical shared food was mother's milk, the original basis for unity of flesh being suckling at the same breast (1894: 178). A shift from womb to breast also displaces the genesis of substance from conception to birth (and thus from blood to land),[123] which was conducive to Robertson Smith's requirement (1885: 107–9; 275) to account for the transition to patriliny amongst nomadic Semitic tribes (for whom, as we saw, the bed of birth and suckling was also that of paternity).

Whilst this shift may have produced a coherently naturalistic theory of patriliny, it did so at the expense of that metaphysical transcendence of the umbilical tie that had accompanied (or, at least, had seemed to accompany) the transition to patriliny in the earlier versions of mother-right. In extending the realm of the concrete to encompass father-right, therefore, Robertson Smith was merely displacing the question of abstraction. For, if the basis of union – and, hence, of sacredness – was shared substance, how was the insubstantial divine party to the union to be accounted for? Time and time again, Robertson Smith came up against a basic logical redundancy: if the mere *act* of eating together – i.e. of sharing anything whatsoever – generated sacredness, how could there be any necessity for a special category of food? What was the ground for an ontology of residual sacredness beyond the act of collective ingestion? Though he never satisfactorily resolved this problem, the debating-effect that he generated in the course of disguising it enables us to see why it was that the totem-sacrament could not be compatible with nescience.

According to Robertson Smith, for the ancient Semites in the desert the principle of shared substance entailed that those who ate together were united, whilst others were enemies, against whom the only sanction was the law of blood-feud. Conversely, the sharing of food with a stranger created a bond of union for as long as it was deemed to remain in the body (hence the importance of hospitality, expressed in the offering and receiving of salt). On this basis, there was no special or reserved kind of food. Furthermore, the principle was explicitly telluric:

> The bond of food is valid of itself . . . religion may be called in to confirm and strengthen it, but . . . the essence of the thing lies in the physical act of eating together. (Robertson Smith 1894: 271)

Thus both the bond of food and the blood-feud constituted 'what must be called a physical unity' (1894: 273).[124]

So far, then, there was solidarity but no metaphysics. The argument required nothing beyond mundane human conditions, or what Robertson

---

[123] In 1867, a patrilineal tie had come to constitute consanguinity for McLennan, the transmitter of maternal substance having shifted from the placenta to the breast, so that, among the matrilineal Irish, 'the tie of milk was superior to the tie of blood' (McLennan 1867: 189). In relation to Australian Aborigines, Elkin was using the same logic in 1933 (Elkin 1933: 15).

[124] For Robertson Smith, kinship admitted no degrees of bonding or obligation – you were either in or out: 'it constitutes what in the language of ethics is called a duty of perfect obligation' (1894: 272). This corroborates Kuper's (1988: 193) tracing of Radcliffe-Brown's 'corporate descent groups' back to Robertson Smith.

Smith called 'natural society', which was common to the ancient and the modern worlds. There was, however, this 'important difference' between the two:

> the tribal or national societies of the ancient world were not strictly natural in the modern sense of the word, for the gods had their part and place in them equally with men. (Robertson Smith 1894: 29)

In other words, no strictness was required – the ancient world was not natural at all, but remained riddled with the supernatural (in Weber's terminology, it remained enchanted). The argument from shared substance could not explain how some entities could boast a supernatural component before they came to participate in the feast.[125] To get around this problem, Robertson Smith enlisted the saga of the Saracen camel.

Whilst the ancient Saracens had had private property in their camels, this did not include the right to kill and eat them on a family basis. Rather, camels could only be slaughtered under conditions of extreme deprivation, when they were to be distributed among the clan, which excluded the wife of the camel owner. Though this nuclear family premise was wholly adventitious, it enabled Robertson Smith to declare a private domestic realm which stood in opposition to the public world of the clan, even though, for other purposes, the clan 'could be treated as parts of one common life' (1894: 273–4). To stay with his argument, however, the reason that clan requirements could override private rights in the single case of the camel could only be that the clan had a special relationship with the camel. This was because a rule barring an individual from an act that only the clan as a whole could perform was a corollary of the blood-feud, when the whole clan stood by an individual member's act. Indeed, it was a direct inversion of the blood-feud: a clan execution of one of its own members, which, like stoning to death among the ancient Hebrews, distributed responsibility equally over the whole clan (1894: 284–5). The consumption of a camel was, therefore, no ordinary meal but a sacrifice involving the sacred blood of the clan:

> Thus the conjecture that sacrificial animals were originally treated as kinsmen, is simply equivalent to the conjecture that sacrifices were drawn from animals of a holy kind. (Robertson Smith 1894: 289)

The holiness of the relevant kind of animal was, of course, anything but simple. By means of it, however, Robertson Smith introduced an element that was central to the totem-sacrament. For, if holy animals were kinsmen, then eating them amounted to cannibalism within the clan. In this respect, there was a further major difference between the Saracen camel and blood-brotherhood, since blood-brotherhood was entered into with outsiders. So, for that matter, were other forms of cannibalism, as Robertson Smith made clear in his *Britannica* article on sacrifice: 'The human wolves would no more eat a brother than they would eat a wolf; but to eat an enemy is another matter' (1885: 136). A human wolf who killed and ate his own would,

---

[125] At one point, Robertson Smith claimed that, though not empirically proven, it was 'morally certain' that the earliest Semites had an institution like the Roman *sacra gentilicia*, where the clan sacrificed both to their gods and to the 'demons' of their ancestors, thus bringing together the whole kin, living and dead (1894: 275–6).

therefore, be a murderer, as Robertson Smith showed by recounting the stoning by worshippers of the priest who had sacrificed to Bacchus (who was represented in the shape of a bull) a bull whose human clothing made it 'of the same race with the god as well as with the worshippers' (1886: 137).

The redundant introduction of an internal (or, to adapt McLennan, endophagic) form of cannibalism was Robertson Smith's crucial move. It enabled him to displace the sustaining effects of collective consumption from the act to its object, producing a collectively edible entity which, by virtue of its consubstantiality with the clan, was already sacred. The sacred principle which was superadded to the camel gave Robertson Smith the third term that he needed to complete the triangular unity of humans, animals and gods which constituted the logic of sacrifice.[126] This sacred principle, duly hypostatized, became the invisible component of the sacrificial triangle. The crucial feature of the third party to the sacrifice was not, therefore, its sacredness – that had been there all along in the shared substance of kinship – but its invisibility, which is to say, its abstractness. Thus the shift to endophagy was an attempt to smuggle in abstraction without resort to animism.

In keeping with his telluric emphasis, Robertson Smith asserted a correlation between the different ways in which abstract divinities could be conceptualized and the different stages of social organization. Thus (in a manner reminiscent of Bachofen) he distinguished between religions appropriate to nomadism, to pastoralism and to agricultural settlement. For instance, the principle of fosterage through shared milk provided by pastoral stock came to supplant identification with a divine animal species:

> the belief in sacred animals, akin to families of men, attains its highest development in tribes which have not yet learned to breed cattle and live on their milk. Totemism pure and simple has its home among races like the Australians and the North American Indians, and seems always to lose ground after the introduction of pastoral life. (Robertson Smith 1894: 355)

Though charting different ways in which abstraction could be conceptualized, however, such sociological conditions still failed to account for its genesis. So, too, did another, strikingly ingenious method for determining the level of development of theological concepts: the more solid the sacrificial offering, the less refined the concept of divinity involved. Thus Robertson Smith traced a progressive evolution of the sacrificial offering (and, therefore, of the being to which it was meant to appeal) from the solid food appropriate to an altogether biomorphic power, through 'more aetherial elements' which, rising up with the sacrificial smoke, were enjoyed by the sense of smell alone, to a point where, as in the case of the ancient Persians, the divinity took the soul of the victim rather than any physical part. In sum, 'the material gift offered to the deity is first attenuated and then allegorized away as the conception of the godhead becomes less crassly material' (1886: 134). This evolution illuminates the subordination of blood to flesh, of which, as seen above, it was but a 'synecdochic expression'. Portia's distinction was hardly

---

126 These were to provide the formative ingredients of Hubert and Mauss (1898).

less significant for Robertson Smith, since, being thinner than flesh, sacrificial offerings of blood – or, to use his own lingering phrase, 'libations of gore' – were a step toward aetherialization, a 'subtle vehicle of the life of the sacrifice':

> Thirst is a subtler appetite than hunger, and therefore more appropriate to the disembodied shades, just as it is from thirst rather than from hunger that the Hebrews and many other nations borrow metaphors for spiritual longings and intellectual desires. Thus the idea that the gods drink, but do not eat, seems to mark the feeling that they must be thought of as having a less solid material nature than men. (Robertson Smith 1894: 235)[127]

Despite the relative viscosity of their oblations, however, the gods who drank were no less abstract than those who merely breathed in the sacrificial smoke – their presence about the stone or earth into which the offering was poured was still invisible. Thus the social and the ideational series did not actually correlate at all. Rather, whereas the sacrificial gifts constituted a spectrum of relative solidity, the presence or absence of metaphysical concepts remained an absolute distinction. As the example of blood-brotherhood made vividly clear, no metaphysical principle followed from the relative thinness of blood. On the contrary, blood-brotherhood was an eminently telluric, pre-metaphorical way of sharing substance: 'two men become brothers by opening their veins and sucking one another's blood' (1894: 314). In the libation of gore, therefore, there was no advance on the problem of abstract thought.

In the end, then, Robertson Smith did not succeed in installing a social ghost in the animism machine. This failure is, of course, trivial (or, at least, general). What is significant is not the failure itself but the procedures that he adopted to cover it over. For the positive form that these procedures took was the concept of the totem-sacrament, which makes full sense once it is understood as an attempt to plug the obstinate gap between animism and social organization.

When it came down to it, Robertson Smith could not avoid animism after all. He was too rigorous a theorist simply to assume the totem habits of thought. Thus he did actually resort to Tylor's explanation – dreaming and all – only in a manner whose staggeredness surely bore the imprint of his mentor McLennan. For animism was inserted into his theory in the second lecture of a series whose crux did not occur until seven lectures later (even in print, the gap is over two hundred densely argued pages). Before moving on to the ninth lecture in the series, therefore, we should note that, in Lecture Two, the genesis of abstract concepts had been unequivocally cognitive, being a consequence of a mentality which was 'incapable of separating in thought between phenomenal and noumenal existence', or even between different categories in nature – and it was this incapacity that ultimately made kinship with non-humans possible. The resultant capitulation to Tylor was unqualified:

---

[127] A diametrically opposed principle could also apply: 'In the more primitive forms of semitic religion the difficulty of conceiving that the gods actually partake of food is partly resolved by a predominant use of liquid oblations; for fluid substances, which sink in and disappear, are more easily believed to be consumed by the deity than obstinate masses of solid matter' (1894: 229).

> A certain crude distinction between soul and body, combined with the idea that the soul may act where the body is not, is suggested to most savage races by familiar psychical phenomena, particularly by those of dreams; and the unbounded use of analogy characteristic of pre-scientific thought extends this conception to all parts of nature which become to the savage mind full of spiritual forces. (Robertson Smith 1894: 86–7)

By the time that Robertson Smith got to the totem-sacrament itself, however, this animistic explanation for the invisible nature of the third party to the sacrifice had become overwhelmed in the telluric argument from shared substance.

The totem-sacrament consisted in the clan's joint consumption of a sacred animal which, being of their own kin, would normally have been proscribed to them. In other words, the logic was precisely that of the Saracen camel. Unlike the material deprivation that had prompted the consumption of the camel, however, the motivation for the totem-sacrament was religious. It was undertaken to 'quicken and confirm the life-bond that already subsists between the parties' (1894: 319). To the principle of abstraction that animism furnished, the totem-sacrament thus added those of collectivity and sacredness. As we have seen, this was achieved at the cost of a single redundancy: the idea that a reinvigoration which could be effected by the mere act of eating together should entail the eating of a particular object. This redundancy was camouflaged by – to put it another way, it motivated – the totem-sacrament. In our terminology, the totem-sacrament was a debating-effect. How, then, did it operate?

Whilst animism provided the abstraction necessary for the hypostatization of the sacred principle of shared clan substance, it was, as already noted, an intellectualist theory that could provide no account of the social bonds that were so important to Robertson Smith. On the other hand, as we have seen, he failed to derive animism from a sociological starting-point. In the event, he played it both ways, separately positing the telluric process of sharing food as well as the animist delusions of the dreamer as first cause. Though placed well apart in his presentation, both beginnings were encompassed by the totem-sacrament, which thus enabled the redundant proposition that a group whose sacredness was presupposed in the very fact of their eating together should eat themselves to achieve sacredness.

The return on this redundancy was, however, that, since both the social and the ideational series passed through the totem-sacrament, it could operate as a syllogistic switch-rail, attaching social origins to the ideational series. Since the abstract notion of a sacred clan principle could be traced back to the totem-sacrament whilst the totem sacrament could, in turn, be traced back to the altogether telluric basis of shared substance evident in such practices as blood brotherhood, collective feasting and cannibalism, it seemed to follow that the abstract idea could be traced back to the telluric basis.

To reinforce this switch-rail effect, Robertson Smith employed language that marks something of a high point in misplaced concreteness. For instance, once the totem-sacrament has been introduced, we find (in Lecture Nine) that the physical act of eating together is no longer 'the essence of the thing' after all. Rather, it has become an advance on an even earlier idea which, though expediently misnamed 'cement', is the very animism that the redundancy in the totem-sacrament has now enabled him to assume:

> In later times we find the conception current that any food which two men partake of together, so that the same substance enters into their flesh and blood, is enough to establish some sacred unity of life between them; but in ancient times this significance seems to be always attached to participation in the flesh of a sacrosanct victim, and the solemn mystery of its death is justified by the consideration that only in this way can the sacred cement be procured which creates or keeps alive a living bond of union between the worshippers and their god. This cement is nothing else than the actual life of the sacred and kindred animal. (Robertson Smith 1894: 313)

If the function that the totem-sacrament performed for Robertson Smith's theory is now reasonably clear, its relationship to Hartland's theory remains to be explained. The difference made by the fact that Robertson Smith's theory was social was that, unlike Hartland's, it could only be read positively as a practice that presupposed a belief, rather than negatively, as an absence that presupposed ignorance. To establish the relationship between the two, however, we need to stay with the positive aspect of nescience, the doctrine of spirit-impregnation which, as shown in Chapter 1, followed directly from Hartland's concept of transformation. The concept underlying transformations – deriving, as we saw, from the idea of an external soul or life-token – was that of a sharing of life between people and other entities. This, of course, was the very logic that underlay the totem-sacrament (so it was no accident that Hartland and Robertson Smith should both have used the term 'substitution'). In its positive aspect as the doctrine of spirit-impregnation, therefore, nescience shared the idea of a mystical kinship between humans and natural entities that Robertson Smith had worked so hard to smuggle into the totem-sacrament. If the two theories were at bottom one and the same, how can they have been incompatible?

As positive theories, they were not incompatible. Rather, the incompatibility arose when spirit-impregnation was read negatively, as an absence of knowledge. In other words, not only the totem-sacrament but spirit-impregnation itself were incompatible with nescience. To appreciate this, it is necessary to clarify quite what nescience signified in evolutionist terms – to put it another way: given evolutionism's implicational economy, what else should have followed from the premise that the Arunta did not understand how women came to fall pregnant?

Totemism and/or Nescience

The theoretical significance of genetic ignorance was that it corroborated the view that the Arunta represented the lowest stage of social development that might still be in existence. Given evolutionist premises, this meant that the Arunta should also evince other characteristics that attached to this lowest stage. For instance (to recall the continuity between evolutionism and the doctrine of *terra nullius*), the Arunta's failure to appreciate the mechanics of conception made it unthinkable for them to have had any inkling of notions such as private property or centralized government.

Evolutionist stages had all the functional containment of the relativized social isolates that were to supplant them in the wake of the paradigm shift, only they were set into a diachronic universal frame. The requirement for different attributes of given societies to harmonize with each other provided endless scope for theoretical competition. Anomalies could almost always be found, in response to which adjustments or higher-level reconciliations had to be made. No other factor used up so much of evolutionism's epistemological slack as this. By the time that the Arunta entered the paradigm, it had almost no dialogic elbow-room left, so that anomaly in a single area could jeopardize the whole system. As a result, every trait attributed to the Arunta had the most far-flung implications.

As we saw in the previous chapter, if the Arunta had been as primitive as Frazer said they were, it would have been anomalous for them to have passed through the transition to father-right. Thus their form of patriliny was declared to be the co-residential kindred tie which, in McLennan's scheme, had been even more primitive than the blood tie that had first held together matrilineal stocks. This, in turn, entailed that their religious beliefs should be correspondingly undeveloped. Accordingly, since Howitt's matrilineal (and thus more advanced) south-eastern tribes had a monotheistic-seeming belief in a primordial All-father, it followed that the Arunta should have a more primitive, plural theology (Frazer 1905: 165–71; cf. Lang 1899a, b; 1904; 1905c; 1907a; 1909, Tylor 1892). Indeed, at their level of development, they should not have had a theology at all, since, to accord with the schedule of epistemological development that Frazer had received from Turgot and Comte, rather than having religious beliefs, the Arunta should have been confined to the realm of magical thinking (Frazer 1905: 162; cf. Spencer and Gillen 1898: 277) that had preceded the development of religion (which, in turn, had preceded the rise of science). One can pursue such implications endlessly, to the point where the question of whether or not a given tribe should have practised, say, circumcision or tooth evulsion could be read off from such factors as its proximity to coastal rains or the number of its marriage classes – not only this, but the respective converses applied as well.[128] Thus it is unprofitable to try to trace the whole recursive system

---

128 In Howitt's (1889: 33–4) estimation, 'This coincidence of advanced social development with fertility of country is not without some significance. The most backward-standing types of social organisation, having descent through the mother and an archaic communal marriage, exist in the dry and desert country; the more developed Kamilaroi type, having descent through the mother, but a general absence of the Pirauru marriage practice, is found in the better watered tracts which are the sources of all the great rivers of East Australia; while the most developed types having individual marriage and in which, in almost all cases, descent is counted through the father, are found along the coasts where there is the most permanent supply of water and most food. In fact it is thus suggested that the social advance of the Australian aborigines has been connected with, if not mainly due to, a more plentiful supply of food in better watered districts'. Howitt's view was, naturally enough, endorsed by Frazer (1905: 463) and, no more surprisingly, opposed by Mauss (1905–6: 226) who claimed that progress was encouraged by hardship rather than by plenty. For his part, Lang reiterated (1905b: xiii–xiv) the observation that the Arunta eightfold system had to be more advanced than a

through. For our purposes, it is enough to have established that the level of primitiveness associated with the failure to appreciate the relationship between sex and conception was incompatible with the holding of religious beliefs.

It should now be clear why the totem-sacrament was incompatible with nescience of principle. As its controversial resonances with the Christian Eucharist attest,[129] the totem-sacrament was a thoroughly religious concept. By contrast, magic did not even require sacredness, let alone hypostatized sacred abstractions. Rather, for evolutionary anthropology, magic merely signified the belief that some humans could affect the operations of nature. For the Arunta to be nescient, in other words, they also had to entertain magical ideas which precluded them from having religious beliefs and, thus, from exemplifying the totem-sacrament.

As noted, however, spirit-impregnation, the positive reading of nescience of principle, was conceptually equivalent to the totem-sacrament. Indeed, before Hartland, Robertson Smith had already enunciated a version of nescience, only in such a sublime context that it seems unlikely that even he appreciated the theoretical implications of his remarks:

> In Christianity, and already in the spiritual religion of the Hebrews, the idea of divine fatherhood is entirely dissociated from the physical basis of natural fatherhood ... God-sonship is not a thing of nature but a thing of grace. (Robertson Smith 1889: 42)[130]

Thus it follows that the positive reading of nescience of principle was incompatible with the negative one. Since the negative reading was propounded by Frazer and Spencer and Gillen, this gave obvious scope to their competitors, an opportunity which was not missed by the likes of Durkheim, who cited (1900–1: 111, n. 2) Arunta conception doctrines as evidence of their relative advancement, or Andrew Lang, whose Arunta, though espousing the same belief as Frazer's, could hardly have voiced it more differently:

> The Arunta philosophers, in fact, seem to concentrate their speculation on a point which puzzled Mr. Shandy. How does the animating principle, or soul, regarded as immaterial, clothe itself in flesh? Material acts cannot affect the incarnation of

---

simple twofold (moiety) division, a conclusion reinforced both by the fact that the Arunta practised subincision rather than tooth-evulsion and by the fact that their social organization was capable of sustaining a four-month-long ritual (Spencer and Gillen's *Engwura* – Lang ignored the sustaining effects of the inducements to ritual that Gillen had provided). With characteristic panache, Lang concluded that 'For all these reasons I must confess that I do not follow the logic of the philosophy which makes social advance the cause of the belief in the All Father, and coastal rains the cause of social advance' (1905b: xvi).

129 Though it was not this theory but his German-influenced text-critical Biblical scholarship that got Robertson Smith into trouble with the Free Church. Beidelman's (1974: 30–1) view was that the totem sacrament's implications for the Christian Eucharist were not so radical as they might seem because 'Smith was able to view "lower" religions sociologically, but as a Christian he viewed Christianity in absolute, intellectual terms'. I find it hard to believe that the worthies of the Scottish Free Church would be inclined to such niceties. It seems more plausible that the totem sacrament caused less fuss because, by the time it appeared, Robertson Smith had left Aberdeen for Cambridge. Beidelman himself noted (1974: 57) that the most explicit connection that Robertson Smith made between Baal-worship and the Eucharist ('That the God-man dies for His people, and that His death is their life, is an idea which was in some degree foreshadowed by the oldest mystical sacrifices' – Robertson Smith 1889: 393) was removed from the second edition (cf. Frazer 1894, Kuper 1988: 88).

130 Since the date is in issue, I have again cited the first (1889) edition here rather than the canonical second one (cf. 1894: 41).

a spirit. Therefore, the spirit enters women from without, and is not the direct result of human action. (Lang 1905b: xix)

In a book published in the same year, Lang seized on Frazer's stretching of the paradigm, asserting that Arunta patriliny was indeed the evolutionary advance on the matriliny of Howitt's south-eastern tribes that Frazer denied. Moreover, this was demonstrated by the Arunta's nescience, to which the south-eastern tribes had yet to progress! As he triumphantly concluded:

> The proof of Arunta primitiveness, the only proof, has been their nescience of the facts of generation. But we have demonstrated that, where Mr. Frazer's alleged causes of that nescience are present, among the south-eastern tribes, they do not produce it; while among the Arunta, it is caused by their system of philosophy, which the south-eastern tribes do not possess. (Lang 1905a: 193)

In this light, far from it being surprising that Frazer should have backed away from his claim that the Arunta bore out Robertson Smith's theory, it is surprising that he should have slipped up so far as to dub them proto-Christians in the first place.[131] Spencer and Gillen were much more cautious. There again, Spencer and Gillen were particularly sensitive to the pedagogical requirement that they should distance the Arunta from any suggestion of religious sentiment – indeed, it was on precisely this ground that the Lutheran missionary Carl Strehlow was to challenge their ethnography.[132] Accordingly, it is consistent that, where the totem-sacrament was concerned, Spencer and Gillen should have been reluctant fulfillers of prophecy, persistently distinguishing what they had encountered in the field from Robertson Smith's model. Thus, although an Arunta man was barred from eating his totem (or, more strictly, was only allowed to eat 'very sparingly' of it), there were

> certain special occasions on which, as a sacred ceremony, he partakes of his totemic animal or plant. (Spencer and Gillen 1899: 468)

Under other theoretical circumstances, this would surely have been enough. Yet Spencer and Gillen seemingly went out of their way to deny the mystic unity with the totem that was essential to the totem-sacrament, carefully pointing out that 'the Arunta native does not imagine that the animal or plant, or some particular one of the species, is his nearest friend' (1899: 468). The phrase 'nearest friend' was one that George Grey had earlier used to describe the 'certain mysterious connection' existing between an Aboriginal family and its *kobong*, which arose from

> the family belief that some one individual of the species is their nearest friend, to kill whom would be a great crime, and carefully to be avoided. (Grey 1841: ii; 228)

Though Grey had not reported any special relaxations of this rule, Spencer and Gillen quoted his report immediately before their own report of the Arunta exception, which makes it at least unusual that they did not pursue the matter. Moreover, they missed other opportunities, even though Frazer pointed them out. For instance, certain Arunta myths apparently portrayed

---

131 For different accounts of Frazer's distancing of himself from Robertson Smith's theory, see Ackerman 1987: 230, R. A. Jones 1984: 49–50, Kuper 1988: 104.
132 For details and sources, see Wolfe 1991: 207; 219–20.

the *Alcheringa* ('dream-times') ancestors freely eating their totems, which Frazer characteristically interpreted as recalling a tribal decree outlawing cannibalism. This interpretation provided an obvious opportunity to pinpoint the emergence of a group's consciousness of the sacredness of its own substance. In contrast, the significance that Spencer and Gillen attributed to these myths was dampeningly prosaic:

> It may be that in the traditions dealing with the eating of the totem, we have nothing more than another attempt to explain the origin of the totem name. (Spencer and Gillen 1899: 210)

The demonstration that nescience and the totem-sacrament were incompatible does not explain which one Frazer, and Spencer and Gillen should have chosen. My concern is not with their individual motives but with the social effects of their ethnography. In this regard, what was the significance of the fact that the Arunta emerged as exemplars of Hartland rather than of Robertson Smith? Whilst it is, of course, hard to say, we should note that, though Hartland's conjecture was autographic in that the bulk of his evidence was derived from pre-Hellenic Europe, 'pre-Hellenic' could go back a very long way indeed. Hartland's reluctance to believe that even the Arunta could have been as primitive as the Europeans whose traces he had discerned in the myths of supernatural births might not have been a reflection of the scale of time-depth that he thought he had succeeded in penetrating. It might just have been a reflection of theoretical rivalry. None the less, we can at least say that the antiquity involved in nescience was much deeper than that involved in the case of a Middle-Eastern ritual which had positive continuity with the Christian Eucharist. At a minimum, in other words, in exemplifying the negative reading of nescience rather than the totem-sacrament, the Arunta exemplified a much profounder removal from civilized society – one which was consistent, moreover, with the differing cognitive implications that the two theories entailed. These two factors reinforced one another. Between the two incompatible theories, therefore, nescience involved the wider polarity and, accordingly, the greater ethnographic achievement.

Though in keeping with Lévi-Strauss' assertion that it was 'not by chance' that Frazer equated totemism with nescience, and endorsing the conclusion that this 'naturalist view offered a touchstone which allowed the savage, within culture itself, to be isolated from civilized man' (Lévi-Strauss 1963: 2), this chapter has focused procedurally on the specific contingencies whereby this touchstone was produced. In the event, it transpires that there was no foreordained necessity that anthropology should produce it. It could as well have produced something else – though whether or not that something else would have been as amenable to ideological appropriation is another question.

In establishing the Arunta's profounder removal, nescience further widened the gap that was held to separate them from whites. Since it was barely two decades since they had been dispossessed and slaughtered in large numbers in the course of the European invasion of their land, the political implications of this separation hardly need elaborating.

— * —

Before returning to anthropology's appropriation in the Australian context, however, we will consider the discursive fortunes of the opposing tendency in anthropological theory. Animism – as transcendent a concept as any – sprang from reflections on the private experience of dreaming and had nothing to do with blood and land. Thus our provisional definition of evolutionary anthropology can only apply to the circumstantial narrative – to the materialist, mother-right, Scottish Enlightenment tradition propounded by McLennan, Morgan (in places), Robertson Smith and, in one of his incarnations, Durkheim. Accordingly, we no longer have grounds for excluding Darwin and Maine from anthropology. Rather, we are left with the tautology that these two patriarchalists were not matriarchalists. Yet they remained a biologist and a lawyer respectively, so we need a definition that can distinguish anthropology from what they did. We also have to deal with Tylor's intellectualism, whereby, rather than accounting for transcendence, he assumed it by means of a psychologism that held no appeal for McLennan. In the following chapter, the last of our three close examinations of the structure of anthropological theory, we will examine Tylor's doctrine of survivals. In stark contrast to totemism – which, lacking a civilized correlate, was xenography in its purest form – the doctrine of survivals was predicated on traits that united rather than separated natives and Europeans. In this light, it is striking that the discourse on totemism should continue into twentieth-century anthropology[133] while the discourse on survivals fell victim to the paradigm shift.

133 Though it should be admitted that it came and went somewhat, coming close to 'fizzling out' (Kuper 1988: 120–1) around the time of World War One. From Radcliffe-Brown on, though (as we shall see in Chapter 6), it staged a solid recovery.

CHAPTER 5

Survival in a Paradigm Shift

E. B. TYLOR AND THE PROBLEM OF THE TEXT

The principle of survival furnished evolutionary anthropology with a distinctive methodology. Thus its significance was as much institutional as it was epistemological. The institutional history of British anthropology's disciplinary establishment has already been well documented (Burrow 1966, Kuklick 1991, Lorimer 1978, Penniman 1935, Stocking 1987; 1995, Urry 1993). This chapter will concentrate on the 'internal' dimensions of that process, on the propositional ways in which anthropology distinguished itself from other forms of knowledge.

As Lévi-Strauss (1963), Bourdieu (1986) and other structuralists have repeatedly demonstrated, identities are distributed on the basis of systematic differentiation. This principle is not peculiar to these theorists' fields of analysis (totemism, taste, etc.) but is a general characteristic of systems. Systemically speaking, identity is difference – one unit is what the others are not, a principle that can readily be applied to the disciplinary configurations developing within late-nineteenth-century British universities. To gain a space within this reformed configuration,[134] a new science had to establish a difference of its own, which is to say that it had to screen off a disciplinary domain that was not already allocated to one of the established disciplines. Since, to this extent, these sciences were relational (or boundary-determined), we should be wary of the essentialism that defines them in terms of putatively natural taxonomies. This does not mean, however, that the disciplines that were emerging in the second half of the nineteenth century were devoid of specific content. On the contrary, the profession of a specialized competence requires that its object be esoteric or cryptic to outsiders. In other words, a new science constructs a laity.

Taken together, these complementary features of disciplinary differentiation – the external or residual one determined by institutional boundaries, and the internal or technical one constituted by crypticity – make up the process that I shall term 'screening'. This concept enables us to go beyond descriptive statements of the type adduced in Chapter 3, where the mother-

---

[134] The period of reform can be dated from the Royal Commissions whose recommendations began to revolutionize Oxford and Cambridge universities from 1851–52 on, producing expanded numbers, internal reorganization and increased public accountability (see, e.g., Berdahl 1959: 32–40, Collini, Winch and Burrow 1983: 342–3, Sanderson 1975: 93–5, Ward 1965: 152–60). It was also characterized by the post-1826 development of provincial English universities, first at London and Durham and increasingly, as the century progressed, in the civic colleges of the burgeoning industrial centres (Birmingham, Bristol, Leeds, Liverpool, Manchester, Newcastle, etc.). See Berdahl 1959: 40–4, Harte 1986: 67–118, Rothblatt 1976: 184–7, Sanderson 1975: 142–66. For anthropology's slow progress in the British academy after the initial success of Tylor's Oxford appointment in 1883 ('By 1906, the teaching of anthropology, particularly ethnology, was established in at least three universities in Britain'), see Urry 1993: 108–9.

right narrative emerged as structured by a thematic alternation of blood and land. Screening specifies the price – that which it concedes to surrounding disciplines – that a discipline has to pay to exist. It enables us to establish disciplinary priorities and, accordingly, to detect the issues over which contradiction will be risked. Thus the concept allows us not only to focus on the founding of a discipline but also to chart its passage into crisis. In the case to be examined in this chapter, a central element in the screening of British anthropology from the 1860s on will be seen to have been the need for a scientific object that was definitively *non-textual*. As will emerge, Tylor's doctrine of survivals constituted an attempt to get around this constraint so as to conflate social and textual logics, a debating-effect that built in unforgiving contradictions that were to surface thirty years later in Spencer and Gillen's fieldwork. The issue goes further than this, however, since the antagonism between social and textual logics was not affected by the paradigm shift, which it transcended. The two logics – that of texts and that of events – were not (and are not) reducible to each other. Rather, they interact. In the process, texts become historical factors in their own right. This does not mean that histories, or social processes as a whole, are like texts. It simply means that texts are among the active ingredients that combine to generate histories.

Rhetoric and Method in Tylor

Tylor's doctrine of survivals forced a union between two strategies, one rhetorical and the other methodological. Though both integral to unilinear evolutionism, the two were normally kept more discreetly apart.[135] Put generally, the rhetorical element was the polemical rationalism of Reform. So far as anthropology is concerned, the significant feature of this creed is that it had a dual application, prescribing enlightened attitudes both at home and abroad. At home, reformers campaigned to rid British society of the irrational, the anomalous, the corrupt, the outmoded – in short, of everything that stood in the way of progress. Where the colonies were concerned, though the great victory of the abolition of slavery had taken place over three decades earlier,[136] reformers of the 1860s were still pursuing its implications. As noted in Chapter 1, from the point of view of anthropology (or, more strictly, ethnology), the issue of slavery had resurfaced in the controversy between monogenists and polygenists, since polygenesis entailed degrees of difference profound enough to be consistent with discontinuous standards of moral treatment. Tylor's response to the polygenists was the principle of the psychic unity of mankind. This principle afforded vital underpinning to Tylor's unilinear evolutionism since, without it, it would not necessarily have been the case that 'we' had once been at the same level of progress as contemporary savages. Thus monogenesis, whose corollary was psychic unity, held together a spatiotemporal triad that theoretically integrated autography and

---

135 Hodgen (1936: 50) saw the immediate prompt for survivals as Tylor's need for an argument to defeat degenerationism.

136 Though trading in slaves had been banned in British colonial possessions in 1807, slavery itself was not banned until 1833, and even then not in the immediatist sense, which had to wait until the ending of apprenticeship in 1838. See Turley 1991: 31–43.

xenography. This triad consisted in 'our' (i.e. Europeans') savage past, 'their' (i.e. colonized natives') ethnographic present, and 'our' civilized present.

The evolutionary triad was, therefore, a key component in the external, or colonial, rhetoric of reform (for all the invidiousness of evolutionism's racial hierarchy, we should not forget what difference had signified in the context of polygenesis). In the concept of survivals, Tylor explicitly combined the three components of the evolutionary triad by means of the argument that irrational features of present-day civilized society were decayed anomalies left over from our prehistoric past, whose counterparts were to be found in their full vitality among contemporary savages. Thus the concept represented a cultural correlate to atavism, a condition that designated the continuation of the past into the present as inherently pathological. Tylor's particular rhetorical target was the 'pseudo-sciences' (he really meant 'anti-sciences') of spiritualism and astrology, which dealt in invisible forces that were unknown to science. This belief in unseen forces he attributed to animism, the most primitive of cognitive operations (cf. Stocking 1971). Tylor's theory of animism was massively elaborated through the two volumes of his canonical *Primitive Culture*, whose thousands of ethnographic examples were regularly and polemically correlated with surviving metropolitan superstitions and which ended with the ringing declaration (Tylor 1871: ii, 410) that 'The science of culture is essentially a reformer's science'.

As polemic, this equation of savagery and civilization was unremarkable, part of the satirical essayist's stock in trade. Moreover, the methodological use to which Tylor put his doctrine was not novel either. Survivals are, however, noteworthy for the open and systematic way in which he combined the two strategies. Methodologically, his polemic against what we might term the Victorian New Age was intended to double as a technique that could enable anthropology to emulate the achievements of the hard stratigraphic sciences. Geology presented a prestigious benchmark against which he could aspire to measure his reformer's science.[137] Despite occasional frauds (such as those perpetrated on the hapless Boucher de Perthes by workers whom he was gullible enough to pay by the find), archaeology had also begun to share in the general prestige attaching to stratigraphy – especially in Britain after 1858, following Falconer and Pengelly's discovery, beneath the Brixham caves, of stratum cohabitation that could hardly have borne out the evolutionary triad more vividly, since it demonstrated that palaeolithic Englishmen had not only lived like contemporary savages, but had even lived with the same creatures – the lions, hyaenas, bears, elephants and rhinos that were presented to startled Victorians as their erstwhile neighbours from rural Devon (Daniel 1976: 58, Gruber 1965).

Though geology could penetrate deeper into time than could any other contemporary science, a corollary was its relatively high degree of semantic imprecision. For geology was above all concrete, its prestige deriving from the plain hardness of its data. Accordingly, though one could hardly go further back than geology did, one could aim to go where no material science could go: into the softer, more elusive realm of metaphysics, which alone contained

---

[137] Tylor's older brother Alfred was a distinguished geologist.

the key to humanity's unique endowment. Thus the patterns that Tylor sought did not show on the face of the earth. Rather, they were those primary mental patterns that had shaped the foundations of culture. Throughout his career, Tylor's writing evinced a desire, which suffuses his language and imagery, to equip metaphysical data with evidenciary credentials to match those of the fossil record. He was trying to annex the empiricist and utilitarian heartland of British philosophy, the Humean problematic of the association of ideas,[138] to the domain of anthropology. In this he was not alone, since the co-emergent discipline of psychology (which, though individualistic, experimental and clinical by comparison, was bound to remain enmeshed with anthropology so long as the evolutionist equation of phylogeny and ontogeny held sway) had the same designs (Donnelly 1983: 110–13, Leahey 1980: 43–125, Lowry 1982: 20–36). Moreover, psychologists shared Tylor's fondness for the most material of natural-scientific metaphors, although their source was characteristically chemistry rather than geology. In both cases, solidity of imagery was designed to compensate for the perceived tenuousness of its referent. This anxiety was a symptom of transition, of the passage into areas as yet unsurely claimed for positivism of what Bob Young (1973a: 353), adapting Gillispie, called the advancing edge of objectivity.

For anthropology, psychology (or, for that matter, any evolutionist discourse which embraced the present) there was, however, a major problem with the notion of survival. This was the problem of selective utility, or function. Shards of pottery or palaeolithic dwelling sites survive despite, rather than as a result of, the routine processes of nature. They are anomalies whose detection is sufficiently specialized to warrant scientific status. The science that discovers them has a requirement for proof, which revolves about the material discovery. Thus archaeology is predicated on destruction, obliteration, decay – all the processes that make the discovery of survivals an esoteric skill. Without the decay, survival would be patent and obvious, so there could be no science of its discovery. The situation is quite different where beliefs, parts of the body, or other components of viable undecayed systems survive into the present. In this case, unless the item cannot be perceived without mechanical aid, the issue is one not of discovery but of analysis and interpretation. For instance, the principle of natural selection was not formulated to facilitate discoveries; it was formulated to account for the characteristics of observable phenomena. According to this principle, biological survivals persisted because they continued to have a function. Despite the terminological coincidence, therefore, Darwin's survivals were the opposite of Tylor's, which somehow persisted despite their loss of function. Being a function as much of the present as of the past, the Darwinian type of survival could not be held to betoken the past alone, so it had no interest for Tylor, who dismissed its superorganic analogues as instances of 'mere permanence in culture' (Tylor 1871: i, 70).

On this basis, a major problem for Tylor's theory was that, had his survivals continued to have utility, they would have cast light on the present rather than on the past. For this reason, survivals had to be in decay. On the other

---

138 Though Tylor was more like Locke – and opposed to Hume – in viewing the association of ideas pejoratively, as a logical weakness, rather than as a general characteristic of thought (in which regard, a worthier anthropological successor to Hume would, of course, be Lévi-Strauss).

hand, since lack of utility meant lack of selection (i.e. non-existence), the persistence of something that did not have utility was hard to explain (here, a Darwinian correlate might be blood groups). For the purposes of the argument to come, this tension between decay and survivals is crucial. As will emerge, it arose as a direct consequence of Tylor's desire to combine methodological and rhetorical strategies within the scope of the single concept. To appreciate the difficulties in which this involved him, we shall first sketch out the discursive context within which he was screening off a distinctive disciplinary space for his science.

Anthropology in Disciplinary Context

Methodologically, anthropology was surrounded by discourses that rescued the remote past by means of secondary material vehicles, both textual and otherwise. The key requirement for rescuing the past, whether by texts or by other vehicles, was pattern. Patterns provided the link between present observation and past object. In this regard, the two master discourses were geology and philology (clearly, what geologists had discovered was not rocks but the significance of patterns that were observable on rocks). Of these two disciplines, though geology provided the ultimate reference point for metaphors of evidenciary solidity, it was the historical achievements of philology that most intimately converged with the semantic concerns of a discourse on primitive culture.

For all their differences, however, geology and philology shared the crucial feature that the patterns that they deciphered were materially constituted. The giants of philological reconstruction – Jones, Bopp, the Grimms and Oxford's German Sanskritist Max Müller, who towered over British philology in the 1860s and 1870s – dealt in texts, overwhelmingly from within William Jones' Indo-European family of languages. They compared historical texts with each other and with contemporary linguistic forms in order to map the occurrence of historical movements, both within language (as in the case of sound shifts) and externally (as in the case of demographic distributions [Olender 1992, Pedersen 1962: 240–339, Whitney 1875]).

Though philology could hardly have provided a better avenue into the semantic concerns of an emergent discourse on primitive mentality, the authority of the established text-based specializations (i.e. besides philology, law, antiquities, political economy, logic, moral science and history) meant that the fledgling science of anthropology could not hope to annex a textual domain.[139] Given the Victorian obsession with origins, however, there had to

---

139 Anthropology was co-emergent with history from the receding discipline of antiquities (or antiquarianism, as it increasingly came to be called). Over an extended time-period, antiquarianism was amateurized in favour of the professionalizing disciplines with scientific pretensions – history, politics, psychology and, later on, archaeology – which emerged out of palaeontology and the old moral science tripos at Oxford and Cambridge. Nature and culture had been epistemologically institutionalized in tandem in 1851 when the Cambridge Natural Science and Moral Science triposes had both been set up (McLachlan 1947), with Moral Science requiring papers in mental and moral philosophy, logic, psychology, history and political philosophy, political economy and jurisprudence (Collini, Winch and Burrow 1983: 345). History had been established a year earlier at Oxford as part of a joint school of law and history (Burrow 1981: 98) (at Cambridge, history was subordinate to law; at Oxford, it was the reverse [Winstanley 1947: 208]). In 1867, history was taken out of the Cambridge Moral Tripos, a Law and History Tripos was set up in 1868 and, in 1873, Cambridge triposes were established both in history and in Indian and Semitic languages (Winstanley 1947: 189; 207–8) alongside other recently

come a point at which philology cast loose from its textual moorings and ventured into the speculative realm of proto-languages. This occurred in the case of Max Müller's famous (1861; 1864) 'diseases of language' theory. For our purposes, the salient feature of this theory is that, in anticipating the ground that anthropology was to make its own, it also anticipated the epistemological structuring of anthropological explanation. Müller's theory was based on the premise that linguistic forms continued to circulate after their original meaning had become lost – or, as he put it, 'withered'. The operative feature is the withering – the decay, distortion or amnesia whereby patterns that had lost their original meanings nonetheless persisted as empty routines which thus, and crucially, constituted traces that could be used to recover the forgotten meanings. The anomalous persistence of the hollow phonological shell enabled the philologist to go back behind textuality and penetrate deep into the prehistory of language. In other words, loss of meaning was a process of becoming cryptic that vindicated a technique of decipherment. Displaced from its specificity to language, this explanatory structure was to constitute Victorian anthropology's disciplinary screen, its proprietary methodology for reconstructing prehistoric culture.

Müller's circular explanatory device had a deep though contradictory affinity with the prevailing ideology of the times. As noted, it harmonized with the Victorian preoccupation with origins, a preoccupation that evinced an arriviste bourgeoisie's anxiety to emulate the ancestral legitimation sustaining the landed order that it had so rudely usurped. Correspondingly, however, the persistence of meaningless outmoded forms was offensive to an entrepreneurial ethic that championed rationality over habit. In both scientific and free-market terms, the Victorian bourgeoisie had no place for that which lacked utility or selective fitness.

In Müller's philological reconstructions, the morpho-semantic disjuncture whereby a word could survive the loss of its original meaning resulted from migration, diffusion and the various other processes that had caused the original Indo-European tongue (which he termed 'Aryan') to fragment into localized offshoots – Sanskrit, Persian, German, Greek, Latin, Celtic, etc. In the course of acquiring its own distinct linguistic, territorial and cultural identity, a given offshoot could lose the descriptive attributes attaching to, say, a divine name, which would either decline into relative insignificance or acquire a new explanatory mythology – one which, under the circumstances, was likely to be garbled and perverse. Accordingly, the bizarre and offensive elements in mythology could be mitigated by an eclectic collateral process whereby their original meanings could be found plausibly and inoffensively persisting in some other branch of the Aryan family, where loss of meaning

---

established ones in philosophy, biological sciences, theology and law (Rothblatt 1981: 184–5). At Oxford, law and history were separated in 1870 (Ward 1965: 279). 'In the 1860s and 70s', as Collini, Winch and Burrow (1983: 209) put it, 'the map of learning seemed, to many members of the educated class in England, about to be redrawn in an exhilaratingly comprehensive and coherent way'. A similar process, it might be noted, was going on in the US – between 1840 and 1905, Yale's eight Departments grew to twenty-two and Michigan's five to thirty-two (Kimball 1986: 163, see also Powell 1965), though anthropology fared much better in the US than in Britain (Urry 1993: 108). Diversification was closely bound up with increasing professionalization. In the course of the nineteenth century, not only did the Oxbridge clergymen give way to dons (Engel 1983, Rothblatt 1981: 90) but, increasingly, it was expected that the liberal curricula that they dispensed would lead to public or professional (or, later, Indian Civil Service [ICS]) careers (Goldstein 1983, Sanderson 1975).

would have affected different elements of the original cosmology. Thus could Müller acquit the Greek gods of the incest, cannibalism, bestiality, parricide and related tendencies that so perplexed the sensitivities of a bowdlerizing age.

As we shall see, narrative details apart, Müller's theory anticipated evolutionary anthropology in postulating a kind of evolutionist semiosis whereby denotation (or surface reference) functioned as a methodological pretext for connotation (or cryptic, inferred reference). The essential feature of surviving patterns, linguistic or otherwise, was their extrinsic signification – mere palimpsests, their referents had otherwise disappeared. The method was by no means particular to Müller – consider, for instance, Bachofen's reduction of the narratival wealth of a huge sample of ancient European mythology to the single implication of mother-right.[140]

By elimination, the patterns that remained available for a new human science to decipher would have to be non-textual and non-material, a consideration which encouraged the emergent discipline of anthropology to go a step further than Müller or Bachofen. Rather than using texts as a springboard backwards into the pretextual, it sought to dispense with them altogether. Though conventionally assimilated to the anthropological canon, Bachofen's theory should be distinguished from anthropology not only for the reasons specified in the mother-right chapter but on the more comprehensive additional ground that it was text-based, which made it the domain of law, antiquities or history. Thus it was not available for incorporation into the proper domain of an emergent science. Effectively barred from textuality and material culture, evolutionary anthropologists found themselves confined to the decipherment of *behavioural* patterns.[141] It is not surprising that this field should have remained unclaimed. Being evanescent in the extreme, behavioural patterns could hardly have been less congenial to a discourse on origins. For all its inherent difficulty, however, the determinate problematic of Victorian sociocultural anthropology can be defined as the project of recovering lost meanings for behavioural patterns that lacked textual or other material support.

Tylor's was one of three theories that together established Victorian anthropology's epistemological repertoire, the other two being those of Morgan and McLennan. In Morgan's case, as we have seen, the behaviour involved was kinship, whilst in McLennan's it was ritual. In Tylor's theory of survivals, it was superstitious practices. In each of these theories, loss of meaning operated as a scrambling device that rendered the behaviour illegible without the aid of the theory, thus constituting a laity and its corresponding science. Here, in other words, was anthropology's screen. Thus the theories of Morgan and McLennan do not comprise a context for Tylor's theory in the conventional sense that Tylor either echoed or rebutted them, but in the symptomatic sense that they were epistemologically co-

---

140 'All these traits join to form a single picture and lead to the conclusion that mother right is not confined to any particular people but marks a cultural stage' (Bachofen 1861: 71).

141 Though it should be noted that anthropology remained intertwined with archaeology until well into the twentieth century. Whilst, in common with psychologists, many anthropologists also engaged in craniometry, this was increasingly marginalized from sociocultural anthropology. Even when included, physical data were conventionally confined to a separate section or chapter.

conditioned. Emerging otherwise independently in the mid 1860s, the three approaches represent alternative realizations of a common strategy. As we shall see, so far as the epistemological structuring of Victorian anthropology is concerned, the least successful of these theories – though, by the same token, the most revealing – was Tylor's.

In Morgan's case, as explained in Chapter 3, the requisite pattern was provided by kinship nomenclature, the element of disjuncture between pattern and meaning resulting from the proposition that kin terms changed more slowly than actual marital practices, lagging behind to provide an index of previous usages.[142] As we saw, there was no doubting the competitive intent of Morgan's theory. Blood lines constituted a more enduring vehicle than texts. Thus kinship furnished an instrument for penetrating prehistory that could 'take up the problem at the point where philology is now arrested' (1871: 506). The patterns that anthropology acquired by virtue of Morgan's kinship systems were not just extra-textual avenues into prehistory, however. They also embodied the crucial quality that they could be turned into texts. Indeed, more positively still, their graphemic potential was such that it subtended the diagrammatic idiom that was to distinguish twentieth-century kinship studies. Understood as commonly fulfilling a requirement for behavioural patterns, kinship and ritual converge, since ritual constitutes patterned behaviour *par excellence*. On this basis at least, therefore, Morgan's theory harmonized with that of his great rival McLennan.

McLennan's theory overtly relied on the spatiotemporal triad that has been noted in relation to Tylor. *Primitive Marriage* opened (1865: 1) with the assertion that the two chief sources of information for 'the early history of civil society' (i.e. our past) were, firstly, 'races in their primitive condition' (their present) and, secondly, 'the study of symbols employed by advanced nations' (our present). McLennan's principal symbol, the rite of mock capture, was in decay – or, as he was to put it a few years later (1869–70: 210), 'facts come first, and symbols are facts in decadence'. The 'fact' that contemporary mock captures preserved was a prehistoric reality in which violence and rapine had been the means whereby men obtained wives. For our purposes, however, the important point is that the only practical function that McLennan's symbols performed was for his theory, where their half-life afforded a means of 'connecting and arranging in their order the stages of human advancement' (McLennan 1865: 1). For the societies that maintained them, these symbols were formal superfluities, devoid of any acknowledged utility or purpose. Thus decay meant that, as in Morgan's theory, patterns could survive independently of their original meanings.

In so controversially undermining the bourgeois family, McLennan's theory had more than purely methodological significance. Here again, the same applies to Morgan, whose indurated nomenclatures attested to primitive marital scenarios that were hardly preferable to McLennan's. As in the case of Tylor, therefore, these theories were of both methodological and rhetorical

---

142 Compare Tylor (1871: i, 16): 'Among evidence aiding us to trace the course which the civilization of the world has actually followed is that great class of facts to denote which I have found it convenient to introduce the term "survivals". These are processes, customs, opinions, and so forth, which have been carried on by force of habit into a new state of society different from that in which they had their original home, and they thus remain as proofs and examples of an older condition of culture out of which a newer has been evolved.'

significance. This is not merely a formal distinction. Rather, the two derive from independently motivated discourses, the rhetorical strategy embodying the politics of liberal rationalism, the methodological one being determined by the presence of epistemological gaps within the institutional configuration of the Victorian academy.

When the manner in which they combined the two strategies is considered, however, a major distinction must be drawn between Tylor's theory and those of Morgan and McLennan. For, in contradistinction to Tylor's direct assault on spiritualism, astrology and other features of the Victorian New Age, McLennan's and Morgan's theories only applied to metropolitan society in an oblique or indirect way. McLennan did not suggest that civilized Englishmen still captured their brides,[143] whilst Morgan's classificatory kinship systems, with their legacy of primitive promiscuity, were at a categorical remove from his descriptive system, which faithfully represented the monogamous ideals of respectable Rochester (1871: 470–1). This is not to say that the rhetorical bite of their theories was less radical than that of Tylor's. A comparison between Tylor and McLennan is instructive in this regard, since they were operating within the same society. Where Tylor came to enjoy an Oxford living as the first reader in social anthropology anywhere, as noted, the embittered McLennan never obtained an academic job. A glance at their theories bears out this disparity. For, even though its application was indirect, *Primitive Marriage* was tampering at the very heart of social values. By contrast, Tylor's targets were themselves anti-establishment. In other words, where Tylor's aspirations were organic to the project of progress, McLennan was desecrating one of bourgeois society's most cherished adornments.[144] All the same, though the rhetorical implications of McLennan's narrative were much more subversive than Tylor's, they were also less immediate. To put this another way, McLennan (or, for that matter, Morgan) was less prepared than Tylor to subordinate his methodology to his rhetoric.

For all the dated evolutionism of their narrative details, Morgan's and McLennan's theories were to be profoundly formative for twentieth-century sociocultural anthropology, especially in Britain and France. Morgan's theory inaugurated the comparative study of formal kinship systems, an achievement that would prompt Lévi-Strauss to dedicate his first great work, *The Elementary Structures of Kinship* (1947), to him ('to pay homage to the pioneer of the research method modestly adopted in this book'). As channelled through the work of his faithful acolyte William Robertson Smith, McLennan's theory was taken up into the ritually-focused anthropology of Emile Durkheim and the *Année Sociologique* school, whence it came to acquire a profound influence on twentieth-century anthropology. Indeed, by investing anthropology with its dual preoccupation with kinship and ritual,

---

143 Although, as we have seen, he was not above using his theory to take a tilt at civilized depravity: 'Savages are unrestrained by any sense of delicacy from a copartnery in sexual enjoyments; and, indeed, in a civilised state, the sin of great cities shows that there are no natural restraints sufficient to hold man back from grosser copartneries' (McLennan 1865: 91).

144 Hence, as Tylor himself observed, in his obituary for McLennan, 'in 1865 he published a law-book which had the natural and immediate effect of losing him half his briefs. This was *Primitive Marriage*' (Tylor 1881: 9–10).

Morgan and McLennan substantially constituted the discipline between them.

When we turn to Tylor's concept of survivals, however, the story is very different. For, though it was initially as influential as the doctrines of Morgan and McLennan, its effects were not to endure. This failure is significant. Tylor's intellectualism distinguishes his theories from those that attempted to derive superorganic culture from material conditions. In the case of animism, as we have seen, he attributed the origin of abstract concepts to responses to the experience of dreaming. The doctrine of survivals was premised on the association of ideas. Yet, whereas blood and land were to enjoy a vigorous twentieth-century career as descent and residence respectively, neither of Tylor's two major theories was to survive the paradigm shift. This lack of selective fitness on the part of these theories enables us to identify sociocultural anthropology's elementary logical structures.

Theory and Doctrine

As explained, the methodological value of disfunction (or, for consistency, of decay) was that, in providing for patterns to survive independently of their original meaning, it provided for overlaps between succeeding social epochs. For the purpose of penetrating prehistory, this enabled the analyst to go as far back as otherwise possible, and then to proceed still further by means of the overlap. Accordingly, it made little methodological sense for Tylor to start with an overlap into the present rather than with one that only just crossed the horizon of our determinable past – especially when both were available for observation amongst contemporary savages. Rather, the worthwhile survivals were those which, having already started to decay by the dawn of recorded history, were no longer to be encountered in civilized usage.

In fact, Tylor did employ just this logic to develop his influential notion of 'adhesions', which, having no immediate rhetorical impact, he did not present as a vindication of the concept of survival. The particular prehistory that Tylor set out to trace was none other than the transition from motherright to father-right, his article (Tylor 1889) being principally renowned (e.g. Kuper 1988: 98, Stocking 1995: 4) for the fact that he adapted Francis Galton's statistical method to do so. The concept of adhesions, which itself echoed the synchronic stratigraphy being developed in archaeology,[145] referred to practices that were observed to correlate with other cultural phenomena in a significant number of cases. Tylor cited the practice of couvade, in which husbands mimicked the process of giving birth whilst their wives were in labour. Methodologically, the significant feature of this custom was that it was not practised in matrilocal societies. Thus Tylor argued that, as an assertion of paternity over the children about to be born, it must have sprung up as part of the transition to father-right, afterwards

---

145 It is unlikely that Tylor had not encountered Pitt-Rivers' (at the time, Lane-Fox's) concept of 'cohesions', first expressed in the closing words of his 1874 lecture 'Principles of Classification': 'Progress is like a game of dominoes. Like fits onto like. In neither case can we tell beforehand what will be the ultimate figure produced by the cohesions; all we know is that the fundamental rule of the game is sequence' (quoted in Daniel 1976a: 172).

fading into an attenuated symbolic form which nonetheless residually testified to the occurrence of the great transition.[146] Despite the statistical innovation, therefore, the methodology was precisely that of McLennan, with couvade replacing mock capture as the tell-tale behavioural pattern. Moreover, any rhetorical implications that Tylor might have intended were left unstated. It is, therefore, consistent that he should have reserved his most confident claim to parity with geology for this moment of methodological purity:

> The argument is a geological one. Just as the forms of life, and even the actual fossils of the Carboniferous formation, may be traced on into the Permian, but Permian types and fossils are absent from the Carboniferous strata formed before they came into existence, so have the widow-inheritance [an ancillary adhesion] and couvade, which if the maternal system had been later than the paternal, would have lasted on into it, prove by their absence the priority of the maternal. (Tylor 1889: 256)

Given his obvious satisfaction with the efficacy of the adhesions method, why did Tylor not hold it out as further support for his theory of survivals? The essential difference between the couvade and survivals was the same as that between marriage by capture or Morgan's classificatory kinship systems and survivals: they were not to be found in the civilized present, so the inference that civilized nations had once practised them could only be obtained by evidence obtained from contemporary savages. This brings us back to our spatiotemporal triad, which the doctrine of survivals rendered oddly redundant.

If prehistory were to be found persisting in the civilized present, then, in theory at least, there should have been no need for ethnographic corroboration (i.e. for auxiliary evidence from 'their' present). A way around this consideration was provided by the notion of decay, whereby prehistory only partly or residually subsisted in survivals, which needed to be supplemented by the fuller picture obtainable from ethnography. But this way out merely compounded the redundancies. For, if survivals really had been in decay, then they would not have warranted the mounting of a rhetorical campaign against them. Despite all Tylor's talk of decay, therefore, the truth was that spiritualism, astrology and the like had survived only too vitally. In fact (and this is the point), *they had not lost their meaning*. On the contrary, they boasted elaborately articulated bodies of doctrine, whose meaning to their practitioners, far from being lacking, constituted the very problem that Tylor wanted to eliminate. The reason why he should have risked such a damaging contradiction will be important when we come to examine his exposition of survivals in detail. As will emerge, his efforts to cover over this contradiction illuminate the epistemological structure of evolutionary anthropology.

For the purposes of historical reconstruction, it was not necessary that survival should continue right into the present. All that was necessary was a series of links connecting a custom to the present (in the case of the couvade,

---

146 Bachofen (1861: 17; 255) had earlier seen the couvade as belonging to a turning-point when the increased level of domestic responsibility associated with developed agricultural settlement caused mother-right to give way to a father-right purged of the sexual promiscuity that had been characteristic of the first, 'hetaeristic' mode of patriarchy that the virtuous mothers had overthrown.

for instance, the way through to modern marriage was clear once father-right and its attendant property arrangements were in place). Thus the reason that survivals stretched on into the present can not have been methodological. Rather, it was the fact (which, as we shall see, Tylor went to considerable lengths to disguise) that they were not actually customs at all. As already observed, the survivals that counted for Tylor were taken from the realm of philosophical associationism. They were articulated ideational phenomena, the heretical *doctrines* on which the spiritualist 'pseudo-sciences' were predicated. The problem that such material presented to Tylor was, therefore, that the vehicle whereby it survived was not behaviour but written documents, which put it outside the epistemological space available to a new science.

As the example of Bachofen illustrates, myths provided abundant scope for penetrating prehistory. But Bachofen's myths had not been obtained ethnographically. Their survival across the millenia was not an achievement of oral tradition but a consequence of the fact that they had been materialized as texts, which rendered them the preserve of antiquarianism. How could the speculations of our prehistoric ancestors be recovered without the aid either of texts that had been written at the dawn of literacy or of other significant icons that were also the province of antiquities? As the detailed analysis of Tylor's exposition of survivals will show, the contradiction from which all the others followed was that he was trying to smuggle texts into the domain of anthropology. Thus the end of his exposition, which culminates in a whole series of ethnographic (and overtly behavioural) examples, consists in a reading from an astrological almanac. Given that his theory was both rhetorical and ideational, this contradiction had to arise, for the simple reason that it is impossible to address modernity without addressing texts. Thus the issue of textuality was the point at which Tylor subordinated his methodology to his rhetoric, and it is this issue that distinguishes his analysis of the couvade (clearly a behavioural pattern) from his survivals.

To explain the contradiction in survivals, it is, therefore, necessary to explain Tylor's doctrinalism. Why, when it came to survivals, was he not prepared to start with ritual and secure the same methodological benefits as McLennan? The argument from disciplinary boundaries cannot explain Tylor's doctrinalism; it merely accounts for his efforts to disguise it. A preference for doctrine over ritual does, however, have a thoroughly Protestant stamp, which takes us to Tylor's Quakerism and, accordingly, to the philanthropic universalism underlying his commitment to the psychic unity of mankind, a principle that he advocated in opposition to the racist doctrines of polygenesis and degeneration. Psychic unity was not some determinate routine that could be demonstrated by means of motiveless behavioural patterns. Thus Tylor's problem was *verstehen*. It was not enough to show what people did – he also needed to be able to demonstrate their reasons for doing so. This entailed articulated propositions and, therefore, language, which inescapably brought in texts as well.

Ultimately Tylor's furtive incorporation of texts was rhetorically motivated. Ironically, however, the philanthropy underlying the psychic unity of mankind was subverted by the denigration of savages entailed in the rhetorical use to which he put them. For the moment, though, the concern is with the methodological contradictions involved, since these cast independent light on the relationship between anthropology and texts. For, quite apart from the issue of disciplinary boundaries, there is a basic incompatibility between doctrines and ritual patterns such as the couvade or McLennan's marriage by capture. This is that, for all Tylor's talk of decay, oral language cannot survive the loss of its meaning. To be preserved, meaningless language requires secondary support, which texts can provide. At this point, therefore, we will turn from the context in which the doctrine of survivals was formulated to the relationship between textuality and ritual in the context of anthropological theory.

Ritual, Text and Epistemology

As observed in Chapter 2, anthropology's ritual emphasis was – with no pun intended – a paradigm survivor, becoming as central to the synchronic approaches of the twentieth century as it had earlier been to evolutionism. We need to consider the grounds for this versatility. Why was a ritual emphasis congenial to two otherwise very different paradigms? In the case of evolutionism, as we have seen, ritual's principal value was methodological, in that it provided the kind of behavioural pattern that could penetrate prehistory without encroaching on the territory of rival disciplines. Ritual was suited to this purpose because it could survive the loss of its original meaning. In other words, ritual was *unforgettable*. Indeed, unforgettability was the quality that enabled ritual to bridge the two paradigms, though it functioned differently in each case. To see how, we need to consider the logic of anthropological explanation.

The mnemonic basis to ritual's unforgettability was that it lacked propositional sequence. To put it, for the purposes of the argument, linguistically: prior to van Gennep's (1909) rites of passage at least, ritual had no syntax. Rather, rites were single items, so the same one could occur independently in different narrative contexts (Welsh marriages, Bedouin marriages, etc.). Thus ritual differed crucially from doctrines (including, in this particular sense, myths), that were made up of strings of words which, being propositionally cumulative, were not interchangeable. Compared to a single word or ritual, the meaning of articulated sentences is overdetermined. This is why, in contrast to ritual, narrative passages cannot survive orally and be in decay (you can refuse to believe in a myth but you cannot refuse to understand what the words mean).

Meaningless strings of words can, however, survive if they are transmitted by way of a secondary vehicle. As observed, this need not be material. A behavioural vehicle – say, a set of gestures or a tune – will do (people sing songs in languages that they do not understand). Mnemonically, therefore, unforgettability – or, for consistency, the capacity to survive whilst decayed – required that doctrines should be backed up by somatic or kinesic complements, from which (and this is the operative factor) they could subsequently become detached. On detachment, it was the complement, rather than the doctrine to which it was ancillary, that survived. (In the case of the song in a foreign language, for instance, phonic and rhythmic qualities survive independently of semantic ones.) For the purpose of survivals, therefore, the medium really was the message. For our purposes, this means that the basis for ritual's capacity to penetrate prehistory was synaesthesia.

Where syntax is concerned, sensory-modal plurality is redundant. Thus language is either heard (speech), seen (writing, Sign) or touched (Braille). Combining these separate modalities only produces redundancy (consider subtitles in the same language as the soundtrack). To say this is simply to say that language has propositional sequence, that it is cumulative and linear. Ritual, by contrast, can equally well be either heard or seen, but it can also combine these and other media without redundancy (adding an accompanying song does not mean that a mock capture need take any longer). Ritual, in short, is a sensory-modal melting pot.

With this observation, we can move from the service that ritual performed for evolutionism to that which it performed for the synchronic paradigms of the twentieth century. For, in either case, it was necessary that a plurality of channels should operate simultaneously. In the case of evolutionism, as we have seen, this requirement arose from the fact that, as the means for penetrating prehistory, secondary vehicles were methodologically indispensible. Now, so far as synchronic analysis was concerned, a corresponding plurality was presupposed in the basic premise of an equilibrium or homology *among the parts* (this applies both to the structuralist requirement for morphological symmetry and to the functionalist one for homeostatic balance). Either side of the paradigm shift, therefore – though for different reasons – a ritual emphasis remained methodologically central to anthropology.

In synchronic analysis, ritual's internal complexity could not provide propositional sequence. On the contrary, as innumerable critics have complained, sequence is precisely what the method omits. In relation to articulate language, which is a progressive linear sequence, a conspicuous property of texts is that they can be held still for the eye to move about them (in this sense, the model of the text is really that of the page – or, more topically, of the screen). By virtue of their materiality, texts can be shuffled, read backwards or sideways, cross-referenced and broken down into any number of lists (columns and rows, presences and absences, syntagms and paradigms, etc.). Thus texts – and especially diagrams – can accommodate the plurality of the elements simultaneously 'thrown together' (the etymology of 'symbol') in ritual. If time is a key variable distinguishing symbol and ritual, then it follows that the two should have been conflated in synchronic analysis. By holding rituals and other activities still, synchronic analysis spread them out cross-sectionally so that they became analytically equivalent to material icons. The point is, however, that there are no alternatives to hearing articulate speech sequentially. Thus, however much synchronic reading can aggregate ritual's complexity, it reduces language to the signifying capacity of just another symbolism. Sequential verbal propositions might as well be so many pictographs or mandalas (in this regard, it is no accident that Saussure's best-known illustration was a railway timetable). This is not to say that language could not constitute synchronic data (given the anthropological status of myth, that would be absurd). It does, however, mean that language had to lose its sequential dimension in favour of signifying sideways. Thus anthropological ears became closed to propositional language – when someone spoke in a ritual, the anthropologist wondered what else they were saying.[147] In other words, like ritual within evolutionism, language within synchronic analysis became an empty palimpsest (hence the alluring formula that myths tell us what natives are really thinking when natives think that myths are what they are really telling).

In one sense, the observation that synchronic analysis robs language of its sequence merely restates the stock objection that the technique is ahistorical. This follows automatically once the technique is shifted from language to society, since the social counterpart to loss of sequence in language is loss of sequence in human affairs, which is to say loss of history. The question of history brings to the fore the spatiotemporal triad that we saw at work in evolutionary anthropology. Despite the equivalence that was held to obtain between European prehistory and contemporary savagery, there were major differences between archaeology and ethnography, in particular where the question of evidence was concerned. Ethnography produced its own flood of material trophies (enough to sustain the late nineteenth-century ethnological museum boom) which were of an ontological order comparable to that of the archaeological find. Such trophies were, however, of a different evidenciary order to archaeological data. Since they were not the only evidence, they illustrated or supplemented – rather than proved – the data of ethnography. If they proved anything, it was the extent of their donor's travels. Moreover, as the nineteenth century drew to a close – and especially once Tylor had enunciated the concept of survivals, which entailed the possibility of doing ethnography at home – the popularity of folklorism (German-style local oral mythography) grew rapidly (Stocking 1987: 163).[148]

In other words, the doctrine of survivals overburdened the link between the reconstruction of European prehistory and the study of contemporary savages, jeopardizing the founding (and thoroughly colonizing) premise of evolutionary theory, the premise that 'their' present was 'our' past: that to travel across space was to travel back in time. Thus it is not surprising that survivals should have succumbed to the paradigm shift, given that twentieth-century synchronic analysis was to shatter the universalism of the evolutionist narrative and replace it with an atomistic plurality of relativized social isolates.

To see how these tensions played themselves out in theoretical practice, we will turn now to the concept of survivals as Tylor enunciated it. As already indicated, when we examine the concept we find not only that it was contradictory but that this in itself casts light on the constitution of

---

[147] This observation is indebted to Maurice Bloch (1974; 1975).

[148] This trend was encouraged by the late-Victorian concern that industrialization was sweeping away local cultural traditions in Britain (Urry 1993: 83–101).

evolutionary anthropology. As we shall see, Tylor was so sensitive to the contradictions in his theory that his exposition of it is best read symptomatically, as a theoretical reaction-formation whose details were determined by the need to disguise contradiction. As we follow his subterfuge, retracing its careful construction, we gain new insights into the theoretical norms that he was transgressing, norms whose satisfaction the subterfuge was designed to feign. To this end, we will closely examine survivals' founding moment,[149] which occurred towards the end of a lecture that Tylor delivered to the Royal Institution of Great Britain on Friday, 15 March 1867.

The Anatomy of Survivals

The full text of Tylor's first exposition of his doctrine is as follows:

> Another subject may be found to throw light upon an early condition of men's minds. We are all agreed that there is a certain mental process called the association of ideas. That we are in the habit of connecting in our minds different things which have, in actual fact, no material connection, we all admit as a matter belonging to this association of thoughts or of ideas. Now we have been taught to keep an eye on the action of the association of thoughts, to recognize it as a fallacious process apt to lead us into all manner of unreasonable opinions. But if we descend to a lower range of civilization, we shall find that the mental association which we tolerate as a sort of amiable weakness, and against which we are at any rate forewarned and forearmed, is the very philosophy of the savage. There is one particularly excellent way of studying the effects of the association of thought. It began to produce, in a time associated with a very low human condition, a set of opinions and practices known as the occult sciences, witchcraft, divination, astrology and the like. The germs of these imaginary sciences are to be found still lively among the lower races. Their development into elaborate pseudo-scientific systems belongs to a period now beginning to pass away; and we can still study them in their last stage of existence, that in which their remnants have lingered on

---

[149] 'Founding moment' in so far as this represents the first occasion on which the doctrine received both its name and a full exposition. At least inchoately, however, the doctrine had been part of Tylor's thought from the very beginning. In his first book, the Mexican travelogue *Anahuac* (1861), he was already using the actual terminology of survival in relation to almanacs – which, as we shall see, constituted the principal rhetorical problematic of the doctrine when it was finally enunciated as a whole: 'there are the almanacks, which contain rules for foretelling the weather by the moon's quarters, but none of the other fooleries which we find in those that circulate in England among the less educated classes. It is curious to notice how the taste for putting sonnets and other dreary poems at the beginnings and ends of books has *survived* in these Spanish countries . . . It is not merely apropos of sonnets, but of thousands of other things, that in these countries one is brought, in a manner, face to face with England as it used to be; and very trifling matters become interesting when viewed in this light' (Tylor 1861: 125, my emphasis). Without its name, the doctrine had received a coherent statement the year before Tylor's Royal Institution lecture in his (1866c) paper 'On Phenomena of the Higher Civilization Traceable to a Rudimental Origin Among Savage Tribes' (cf. Leopold 1980: 49). Well before Tylor, Herbert Spencer (1854) had spelled out the essential principles of the doctrine. Hodgen (1936: 70–1, n.) managed to accord Tylor priority over McLennan in this regard by misdating McLennan's *Primitive Marriage* (actually, by citing the date of its 1876 reprint), a mistake which she did not make when citing *Primitive Marriage* for a different purpose, when the correct first-edition date of 1865 was given (Hodgen 1936: 91). In general, Hodgen would seem to have had it in for McLennan. Thus a list of classical precedents (Thucidydes, etc.) that she cited (Hodgen 1936: 44–5) had actually been lifted without acknowledgement from McLennan (1896: 24). Among contemporary precedents, the one most likely to have impressed Tylor (because it was based on archaeology) was Sven Nilsson's (1834) 'comparative method' (see Daniel 1976a: 48–9).

into a period of higher mental culture, and have become survivals, or, as we call them, 'superstitions'. In producing the occult sciences, the association of thought works in ways most distinctly recognizable. When the Polynesian weather-maker practises on his sacred stone, wets it when he wants to produce rain, and puts it to the fire to dry when he wants dry weather; and when in Europe water is poured on a stone, or a little girl led about and pails of water poured on her that rain may in like manner be poured down from the sky, we have practices resting on the most evident and direct association of thoughts.

Thus we may see a Zulu busy chewing a bit of wood, and thereby performing an ideal operation, softening the heart of another Zulu with whom he is going to trade cows, that he may get a better bargain out of him. So it is when we find lingering in England a practice belonging thoroughly to the savage sorcerer, that of making an image representing an enemy or part of him, and melting it, drying it up, or wounding it, that the like may happen to the person with whom it is associated. From time to time there is still found hidden about some country farm such a thing as a heart stuck full of pins, the record of some secret story of attempted magic vengeance.

In the ancient and still existing art of astrology, we see the same early delusive association of ideas producing results so perfectly intelligible to us, that it is really difficult for educated people to have patience to study its details. An astrologer will tell us how the planet Jupiter is connected with persons of a bold, hearty, jovial temperament; and how the planet Venus has to do with love and marriage; while to us the whole basis of this theory lies in the accident of the names of certain gods having been given to certain stars, which are therefore supposed to have the attributes of these gods. The wonder is not that much of the magician's sham science is inexplicable to us, but that the origin of so many of its details is still evident.

(An extract from Zadkiel's almanac was here read, with the object of showing the principle on which the astrologer's deductions are still made, the movements of the heavenly bodies being simply taken to symbolize human action, virtue and good fortune being connected with the aspects of the Sun and Jupiter (sunny and jovial influences), &c., the working of the early childlike principle of the association of ideas being thus traceable through the occult sciences from their rise among savages to their decay among educated men.) (Tylor 1867: 91–2)

It is ironic that Tylor should have been concerned about misleading associations, since his own discussion is meticulously contrived to produce a web of associations whereby he could situate an astrological text within the preliterate realm of savagery. Though the whole excerpt contributes to this end, the crucial movement occurs in the passage that extends from the Polynesian weather-maker to Zadkiel's almanac (Polynesian weather-maker – European water-rites – Zulu chewing bit of wood – English pin-stuck heart – astrology, including Zadkiel). Between these two points, Tylor effects a fusion of savage ritual and European text. As we shall see, he achieves this effect by shifting the connecting term from materiality to pattern.

As observed, astrology, being textual, could not decay in the same way as other survivals which were behavioural. In terms of Tylor's theory, this amounts to saying that astrology only boasted two of the three phases that he assigned to survivals (as stated in the middle of his first paragraph, survivals originated as savage 'germs' – i.e. in the Lamarckian idiom invoked, maximally simple – which arrived in the present by way of an intervening 'pseudo-scientific' phase). Yet, when it comes to *astrology*'s first phase, apart from the (duly capitalized) Sun, the only germs that Tylor has to offer are two highly elaborated (and, of course, textualized) high gods of Roman antiquity, Jupiter and Venus. What is more, he can offer no contemporary savage counterpart to astrology's detailed specificities. Thus, in addition to lacking one of survivals' three phases, astrology is a purely European phenomenon that misses the ethnographic element ('their' present) from the evolutionary triad.

The mere fact that Tylor was prepared to tolerate such problems demonstrates the rhetorical motive behind his doctrine. His intention was to rid civilized society of survivals by assimilating to them the opprobrium that attached to savagery. Accordingly, despite the stock primitiveness of his preliminary examples (rain-making, effigies, etc.), he reserves his exasperation for astrology, whose details 'it is really difficult for educated people to have patience to study'. The genealogy of those survivals that counted for Tylor was confined to the historical civilization of Europe.

Of the survivals that did not count, many were simply too trivial to be exceptionable. Etymologically, phenomena left 'standing over' from the past already had a name as 'superstitions'. From his specification of the occult sciences as comprising 'witchcraft, divination, astrology and the like', there was hardly a need for him to coin a theory to discredit witchcraft, since this was already the subject of established and active suppression,[150] whilst divination was innocuously rustic. Thus his real targets were astrology 'and the like' ('the like' consisting principally of spiritualism, against which Tylor was directing his other great concept, animism, which he had expounded earlier in the presentation [1867: 87–90]). To sustain his reformist critique of astrology, Tylor attempted to suppress its textual status by placing it at the end of a series of otherwise typically savage examples. If we reverse this process and start with his treatment of astrology, the rhetorical structure of survivals emerges quite clearly.

On moving backwards from astrology to the preceding examples of the 'association of ideas',[151] it is striking that the entities connected together are obvious primary quantities such as water and rain rather than derived doctrinal constructs. The contrast reveals Tylor's problem quite clearly: the occult discourses that formed his target were too complex to be characterized

---

150 Though witchcraft had ceased to be a statutory offence in Britain, and penal sanctions against it had been abolished in 1736, as Hole (1945: 148) notes, this was not enough to entirely 'protect suspected witches from the fury of their neighbours when these, no longer able to seek legal redress, took the law into their own hands. The passage of many years and innumerable prosecutions for assault were needed before the average man could be persuaded that to swim a witch or draw his blood was anything but a time-honoured and quite justifiable remedy for a known and dreaded evil'. Hole (1945: 148–53) and Crow (1968: 243) both cite late nineteenth-century cases of witches being killed in Britain.

151 The term was not, of course, Tylor's. Though an Aristotelian concept, the association of ideas was so named by Locke (Leahey 1980: 43, Lowry 1982: 20–1).

by means of the simple reductionism of germs. Thus the 'pseudo-scientific' median phase of the tripartite career of survivals was pedagogically necessitated by astrology's need to have a germinal origin. A corollary to this is that the other survivals had missed out on the pseudo-scientific phase, lingering on in rural Europe with their primitive rudeness intact. Thus astrology had a pseudo-scientific phase but no germs, whilst the other survivals had germs but no pseudo-scientific phase. What separated them, therefore, was the pseudo-scientific phase – which, as will become increasingly clear, was simply a cover for textuality. If we now follow Tylor forwards through his examples from the rain-making to Zadkiel's almanac,[152] it becomes easy enough to pick out the moves that were critical for connecting up the whole.

A significant feature of rain-making is the fact that water evaporates. It leaves no trace. So far as the balance of pattern and materiality is concerned, therefore, rain-making is all pattern. An arrangement of gestures, it vanishes into thin air. In this sense, rain-making contrasts with the subsequent effigy examples, which, though no less 'savage' (after all, a Zulu is involved), move unequivocally into the realm of the concrete (the bit of wood, the pin-stuck heart). Quite apart from the axis of materiality, though, the savages' modern counterparts are located progressively closer to home. Thus, where the local rain-makers are situated, with noticeable vagueness, 'in Europe', the pin-stuck heart, which corresponds to the Zulu's bit of wood, is to be found in the depths of England herself. The rain-making quasi-Polynesians' location 'in Europe' considerably narrows the gap between savagery and England, making it more susceptible to final bridging by the succeeding (and crucial) analogy, that linking the Zulu's wood-chewing to the pin-stuck heart. That this is *the* crucial move is clear from the positioning of the various examples in the series. The shift from Polynesian to European rain-making is not a leap into textuality. That leap only occurs somewhere between the Zulu's wood-chewing and astrology, which means that it must be effected by means of the pin-stuck heart. To locate Tylor's key move, therefore, we should ignore the diversions of geography and focus in on the pin-stuck heart.

While the Zulu's bit of wood was material evidence, it could not speak for itself. You needed to be there to appreciate the difference between one chewed remnant and another ('thus we may see a Zulu busily chewing . . .'). With the pin-stuck heart, however, this was not the case. Here, if the finder knew of the practice, even after the event its traces could not be in random conjuncture. They were a self-evident *pattern*. The difference between observing and finding (or collecting) summarizes that between ethnography and archaeology. The difference is that, since the observer can see a practice being performed, its remnants (so long as it is a continuing practice) serve as illustration rather than as proof. Accordingly, since a practice was available to be observed 'lingering in England', Tylor should not have needed recourse to its material trace. Indeed, the whole point of his rhetoric would have been lost if the survivals concerned had not been observable anomalies in civilized life.

[152] Polynesian rain-making – European water-ceremonies – Zulu chewing wood – English pin-stuck heart – astrology plus Zadkiel's almanac.

To get around this problem, Tylor made the surviving practice so secret that its occurrence in England, though undoubted, could not actually be observed after all. Pin-sticking was, in fact, witchcraft without a name (and, therefore, subject to established suppression). In other words, Tylor introduced furtiveness into his anthropology in order to generate there the same necessity that was generated in archaeological antiquities by the passage of undocumented time: in both cases, the result was a necessity for *proof*. In the case of this particular survival, therefore, even though it took place in the present, it was still necessary for it to produce a material trace. Thus the essential difference between the pin-stuck heart and the preceding survival is that, since rain-making was not proscribed, it would have been redundant for it to have had to leave a trace.

In addition to this, though, Tylor had a deeper motive for constructing the pin-stuck heart. For, though it was categorically not a text itself, it shared with textuality the quality of combining pattern and materiality, which meant that it could provide a bridge from savagery to Zadkiel's astrological almanac. Lacking an ethnographic counterpart, astrology's genealogy could only be known vertically, through documents that were the preserve of antiquities. Leaving no trace, rain-making could only be known horizontally, through ethnographic observation. Pin-sticking combined – or, more accurately, mediated – the two. Tylor's problem was, therefore, that, having removed pin-sticking from the gaze of the present by making it secret, he had to return it or it could not afford proof of the surviving practice. The only vehicle available to return it to the present was its trace. Thus the trace had to belong in the present. For once, therefore, he did not want prehistoric data. On the contrary, he had the paradoxical task of producing material remains that would testify to a *lack* of history. The resolution of this paradox was an evidenciary limbo of perishable, fleshy material mid-way between evaporating water and the durable data of archaeology. Since flesh is only evidence for a short time, it is simultaneously evidence *of* a short time. Thus the pin-stuck heart belonged in the present.

Ironically enough, Tylor's own association of ideas was less sophisticated than that of his conjectural Zulu. The Zulu's middle term – softening – was both general and processual. It linked two superficially distinct phenomena (bit of wood, heart) on the basis of their common susceptibility to the one process. By contrast, Tylor's own association relied on the superficial coincidence of hearts being the goal of both Zulu and English practitioners. Moreover, where the Zulu's effigy was metaphorical (the bit of wood stood for the heart), the English one was crudely metonymic. Tylor could not make wood his middle term because it lasted too long, whilst the general principle of substitution underlying the use of effigies did not necessarily lead him to flesh, which was the middle term that he needed to soften us up for astrology.

So long as it did not decay too much, the pin-stuck heart betrayed a present concealed within the present. This – regardless of the substitution of secrecy for prehistory – represents the essential, tip-and-iceberg structure of survivals. The essential element, the water obscuring the iceberg, is the presence of an intervening barrier to make the data cryptic, whether that barrier be secrecy, the passage of uncharted time, or post-Oedipal maturation.[153] In ordinary, non-secret survivals, this was provided by the pseudo-scientific median phase, which (ostensibly at least) scrambled the savage germs so that their provenance was not too obviously manifest in the present. Had this provenance been plain for all to see, there would have been no role for anthropology. Thus the median phase, during which the germs became cryptic, provided screening for the science that deciphered them.

As Tylor's almanac-reading demonstrated, however, astrology's provenance was by no means cryptic. Thus astrology was not only lacking a germinal phase – it was not even in decay (indeed, as observed, had survivals really been in decay, there would have been no point in campaigning against them). Tylor tried to avoid this problem by switching between doctrinal and demographic criteria. Thus, though rain-making and pin-sticking were both doctrinally robust, their impact was attenuated by virtue of the fact that their rustic *practitioners* were marginal to civilization. When it came to astrology, however, this tactic was not available, since the whole point of Tylor's rhetoric was that astrology's presence *within* civilization was anomalous. Moreover, as argued above, doctrines cannot both decay and survive. With astrology thus resisting both demographic and doctrinal attenuation, Tylor was reduced to parading injury as advantage:

> The wonder is not that much of the magician's sham science is inexplicable to us, but that the origin of so many of its details is still evident.

For the purpose of evolutionary reconstruction, the problem with doctrine is that (as opposed to McLennan's mock captures) it has intrinsic – or 'unforgotten' – significance, which means that, rather than furnishing a secondary vehicle with which to penetrate prehistory, it casts light on its contemporary adherents. To operate extrinsically, meaning has to become indefinitely compressible (no matter how much Bachofen extended his collection of myths, for instance, it just went on signifying mother-right). In this regard, it is noteworthy that the details of Zadkiel's almanac were immaterial – having paraphrased it minimally, the editor simply bundled it up in brackets.

No such contrivance had been necessary in the case of the pin-stuck heart, whose significance was patently extrinsic. Though neighbours in Tylor's series, the pin-stuck heart and astrology were separated by the chasm of textuality. Though textuality constitutes a specific mode, this does not mean that the opposition between textual and non-textual icons is constant. Rather, as the skilful positioning along Tylor's series demonstrates, some icons are more like texts than others. The pin-stuck heart links the chewed bit of wood to astrology. As observed, however, there is a major difference between the bit of wood and the pin-stuck heart, which is that the bit of wood can only illustrate rather than prove (you need to be there to know it from a bit of wood chewed for a different purpose). To put this another way, the bit of wood is no evidence at all. For that matter, nor is the act of chewing. For the

---

[153] Survivals' individual (i.e. ontogenetic) correlates were to surface in psychoanalysis as parapraxis and the mystic writing-pad (Freud 1901; 1925).

event to have meaning, the chewer needs to explain it. With the pin-stuck heart, however, the assemblage of elements is not random, so its purpose is explicit, even to a fine degree (thus the practice that it denotes is not, say, cooking, sewing, taxidermy or acupuncture).

The important factor is not, therefore, materiality alone, but its combination with pattern. Voices vanish without trace, as do other unfixed patterns such as hand or smoke signals, whilst, alone and unshaped, a fetish is no different from any other stone. Immaterial patterns can only be observational data – you need to be there. Thus the issue is not language, nor even writing *per se* – since, whilst writing entails the possibility of permanence, its survival also depends on the materials that are used.

The shifts between pattern and materiality whereby Tylor linked the bit of wood to astrology are mediated through the pin-stuck heart. On the axis of materiality, the bit of wood, being solid, is comparable to the heart, the two being commonly opposed to the water featured in the previous example. The two differ, however, on the basis of pattern (which, in the case of the bit of wood, is not legible). To get from the pin-stuck heart to astrology, therefore, we have to switch axes from materiality to pattern, whereupon the pin-stuck heart and texts can be seen to share the property of encoding purpose in a manner independent of observation (in both cases, you don't have to be there). Thus the pin-stuck heart constitutes a shifter between behaviour and texts.

Though the pin-stuck heart is like a text in that it expresses a doctrine, it does so because we are already familiar with it – it *reminds* us of the doctrine. The crucial difference between extrinsic signification (pin-stuck heart) and intrinsic signification (language) is that language is the only one that can provide us with new information. Thus we are back to the propositional function of language, as well as beginning to move into the paradigm shift. Extrinsic (or connotative) meanings are congenial to synchronic analysis because they do not introduce anything that has not already happened (i.e. they do not introduce change). Since extrinsic meanings had also been congenial to evolutionism as aids to recovering the past, there were grounds for a ritual emphasis on either side of the paradigm shift. As we have seen, Tylor's motive for abandoning the methodological security of ritualism in favour of the hazardous terrain of texts was polemical. When his concerns were methodological, as the example of the couvade illustrates, even Tylor's needs were fully met by behavioural patterns. Then, being patterned behaviour *par excellence*, ritual constituted an ideal object (indeed, he was to dub it 'the gesture language of theology': 1871: ii, 328).

We can thus confirm the text-exclusive definition, consistent with the concept of screening, that specifies sociocultural evolutionary anthropology immanently, as the project of recovering lost meanings for behavioural patterns. To this it might be objected that anthropology was not the only discipline emerging in the last third of the nineteenth century. In particular, psychology was not merely co-emergent with anthropology (though, in Britain, more hesitantly: Hillner 1984: 65) but was also laying claim to the domain of behaviour (Hearnshaw 1964, Leahey 1992: 172–3, Murray 1988: 161, Young 1973b: 162–3). For most of the century, anthropology and psychology were indistinguishable, as is evident in their shared propensity for skull-measuring. Since both were emerging from a common humanist discourse that embraced individuals and the species alike, the basis for their demarcation is obvious. It concerned scope rather than epistemology – where anthropology became xenographic and collectivist, psychology developed the autographic and individualist applications of the same narrative, whilst sociology developed the autographic and collectivist ones (the fourth possibility – combining xenography and individualism – was to remain beyond institutional imagining). This explains what happened to Tylor's two great concepts, animism and survivals, neither of which survived the paradigm shift. They did not simply vanish. Rather, they only vanished from anthropology, since they became hived off into psychology (specifically, into psychoanalysis). By way of parapraxis, extrinsic meaning came to attach to civilized language too (whereupon it duly became discontented). The underlying template was associationism, the master-narrative of connotation and all forms of lateral signification, whether mediated by culture or by the unconscious. Although I cannot do justice to the topic here, I raise it in order to suggest the discursive scope of the extratextual realm, so that it can be seen to be more than a merely negative determination.

It remains, therefore, to leave Tylor's text – and, accordingly, a text-appropriate analytical mode – and to move on to the 1890s and the paradigm shift in a different, and appropriately historical, manner. To start again from Tylor's text with this in mind, it is apparent that, as an icon embodying ethnographic traces in its own materiality, the pin-stuck heart anticipated anthropological field photography, the ultimate salvage technology. Needless to say, the rise of photography revolutionized the question of evidence across a whole range of disciplines. So far as ethnography is concerned, field photography (which, as we shall see, did not really develop until the end of the century) made all the difference in relation to a particularly delicate evidenciary issue, since, unlike ethnographers, the camera could not tell a lie.[154] For scientific purposes, therefore, the camera rendered survivals' supplementary or corroborative function obsolete – given the material verisimilitude of photography, there was no need to replicate ethnographic findings at home. Thus field photography supplanted survivals' methodological aspect and, with it, evolutionism's spatiotemporal triad (in the process, of course, it also took the rhetorical bite out of anthropology).

Analytically, therefore, it is only to be expected that there should be tension between survivals and photography. Clearly, anthropology did not simply shift from being a Eurocentric discourse that employed the concept of survivals to being a colonial one that replaced survivals with photography. Nonetheless, this formula is not so much inaccurate as incomplete – though the demise of survivals was not simply an outcome of the advance of photography, the two developments were actively related within the complex process that constituted the paradigm shift.

154 Or so it was believed in a pre-UFO era when manipulation was in its infancy. This is not to say that photographs could not mislead or puzzle, as the various claims to have photographed fairies, ghosts, etc. attest.

Unlike other material traces, photographs were made by the ethnographer rather than by the native. Furthermore, unlike drawings or other illustrations that could be made by the ethnographer – but like archaeological or ethnographic trophies – photographs maintained a material community with their object. Thus photography collapsed the distinction between observing and collecting. In this regard, there is a major difference between studio and field photography. Studio photography is collecting rather than observing. In the tradition of Montaigne's cannibals, its savages were imports into the realm of civilization. This lodgement of the savage within civilization was, therefore, different to that theorized by the doctrine of survivals since, unlike its surviving counterpart, the imported savage – studio or otherwise – was not indigenous to civilization. Studio savages resembled survivals, however, in that they were merely decontextualized traces, savages detached from their savagery (hence the giveaway semiology of nineteenth-century attempts to make studio savages look as if they had been photographed in the field). Only field photography combined the xenographic context of observation with the (im)portability of trophies.

Given collodion, or wet-plate, photography, though, there was good reason for bringing natives into the studio. Taking the camera to the native not only meant taking along a portable dark room, together with equipment and chemicals weighing over a hundred pounds, it also meant developing on the spot, whilst the collodion was still moist (Eder 1945: 344–7; 357–60). In the 1880s, however, George Eastman was effecting the series of innovations that were to enable his momentous breakthrough into portability. On 14 September 1888, the name Eastman had thought up for his new handy camera received a trademark, whereupon the first Kodak, a two-spool box camera with nitro-cellulose film which could be sent back for processing, was launched to the tune of Eastman's winning catch-cry: 'You press the button – we do the rest' (Eder 1945: 440; 486–9, Gernsheim 1955: 302).

Field photography validated ethnography. It demonstrated to imperialist eyes that the ethnographer had penetrated. In this sense, observing and collecting amounted to getting there and capturing the image. Both were essential. For ethnography, then, the salient technological revolution took place not only in photography but in transport as well – first the motor car and then the aeroplane. We are into history. In the section that follows, we will consider the principal consequences that turn-of-the-century developments in transport and photography generated for anthropology.

Ethnography, Texts and History

There had never been anything like the profusion of astonishing photographs that crowded the pages of Spencer and Gillen's two great books. Yet these photographs were produced from plates that had been processed on the spot – not because Spencer was any stranger to technological innovation, but because the conditions ruled out keeping unprinted plates for later developing. On the Horn Expedition, these plates and their attendant paraphernalia were carried by camel; on the Northern Tribes expedition, by horse and buggy. In heat that threatened them and sand that stuck to them, they were developed and printed in tents and under blankets draped from trees (Mulvaney 1987: viii). The achievement makes the results anomalous – dry gelatine photography combining the mobility of roll film with the cumbrousness of wet plates.

Fittingly enough (since Gillen had meanwhile died) for Spencer's next major foray into ethnography, which culminated in 1912, he took a Kodak (Mulvaney 1987: ix). As if symbolically marking the paradigm shift, on 2 September 1912, he set off with Administrator Gilruth on a car ride. It may have been only the third car ride in the Northern Territory. It was certainly only the second away from Gillen's overland telegraph track and into the bush – the first having been a trial run on which Gilruth had been accompanied by the woman who would later become Malinowski's wife (Mulvaney and Calaby 1985: 296–7).

Field photography enabled the capture of ethnographic trophies with their contexts still attached. In attempting to fabricate these contexts, studio savagery had anticipated twentieth-century museology's attempts to recreate the settings in which trophies might have been observed 'in real life'. Here again, Spencer's role was transitional. As noted, before leaving England for Australia, he had worked with Tylor on reinstalling the Pitt Rivers Museum, which had hypostasized progress in glass. Whatever their contexts of use or acquisition, items had been displayed as so many points along evolutionary continua. Though Spencer retained this policy when it came to installing his and Gillen's anthropological trophies in the course of his reorganization of the ethnographic collection at the National Museum of Victoria, he also included that collection with Australian flora and fauna rather than with the rest of humanity. Whilst the resulting macro-contextualization was possibly unintentional, it nevertheless echoed a quite deliberate modification of Pitt Rivers'-style linearity where other flora and fauna displays were concerned. For these, he created synchronic eddies in the evolutionary stream through the introduction of cases containing habitat groups (Mulvaney and Calaby 1985: 246–7).

Field photography and ethnographic museology differed crucially, however, when it came to the issue of renewability. Given the durability of relics, archaeologists could reasonably expect to keep on finding them. By contrast, the very revolutions whereby ethnographers got to the field and captured their object in its context simultaneously destroyed that object. The salvage metaphor (Gruber 1970, Clifford 1987) does not do full justice to this irony. We need to develop it to express the lethal quality of the ethnographic gaze. Like Orpheus with Eurydice, it was a look that killed what they, the ethnographers, were rescuing (in their case, from a palaeolithic underworld). I will adopt the analogy, since I know of no other term that combines the four distinctive features of the project. By 'orphism', therefore, I mean (1) an ocular enterprise that (2) brought savagery and civilization into an otherwise anomalous interface that (3) presaged the imminent destruction of the savage party to the encounter, but not before (4) their savagery had been captured and inscribed for posterity. Spencer and Gillen's photography constitutes a type-case of orphism, a swansong endlessly playing at the edge of acculturation.[155] Though, like the pin-stuck heart, the photograph remains as a trace of those who have disappeared, orphism is premised on rupture rather than continuity, so it constitutes the antithesis of survivals. Since what Spencer and Gillen observed was inherently unrepeatable, their photographs constitute(d) proofs of what had been but not illustrations of what continued to be. On both counts, therefore – as xenography rather than as autography and as proof rather than as illustration – Spencer and Gillen's photography represents the negation of survivals.

In the wake of orphism, what persisted was not survivals but ethnographic equivalents of Tylor's 'mere permanence' – an empirical persistence on the part of some of field photography's human substrates which, however decayed, were of no value to anthropology. Indeed, acculturation threatened to compromise anthropology's validating screen of otherness, a consideration that obliged most field photographers to disguise the acculturation of their savages. Readers of Spencer and Gillen, for instance, whose (1899) Arunta photographs far exceeded anything that had gone before, could be forgiven for not realizing that the Arunta had been missionized for well over a decade. Thus it was fortunate for Spencer and Gillen that, when the German Lutheran missionary Carl Strehlow produced a compendious rival ethnography (Strehlow 1907–20), it was not translated into English, since the photographic disparity between his Aranda and their Arunta was truly startling (Figure 2).

These discordant representations reflect the opposing professional interests of the competing ethnographers. Strehlow's primary concern was to uplift and civilize, a project whose undertaking his camera corroborated, whilst Spencer and Gillen's object was uncontaminated savagery. The threat that Strehlow's photography could have posed to Spencer and Gillen's credentials stemmed from the fact that Strehlow was located in the field.[156] This consideration is central to the paradigm shift. Tylor's armchair anthropology had drawn on evidence collected from people who were primarily in the field for other purposes. By contrast, for structural-functionalists such as Malinowski and Radcliffe-Brown, being in the field would become a scientific procedure in its own right.[157]

In starting planned fieldwork among the Arunta in September 1896, Spencer and Gillen, scientist and local man, separately contributed the twin

---

155 For a limiting case, see, e.g. 'Humboldt saw in South America a parrot which was the sole living creature that could speak the language of a lost tribe' (Darwin 1871: 236).

156 Thornton (1981: 14, cf. Cocks 1995: 102) argues that missionaries' ethnographic salience 'cannot be ascribed simply to the fact that missionaries happened to be "there" for other reasons of their own. Both science and salvation, and the practical activities associated with these ideas, "research" and "mission", are generalizing and universalizing.'

157 Precedence in this procedure has been variously attributed to Tylor and Boas, to the Cambridge Torres Strait expedition of 1898, and to others (e.g. Clifford 1988: 24–5, Kuklick 1991: 139, Kuper 1983: 6, Langham 1981: 66, Stocking 1983: 71–5). Von Humboldt, Bastian and Morgan would seem to have been prior candidates. Be that as it may, Boas clearly beat Spencer and Gillen to it. Moreover, unlike Boas, Spencer did not set about prescribing ethnographic techniques and training successors. Nonetheless, being more immured in evolutionism than Boas was, Spencer better embodies the *transitional* nature of the 1890s (here I concur, albeit on different grounds, with Morphy 1996; 1997). Though, in 1894, he had joined the Horn Expedition as a scientist but not as an anthropologist, he had come back planning ethnography (Mulvaney and Calaby 1985:

Die vier Schwarzen, die die meisten Sagen erzählt haben.

Figure 2. From Carl Strehlow's *Die Aranda- und Loritja-Stämme in Zentral-Australien* (1907) and from Spencer and Gillen's *The Native Tribes of Central Australia* (1899)

qualifications that were to be combined in the ideal of participant observation that was to become a distinctive feature of the synchronic paradigm (Morphy 1997: 43).[158] With professional ethnography, all the questions of authenticity of witness come into play. Hence Spencer's stressing of Gillen's long-term familiarity with the Arunta, who, he claimed, regarded Gillen and himself as initiated members of the tribe (Spencer and Gillen 1899: vii; 1904: x). This last qualification establishes an important difference between Strehlow and themselves. For, whilst missionaries could and did become as fluent in native idioms as others in the field, they could not, for obvious reasons, claim to have submitted to pagan rites (a factor that provides a further motive for anthropology's ritual emphasis).

Though claims to ritual status were unavailable to missionaries, there was no reason (in theory, at least) why secular colonizers should not accept initiation if it were offered. Unlike at least some missionaries, however, such people tended not to be people of letters, so their access to native culture did not pose the same threat. With twentieth-century anthropology, in other words, there was a change of boundary rivals. Where Tylor had defended a disciplinary space hemmed about by antiquities, philology, law, history and the like, the competition that a later and more securely established anthropology would have to repudiate was ethnographic, with rival claims to have got there, observed and recorded (cf. Clifford 1988: 13–15). The new threat did not come primarily from missionaries, who had been there all along, but, appropriately enough, from the same innovations in transport and photography that had revolutionized ethnography itself. The twentieth-century threat to anthropology was that increasing numbers of people could get to the field and take photographs. Thus an established anthropology still needed a screen, only one to keep out journalists, colonial administrators and tourists rather than antiquarians and philologists.

The new rivals encompassed a much wider social range than had the old. Accordingly, though new screens were constructed somewhat differently by Malinowski and by Radcliffe-Brown, they shared the characteristic of excluding a much wider range of discourse. To generalize well-known information roughly, Malinowski's participant method eschewed the hit-and-run ethnographic questionnaire, requiring self-immersion in the field for much longer than would have been practicable for journalists or tourists and at a much more intimate level than would have been appropriate for officials (cf. Kuklick 1991: 189–90), whilst Radcliffe-Brown's theoretical reportage made for findings that were indigestible as popular fare. With structural-functionalism, therefore, anthropology became technical (Figure 3). Thus it was not to inspire the cult of drawing-room bibliophiles who had wondered at *Primitive Culture* or *The Golden Bough*.

167–9). Three years before the Torres Strait expedition, he was in correspondence with Gillen in preparation for a return to the field for specifically ethnographic purposes, quite distinct from other scientific trips that he continued to make, even to the same region (Mulvaney and Calaby 1985: 171). In addition to working with Gillen, he was consulting both Tylor and Frazer in relation to the project's theoretical objectives (Marett and Penniman 1932: 9–10).

158 '[W]hen the book of Messrs. Spencer and Gillen is before the world, I think it will be admitted that in them we have the ideal men for the work. The long and intimate familiarity of the one with the natives, and the trained scientific powers of the other, make up a combination of talent which in anthropological research, so far as my knowledge goes, has never been surpassed' (Frazer 1898: 281).

THE SOCIAL ORGANIZATION OF AUSTRALIAN TRIBES

It will be readily seen that this system of four sections involves a division of the society into two matrilineal moieties and also a cross division into two patrilineal moieties. Thus in the diagram the sections A and D (Banaka and Palyeri) constitute one patrilineal moiety, and B and C (Burung and Karimera) the other. While A and C constitute one matrilineal moiety and B and D the other. In many of the tribes of eastern Australia there are names for the matrilineal moieties in addition to the names for the sections. It is important to remember that the moieties exist in every section system whether they are named or not.

A still more complex system is that in which the tribe has eight subdivisions. These will be called *subsections*, since they can be shown to be subdivisions of the sections of the four-section system. The following diagram shows the rules of marriage and descent in the system of eight subsections:

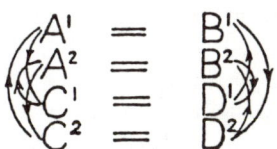

$$\begin{pmatrix} A^1 & = & B^1 \\ A^2 & = & B^2 \\ C^1 & = & D^1 \\ C^2 & = & D^2 \end{pmatrix}$$

The sign = connects two intermarrying subsections. I shall speak of two such together as an *intermarrying pair* or simply a *pair*. The lines at the side connect the sub-section of a woman with that of her child, the arrow indicating the direction in which the line is to be followed. Thus, reading the diagram we have

A^1 marries b^1 and the children are D^2 and d^2
A^2 ,, b^2 ,, ,, ,, D^1 ,, d^1
B^1 ,, a^1 ,, ,, ,, C^1 ,, c^1
B^2 ,, a^2 ,, ,, ,, C^2 ,, c^2
C^1 ,, d^1 ,, ,, ,, B^1 ,, b^1
C^2 ,, d^2 ,, ,, ,, B^2 ,, b^2
D^1 ,, c^1 ,, ,, ,, A^2 ,, a^2
D^2 ,, c^2 ,, ,, ,, A^1 ,, a^1

I shall speak of the subsection of a father and the subsection of his child as together forming a *couple* of subsections. Thus the couples are $A^1 D^2$, $A^2 D^1$, $B^1 C^1$, $B^2 C^2$. If a man belongs to one subsection his child belongs to the other subsection of the same couple.

Figure 3. From Radcliffe-Browne's 'The Social Organization of Australian Tribes'

Given the inherent tension between conviviality and scholarship, twentieth-century anthropology's fusion of science and participation was bound to be problematic. After the paradigm shift, ethnography became so technical that merely being an old-style gentlemanly amateur, as missionaries often were, was not sufficient qualification. Before the paradigm shift, on the other hand, merely being on the spot had not enabled anyone to hold a candle to Tylor or Frazer, who, from their armchairs, had surveyed and reconciled all spots at once. Thus missionary ethnographers threatened neither a (relatively) non-technical but universal evolutionism nor a locally particular but technical structural-functionalism.

Spencer and Gillen's reprieve from the threat posed by Strehlow's camera did not affect the principle of professional ethnography's vulnerability to photography. Indeed, to the claim that nothing like their photographs had been seen before, we can add the rider that, in structural-functionalism at least, nor would anything quite like them be seen again.[159] Even the photographs of Malinowski, the high priest of ethnographic presence, do not match up, and certainly not those of Radcliffe-Brown.[160] Within the local tradition, Warner, Kaberry, Pink, McConnell, the Piddingtons, Stanner, the Berndts, and their successors never produced anything to compare, whilst the bulk of Donald Thomson's magnificent Arnhem Land photographs were not published until half a century after he took them (Peterson 1983). Elkin's various publications are instructive in this regard, since, while his popular general manual, *The Australian Aborigines: How To Understand Them*, which appeared first in 1938 and in new editions regularly thereafter, is relatively well endowed with photographs, his more specialist publications, in the journal *Oceania* and elsewhere, are not.[161]

Structural-functionalism's eschewal of photographs in favour of technical discussion (which photographs served at best to illustrate but not to prove) reflects the disciplinary undesirability of authentic data that all manner of people can collect. Thus photography shares with survivals the characteristic that, so far as observation is concerned, neither is esoteric. Just as anyone could take a photograph, so were survivals visible features of civilized society. Accordingly, quite apart from the fact that an explicitly historical concept was incompatible with a synchronic framework, there was no place for survivals in structural-functionalism for the reason that they derived from general, non-specialist observation. Structural-functionalism was, therefore, a symptom of the shrinking world of the twentieth century. The technological innovations that revolutionized ethnography also compromised its distance from home (this was a practical concomitant to the colonial incorporation of hitherto external worlds). Internal colonization compounded the need for ethnography, which lacked the screen of prehistoric time, to close off its mode of observation to outsiders. In this

---

159 Thus I should register a minor reservation in regard to Stocking's (1995: 95) observation that, one third of the way into Spencer and Gillen (1899), when the text begins to be 'thickened' with photographs, 'one feels that one has stepped into the ethnographic world of the next century'.

160 It is, however, notable that the proto-functionalist Radcliffe-Browne of *The Andaman Islanders* (1922) was much more given to photographs (though they significantly cluster in two chapters devoted to 'superorganic' phenomena, 'The Social Organisation' and 'Ceremonial Customs').

161 This is not to ignore the economic considerations militating against the inclusion of photographs in journals.

regard, admission to secrets represents the ultimate accolade for extended, Malinowski-style participant observation.

Photography is the supreme secret-breaker. Under the regime of a recently adopted sensitivity, Spencer's Museum of Victoria now (in the 1990s) subjects ageing anthropological photographs of certain Indigenous ceremonies to the same restrictions as those which apply to secret-sacred objects that were made by Indigenous people themselves. Curatorial staff, Indigenous and settler alike, affirm the common categorization of these two different modes of materializing the sacred – as, apparently, do the cultural owners of the trophies concerned. So far as ethnographic credentials are concerned, however, for all the damage that photographs can do to Indigenous people's sensitivities, their anthropological value is not as proofs of certain mysterious occurrences. Rather, they prove the admission to the secret event of the person holding the camera. The ultimate penetration of the savage world is, of course, to become a savage oneself (hence the corroborative value of Spencer and Gillen's claim to initiation). In this regard, nescience is ancillary to a most graphic enactment of the charged relationship between photography, secrets and ethnographic authority.

Carl Strehlow's son, Theodor, could not have had stronger ethnographic credentials. He was not just adopted into a tribe. He was actually born an Aranda since, according to the relevant calculations, the time of his birth signified that his mother, Frieda Strehlow, had been entered by a *ratappa* in Aranda country. Thus Strehlow the younger's ethnographic debt to nescience was even greater than that of Spencer and Gillen. Despite the legitimacy of his provenance, however, Theodor (Ted) Strehlow was to grow up to abuse his position. His photography was very different from his father's. In August 1978, he sold secret-sacred Aranda photographs, that only he could have taken, to the German magazine *Stern*, who syndicated them to the weekly pictorial *People*, who published them in Australia. At this point, my innocence of ethnography breaks down.

In September 1978, Indigenous activist Ambrose Golden Brown, who was visiting Melbourne to address a land-rights campaign meeting that I attended, informed those present that, for his treachery, Ted Strehlow had been 'sung' (i.e. metaphysical retribution had been launched against him). On 3 October 1978, Strehlow collapsed and died, five hours before he was due to attend the official opening of his anthropological memorial to his own family, the Strehlow Research Foundation, that the sale of the photographs had been intended to finance.[162]

Twenty years on, I still do not know what to make of these events. Like Tylor, I find my method at odds with my politics. On the one hand, my lapsed-Catholic rationalism is averse to the idea that there could be more to it than coincidence. On the other, there is justice in the possibility that, in spite of everything, there could still be some areas in which an Indigenous writ might run. My ambivalence is of more than merely individual significance, however. In so far as it exemplifies a dilemma between the quantifiable and the interpretable, it goes to the heart of the ethnographic project. This is

---

162 For details of the T.G.H. Strehlow story, see McNally's somewhat journalistic (1981) account. Cf. Berndt 1979.

because that which is irreducibly ethnographic about this story is precisely that which resists being photographed or otherwise materially registered. Even if the pin-stuck heart had really worked, neither photography nor the naked eye could have caught the invisible force connecting it to its living counterpart. Spencer and Gillen actually took shots of the procedure of singing (the particular method adopted being pointing the bone – one of the targets was even a heart). The pictures that they secured[163] are remarkable for the absence of the metaphysical ballistics that framed the depicted events. These photographs are not self-evident. We have to be told what is going on.

The conspicuous absences in photographs of metaphysical practices demonstrate that photography could never usurp the scope of ethnography. From an external perspective, the event itself is liable to be prosaic, even banal – we see only the outward sign, not the inner significance. There will always be abstract or secret significances, invisible to eye or to camera (and therefore to journalist or to tourist) that only time, intimacy or theory can penetrate. The fact that such professional credentials are primarily abstract and secret is a further, powerful motive for anthropology's ritual emphasis. In this regard, the more abstract and the more secret a phenomenon the better. In Victorian public discourse, hardly any topic was more restricted than sexual connection.[164] Thus Spencer and Gillen's ethnogenetic revelations demonstrated their entry into a most sensitive area, one that neither camera nor other material technology could reach. In this respect, too, they anticipated what was to come, since, in common with their claim to have been initiated, these revelations exemplified an ideal of ethnographic penetration that was much closer to participant observation than to the contextual insouciance of evolutionism.

No one would have needed to buy photographs of survivals, since their whole point was that they could be observed, in all their anomaly, in civilized society. Though closer to journalism than to professional anthropology, therefore, Strehlow's photographs represent a polar inversion of the doctrine of survivals. Despite his own interiority to Aranda society, they depended for their effect on his also sharing his audience's exteriority to it. They constitute pure xenography in that they could not run more contrary to the autographic reference that was essential to survivals. Journalism or no, therefore, the photographs encapsulate another of the essential features of the paradigm shift, which is that it was a movement from unilinearity to difference.

The shift away from survivals – and, as I contend, the paradigm shift as a whole – is encapsulated in Spencer and Gillen's ethnographic realization of Hartland's prophecy. When first published in 1894, Hartland's speculation was based on mythic echoes from the prehistory of civilized Europe. These echoes even had contemporary exemplars, in the form of tales about storks and the like. At that moment, therefore, an appropriately heterodox instance

---

163 I trust that the relevant content of these photographs can be well enough imagined for the point to be made without reproducing them.

164 Alternatively – following Foucault's (1979) debunking of the repressive hypothesis – it might be held that the operative principle was not the restriction of discourse but the incitement to it. Ironically perhaps, it makes no difference, since the *frisson* that incites garrulousness about sex could not operate without some measure of a transgressiveness in which restriction is presupposed.

of ethnogenetics could have completed the evolutionary triad in a way that Tylor's astrology could not do, since, unlike the classical Romans' belief in their gods, the state of consciousness that Hartland had divined in his myths was prior to the invention of writing.

Tylor should have thought of that. For the purpose of survival, the sublime virtue of something that does not even exist is that it is *impervious to decay*. Read negatively, as a missing idea, nescience was simultaneously both doctrinal and non-textual. Moreover, as a mere absence, it had no internal content, so its significance was purely extrinsic. In discovering ignorance, therefore, Spencer and Gillen could finally have furnished a doctrinal correlate to the meaningless behavioural palimpsests that had enabled McLennan and Morgan to plumb the past. It would have been the ultimate survival. As it was, however, when Spencer and Gillen made Hartland into a prophet, nescience did not figure as a glimpse into European prehistory, but as an ethnographic coup that testified above all to the unparalleled abasement of the Arunta. What implications did this have?

As a survival, nescience (like the totem-sacrament) would have narrowed the gap between the Arunta and civilization. But Spencer and Gillen chose xenography. Accordingly, though the material that they and Hartland publicized shared phenomenal characteristics, the technique that it served to validate was different. Neither Hartland nor Spencer and Gillen had any particular interest in genetic theory *per se*. For Hartland, it provided a means for mythography to go deeper in time than history or philology could go. Conversely, at the very point where Spencer and Gillen could have completed this project, they chose instead to extend the outer edges of ethnographic difference.

The proposition that the demise of survivals coincided with the rise of an anthropology predicated on difference is not only historically consistent with the way in which synchronic relativism was to insulate and relativize the societies that it would construct. It is also dialectically consistent with the rhetorical linkage between survivals and the psychic unity of mankind. On the basis of this linkage, it would be consistent for the demise of survivals to have signalled psychic disunity. Here, then, nescience becomes foreordained in a further sense, as a dialectical antithesis to the monogenetic doctrine of survivals (perhaps, therefore, Tylor had thought of it after all).

In the event, both texts and folklore were categorically excluded from a rigorously xenographic (which is to say colonial) anthropology. Survivals went down with evolutionism, whilst, for Morgan's and McLennan's theories, there was life after the paradigm shift in the form of anthropology's continuing preoccupation with kinship and ritual. There again, back in the 1860s, when anthropology had been screening off a disciplinary space of its own, Morgan and McLennan had obeyed the rules.

— * —

With the paradigm-survival of ritual and kinship discourse, we have reached the theoretical conditions for *homo superorganicus*. As the next chapter will show, this anthropological construct was to have major ideological consequences in twentieth-century Australia. In this later period, we find that the relationship between anthropological theory and Aboriginal policy differs markedly from the fairly straightforward ways in which evolutionism legitimated the territorial dispossession that frontier expansion entailed. Yet, just as the establishment of the modern nation-state required those prior acts of dispossession, so did synchronic relativism depend on the demise of the evolutionist paradigm. It did not simply spring up *de novo* in its wake. For instance, as we saw in Chapter 3, social fatherhood emerged out of the contradictions that brought down the doctrine of mother-right. In its positive aspect, however, social fatherhood was to ground Radcliffe-Brown's theory of Aboriginal social organization, a theory which, as will emerge, was to be directly incorporated into Australian land-rights legislation. As we shall also see, in twentieth-century Australia, the theoretical isolation of Aboriginal society, its thoroughgoing detachment from European civilization, was to be important for anthropology and state ideology alike. The same can be said for the ahistoricity or timelessness that was axiomatic to a synchronic paradigm. Having traced the theoretical conditions under which these features of synchronic relativism developed out of evolutionism's terminal crisis, we are now in a position to return to the political conditions under which this independently generated body of anthropological theory came to be appropriated into Australian settler-colonial politics. As the preceding three chapters have now demonstrated, there was nothing necessary or foreordained about anthropology's conformity to Australian political requirements. Rather, the development of anthropological theory was to a large extent autonomous. Moreover, not only did anthropology undergo a paradigm shift, but Australian policies on Aborigines were successively reconfigured. In the following and final chapter, we shall try to conceptualize the changing relations whereby affinities were maintained between a developing anthropology and an independently developing series of settler-colonial strategies.

CHAPTER 6

Repressive Authenticity

The aim of this final chapter is to trace discursive relationships between the anthropological tradition that we have been examining and changing regimes that Australian society has sought to impose on Indigenous people. In the process, we will evaluate the claim that recent reforms in which anthropological discourse has been crucially involved – in particular, the Australian High Court's Mabo judgement and the Labor government's 1993 *Native Title Act* – effected a historical rupture that was sufficient to reconstitute the relationship between Indigenous and settler societies. For such a claim to be evaluated, it is necessary to analyse the deep structures of the Australian colonial project. To this end, a broad overview was outlined in Chapter One. Having proceeded this much further with the argument, we can now restate and develop that overview.

The determination 'settler-colonial state' is Australian society's primary structural characteristic rather than merely a statement about its origins. The primary object of settler-colonization is the land itself rather than the surplus value to be derived from mixing native labour with it.[165] Though, in practice, Indigenous labour was indispensible to Europeans, settler-colonization is at base a winner-take-all project whose dominant feature is not exploitation but replacement. The logic of this project, a sustained institutional tendency to eliminate the Indigenous population, informs a range of historical practices that might otherwise appear distinct – invasion is a structure not an event.

If the historical surface is complex, it might seem doctrinaire to insist on the primacy of an underlying polarity. The motivation is, however, empirical. Retrospectively, polarity is indisputable – back from a certain point, there can be no question as to the mutual separateness of the two principal parties to the Australian colonial process. The differences within them were smaller than the differences between them. Thus the empirical question is whether or not (and, if so, when and where) that initial polarity came to be dissolved. There is no justification for simply assuming that it did. To this it could be argued that, in from the beach that momentarily separated the watching Gamaraigal from the First Fleet, there never was a clear line between white and black – rather, colonial settlement involved a range of mediations, from agencies such as the diseases and trade goods that preceded the escaped convicts, explorers and other colonial advance guards through to the extreme of incorporation attained when neither physical nor cultural differences are mutually acknowledged. Whilst this no doubt represents an influential

---

[165] The different colonial formation obtaining in the Torres Strait will be discussed below.

perception of the situation, to assume that the opposing identities[166] became merged in keeping with it is to underwrite assimilationism, a phenomenon that we should be analysing rather than practising. In other words, one's position on binarism cannot be innocent. Accepting this, my analysis is consciously oppositional in that, rather than asking why polarity should be asserted in the face of surface complexity, it asks what grounds there are for crediting the rhetoric of assimilationism with historical fulfilment. In finding none, it finds that the recent reforms were not enough, a conclusion which indicates that, whether or not these reforms survive the current conservative campaign against them, the 'Aboriginal problem' will continue into the future.

The question of polarity is closely tied to that of gender. Indigenous men, Indigenous women and Indigenous children have been invaded in different ways – not only on the basis of gender but in terms of their positioning in relation to the settler economy (within or without the domestic sphere, etc.), whilst white men and white women have invaded in different ways. Such factors can produce practical contradictions. I will argue that the single most important contradiction to have obstructed the logic of elimination was quintessentially gendered. This was the sexual abuse that male colonizers have visited on Indigenous women everywhere. The systematic nature of this abuse has prompted some to set up a competition between territoriality and sexuality so as to champion the priority of their own preferred determinant, as in Ann McGrath's partisan (1990: 206) claim that 'The women would be first, the land next'. Quite apart from its dubious empirical basis (it was certainly not the case, for instance, when the First Fleet established their beachhead), such assertions miss the foundational genderedness of settler-colonialism as a world-historical project, on which basis it is only to be expected that its contradictions should also operate in gendered ways.[167] As a direct articulation to land, which it claims to render productive, settler-colonialism is gendered in a peculiarly thoroughgoing way. Hence the ubiquitous rhetoric of interiors waiting to be opened up, a process in which the expansion of the frontier figures as a fertilizing penetration.[168] In Judaeo-Christian culture, the theme could hardly run deeper – Eve, after all, means both woman and land. So far as Australia is concerned, there has been no shortage of gendered expressions of settler-colonialism, as Marcus (1988), McGrath (1990), Schaffer (1988) and others have shown. In this broadest of

---

166 As will become increasingly clear, I use the term 'identity' to signify a subject-position that Australian state discourse seeks to repress rather than a subjective (which need not mean individual) self-representation. For a concise statement of the problems involved in scholars' uncritical acceptance of notions of 'identity', an acceptance that risks 'celebrating in a scientistic jargon that too frequently legitimizes what it names', see Handler 1994.

167 Gender is not, of course, restricted to women. Rather, as Joan Scott so influentially stated (1988: 28–52), it is a way of encoding power relations (a major precedent for this style of analysis was Ortner 1974). Accordingly – and as we shall see below – we should not conceptualize gender as being restricted to a realm of signification that can be separated from that of power. Rather, gender takes place as power.

168 Following up some hints in Said's *Orientalism* (1978, e.g. p. 6), a number of scholars have analysed the inherent genderedness of the colonial project. This has been most apparent when colonialism has functioned as a discourse on land, which, in settler colonies in particular, has figured as waiting to be penetrated, opened up, made fertile and so on ('Guiana...', as Raleigh remarked, 'hath yet her maydenhead' [Montrose 1991: 12]). As gender provides a model and precedent for the dominated, so, by the same logic, does it construct the dominator as male – or, in Hall's more complete (1992) formulation, as white, male and middle class.

senses, the gender of individual Indigenous people and individual colonists becomes irrelevant – Europe is male, the conquered land is female, and ever the twain shall meet. For historical purposes, however, such metaphors do not get us very far. They are too general and too archetypal to evince any contingent development. We need to go beyond the metaphors to discern the social processes that give them life and form in particular contexts. As will become clear, at a particular stage in its development the colonial contest in Australia became concentrated on the colour-coding of bodies that testified to sexual relations between male colonizers and Indigenous women. In this most material of contexts, it would be perverse to separate territoriality from gender, since we do not encounter one without the other.

To analyse the historical development of Australian settler-colonialism, we will start with its primary paradigm, the frontier, a classic binarism that counterposes two pure types (civilization vs. savagery, etc.) and admits a multitude of variants. The reality accompanying the idea of the frontier is that of invasion. Invasion is not as tidy a process as the representation would suggest. In practice, rather than fixed (as in the visual metaphor of the dividing line), the Australian 'frontier' was shifting, contextual, negotiated, moved in and out of and suspended (McGrath 1987). As Jan Critchett (1990: 23) pithily observed, are we to think of the frontier as running down the centre of the bed shared by a white man and a black woman? – to which we might add, are we to think of the frontier as running through people's veins? In short, it is necessary to distinguish between the misleading or illusory nature of the concept of the frontier as a representation and the social effects that were sustained by the currency of that representation. Though it is not possible to fix the precise extent of the process at any point from the landing of the First Fleet onwards, the idea of the frontier expresses the fact that, between the last quarter of the eighteenth century and the first quarter of the twentieth, 'Australia' was almost completely invaded. Moreover, as will be explained, the idea itself consolidated this process. Thus the point is not simply that the idea of the frontier was misleading. What matters is that it was a performative representation – it helped the invasion to occur.

The product of the Other is, of course, self. In a settler-colonial context, this means that the frontier binds together a divided colonial fragment in common opposition to the natives on the other side. This is easy enough to see when an advance party, with its back to the sea, is only just beginning to fan out, but ideologies of encirclement naturally fall victim to their own success as the invasion becomes consolidated and settlement securely established. Thus we need to distinguish different discourses on Aborigines and relate them to corresponding stages in the colonizing process. We also need to keep sight of the constants. This will not only give us a consistent framework for Australian settler-colonial history from the landing of the First Fleet to the present. A demonstration of the persistence of the logic of elimination will also bring out what periodized studies miss: that the foundations of the Australian state continue to inhere in its articulation to Indigenous societies.

Another Side of the Frontier

Whatever their motivations, periodized studies run the risk of confirming the ideological rupture whereby the 'post'-colonial state distances itself from its foundations. The line that the frontier represents is doubly misleading, since it not only constructs a hermetic division in space but also inserts a partition into Australian historical consciousness, rendering expropriation a past event rather than an ongoing practice.[169] Moreover, when frontier historiography doubles as an advertisement for its presenter's moral credentials, as it too often has done, this has the ideological effect of co-constructing writer and reader as fellow citizens of a consensual culture ('enlightened Australian opinion') which thereby revalorizes itself. Being beyond social determination, this transcendent moral community is blind to its own involvement in the subtly developing histories of expropriatory discourse. The moral detachment thus afforded compounds the historical detachment that flows from frontier periodization.

Admittedly, Henry Reynolds' frontier studies (amongst others) provided a corrective to the impression of hapless Aboriginal victimage that could be gained from accounts such as those of Rowley or Biskup.[170] Nonetheless, the martial emphasis brought problems of its own, quite apart from those just mentioned. Given such strategic acumen, for instance, it is sometimes hard to see how Aboriginal resistance could ever have been contained. Moreover (and particularly in the case of Robinson and York), the romantic evocations of Viet Cong-style heroics were too rhetorically opportune to be credible. In the wake of the 1970s, widespread dissatisfaction with the behaviourist simplicity of the frontier-resistance model set in, with scholars such as Barwick, Reece, McGrath, Fels, Attwood and Reynolds himself emphasizing more complex and mobile Aboriginal practices involving adaptation, accommodation and synthesis.[171]

Whilst many of these analyses had the virtue of stressing the continuation of Indigenous life beyond the frontier, the implication that resistance and accommodation are separate alternatives is quite wrong (Genovese 1974: 78, Goodall 1996, Morris 1988: 53). Indeed, to the extent that this implication renders Indigenous people part of Australian society by analytical fiat, it is insidiously assimilationist. Since our focus is on the continuity of settler colonialism, Indigenous discourse is peripheral to this analysis. Thus I am deliberately repeating a familiar historiographical structure, one that C.D. Rowley and others effectively discredited in the 1970s. Unlike the marginalization or suppression of Indigenous discourse in traditional Australian historiography, however, its avoidance here is open and acknowledged. It reflects the continuing historical contest of settler-colonization, a contest to which the separation of Indigenous and settler identities is central.

---

169 An example of the hazards of periodization is Attwood's (1989) decision to begin his mission study after Victoria's 'killing times', as if recent decimation could have failed to be the most decisive of continuing cultural determinants.

170 Although Rowley's work should not be contrasted too neatly with that of Reynolds in this regard. See Rowley 1970: 5–6; 112–14.

171 See, e.g., Barwick 1972, Reece 1984, McGrath 1987, Fels 1988, Goodall 1996, Attwood 1989, Reynolds 1981; 1991. Cf. Robinson and York 1977.

A one-sided analysis of Australian strategies for dealing with Aborigines might seem to run the risk of negating Indigenous agency, representing domination as unidirectional and, accordingly, as total (cf. Foucault 1980: 88–9). If (heaven forbid) I were analysing the nature or practice of Aboriginality, this would clearly be the case – my analysis would be guilty of constructing Indigenous people, as Beckett (1988: 192) put it, 'in their absence'. But I am not analysing such things. Rather, in the logic of elimination, I am analysing what might be called the settler-colonial will, a historical force that ultimately derives from the primal drive to expansion that is generally glossed as capitalism. Though capitalism has energetically constructed and thrived on a host of alterities, it is not ultimately dependent on them. In the final analysis, its greedy dynamic is internal and self-generating. In the same sense, settler-colonial expansion was prior to and exceeded the myriad uses to which it has put Aborigines and Aboriginalities. This is not to say that Australian history would have developed in the same way if there really had been no prior owners. It is rather to isolate a constitutive characteristic of settler-colonialism that preceded the process of mutual formation that has been in train since the invasion commenced. Thus the logic of elimination is not some extra-historical teleology, unfolding independently of human practice. It is, however, a force that cannot be reduced to Australian motives – no matter how profoundly the parties to the Australian colonial relationship have impacted on each other, this alone is not enough to account for the logic of elimination.

In so far as it exists independently of Australian historical factors, the logic of elimination constitutes a settler-colonial residue. Doubtless, there are also Indigenous residues, traits that lie beyond the interpellations and appropriations of settler-colonial discourse. To say this is not, of course, to deny European agency. If anything, it is to emphasize it, since it is in relation to European agency that Indigenous residues emerge as such striking cultural achievements. Indigenous residues exist in spite of, rather than as a result of, colonization. In analysing the elementary structures of the settler-colonial mentality as it enters into dealings with Indigenous people, therefore, I am not only engaging in a kind of white Australian auto-ethnography. I am also refusing the assimilationist denial that Indigenous discourse(s) can exceed the one-sided 'dialogue' between Indigenous people and colonizers. If the idea of the frontier has anything left to express, it is that contact presupposes independence.

For all its resonances of the binary ideology of the frontier, there are good reasons for insisting on a binary approach to settler colonialism. In particular, such an approach undoes a strategic pluralism whereby the logic of elimination has been implemented in recent Australian government policy. As will be argued, successive Australian governments have sought to blur the polarity of the relation of invasion by means of an intermeshing of binary and plural (or exclusive and inclusive) representations. In relation to this state strategy, the binarism of frontier ideology has its merits after all. Conversely, it could be said that latter-day official pluralism makes visible the divisions that the concept of the frontier ideologically suppressed. The key to such apparent paradoxes is the relative status of the divisions concerned. Thus the 'truth' of the frontier was that the primary social division was encompassed in the relation between natives and invaders. This notwithstanding, the suppression of divisions within settler society was an ideological effect of the concept of the frontier. Correspondingly, though the 'truth' of present-day multiculturalism is a racially divided society, the reduction of the primary Indigenous/settler divide to the status of one among many ethnic divisions within settler society is an ideological effect of multiculturalism.[172] The consequences of this play between exclusion and inclusion will become clearer as the discussion proceeds.[173] For the moment, the point is that, postcolonialism notwithstanding, a consequence of settler-colonialism is that thinking against its grain can mean recuperating an empirical binarism.

Frontier, History and MiscegeNation

As sketched in Chapter 1, Australian settler-colonial strategies can be categorized into three principal modes. To begin to develop these modes, I shall term them confrontation, carceration[174] and assimilation. Of these, the first and the last represent opposite ends of a historical transformation during which Aborigines' relationship to European society shifted from one of exteriority to one of interiority. This fundamental shift is culturally acknowledged in the idea of the frontier. The demise of the frontier means the incorporation of all Aboriginal tribes and groupings. This demise – or, which is the same thing, the completion of the invasion – is also a prerequisite to the establishment of the nation-state, with its stable territorial basis. For state-ideological purposes, therefore, we can date the demise of the frontier from the foundation of the Commonwealth of Australia in 1901. This is not to say that there were no unincorporated Indigenous groups left anywhere – some survived into the 1950s. It is not even to say that frontier massacring came to an end – this practice continued into the 1920s. Rather than an empirical claim in relation to an inherently indeterminate condition, to equate the end of the frontier with the beginning of the nation-state is to make a statement about official ideology. From 1901, despite the remaining blanks and smudges on the map, Australia's political and geographic constitutions

---

172 Thus the Indigenous/settler relation does not conform to the 'cultural division of labour' that characterizes Hechter's influential (1978) definition of internal colonialism. Rather, cultural pluralism is itself celebrated by an assimilationist discourse that seeks to lose Indigenous specificity in amongst the ethnic heterogeneity of immigrant populations.

173 I am grateful to Jeremy Beckett, who, in commenting on an earlier version of this chapter, pointed out that, in stressing the discourse of exclusion, I had dealt inadequately with its contradictory relationship with the coexistent one of inclusion.

174 This second phase might itself be subdivided into two modes, segregation and reservation, which are distinguishable on the basis of the presence or absence of formal compulsion. Segregation, which is characterized by the lure (blankets, rations, social security payments, etc.) maintains an aura of voluntarism that is lacking in explicitly coercive measures providing for Indigenous people's confinement to reserves. Whilst it may seem that there is little practically distinguishing this formal coercion from the indirect or de facto coercion of the lure, its significance becomes clear when it is compared to assimilationism, which initially consisted in a partial inversion whereby, rather than simply being confined to reserves, Indigenous people could also be excluded from them.

were officially treated as homogeneous.[175] Thus it is no coincidence that the few years around the founding of the nation state should witness a rash of assimilationist legislation.

For the purpose of establishing cultural continuities, the crucial shift is that from carceration to assimilation. As previously observed, carceration was directly continuous with the homicidal activities of the confrontation stage — though associated with markedly different rhetorics, both had the effect of vacating Indigenous territory in a manner consistent with the logic of elimination. To establish a link between carceration and assimilation is, therefore, to establish a continuity between the confrontation stage and assimilation. Moving on from there to the other end (as it were) of assimilationism, we enter into the present, into and beyond the era of self-determination and land rights that was inaugurated in the 1970s. To complete the cultural continuum, therefore — which is to say, to preserve the strategic consistency linking present-day practice to the initial invasion — it will also be necessary to show the conformity between assimilationism and current Australian policies.[176] To proceed from the first two fairly straightforward modes to analyse the cultural logic of assimilationism, we shall start again from the concept of the frontier.

The principal ideological effect of the frontier was that it rendered spatial coexistence anomalous. As a linear metaphor that expressed the invasion's zero-sum polarity, the frontier divided 'us' and 'them' into discrete and homogeneous domains whose relative proportions were constantly shifting in favour of 'us'. This does not, of course, mean that there were no Indigenous people left 'this side' of the frontier. It simply means that their presence was anomalous. In fact, though massacres in the conventional sense — the indiscriminate killing of numerous people on single occasions — were

---

175 In so far as *terra nullius* – or, nowadays, the radical title vested in the Crown – is concerned, it could be argued that this homogeneity obtained from 1770 or, at least, from 1788. This may be so. None the less, 1901 clearly constitutes a watershed in the normalization of that principle.

176 So far as its initial phases are concerned, the typology presented here is comparable to a number of earlier ones. For instance, Peter Read (1988: 1) specified four methods that whites have adopted for 'subduing the Aborigines' – extermination, concentration, separation and indoctrination – whose initial three terms would seem to be reducible to my first two (of which the second is anyway subdivided). I differ from Read, however, in that I see indoctrination as an element in assimilationism and, more importantly, in that I see assimilationism as continuing into the present. Accordingly, though acknowledging the shift – from an official policy of assimilation to one of welfare colonialism – that Beckett dates (more plausibly than Read's 1968) from the 1972 election of the Whitlam government, I cannot accept that this shift is of the same order as Beckett's earlier three phases (act of dispossession, protective segregation, assimilation) with which mine otherwise broadly concur (cf. Beckett 1989). The case of David Drakakis-Smith's (1984) model is rather different. Whilst, in common with others, he starts with the original expropriation, Drakakis-Smith stresses the territorial nature of this process so as to contrast it with a subsequent phase in which the primary focus is on the exploitation of Aboriginal labour (a possibility that remains, as he might have noted, dependent on their loss of land). Thus he fails to accommodate the carceral nature of most Indigenous people's post-confrontation histories (a consequence, no doubt, of his fieldwork being conducted in central Australia). As a result, he fails to recognize the generality of his third – and, for him, only recent – phase (Aborigines as consumers of white-provided services) which comprises an 'institutionalization of Aborigines within a dependency framework, following the appropriation of their land and labour power' (1984: 100). Such problems notwithstanding, Drakakis-Smith's analysis bears out one aspect of the continuum that I am proposing here – its reluctance to make the north-Australian cattle industry a special case – since it emphasizes northern and western Australia's conformity with the general model once the distorting influence of local labour-market factors (ecology, lack of convicts, etc.) was removed as a result of wage-parity legislation.

standard practice, they were not daily events. None the less, they were continuous with the routine process of casual homicide whereby Indigenous people were killed on sight in the vicinity of sheep or cattle runs, so the definition of massacre needs to be extended to include a serial or cumulative dimension.[177] Chronologically too, therefore, the clear division effected by the frontier is misleading. All the same, even allowing historical leeway for the consolidation of the initial invasion, a number of Indigenous people managed to survive within the margins of settlement. In many cases, their resourcefulness was abetted by tensions or contradictions within colonial society. For instance, the near-realization of genocide in Van Diemen's Land (later Tasmania) was one of two signal scandals of the day (the other being the slaughter of the so-called 'Cape Kaffirs') which strengthened the hand of a liberal-philanthropic faction in the British House of Commons who had been buoyed by the success of their campaign to put an end to slavery in the British Empire. Prompted by the Exeter Hall group, the Secretary of State for the Colonies in 1838 issued instructions for protectorates to be established in the Port Phillip District (later Victoria) and in Queensland (Moreton Bay). Under a variety of names and institutional guises, Indigenous people were then 'protected' (or, as the wags put it, colonists were protected from them) by means of a series of institutionalized inducements that were provided on stations and reserves set aside for the purpose (Christie 1979: 81–106).

Once land is set aside for them, however temporary an expedient for managing a dying race it is seen to be, Indigenous people have begun to move into settler society. This development did not disturb a representational tradition of noble savagery that had flourished since the early days of the invasion. Nobility was, however, a function of distance. Thus romantic depictions of savage life coexisted with an opposing, vicious-savage idiom that had both wild and domesticated modes. In its wild version, predictably enough, a treacherous, anonymous and warlike savagery was counterposed to the steadfastness of resisting pioneers (Figure 4). The domestic counterpart to this threat was a kind of Hogarthian grotesque which, though still vicious, substituted absurdity for menace and bottles for spears, as in the ragged spidery degenerates that Fernyhough and Rodius depicted leering, importuning, fighting and collapsing in Sydney streets (Figure 5). In this domestic mode, however, the field of difference is narrower. Where, after all, did the bottles come from?

In addition to agreeing as to native viciousness, both the steadfast-pioneer and the degenerate-spider idiom signify colonization. An opposing, romantic genre, which can (but does not have to) omit all signs of Europeans, is an iconography produced by people who do not live in proximity to its Elysian savages' empirical counterparts (nobility, again, is a function of distance).

177 A local example was publicized by the Melbourne *Age* newspaper, quoting from a collection of letters between officials of the Port Phillip District Protectorate which the Victorian Government auctioned in 1991. On 20 July 1839, Assistant Protector Edward Parker wrote to Protector George Augustus Robinson: 'in the month of July last, the Aborigines carried off a flock of sheep belonging to a Mr. Bowman. They were pursued by an armed party and (it is alleged) on their showing signs of resistance were attacked and slaughtered in great numbers. One of the persons engaged on this occasion informed me that upwards of 90 rounds of ball cartridge were expended. I am also informed by Mr. Yaldwyn, a magistrate of the colony, that after this occurrence, Mr. Bowman was accustomed to shoot every black man, woman or child whom he found on his run' (*Age*, 15 April 1991: 6).

PALMER GOLD FIELDS, QUEENSLAND.—DIGGERS PREPARING FOR DEFENCE.

Figure 4. Artist Unknown, *The Dangers of the Palmer – A Native Attack*. From *The Illustrated Sydney News*, 22 July 1876

Figure 5. W.H. Fernyhough, *Natives of New South Wales Drinking 'Bull'*, and Charles Rodius, *Scene in the Streets of Sydney*

The significance of the vicious genre's routine incorporation of some sign of the invasion is that, in the absence of so much as a partly-glimpsed chimney stack or an overturned billy can, savages are outside history – without a target, they cannot be marauding. It may, therefore, seem contradictory that settler colonialism should produce pictures of Edenic savages who were monarchs of all they surveyed (Figure 6).[178] The romantic genre is, however, an urban creation which, in the course of the twentieth century, has sustained an official Aboriginality that has been an important element in the Australian state's construction of itself. The romantic genre is important to national ideology because the parallel coexistence that it depicts is consistent with the legitimating illusion that Australia was not founded on homicide and theft. Correspondingly, the vicious genre furnished a justification for these foundations, which were ideologically insulated within the liminal space of the frontier.[179] In the nineteenth century, the two genres were spatially correlated, the vicious covering areas already claimed for white settlement whilst the romantic represented an appropriately distant region behind the frontier which, though imaginary, had some empirical reference. This should not, of course, disguise the frontier's ideological function as a limit of otherness that contained the colonizing society through its subsuming of internal divisions. This function was not dependent on geography. Indeed, it not only survived the frontier's loss of empirical reference but kept intact the parallel coexistence of the romantic genre.

The most important feature of this imaginary coexistence is that space is not shared – as observed, the Aborigines are always somewhere else. Thus the frontier's loss of empirical reference simply made it entirely, rather than partly, mythic. The significance of this is that both of our anthropological paradigms rendered it anomalous that historical Indigenous people should exist in the same space as white people, which is to say that the two modes differentially underwrote the logic of elimination. This point requires elaboration.

Evolutionism's spatial implication, the premise that another country was the past, did not mean that different societies would never meet up. Rather, it meant that, when they did meet up, the consequence for the lower party to the encounter would be that the developmental history separating the two would be flattened out. Thus the impact on the lower party would be proportionate to the scale of the developmental gap. According to this

---

[178] The disagreement over the captioning of Fig. 6 nicely illustrates the point, since, though championed by art-historical specialists (Bruce et al. 1982: 184) the alternative name for the painting – 'Aborigines Met on the Road to the Diggings' – has simply failed to catch on. Whilst these natives conform closely to a well-established subject-position that the romantic genre has routinely reproduced, this subject-position could hardly be less compatible with the blunt instrumentalism sustaining the discourse of gold-digging.

[179] Creole status – being born in the settler colony – is a significant element in the ideological insulation of the original seizure of territory. The frontier functions as a liminal zone that stands apart from the orderly flow of colonial succession. As diasporan exiles, the first invaders are neither of the mother country nor of the colony. The legitimate genealogy that the emergent nation-state continues passes through the succeeding generation of settlers or through those who emigrated to post-frontier regions (explorers, by contrast, are pre-frontier). As Howitt's father put it, Australia 'is a strange land, to the next generation it will be the native land' (Howitt 1855: ii, 425). Anxiety in regard to the effectiveness of this insulation still permeates Australian country music, which endlessly speaks (or sings) as native son, one who was born with the land in his blood. In keeping with the thoroughgoing genderedness of the settler-colonial project, this vascular condition does not, so far as I am aware, affect women.

Figure 6. Eugène von Guerard, *Natives Chasing Game* (1854)

rationale, Aborigines confronted their far-distant future in the whites, a strain whose superiority exemplified the cumulative operation of selection in a whole range of ways, from cranial enlargement to the institution of private property.[180] Hence the ensuing doom of the Aborigines was a result inscribed in the natural order of things and bound to accrue once others had reached a level of progress that enabled the crossing of barriers that were at once both geographic and phylogenetic.

Thus evolutionism performed one of the basic functions of ideology, that of naturalizing. Though, in common with many other facts of nature, the spectacle of extinction was undoubtedly cruel, it did not figure as the consequence of any volitional human activity. Rather, it was a foregone conclusion whose implementation, being in higher hands, left no more to be done than the alleviation of its symptoms. The certainty that Aborigines were a doomed race sustained the philanthropic project of 'smoothing the dying pillow' (Harris 1990: 549–53), which was, therefore, a way of stating that spatial coexistence was anomalous in a language that was common to evolutionary anthropology and to settler-colonial policy alike. The concrete institutional expressions of this anomalousness were the missions and reservations on which Indigenous people were sequestered. Less direct than the elimination methods of the confrontation phase, they were, nonetheless, antechambers of extinction, so their operations did not conflict with the logic of elimination. Thus the significance of expelling certain Indigenous people on the basis of their having some European descent is that, for official purposes, this meant that such people ceased to be Aborigines. Needless to state, this remained an official fiction, since, on the practical day-to-day level, Indigenous people and colonists knew full well who each other were.[181] As in the case of the frontier, however, descriptive inadequacy is not the point. In constructing an Aboriginal category defined on the basis of racial purity, the policy initiated by the 1886 Victorian Act split Indigenous people into two groups, of which only one was treated as Aboriginal. At a stroke, in other words, a substantial proportion of the Aboriginal population was officially eliminated. In so far as the assimilation policy sought to minimize the number of people who might be accounted Aboriginal, it was no less eliminatory – albeit less crude – than the more directly physical methods of the first phase. This is not to suggest that assimilation was less than physical, some mere sleight of bureaucratic tabulation. On the contrary, children were snatched from schoolyards, torn from their mothers' arms and ambushed at play, often never to be seen again. The point is rather that assimilation was premised on a classificatory

---

180 So pervasive was the ideology underlying *terra nullius*, however, that the universality of natural selection could become subordinate to it, even in the writings of Darwin himself. Consider, for instance, the following, which seems as remarkable from the scientific as from the political point of view: 'When we see in many parts of the world enormous areas of the most fertile land peopled by a few wandering savages, but which are capable of supporting numerous happy homes, it might be argued that the struggle for existence had not been sufficiently severe to force man upwards to his highest standard' (Darwin 1871: 180). That this was not an uncharacteristic slip of the pen is apparent from the revised version of the *Descent*, where Darwin carefully reordered the wording of this particular sentence whilst leaving the sense intact (Darwin 1896: 142).

181 As Peter Read (1984: 49) observed in relation to the New South Wales town of Yass, in 1919: 'Managers were instructed to discourage "half-castes" from entering reserves; yet the townsfolk of Yass could not allow these same people, who by association and culture were commonly regarded as Aborigines, from [sic] entering the town.'

scheme, a definition of authentic Aboriginality, that would have been altogether superfluous in the first phase.

A number of related points might be made here. First, so far as Australian ideology is concerned, the assimilation policy was not held out as a strategy for eliminating the Aboriginal population. On the contrary, it was almost invariably couched in a rhetoric of improvement that recapitulated the missionary project of uplifting and civilizing. Whether reserve rejects of the 1880s or stolen children of the 1960s, they were to be privileged with the same opportunities as whites.[182] Second, the idea of introducing a hard and fast division between Indigenous people, or even between officially constructed Aborigines and whites, was not only unworkable. It was not even meant to work. The rhetoric of improvement notwithstanding, the practical logic inspiring the construction of a racially homogeneous Aboriginality was that it provided for an ever-dwindling category.

This last consideration explains how child abduction, the centrepiece of the developed assimilation policy, constituted an extension of the 1886 Victorian Act. Simply excluding certain Indigenous people left the excluded in a kind of official limbo somewhere between the authenticated Aborigines remaining on the reserves and the white population. The problem with such legislation is, therefore, that, as noted above, it fails to work in practice, since it does not change the identities that govern the daily transactions of local life. The outcome is a liminality – a category that is officially not black and descriptively not white – which came to be spatially symbolized in the image of the 'fringe-camp'. It is, obviously, impossible to conceal from fringe-dwelling adults their kinship with the rest of their family who are (ideally at any rate) back on the reserve. With abducted children, however, the situation is different. Moreover, so long as reserves remain practically porous, so the thinking went, they will continue to provide abductable children, whilst racially homogeneous children will not, by definition, be born in the fringe-camps. 'Ultimately', as Professor Cleland put it to the 1937 Conference on Aboriginal Welfare, 'if history is repeated, the full bloods will become half castes' (Commonwealth of Australia 1937: 21). Given the refinement of child abduction, therefore, within the space of two or three generations, assimilation completes the project of elimination. Since, put this way, the pattern seems so obvious, the question arises of the mechanisms that enabled such a logic to coexist with official expressions of enlightened concern. Thus the question is one of ideology, or, more precisely, of the extent of ideology's effects. For, without wishing to engage in a naïve humanism, the Australian experience provokes inescapable questions as to the extremities that rationalization can encompass. Even leaving aside the intimate procedures involved in massacring, the disease component of the confrontation phase meant that pioneering colonists moved about a landscape that was alive with

182 As Elkin put it, in the introduction that he contributed to Neville's (1947) apologia for assimilationism: 'While we hold the mixed-bloods at arm's length, few of them will rise in the social and economic scale; they will be hangers-on and parasites. The circle is a vicious one. Let us break it. This means enforcing [sic] *through the same channels as in the case of our own white folk*, decent housing, cleanliness, regular school attendance in our schools (as at Alice Springs, for example), orderly behaviour and voting. At the same time, it means opening to them the door of opportunity through higher education, through training for professions (teaching, nursing, and others), through membership of trade unions (wherever this is barred), and in recreation and Church-life' (Elkin 1947: 15, original emphasis).

a suffering that so harrowed every sense that their descriptions of it are replete with cameos that are as shocking as the death of Damien, only generalized. Much closer to the present, how are we historically to situate ideologies that enabled officials with a post-World War Two awareness of the implications of racial hygiene to drive away cars full of terrified 'mixed-race' children? – officials who, in some cases, still (in 1998) work in Aboriginal affairs?

With regard to ideology, the significance of evolutionary anthropology is that it gave an impartial scientific warrant to (which is to say, it naturalized) the binary opposition between pure types that the idea of the frontier represented. What is more, the paradigm shift in anthropology encompassed the same shift from externality to internality as that encompassed in the colonizing typology that has been set out here. Thus we come closer to appreciating the ways in which, in the Australian context, the two cardinal modes of anthropology differentially underwrote the logic of elimination.

I specify 'cardinal' because it is clearly not the case that anthropologists unanimously participated in shaping government policy. Throughout the history of Aboriginal anthropology in Australia, there have been major factions and schisms – one has only to think of Howitt versus R.H. Mathews; Spencer versus Carl Strehlow; Donald Thomson versus Radcliffe-Brown; Elkin versus Thomson (or even, more mutely, versus the half-life of Radcliffe-Brown); Tindale and his South Australian Museum colleagues versus almost everyone,[183] and so on. Again, therefore, what is significant in the present discussion is not anthropology as some of its practitioners might have wanted it to be (or tried to make it). To view the question thus would be to coin a sociological version of the intentional fallacy, an error whose denunciation tends to reconcile anthropologists. Anthropology is, rather, significant as a *discourse appropriated into state practice*. In this regard, professional schisms, far from weakening the political efficacy of a co-opted anthropology, grant it further legitimacy as the outcome of open debate. For social and historical purposes, we are concerned with effective outcomes. In the discussion to come, we will shift from the nineteenth century and evolutionism to twentieth-century political developments in which Australian anthropology has played a decisive role, in particular to land-rights legislation. In this regard, the first land-rights legislation to be passed by the Australian government was substantially influenced by an understanding of Aboriginal land tenure that had been derived from Radcliffe-Brown and was held with significant unanimity by Stanner and R. Berndt, a view whose previous failure to impress Justice Blackburn, in the Gove land rights case of 1971, had resulted (*inter alia*) from its inconsistency with the Yirrkala plaintiffs' own account. As we shall soon see, it is easy enough to cite a number of anthropologists who disagreed with Stanner and Berndt. Indeed, if one were writing a history of Australian anthropology for its own sake, one would no doubt concentrate on doing so. But I am not writing such a history. I am writing a history of discursive appropriation, a history which, as I have been trying to demonstrate, involves the reconstruction of affinities that have been

[183] Howitt 1908, Wise 1985: 98–9; 131–2; 143, Elkin 1956; 1975, Jones 1987.

mobilized in the realm of cultural logic. In this connection, whatever the intrinsic merits or lack of them of the dissenting theories, their salient feature is the fact that, unlike Stanner's and Berndt's views, they were not incorporated into official discourse. This simple observation has a crucial consequence for the politics of anthropological practice. This is that reforming anthropology does not address the problem of its own political misappropriation. The problem lies elsewhere (hence the reformed anthropology simply fails to get appropriated). This point is regularly demonstrated at land-rights and native-title hearings, when radical anthropologists suddenly start to sound like Stanner and Berndt. I am not suggesting that it is wrong for them to couch their evidence in the idiom that is appropriate to the discursive context concerned; merely that the idiom's selection is not an internal anthropological matter. It follows that a responsible anthropology should expand its scope so as to take in the total social process in which it participates. Rather than silencing anthropology, this project will give it more to say.

On this basis, in the Australian context, the significance of anthropology is that it has provided – though not exclusively – narratives that have been selected in furtherance of the logic of elimination. Thus, as the mother-right chapter showed, evolutionist categories precisely replicated those of *terra nullius*, installing a bourgeois discourse on territory at the basis of its definition of human society in such a way that nomadism figured as presocial and lacking any basis whereby property rights might accrue. This much, perhaps, is only to be expected. The point is, however, that the underwriting survived the paradigm shift. This is not to say that synchronic relativism retained the narrative details whereby evolutionism had reinscribed *terra nullius*. On the contrary, mother-right was abandoned. None the less, in constructing a superorganic Aboriginality that excluded historical and economic factors, post-paradigm shift anthropology denied Indigenous people's historical productivity in a way which, though transformed, still promulgated the transparent Aboriginality of the *terra nullius* doctrine.

In the wake of invasion, pacification and the consolidation of pastoral settlement, Indigenous people who survived the abolition of their traditional modes of production could be put to work to serve the requirements of the introduced economy. Yet other aspects of Indigenous people's precolonial lives did not necessarily conflict with their participation in that economy. Accordingly, these aspects did not need to be effaced or reconstituted to the same extent (in this regard, missionaries often exceeded the basic requirements of settler colonialism). Thus the colonizing society remade indigenous life in its own likeness, imposing on Aboriginal societies a severance between economic and other social spheres that was characteristic of European capitalism. Following this severance (or disembedding) of economic life, ritual and kinship patterns of the conquered culture became residual, since they did not function to reproduce the dominant sphere. Thus blackfella business became what was left over – wet-season business, by definition (or, rather, by elimination) marginal and non-pragmatic. Appropriated into settler-colonial discourse, this innocuous remainder provides *homo superorganicus* with its empirical alibi, a truncated life-world whose continued coexistence need not pose any threat.

In relation to settler colonialism, therefore, synchronic relativism had the ideologically valuable consequence of constructing Aboriginal and European societies as occupants of discontinuous spheres, with the Aboriginal one hovering in an apparently self-sufficient ritual space that did not conflict with the practical exigencies of settlement. After the geographical and theoretical paradigm shifts of the early twentieth century, though spatial coexistence remained anomalous, the undeveloped savagery that evolutionism had located over the frontier persisted within as the authentic ritual Aboriginality of synchronic relativism. Whilst, from the synoptic perspective of the analyst, this means that the authentic Aboriginality must exist nowhere, this is not the native's point of view. Rather, for local Australian subjects, Aboriginality is severally constructed as somewhere else.

In the cities of the south-east, where the majority of the Australian population lives, authentic Aboriginality is located, somewhat vaguely, to the north and west. You can visit it, and – if local Indigenous people are prepared to co-operate – even find it. Here again, this much is only to be expected. To cite another ethnographic observation of my own, however, the phenomenon obtains in bush and outback Australia too. Although in racist outback pubs it is initially surprising to hear the virtues of 'bush blacks' or 'the real blackfella' being extolled, the classification rapidly makes sense. Without the ever-absent good black, there would be no basis for condemning the ever-present bad black. Indeed, the Aboriginalization of Kakadu, though virulently opposed by Australian racists at the time, has since come to invest the mythical good black with a concrete locale.

Repressive Authenticity

From the beginning, authentic Aboriginality has been an official way of talking about the repression of Indigenous people. With half an eye to Herbert Marcuse (1965), therefore, I shall term this strategy 'repressive authenticity'. Repressive authenticity cannot be understood by studying the symbols that it promulgates. Rather, the reverse is the case, since attracting attention to its symbols is the whole point of the strategy, whose real effects are thereby excused attention. To understand repressive authenticity, we have to attend to the consequences for those whom it renders *in*authentic – historical Indigenous people who do not embody the construction.

To cut a rather obvious progression short, this leads us back to binary oppositions – authentic Aboriginality is everything that 'we' are not and vice versa. Thus inauthenticity results from straddling this dichotomy, a situation that can be expressed genetically or culturally or both. European society was unified in contradistinction to the Aborigines and vice versa; the two categories mutually constructed each other. Thus hybridity was repulsive because, in threatening the black category, it thereby threatened the white one as well. This received its most public expression where 'miscegenation' was concerned, to the extent that 'mongrel' remains one of the most potent insults in the settler repertoire. Though readily obfuscated by race, the essential feature of European society was not, however, its colour but the fact that it was the expropriating party. Thus ambiguity as to whether people were whites or Aborigines should be understood as an ambiguity as to whether or not they were being expropriated, with corresponding implications for the legitimation of settler-colonial society.

Ideologically, therefore, representations based on race or colour obscure the primary historical relationship of invasion. Given a dichotomy of white and black, Chinese, Indians and others can be anomalous. But Chinese and Indian children were not officially abducted on racial grounds, so their anomalousness was of a secondary order, one peripheral to the primary terms of the underlying invader/invaded opposition. Where Asians were neither white nor black but neither, 'half-castes' were neither white nor black *nor* neither.

Repressive authenticity presents a complex set of histories as an eternal dichotomy. Shared features are anathema. Since the feature most crucially shared by Indigenous people and colonizers is an economic interest in the same land, it is only to be expected that the symbols of Aboriginality that figure most prominently in repressive authenticity are precisely those that least conflict with settler-colonial economics. In underwriting the mythical Aboriginality of repressive authenticity, therefore, *homo superorganicus* did not merely endorse a misleading idea. Rather, it sustained the most material of constructions, whereby a population was to be genetically eliminated. The genetic counterpart of the ritually constituted stereotype was, of course, the 'full-blood'. Moreover, the genetic and cultural codes recapitulated each other. For instance, it had long been asserted (e.g. Howitt 1904: 50) that 'half-castes' were not admitted to Aboriginal ritual or marital categories. Indeed, as noted in Chapter 1, complicity in the logic of elimination was even alleged of Aborigines themselves, who, it was claimed, killed off 'half-caste' babies at birth (Beckett 1988: 198, n.10). Thus the genetic coding of assimilationist rhetoric disguised the multidimensional construction of inauthenticity. In the twentieth century, many very dark children were abducted, on social rather than racial pretexts (usually some version of parental neglect, even though, in some cases, 'being an aboriginal' was considered sufficient for the purposes of the relevant certificate [Read 1983a: 6]). Correspondingly, where a child was lighter, no amount of ritual eminence could have made it Aboriginal. In short, genetics was an all-purpose metaphor.

Genetics had also been the pretext on which the 1886 Act had provided for the break-up of the troublesome Victorian reserves. At this point, it is necessary to keep in mind that to view the legislation as breaking up communities is to view it from an Indigenous perspective. From the perspective of the legislators of the colony of Victoria, the only way out was in. To repeat, there was no Aboriginal category within colonial society, merely a non-social anomaly that was quarantined off to die away on missions and reserves. If this anomaly were not to die, there would be no social category for it to occupy. In other words, the non-social could either disappear by natural means or be made social. To leave a reserve was to join society. This is why the 1886 Victorian Act was the first official expression of the national policy of assimilation.

The 1886 Act marks the onset of an official panic which, over the following half-century, engulfed the continent as the realization set in that the dying of the dying race was not merely slowing down but reversing. In fact, more than just reversing – given Australian society's inability to moderate the sexual bombardment that white men were visiting on Indigenous women everywhere, the so-called 'half-caste menace' was threatening to explode uncontrollably. As noted, the sexual component of the confrontation stage was antithetical to the other three. From the outset, the chronic negator of the logic of elimination had been the white man's libido. The consequence was a disruption of the course of genocide. The missions and reserves were central to this disruption, giving anomaly the security of a physical shelter. For analytical purposes, the key moment in this whole process is the switch from 'dying aborigine' to 'half-caste menace'. This switch expressed a transformation in which missions and reserves changed from being sanitary disposal outlets to being sources of contagion, a crisis whose remedy was assimilation.

But notice the profundity of the categorical rearrangement that assimilation conceded. For all its ostensible belligerence, official talk of a 'half-caste menace' merely made two anomalies where there had previously been only one. Where, before, there had been a duality which counterposed a mythic Aboriginality over the frontier to the colonial subject on this side and produced the short-term anomaly of the dying Aborigine, the 'half-caste menace' brought duality this side of the frontier. For the duality in which the 'half-caste menace' was anomalous was not one between whites and mythic figures over the frontier, but, rather, one between whites and *'full-bloods' on the reserves*. In other words, a contradictory effect of the sexual dimension of the invasion was the eruption of an officially conceded Aboriginality this side of the frontier. As will emerge, this concession provided the demographic ground for the inclusive discourse of Aboriginality which, in the wake of the achievement of nationhood, the Australian state would contradictorily combine with the logic of elimination.[184]

The narrative structure of repressive authenticity is the excluded middle. The more polarized the binary representation, the wider its intervening catchment of empirical inauthenticity. This is why, to appreciate the operation of repressive authenticity, it is necessary to reverse its values, to see it as the positive production of genetic or cultural *in*authenticity, a condition that it is appropriate to eliminate. In its genetic application,

---

184 Cf. 'Unlike the Indian, . . . [the 'half-blood'] . . . could not be treated evasively because, whereas the full-blood Indian could be restricted to America's prehistory or history, could be safely confined to the past, the mixed-blood Indian belonged very much to the present and quite possibly to the future of America. The Indian, therefore, might be (in the white American mind) doomed to extinction, but the half-blood represented a new force, perhaps even a new race on the frontier. Since the frontier was, for nineteenth-century white Americans, inextricably (if ambiguously) related to the future of the nation, the half-blood, as a unique manifestation of the frontier, seemed a very immediate reality which could not be ignored' (Scheick 1979: 2).

Figure 7. Two-Dollar Coin

repressive authenticity mobilized the figure of the 'full-blood' to construct an official polarity that licensed child-abduction. In its latter-day culturalist application, repressive authenticity converts invadedness into a welfare issue. Accordingly, though the official rhetoric of land rights (or, for that matter, of the two-dollar coin) is ostensibly benign, the rarefied traditional Aboriginality that it dispenses perpetuates the logic of elimination (Figure 7). This continuity reveals the fullness of identity politics, which are in no sense merely aesthetic or superstructural. On the contrary, the sum of settler-colonial history is simultaneously present at each assertion, enactment or refusal of an Indigenous identity.

The battleground of repressive authenticity is that of Indigenous 'post'-colonial identities, which strive to historicize the mythical duality that the discourse propounds. The further from the pole of mythic authenticity that an Indigenous identity can be asserted or reclaimed, the greater the ideological danger that it presents. An Aboriginality that can be identified but not seen represents the ultimate threat to legitimation. At the price of conceding a limited Aboriginality, assimilationism created a non-category, a new *terra* (or, rather, *corpus*) *nullius* that could legitimately be claimed for settler society. This is the descending opposition that we encountered in Chapter 1, whereby 'part-Aboriginal' means 'non-Aboriginal'. Taking the children away was not represented as cutting them out of families and communities but as bringing them into them. As observed, the only way out was in – a single movement whereby children out of the reserve had no social existence until it had been completed. In other words, the car rides were rites of passage – insulated journeys from out of non-existence into social existence as orphans, more like circumcision than excision.

Though on different sides of the paradigm shift, the dying Aborigine and the car rides were alike facilitated by anthropology's ideological appropriation. This is so even though the mode of subjection that was constructed differed markedly between evolutionism and synchronic relativism. Whilst the evolutionist paradigm constructed a rationale for domination that accounted for the deaths of refractory savages, synchronic relativism recruited living subjects for colonial society by disqualifying them from a mythical parallel realm.[185] Though one excluded and the other included, therefore, they had the identical effect of eliminating the non-social.[186]

---

185 Despite the dominance of essentialist attitudes, Australian Aboriginal anthropology has boasted a few figures who have taken the cultural dynamics of 'post-traditional' Indigenous communities seriously. As early as 1935, for example, Caroline Kelly (1935) reported that 'half-castes' in Queensland were integrated into the ritual and kinship systems. Marie Reay's pioneering contributions are probably more significant in this regard, however (see Reay 1945; 1951, Reay and Sitlington 1948). In the wake of Reay, the two contributions which, with hindsight, instigated the major shift away from essentialism and towards more dynamic culturalist analyses were the work that flowed from Jeremy Beckett's MA thesis (Beckett 1958) and from Diane Barwick's PhD thesis (Barwick 1962). This kind of work should be distinguished from anthropological reports on 'mixed-race communities' which sought to elucidate policy problems for assimilationism rather than to attain ethnographic insights into intra-community cultural processes (cf., in this regard, Bell 1956, Calley 1956; 1957, Fink 1957, Le Gay Brereton 1962).

186 Accordingly, to return to the point that was made in Chapter 2 in relation to structural-functionalism's role in the colonization of Africa (cf. Barnett 1956), the fact that anthropology was not seen to have a comparable role in Australian Aboriginal administration does not mean that it was not instrumental in the settler-colonial project. Thus those (e.g., Gumbert 1984: 60, Peterson 1990: 12–13, cf. Radcliffe-Brown 1930, Firth 1931) who have concluded that structural-functionalism could not make a contribution in Australia that might compare to the service that it could offer in franchise colonies such as New Guinea have not taken a sufficiently

Thus we are beginning to move back to the coexistent discourses of exclusion and inclusion. Having reconciled genetic and cultural strategies, we can begin to discern the deep genealogy of the benevolent turn in some recent Australian government policies on Aborigines. We can also begin to bring nescience back into the account. For, though inauthenticity could be constituted culturally or genetically or both, it is not the case that the cultural and genetic narratives were procedurally as well as structurally symmetrical. As opposed to genetic heredity – an individual attribute whose temporal units of change cannot be reduced to less than one generation – cultural authenticity constitutes a generalized condition that can be vitiated very rapidly. In this respect, it is hard to imagine a more fragile condition than nescience. Indeed, on a scale of suddenness, Spencer's observation that it was one of the first things to be modified after contact provides a cultural analogue to the sudden death that characterized the confrontation phase.[187] Thus nescience was not just a high point of orphism. It also established a rather comprehensive two-way loss whereby, if Aborigines were not nescient (with all the moral, cognitive and selective implications this entailed), then they were inauthentic. Either way, their expropriation was warranted. Thus it is important not to be misled by the biological cast of assimilationist rhetoric. For all the talk of 'half-castes', 'full-bloods' and the like, Aboriginality was an ideological rather than a biological threat.

Given a cultural criterion for Aboriginality, the dying Aborigine could be already dead.[188] Though seemingly self-evident, this observation is basic to an understanding of assimilationist ideology. This is because it detaches Aboriginality from the body. No matter how much, say, Tamils or Maldivians might look like Aborigines, they could not pose the same genetic threat. That threat was, rather, posed by something invisible – a fetishized particularity residing behind the bodily surface. As observed, the essential difference between Europeans and Indigenous people stemmed from the relation of invasion, a fact that the various discourses on race and colour sought to disguise. Beneath assimilationism's biological phrasing lay a mystical fear of invadedness – and, reciprocally, the status of invader – being transmitted in the genes. To explain this, it is first of all necessary to distinguish the cultural and biological criteria that assimilationist rhetoric sought to confuse.

To start, appropriately, from the primary social reality of invasion, colour or non-European race are extraneous factors. This does not mean that white Australia was not racist – it simply means that racism that was not predicated on the invasion (which is to say, racism that was not directed against

anthropological view of the situation. The same might be said of Maddock's (1980: 55) statement that 'Needs claims are discussed in the Woodward Commission's reports, but I shall ignore them, for they have not been provided for in the Land Rights Act and they would not have involved the interplay of anthropology and law in which we are interested'. The point – which will be elaborated below – is that the exclusion of a pragmatic needs criterion has everything to do with the interplay of anthropology and law.

187 In this regard, the cultural ramifications of nescience in Australia were quite different from those attaching to analogous surface narratives that were reported in different colonial settings such as the dependent setting of Malinowski's (1916) Trobriand *Baloma*.

188 And, therefore, impervious to a turn-around such as the increase in 'full-blood' numbers after World War Two (Beckett 1989: 125).

Indigenous people) was secondary.[189] In other words, Aboriginality is a matter of history; Indigenous people can be defined as that group which settler-colonial society has attempted to eliminate *in situ* (other groups have alternative social bases[190]). In a non-circular sense, therefore, Aborigines can be designated in terms of the logic of elimination. Thus the primary object of white Australian hostility should not be defined in terms of race or colour but in terms of prior entitlement, of being there from the beginning (*ab origine*). In this context, the significance of a genetically constructed notion of race is that – unlike, say, consciousness or memory – it is *mathematically divisible*. Parents are halves, grandparents are quarters, and so on. This simple fact was institutionalized in assimilationism's oddly precise racial quantifications – the fine calibrations of 'quadroon', 'octoroon' and the like. The precision is odd because it had no bureaucratic substance. People were not deemed to be 'octoroon' because state records showed that they had one Aboriginal great-grandparent. Rather, they were so deemed because that was the snap judgement of some official on the spot (Rowley 1970: 354). Why, then, the elaborate charade of mathematical finesse? This question takes us to the core issue of Indigenous identity, and of the Australian state's attempts to eliminate it.

Despite appearances, genetic arithmetic was not a measure of static racial proportions. Rather, it was a colour-coded lap count along the course of elimination. This course lasted three generations (Figure 8), respectively termed 'half-caste', 'quadroon' and 'octoroon'. Crucially, there was no fourth-generational, one-sixteenth category. Beyond octoroon, therefore, one had been bred white, a condition officially vouchsafed by scientifically-couched assurances that Aboriginal genes were not liable to produce atavistic throwbacks in subsequent generations.[191] With each succeeding generation, then, this spectrum of bodily signs provided for the anomalous Aboriginality to be halved as a result of the sexual activities of white men. Thus there was no tolerance of a 'three-quarter' category, which would have involved a 'half-caste' 'going back to the black'.[192] Similarly, the status of being 'half-caste'

---

189 Thus racist categories that are sometimes deployed within Indigenous societies ('Yellafella', etc.) do not correspond to the primary form of Australian racism.

190 By the same token, nor could Aborigines be deported or repatriated in the manner of those Pacific Islanders who were expelled after December 1906 under the terms of the White Australia Policy (Willard 1974: 182–6). A corollary of the same general point is that, whereas migration constantly swells the settler population, migration or adoption into Aboriginal societies is precluded.

191 'Time and time again I have been asked by some white man: "If I marry so-and-so (a coloured person) will our children be black?" As the law imposed upon me the responsibility of approving or objecting to the proposed marriage, I felt I had to give an answer to that vital question. The answer, of course, depended upon whether the woman was of purely [!] European-Aboriginal descent. If that was so, I felt I could safely reply that while no one could be definite in such a case, I thought the chances were all against it happening. That the children would be lighter than the mother, and if later they married whites and had children these would be lighter still, and that in the third of fourth generation no sign of native origin whatever would be apparent. Subject to this process a half-blood mother is unmistakable as to origin, her quarter-caste or quadroon offspring almost like a white, and an octoroon [sic] entirely indistinguishable from one . . . While it is with the people of European-Aboriginal descent that I am most concerned here as regards intermarriage, the implications are that if a white man marries a coloured woman of Aboriginal descent also possessing some Negro, Asiatic, Indian or other coloured ancestry, then he must take a greater risk of atavism in any children of the union there may be' (Neville 1947: 58–9, see also Bleakley 1961: 318).

192 Where this possibility was officially acknowledged, the logic of the system became explicit: 'The number of half-castes in certain parts of Australia is increasing, not as a result of additional influx of white blood, but following on intermarriage amongst themselves, where they are living under protected conditions, such as

was not deemed to result from having two 'half-caste' parents but from having one who was 'full-blood' and one who was white. The 'half-caste' with two 'half-caste' parents shared with the three-quarters and the one-sixteenth non-categories the property of taking more than three generations to be bred white. Thus they were extending the life of the fringe-camp. In other words, the system sought to impose a negative or descending exogamy, a *nubium* without exchange whose target was not black genes but Indigenous community, not physical but social relations.[193]

Genetic arithmetic represents an obsessive form of applied structuralism in which anomaly can be proportionately expressed as the degree of overlap between two ideally discrete sets. Yet, since such a formula assumes symmetry, it ignores power (this is a major difference between academic structuralism and the official mentality that I am reconstructing here). For the whole point of assimilation was not that mixtures of black and white were anomalous. On the contrary, as the abductions demonstrate, it was quite acceptable to introduce black into the white. It was the converse – white augmenting the black – that was anathema. Though this asymmetry is simply an expression of the logic of the descending opposition, it also demonstrates that biology cannot have been the problem. If Aboriginal genes had really been believed defective, the system would not have sought to incorporate them into the white stock. Thus we need a refinement that can account for two concurrent oppositions: a real – asymmetrical or descending – opposition, together with its ideological disguise – a balanced polarity in which anything interstitial was anomalous.

The distinction in question is expressed in logic as the difference between a contradictory and a contrary opposition. A contradictory opposition includes the whole world and excludes middle terms. An example is white versus non-white. A contrary opposition admits middle terms. An example is white versus black. As the arithmetic of assimilation demonstrates, colour (or race) is a contrary opposition. It has degrees and proportions. Accordingly, it cannot account for the asymmetry whereby, though the category 'white' can stand admixture, the category 'black' cannot. As before, therefore, we should return to the relation of invasion, governed by the logic of elimination. Here, the opposition is straightforwardly contradictory: one or the other, invader or invaded. To specify the cultural logic of assimilationism in relatively formal terms, therefore, we can say that the asymmetry in the contrary (race/colour) opposition demonstrates the priority of the contradictory (invasion-related, zero-sum) opposition, with which the

---

at the Government aboriginal stations at Point Pearce and Point McLeay, in South Australia. This may be the beginning of a possible problem of the future. A very unfortunate situation would arise if a large half-caste population breeding within themselves eventually arose in any of the Australian states. It seems to me that there can be only one satisfactory solution to the half-caste problem, and that is the ultimate absorption of these persons in the white population' (Cleland in Commonwealth of Australia 1937: 10). Bleakley was consistently less concerned about this issue (see, e.g., 1961: 315). In his 1928 report to the Federal Government (Bleakley 1929: 17), he divided the inmates of the 'Half-Caste Bungalow' in Alice Springs into four categories rather than the usual three, recommending that the 'three-quarter-caste aboriginals' be treated as Aboriginals. Though admittedly exceptional, Bleakley's policy still strove to maintain the assimilationist polarity.

193 Assimilationism classically operates to strip individuals of their collective identity, as in Clermont-Tonnerre's famous statement that the Jews 'must be refused everything as a separate nation and granted everything as individuals' (Davies 1996: 843).

THREE GENERATIONS
(Reading from Right to Left)

1. Half-blood—(Irish-Australian father; full-blood Aboriginal mother).
2. Quadroon Daughter—(Father Australian born of Scottish parents; Mother No. 1).
3. Octaroon Grandson—(Father Australian of Irish descent; Mother No. 2).

Figure 8. From A.O. Neville's *Australia's Coloured Minority* (1947)

insolubility of the black category is consistent. Thus we can say that the official rhetoric of assimilation misrepresented the contradictory relation of invasion as a contrary one of race. A revealing clue to the working of the system is provided by the fact that white families who received abducted children were either not told the children's background or, more usually, instructed to conceal it from them.[194] The outcome could not be clearer: what was being assimilated was *the colour not the Aboriginality*. The Aboriginality was to be left behind, insulated from the abducted body by secrecy and by the series of rites of passage (car ride, reception centre, children's home, new name, etc.) which intervened between fringe-camp and white society.[195]

Culture results from sharing history. The Aboriginality left behind in the camp constituted a cultural archive in which the illegitimacy of the Australian state was comprehensively inscribed. As observed, unlike genes, such consciousness is not mathematically divisible. Durkheim made the same observation in relation to another sacredness when he noted that it does not take a whole flag to symbolize a nation – in the right circumstances, the merest of tattered remnants, like each single drop of wine in a Communion chalice, has all the power of the whole. Analogously, the issue of the social is an issue of consciousness, which, unlike genes, is unquantifiable. On operative, social-definitional terms, then, blackness was not disguised. Rather, Aboriginality was disguised as blackness. In other words, history – invadedness, non-socialness – is essential, whilst biology is accidental. Kinship is historical. Thus abduction was actually a purer form of the logic of elimination than massacre, since, like a kind of social neutron bomb, it abstracted only the non-social essence, leaving intact a bodily vehicle that was still available for labour and other civic purposes. Since the requirement for legitimacy rendered massacres relatively inefficient, abduction represents a purer solution to the same social imperative.

In declaring that Aboriginality was a quantity that came in four reducing proportions, assimilationism precluded the one-sixteenth category. That is to say, it denied the possibility that a child born as a result of a sexual

---

[194] Pre-World War Two, abducted children were generally taken to boys' or girls' homes for training in menial occupations (as labourers or domestics) before being committed to white employers at the age of twelve or thirteen (Mulvaney 1989: 199–205). For Margaret Tucker's experiences of this system, see her (1977: 81–144) *If Everyone Cared* and the film *Lousy Little Sixpence* (Morgan and Bostock 1984).

[195] Though I am unimpressed by the definitional juggling whereby Orlando Patterson claims to have arrived at a transcultural and transhistorical definition of slavery, his specification of the 'social death' that is central to slavery applies very well to assimilationism, expressing both its continuity with and its distinction from the purely physical death of the confrontation phase. Patterson's social death has three defining characteristics, one political, one cultural and a third problematically termed psychological. The first refers to a domination that ultimately rests on violent coercion. The second, 'natal alienation', refers to the way its victims became genealogical isolates, liable to be detached from their kin at will. Patterson's (1982: 5) characterization of natal alienation could well be applied to assimilationism: the slave 'had a past, to be sure. But a past is not a heritage. Everything has a history, including sticks and stones. Slaves differed from other human beings in that they were not allowed freely to integrate the experience of their ancestors into their lives, to inform their understanding of social reality with the inherited meanings of their natural forebears, or to anchor the living present in any conscious community of memory'. Patterson's specification of the third characteristic of slavery, 'generalized dishonour' as psychological is problematic because, despite disclaimers (e.g. 'There is absolutely no evidence from the long and dismal annals of slavery to suggest that any group of slaves ever internalized the conception of degradation held by their masters', p. 97) the designation 'psychological' can hardly fail to suggest internalization, especially since Patterson is unclear as to whose psychology he means. As discursive rather than psychological, though, generalized dishonour was certainly a feature of assimilationism.

encounter between a white man and an 'octoroon' woman could live with its family in the Indigenous community.[196] Beyond even the furthest calibration of anomaly, then, was a being who looked white and lived Indigenous, with Indigenous kin, an Indigenous history and, accordingly, an Indigenous consciousness. Since consciousness is indivisible, genetic arithmetic should be seen as an exercise in containment. The implications of an irreducible, non-proportional historical consciousness are startling – in the case of the one-sixteenth person, for instance, it means that one Indigenous unit prevails over fifteen white, with succeeding ratios proceeding in a series 1>31, 1>63 . . . On this basis, white society becomes reinvaded in the space of the very three generations within which the black was meant to be bred out, which renders Australian society still dependent on the practical realization of assimilationist mathematics.[197] Hence, as stated above, the further from the pole of mythic authenticity that Indigenous identities can be asserted or reclaimed, the greater the ideological threat that they pose.

The threat that assimilationist mathematics strove to contain received cultural expression as a fear of engulfment that attributed supernatural (or, at least, hyper-Mendelian) potency to 'miscegenation'. For instance, Bates (1938) attributed the widespread blondness among Indigenous children to the genetic legacy of two Dutch criminals whom the navigator Pelsart had marooned on the west 'Australian' coast in 1627.[198] In official discourse, this hyperpotency figured as a threat to the integrity of both white and black. Without a deconstruction[199] of the assimilationist duality, the following statement seems to contradict itself. It was made by B.S. Harkness, a New South Wales state government representative at the national conference on Aboriginal welfare that was held in Canberra in 1937. Without explanation, I have presented this statement to a number of lecture groups. In each case, a clear majority believed that there had been some mistake; that its two sentences negated each other. Yet the 1937 delegates needed no explanation. Thus the statement gives us a clear insight into the assimilationist mentality:

> It is awful to think that the white race in the Northern Territory is liable to be submerged, notwithstanding that on this continent 98 per cent of the population is of British nationality. If we remain callous we shall undoubtedly see the black race vanish. (Commonwealth of Australia 1937: 14)

196 Indigenous children with non-Indigenous mothers could be dealt with according to standard procedures for children in need of care. Again, the point is not that Indigenous children were the only targets for adoption in an era when state intervention into child-rearing was of a level comparable to the nineteenth-century regulation of working-class women's sexuality (see, e.g. van Krieken 1992). It is, rather, that Indigenous people were alone in being so targeted on the ground of *race*.

197 This is, of course, an expression (or logical conclusion) of Australian state discourse rather than a statement about the empirical incidence of Indigenous community endogamy.

198 'There was no mistaking the flat heavy Dutch face, curly fair hair, and heavy stocky build' (Bates 1938 [1966]: 107).

199 Since the term 'deconstruction' is so generally abused, I will follow Eve Sidgwick in specifying the strict sense in which I employ it (her duality is sexual): 'The analytic move it makes is to demonstrate that categories presented in a culture as symmetrical binary oppositions – heterosexual/homosexual, in this case [white/black in mine] – actually subsist in a more dynamic tacit relation according to which, first, term B is not symmetrical with but subordinated to term A; but, second, the ontologically valorized term A actually depends for its meaning on the simultaneous subsumption and exclusion of term B; hence, third, the question of priority between the supposed central and the supposed marginal category of each dyad is irresolvably unstable, an instability caused by the fact that term B is constituted as at once internal and external to term A' (Sidgwick 1992: 9–10).

What Harkness meant – and the 1937 delegates perfectly understood – was, of course, that white and black were both liable to be submerged by a category that was neither one nor neither. Repressive authenticity should, thus, be understood in relation to the threat posed by a multiplex, heterogeneous and, above all, *historical* set of Aboriginalities that refuse to be contained within the ideal polarity that the logic of elimination requires. Although in recent years Australian state strategies have been culturally rather than genetically coded, their logic has remained consistent. In this regard, nescience constitutes something of a high-water mark, a maximally pure and monolithic condition that was instantly susceptible to contact. For, as distinct from alternative signifiers of otherness, it was contradictory rather than contrary, admitting no middle term (you can be semi-nomadic, semi-civilized and so on, but not semi-nescient). As the least mediated of oppositions, therefore, nescience represents the purest expression of repressive authenticity.

In this culturalist sense, Australian land-rights legislation continued the logic of elimination that the initial invasions had expressed. Though heralded as overdue justice to Aborigines, the introduction of land rights was not a repudiation of *terra nullius*. On the contrary, rather than acknowledging entitlement on the basis of continuous residence of immeasurably longer standing than the common law itself, the Land Rights (Northern Territory) Act of 1976 breathed juridical life into the ritually-constituted *homo superorganicus* of the anthropological imagination, specifying almost exclusively ritual criteria for entitlement. Moreover, the categorical structure of land-rights legislation replicates (only in the idiom of culture rather than in that of genetics) the dwindling rump of authentic Aboriginality that assimilationism has always produced. Thus we will turn now to examine the relationship – a particularly direct instance of political appropriation – between this legislation and synchronic anthropology.

Radcliffe-Brown's Horde: In Theory and Out of Practice

Radcliffe-Brown's model of Aboriginal society, 'The Social Organization of Australian Tribes', was serialized through the first (1930–31) volume of the journal that he launched whilst he was in Australia, *Oceania*. Despite significant anthropological disputation over it – including reservations on the part of no less than A.P. Elkin – forty-six years after its initial publication it was a received version of this model that came to be enshrined as the Australian government's first land-rights legislation. This came about as a result of the weight that land-rights commissioner Woodward had attached to the anthropological advice of Professors Ronald Berndt and W.E.H. Stanner, according to which the 'local descent group', a version of Radcliffe-Brown's 'horde', constituted a coherent land-owning unit in Aboriginal society. Yet, only a few years earlier, Stanner himself (1965a: 15–16) had dismissed as 'one of Aunt Sally's most persistent creations' the idea that the horde constituted the stable discrete grouping that, as Elkin had put it, 'some textbooks imply'.[200] Stanner was not, however, as inconsistent as this might suggest, since his earlier purpose had not been to subvert the local integrity of the horde but rather had been to limit the compromising of that integrity to the minimum extent necessary to maintain it in the face of an empirical attack by Les Hiatt (1962), who had depicted Warlpiri local organization as labile and emergent.[201] Again, therefore, the picture that anthropology presents is by no means straightforward, and is certainly not one of homogeneous compliancy. Rather, the Radcliffe-Brownian paradigm was highly polysemic, bearing a number of tenable readings, one of which became appropriated into land-rights legislation. Thus the question is not whose interpretation was the 'correct' one but how the one model so fruitfully sustained a number of readings.

In 'The Social Organization of Australian Tribes', subsistence production takes place in the 'family', a group 'formed by a man and his wife or wives and their dependent children' (1930–31: 435). At the next level up, families combine into 'hordes', which consist in localized groupings of patrilineally related men together with the other members of their respective families:

> The basic elements of social structure in Australia are (1) the family, *i.e.*, the group formed by a man and his wife and their children, and (2) the horde, a small group owning and occupying a definite territory or hunting ground. Together with these there is, of course[!], a grouping for social purposes on the basis of sex and age. It is on the basis of the family and the horde that the somewhat complex kinship organizations of Australia are built. (Radcliffe-Brown 1930–31: 34)

That, it might seem, should have been that – were it not for the seemingly innocuous qualification involving a further grouping 'for social purposes'. On inspection, these purposes turn out to be the whole superstructural complex of marital and ritual categories whereby Aboriginal society was organized at higher levels, to whose analysis the subsequent discussion was almost exclusively devoted. The term which enabled this was the horde, since, though made up of families, the horde was also connected – at the opposite end, as it were – to the 'clan', which was a marital and ritual grouping. In other words, in Radcliffe-Brown's scheme, the horde performed the same switch-rail function as the totem sacrament had in Robertson Smith's. Since the clan was linked to the horde and the horde was in turn made up of families, there appeared to be a link between the family and the clan. As will emerge, however, there was no such link, which means that, rather than forming the basis of social structure (in Radcliffe-Brown's sense), the family – and, with it, pragmatic existence – was outside (or, perhaps, prior to) social structure.

To turn, therefore, to the clan: the demographic difference between a horde and a clan was genealogical – clan membership was permanently determined

---

200 Stanner also quoted (1965a: 15–16) from Barnes, 'It is probable that for much of Australia the notion of discrete permanent local groups each keeping within its own clearly defined territory must be abandoned', continuing, in defence of his teacher, 'What must also be abandoned is the idea that Radcliffe-Brown was responsible for any such view.'

201 The debate, which also involved Megitt (1962; 1963) and Birdsell (1970), can reasonably be said to have continued to the present (see, e.g., Sansom 1980: 259–67, Maddock 1980: 30–55, Gumbert 1981; 1984, Hiatt 1982; 1984; 1996: 21–6, Rumsey 1989, Morphy 1990, Rowse 1993b: 54–68). For Hiatt's reply to Stanner, see Hiatt 1966.

by birth, whilst, for women, horde membership changed on marriage, which entailed their abandoning their fathers' hordes for their husbands' (i.e. it entailed their shifting from patrilocality to virilocality):

> A horde changes its composition by the passing of women out of it and into it by marriage. At any given moment it consists of a body of people living together as a group of families. The clan has all its male members in one horde, but all its older female members are in other hordes. It changes its composition only by the birth and death of its members. (Radcliffe-Brown 1930–31: 59, n.)

Despite the fact that there was major demographic overlap between horde and clan (i.e., all males plus a significant proportion of females) and despite the fact that this overlap was substantial enough to warrant androcentric references to the 'local clan', the determination of the clan was categorically not geographical but 'social' – the clan being constituted as a ritual (totemic) and marital (exogamous) grouping. It would have been quite incoherent to talk of an exogamous horde (though this did not stop some anthropologists from doing so[202]) for the simple reason that many of the horde's women were actually prevented from marrying out because they had already married in (indeed, in many – i.e. moiety – cases, marriage back out again could only have been incestuous).[203] It was, therefore, paradoxical that Radcliffe-Brown should not have made the same distribution apply in the ritual realm, so that affiliation to 'totem centres' would replicate clan membership. Rather than this, though, totem centres were represented as a function of horde membership. In the case of the women who could not marry out because they had already married in, this could only mean that, whilst their marital identity remained constant, their totemic identity had changed upon marriage – a fact which would necessarily have divorced totemic identity from membership of clans whose composition, as we have seen, could only be reduced by death.

With such contradictions gathering about him, Radcliffe-Brown was reduced to switching terms with all the resourcefulness of a McLennan (their minds are compellingly similar). When he introduced the concept of the totem centre (which, as we shall see, was to become crucial to land rights), he described it as a four-way nexus associating a sacred spot with mythical ancestors, natural species and a social category. Whether or not this social category was demographically labile, it certainly was definitionally so. On the same page (1930–31: 61) as it started life as a horde,[204] it

---

202 For which they can hardly be blamed, since it did not stop Radcliffe-Brown: 'In certain tribes there are factors at work which may result in destroying the exogamy of the horde' (1930–31: 438).

203 At first sight, this may read as if I am simply trying to pull a fast one back on Radcliffe-Brown. Endogamy and exogamy are, clearly, conditions that refer to marital eligibility, which is to say that they apply to premarital rather than to postmarital statuses. But the incoming bride's change of horde identity changed this too. The levirate (marriage to a dead husband's brother, which Radcliffe-Brown discussed [1930–31: 429–30]) is a complete illustration: if the horde really had been exogamous, the levirate, which unambiguously provided for marriage within the horde, would have to have been incestuous. To confirm my point, it can be put the other way round, since Radcliffe-Brown's clan *was* unambiguously exogamous. Thus not only did incoming brides not change their clan affiliation, but this means that the levirate, operating within the horde but involving those of its women who were not born into it, did not violate *clan* exogamy.

204 'Every totem centre lies, of course, in the territory of some horde, and there is therefore [!] a special connection between the members of the horde and the totem' (Radcliffe-Brown 1930–31: 61).

immediately became a *clan or horde*, with the significant addition of a 'tribal' context:

> In most of the tribes that have this form of totemism there is a system of localised rites for the increase of natural species, each local totem centre having its own rite, performed usually by members of the clan or horde to which the totem centre belongs. (Radcliffe-Brown 1930–31: 61)

This shift occurred in tandem with a further one, since these lines only took up one vertical portion of the page, the other side being given over to a diagram in which the social party to the four-way association was termed a 'patrilineal local group'. A few lines below, a motive for the addition of the tribal dimension emerges, in a context where the contradiction involving changing totemic identities would have been precipitated by none other than spirit-conception:

> In some of the tribes having this totemism of local totem centres there is a special connection between each individual and some one totem. This may take the form of a conception that the individual is a reincarnation of one of the totemic ancestors or the incarnation of an emanation from the totem centre. (Radcliffe-Brown 1930–31: 61–2)[205]

Patently, such an identity was not transferable, and Radcliffe-Brown made no attempt to make it so. Hence his sudden promotion of local totem centres to the higher encompassing level of the tribe – brides who changed hordes did not thereby change tribes, so the problem of totemic identity disappeared.

Before moving on to the tribe, however, it would be as well to step back for a moment. There is no point in trying to chase Radcliffe-Brown to the limits of his endless system because all that we get is more of the same – shifting terms, discontinuous levels and staggered sets that do not quite map onto each other. Thus it is worth recalling that the point is not to invalidate or to rehabilitate Radcliffe-Brown's theoretical model. It is, rather, that his Australian successors tended to be less brilliant and more empirically motivated than he had been. Long after he left Australia in 1931, they were seriously trying to reconcile his creation to the post-invasion realities of fieldwork observation. To this end, one aspect of the model was ironically congenial, since the theoretical erasure of local organization corresponded to the settler-colonial erasure of its practical conditions.[206] In labouring to reconstruct functioning social wholes from the transformed articulations that they encountered in the field, however, it is as if, in their undoubted earnestness, Radcliffe-Brown's Australian disciples did not take account of the schematizing passion that had driven the master system-builder.

Turning, then, to the tribe, we reach the limit of deferment, the 'point' beyond which the model allows itself to take for granted the material groundedness of the family/horde/clan complex and move on to the abstract spatiality of formal kinship systems. Thus the tribal level is the last chance

---

205 The passage continues: 'This form of totemism seems to be very widespread in Australia. It was first studied in detail in the Aranda tribe by Spencer and Gillen.'

206 'In more recent years the more or less total collapse of local organization has also dissuaded some fieldworkers from serious attempts at reconstructive study' (Stanner 1965a: 4).

for resolving the aporias left over from the preceding mismatches of family, horde and clan. The tribe was made up of a number of component hordes, on which basis it should have been territorially definable. This would have enabled significant correlations to be made between, on the one hand, territoriality, and, on the other, boundaries of custom, language and kinship organization, each of which Radcliffe-Brown also associated with the tribe, although with a modicum of overlap. For our purposes, the significance of this modicum is that it provided a pretext for a corresponding territorial overlap, the supposed local fixity of the tribe's component hordes notwithstanding:

> A tribe is commonly spoken of as possessing a certain territory, and is regarded as a land-holding group. So far as Australia is concerned, this is not quite accurate. It is true that each tribe may be regarded as occupying a territory, but this is only because it consists of a certain number of hordes, each of which has its territory. The territory of the tribe is the total of the territories of its component hordes. Moreover, in some instances at least, the boundary between one tribe and another may be indeterminate. (Radcliffe-Brown 1930–31: 36)

At this stage, a reminder may help. We are discussing Radcliffe-Brown's system rather than the empirical constitutions of actual Indigenous mobs. It may well be that certain mobs were shifting and labile – or, for that matter, otherwise – in the 1920s and 1930s. This, however, is a separate issue, for, as we see, the instability of Radcliffe-Brown's categories would have occurred anyway, regardless of the empirical situation, since it was independently motivated by his requirement to subordinate pragmatic conditions to the determination of a superorganically constituted model of social structure. Crucially, this means that the model's instability is impervious to definition or lack of it on the part of empirical mobs. Accordingly, no matter how much Stanner and Hiatt might have argued three decades later about the boundedness of local-group organization, this could not have affected the primary determination of the superorganic bias (indeed, in this respect, Hiatt wanted to increase, rather than reduce, Stanner's ritual emphasis). Nor, confronted with terminological subterfuge as thoroughgoing as Radcliffe-Brown's, could anything be gained by quoting supportive definitions, since an opponent could always counter with conflicting ones, perhaps even from the same page. In short, trying to find the lost horde will get us nowhere. We have, rather, to isolate the point at which Radcliffe-Brown took back the analytical primacy that he had earlier granted to the pragmatic territoriality that had initially defined the family (thence the horde, thence the tribe).

As we have seen, the family, the site of material production and reproduction, had no ritual or kinship role. The family fed into one 'end' of the horde. At the other end, the clan connected the horde up to the totemic and marital system(s). In linking the family to the clan, therefore, the horde was the shifter between the organic and the superorganic. We have seen how the horde and the clan were assimilated to each other by the simple expedient of terminological switching. Conversely, therefore, how was the thussuperorganicized horde reconnected to the family so that it could combine the family's pragmatic properties with the metaphysical dimensions that the clan supplied? The moment where this occurs is surely the loopiest of recursions:

> While the family is the primary economic unit in both production and consumption, the horde unites a number of families in a wider economic group in which there is regular co-operation in hunting and other activities, and a regular sharing of food. Thus the particularism of the family whereby it might tend to become an isolated unit is neutralised by the horde solidarity, which is itself based on family solidarity. (Radcliffe-Brown 1930–31: 438)

In other words (to share ground with Hiatt, only for different reasons) the horde was Radcliffe-Brown's debating-effect. It enabled him to link the family to the clan, which is to say it enabled him to subsume material production and reproduction to the formal metaphysics of his theoretical system.[207]

It would take too long to catalogue all the twists and turns in a text as complex as 'The Social Organization of Australian Tribes'. Thus the foregoing constitutes a kind of procedural sample – it is meant to exemplify a cast of reading that should elucidate Radcliffe-Brown's manoeuvres in other parts of his text as well. The *arché* motivating the whole system was the superorganic bias whose theoretical development we have observed in previous chapters. We need to know why. He can hardly have decided to attenuate land rights half a century in advance, so what was the reason for his determination to privilege metaphysics? The answer can only lie in the sketchily depicted family, since everything else just leads somewhere else.

It was not so much that Radcliffe-Brown was averse to the material production that the family effected. It was rather that, systemically speaking, there was not much to be said about it. Compared to the Gordian intricacies

---

[207] To keep the exposition to manageable limits, I have only shown how the horde connects the family up to the ritual (totemic) system. Radcliffe Brown also connected it up to the kinship system, by means of some term-stretching which, I hope, it is by now enough simply to indicate. Thus the family remained definitionally pragmatic: 'it should be noted that the family, *i.e., the group formed by a man and his wife or wives and their dependent children*, is certainly not less important amongst the Australian aborigines than it is amongst ourselves . . . The important function of the family is that it provides for the feeding and bringing up of the children [i.e., unambiguously, production and reproduction]. It is based on the co-operation of man and wife, the former providing the flesh food and the latter the vegetable food, so that quite apart from the question of children a man without a wife is in an unsatisfactory position since he has no one to supply him regularly with vegetable food, to supply his firewood and so on' (1930–31: 435, emphasis added). Two pages later, we find this strict definition strategically relaxed so that an English vernacular family model can let in a fraternal bridge to the kinship system, one that unequivocally exceeds the Cyclopean structure of the pragmatic family of the original definition: 'Not only is the Australian kinship system at the present time actually based on the family and on genealogical relations having their origin in individual relations of parents and children, but also in the analysis given above I have tried to show that the active principles at work in determining the system are the result of the strong solidarity of the individual family. Thus the essential character of the classificatory terminology, according to the interpretation here offered, is the recognition of the bond between two brothers born of the same parents as one of such strength and intimacy that any social relation with one of two brothers necessarily involves a somewhat similar relation with the other. The very intimate relation between a man and his mother's brother [n.b. different horde, different locality, no shared subsistence] is an example of the same process' (1930–31: 437). This, though, is just a beachhead. Where the economic dimension is not actually on the point of being smuggled in, the connection into the kinship system is much more direct: 'By kinship is here meant genealogical relationship recognized and made the basis of social relations between individuals. Genealogical relationships are those set up by the fact that two individuals belong to the same family' (1930–31: 42). Even apart from the abstract nature of the diagrams, therefore, *homo superorganicus* is as much a product of kinship discourse as of the ritual bias.

of his diagrams, families were structurally simple and homogeneous. Being patrifocal or Cyclopean – which is to say, ironically enough, being nuclear – they exhibited none of the morphological variation that distinguished kinship systems. In short, since variety stopped where material production and reproduction began, routine existence offered Radcliffe-Brown nothing to theorize about. In the event, it was not that he denied pragmatic factors. It was simply that his *theory* had no place for them. It stood for something else – 'social structure'. As a result, it did not have a place for the consequences of a colonialism that could transform the pragmatic basis to family life whilst leaving intact the prescriptive representations that regulated kinship systems. Here again, nescience – in this case, as in that of the later Hartland, forming the basis for social fatherhood – was the prime exemplar. As we have already seen, the European invasion was manifest on the level of kinship as 'miscegenation'. Accordingly, just as Radcliffe-Brown's theory could not register the economic transformation of family life, nor could it register the invasion's concrete genetic dimension. In other words, the failure was not simply a consequence of some distaste for economics or genetics on Radcliffe-Brown's part. It was the systemic outcome of a model that had no place for material production or reproduction. Its premises should be familiar:

> In Western civilization we normally think of genealogical relationships in terms of what are commonly called biological, but may perhaps better be called physiological relationships. There is an obvious physiological relationship between a woman and the child to which she gives birth. For us there is also a physiological relationship between a child and the man who is the genitor. The first of these is recognized by the Australian native, but the second is not recognized. In some tribes it seems to be denied that there is any physiological relationship between genitor and offspring. Even if in any tribes it is definitely recognized it is normally, or probably universally, treated as of no importance.
>
> In modern English the word 'father' is ambiguous. It may be used as equivalent sometimes to Latin *genitor*, sometimes to Latin *pater*. Thus we speak of the 'father' of an illegitimate child. Such a child necessarily has a *genitor* but no *pater*. On the other hand, when a child is adopted the male parent is his 'father', *i.e.*, *pater* but not *genitor*.
>
> In Australia fatherhood is a purely social thing. *Pater est quem nuptiæ demonstrant.*[208] The father and mother of a child are the man and woman who, being husband and wife, *i.e.*, living together in a union recognized by other members of the tribe, look after that child during infancy. Normally, of course, the mother is the woman who gives birth to the child, but even this is not essential as adoption may give a child a second mother who may completely replace the first. (Radcliffe-Brown 1930–31: 42–3)

In this as in many other discernible regards, Radcliffe-Brown's theory presupposed and ingested the evolutionist debating that we have been unpicking in previous chapters. As we have seen, this debating was not predetermined by Australian politics. At various junctures, however, different

---

208 'The father is he whom marriage certifies' (PW).

aspects of it were appropriated into Australian politics, where they were invested with local lives of their own. Thus it is important to repeat that these appropriations were not inherent in the theories concerned; they were, rather, motivated by local political exigencies. There is no reason why these exigencies should prioritize those features of a given theory that anthropologists might regard as the most significant. 'The Social Organization of Australian Tribes' is a case in point. Consequential though this series of articles was to be for Australian politics, anthropological aficionados of Radcliffe-Brown are hardly likely to regard it as occupying a status comparable to his work on, say, segmentary lineages or joking relationships. Be that as it may, I have no quarrel with such views; I am simply discussing a different issue.

With this in mind, it should be noted that, for all his protestations to the contrary, Radcliffe-Brown was, in fact, engaged in reconstructive history. Thus he made no bones about the colonial impact. He just left it out of his theory. As opposed to a social process to be described, colonization came between the anthropologist and his social structure, which lay emphatically behind it. Thus the ethnographic difficulties involved in giving an account of local organization in Australia were 'greatly increased when the country has been occupied for some time by the white man, for the local organization is the first part of the social system to be destroyed by the advent of the European and the expropriation of the native owners of the land' (1930–31: 35). Such terminology (especially the unqualified reference to 'owners') was by no means uncontroversial in 1930.[209] Thus it is not as if Anarchy Brown was simply an apologist for imperialism. Indeed, it is not even as if there was anything intrinsically oppressive about reconstructive history. It is, rather, that his theory was one thing for the purpose of salvage and quite another when it came to be appropriated by the Australian state for the purpose of delimiting Aboriginal entitlement. In this latter context, rather than a method for recovering the past, it became a means of invalidating the present. For, once operationalized, the theory's blindness to pragmatic existence rendered claimants' entitlement to land dependent on their conformity to an ideal model which, as we have seen, excluded those who had been touched by history.

Again, therefore, my object is not anthropology in itself so much as its recruitment to hegemonic ends. Indeed, my approach patently derives from anthropology in a number of ways (in this sense too, my tribe is the anthropologists). Anthropology has not stood still in the face of the postcolonial challenge. If anything, the condition of being a discipline in crisis has proved creative, with many of the most productive critiques of anthropology's compromised inheritance coming from within.[210] As

---

209 It would still cause controversy during the pleading of the momentous Gove land-rights case (Milirrpum v. Nabalco) in 1971. See Maddock 1980: 21–3.

210 Even without those whom I have already mentioned (Asad, Beckett, Bloch, Lattas, Leach, Rosaldo, Taussig, and others) the list is such a long one that it is hard to know where to start. Post-World War Two, it seems appropriate to mention Gregg and Williams 1948, Leiris 1950, Hooker 1963, Worsley 1966, Galtung 1967, Berreman 1968, Gjessing 1968; Gough 1968; Banaji 1970; Mafeje 1971, Leclerc 1971, Obeyesekere 1992 and the anthropological contributions to Huizer and Mannheim 1979, Stocking 1991, Pels and Salemink 1994. Before World War Two, though, Julius Lips' (1937) *The Savage Hits Back, or the White Man Through Native Eyes*, to which Malinowski contributed an introduction, already evinced an appreciable measure of postcolonial

observed, though, once a narrative has been appropriated, its discursive fortunes do not remain within the control of its framers' disciplinary successors. In any event, it is not as if Australian history, with its silences – or, for that matter, psychology, archaeology, law, criminology, geography, town planning, comparative anatomy or political science – could claim to have been any less complicit. Being more systematic in its engagement with otherness, however, anthropology has more to reveal. How much, after all, is there to be said about history's inexcusable silence?[211]

In excluding history, *homo superorganicus* replaced it with temporalities of its own, ritual time and an untheorized pragmatic time. Ritual time is not so much the ever-present possibility of Eliade's eternal return as one limit of an oscillation that moves between the scattered and the condensed.[212] Pragmatic subsistence takes place in family groups – minimal, undifferentiated clusters, scattered over the landscape, whose cellular symmetry evinces none of Radcliffe-Brown's social structure. As observed in relation to the model of the text, however, ritual brings it all together – or, to be more faithful to ideology, brings it all back together. In ritual space, clan alignments, cosmology – the whole superstructure – are present at once. An archetype on parade, it dissolves on dispersal; its temporality is at once both episodic and eternal. It persists in a frozen parallel realm that is impervious to the vagaries and mutations of pragmatic existence. The same property makes it amenable to the diagrammatic regime of the page – it holds still. Hence the ever-popular ethnographic 'camp', whose layout expresses a whole society and its cosmology, is not a feature of workaday life (at least, it only becomes so when settler-colonization imposes a carceral stasis that ironically realizes the structuring of the model).

Structural-functionalism's theoretical universalizing of ritual temporality came to acquire the most concrete of practical implications in what is generally known as the Gove land-rights case (Milirrpum vs. Nabalco, 1971), when Aboriginal land rights were first pleaded in an Australian court. As already noted, the model of Aboriginal society – including its system of territorial entitlements – that the lawyers for the Yirrkala plaintiffs presented was fundamentally that of Radcliffe-Brown, which the anthropologists

---

positionality. So far as the current critique within Australian Aboriginal anthropology is concerned, Marcia Langton's (1981) 'Urbanizing Aborigines: The Social Scientists' Great Deception' is particularly significant, not only because (contra Rowse 1993b: 132 and even, so it seems, contra Langton herself [1993: 7]) it was the first in the field but because, being Indigenous herself, Langton, in common with Asad, Mafeje, Rosaldo and others, personally confounds anthropology's traditional subject/object boundary. Apart from Langton's critique (and that of Jones and Hill-Burnett [1982] which was also early), though I am averse to setting myself up as a dispenser of laurels, it seems reasonable to follow Rowse in assigning significance (though not priority) to Gillian Cowlishaw's (1986a) 'Aborigines and Anthropologists' (see also Cowlishaw 1986b, 1990, 1992). It would also seem that any survey should include at least some of the anthropological contributions to Beckett's (1988) *Past and Present*, David Hollinsworth's (1992) response (together with the responses appended to it) to Kevin Keeffe's (1988) 'Aboriginality: Resistance and Persistence' as well as the articles in the *Oceania* special edition (no. 3 of 1993) guest-edited by Cowlishaw and entitled *The Politics of Representation and the Representation of Politics*.

211 In one sense, the question is rhetorical, since, as Tom Griffiths (1996) and Chris Healy (1997) have both argued, in Foucauldian vein, Stanner's (1968) 'Great Australian Silence' in Australian history-writing was more a babble than a silence, a 'white noise' whereby history-makers produced an endless din designed to overlay and deny the 'lurking colonial shadows of bad blood and bad deeds' (Griffiths 1996: 106).

212 The allusion to Boas' 'eskimoes', with their summer/winter, tundra/igloo oscillations, as developed by Mauss (1904–5), is not accidental – the same narrative structure clearly linked Radcliffe-Brown's student Evans-Pritchard's celebrated (1940) analysis of the Nuer to the *Année Sociologique* school.

Stanner and Berndt recommended to the court. The ensuing debacle, in which the plaintiffs testified to a social life whose routine arrangements contradicted the two expert witnesses' version of how they should have been organizing themselves, has been influentially attributed to an empirically misleading boundedness on the part of the horde concept (e.g. Hiatt 1982, Gumbert 1984, cf. Maddock 1980: 30–55). Without rehearsing the technicalities involved, it should be clear by now that behind the problem of territorial definedness lies the dominance of *homo superorganicus*, which no amount of boundary-fiddling could resolve. Since the Yirrkala plaintiffs did not spend their pragmatic lives in the anthropologists' ritual temporality, they spent most of their time in the wrong time. In finding for the mining company, the judge could scarcely have put this more clearly. He was unable, he held, to

> feel satisfied that a band spent a significantly greater portion of its time in the territory of any clan than in that of another, or that a band regarded itself as based in the territory of any particular clan. (Blackburn 1971: 171)[213]

To cut a long, but well documented, story short, the court found against the Yirrkala plaintiffs. The following year, in the wake of the Vietnam moratorium and the Aboriginal Tent Embassy on the lawns of Parliament House, a Labor government was returned for the first time in nearly quarter of a century. Amidst a flurry of reforms, which included an overnight disengagement from the Vietnam war, one of its first actions was to commission Edward Woodward, who had been the unsuccessful leading counsel for the Yirrkala in the Gove case, to hold an inquiry which would report back to the government on procedures for implementing Aboriginal land-rights legislation (i.e. its brief was how best to introduce land rights, not whether or not they were desirable). Woodward maintained his commitment to the model that Stanner and Berndt[214] had presented at the Gove case, with the result that, with one highly significant exception, his recommendations bore the clear imprint of Radcliffe-Brown, prescribing ritually-determined grounds for Aborigines to lay claim to certain categories of public (mainly Aboriginal-reserved) land in the Northern Territory. The significant exception (which had been provided for in the Letters Patent setting up the Woodward Commission) was a 'needs criterion' whereby pragmatic exigency could constitute grounds for land grants to the dispossessed ('town campers', 'station Aborigines', etc.). Before the Labor government could pass the Woodward Commission's recommendations, it was ejected by a constitutional *coup d'état* in 1975, whereupon the incoming conservative coalition

---

213 Clan and band could not have broken Radcliffe-Brown's horde into ritual and pragmatic categories more clearly (clan:band::ritual:pragma). What is more, Blackburn went on explicitly to undo their union as it had been presented to him by Woodward on the basis of Stanner and Berndt's advice: 'I consider that the suggested links between the bands and the clans are not proved. I find it more probable that the situation was not as Mr. Woodward contended, but rather that neither the composition nor the territorial ambit of the bands was normally linked to any particular clan. My finding is that the clan system, with its principles of kinship and of spiritual linkage to territory, was one thing, and that the band system which was the principal feature of daily life of the people and the modus of their social and economic activity, was quite another' (Blackburn 1971: 171).

214 Though I have concentrated on Stanner, Berndt's role, especially as far as the ritual emphasis is concerned, was complementary. Thus, in his report, Woodward (1974: 32) cited Berndt as assigning the following priority: 'there are for Aborigines two levels of ownership, the primary or religious level and the secondary or economic level'.

passed them substantially unchanged except for the removal of the needs criterion.[215] Thus the *Northern Territory (Land Rights) Act* of 1976 constitutes the formal moment at which the Radcliffe-Brownian paradigm became appropriated by the Australian state. In its wake, a largely new breed of anthropologists, encouraged by generally sympathetic (in the case of Mr Justice Toohey, particularly sympathetic) land-rights commissioners, did their best to broaden the terms under which land rights could be recognized, especially in so far as both pragmatic and matrilineal entitlements were concerned. Despite their efforts, which achieved considerable success in relation to the gender issue, the crucial definition of 'traditional owner', though loosened, remained an emphatically ritual concept (Neate 1989: 302–3). The details of land-rights pleadings under the 1976 Act (in particular, the key distinction between owners and managers) are complex and, since they do not affect the primary question of cultural logic, I do not wish to rehearse them here. None the less, there is one detail that, for obvious reasons, should be taken up.

Despite the references to spirit conception in the Woodward Commission's second report, the land-holding unit that was recognized for land-rights purposes under the 1976 Act did not include people who were spiritually conceived on the land in question without belonging to the relevant clan or local descent group (i.e. it did not include people whose mothers had been just passing through). In the first claim to come before the newly established Aboriginal Land Commission (the Borroloola claim) the Commissioner (Toohey 1978a: 9–10) specifically excluded such people, since, though their tie to the land was not in dispute, it was not one which had arisen as a consequence of clan membership. But the issue kept returning. In the following (Warlpiri) claim, Toohey seemed for a while to be wavering ('there are ways by which people possessing no blood relationship to traditional owners may in fact come to be recognised as such. I instance conception filiation' [1978b: 3]) but, in the following (Alyawarra) claim, reconfirmed the requirement for clan membership, specifically excluding non-clan members with rights arising from spirit-conception (1979a: 5). A breakthrough occurred, however, with the Ayers Rock (Uluru) claim, when ambilineal (i.e. both paternal and maternal) descent was recognized (Toohey 1979b: 8). The proliferation of rights that could have ensued as a result of ambilineal entitlements being compounded through the generations was curbed by the principle that a person inherited ambilineally (i.e. from both father and mother) but transmitted unilineally (i.e. only passed on either the maternal or the paternal inheritance to a child). This inroad into anthropological and juridical androcentrism opened the door to spirit-conception, which could provide the basis for a maternal inheritance. It has been necessary to dwell on this detail because the fact that spirit-conception came to be admitted both as an afterthought and as a secondary consequence of the gender-balancing shift to ambilineality would seem to negate the centrality of nescience to land-rights discourse. This is not, however, the case, since the social fatherhood on which (patri)clan membership depended was, as we have seen,

---

215 Maddock 1980: 16, Peterson and Langton 1983: 4. It should be noted that the Woodward Commission had provided for land rights to be recognized on the basis of need (Woodward 1974: 2).

constructed in opposition to physiological paternity (this is quite apart from the fact that clan members whose mothers had not happened to be passing through somewhere else would be affiliated to the totemic population of its land[216] by the positive mechanism of spirit-conception). In any event, even if this particular detail had not eventuated (i.e., even if spirit-conception had been altogether missing from land rights) this would not have altered the hegemony of the discourse of *homo superorganicus*, in the construction of which spirit-conception had been a central element.[217] And this, clearly, is the main point, the one that enables us to focus on the broader phenomenon of cultural logic.[218]

As noted above, of itself nescience holds no more interest for me than it did for Hartland or for Spencer. In each case, its significance has been extrinsic, a means to an end. In Hartland's case, that end was his own European prehistory; in Spencer's case, it was the other's ethnographic about-to-be-past; in my case, it is my own settler-colonial past, present and future. To this end, I have found nescience to be well placed for the purpose of unravelling the cultural logic whose construction I wish to understand. Cultural logics are both more diffuse and more resilient than the formal provisions of juridical or legislative determinations. Thus we may abolish *terra nullius* at a stroke, but this does not simultaneously dismantle the cultural, economic and myriad other structures of practical disenfranchise-

---

216 I.e. to its 'estate'.

217 As a ritually constituted basis for entitlement, nescience perfectly exemplifies the two-way loss produced by settler-colonialism in general and *homo superorganicus* in particular. Read negatively, as an absence of knowledge, nescience symbolizes a primitive irrationality around which moral and cognitive discourses unite. Read positively, as a metaphor for transcendence, spirit-conception is a pre-eminently mystical discourse that is at odds with instrumental-pragmatic use of the land. This closure is perfected on the basis of repressive authenticity, whereby, if neither of these options apply – which is to say, if Aborigines are not ignorant after all – then they are not traditional and thus, it follows, not entitled. Double jeopardy had, however, been a feature of nescience from the outset. Thus, though Radcliffe-Brown (1912b: 181–2) was neither the first nor the only one to allege that certain ritual enactments presupposed ritual knowledge (e.g., Purcell 1893: 288, Basedow 1925: 291–2, Thomson 1933; 1936, Berndt 1951: 32; cf. Roheim's [1925: 151–2] psychoanalytic explanation), the fact that the evidence is ritual evidence merely sustains the ideological closure. Similarly, some missionaries argued (e.g. Frodsham quoted in Frazer 1910: 577, Strehlow in Malinowski 1913: 20, Read 1918: 151) that the old men knew the truth but kept it from women and girls so as not to jeopardize their sexual compliance (cf. Meggitt 1962: 272–3), an evangelical analysis that located correct knowledge within a well established discourse on gerontocratic nefariousness (see also Porteus 1931: 217). Similarly, the claim (Malinowski 1913: 211) that Aborigines were only nescient about themselves but not about animals (or, in some accounts, about white men) merely compounded their illogicality. Even where there seemed to be glaring inconsistencies, these could be reconciled by shifting between *genitor* and *pater*. How else are we to account for blithe assertions such as the following? – 'So far as the phratry is concerned, the matter of descent is comparatively simple – the child goes into that of its father' (Spencer and Gillen 1897a: 20). All this is not only ironic in view of the fact that, as Barnes (1973: 66–9, see also van Gennep 1906b: lix–lx) noted, 'correct scientific' genetic knowledge was only just over a century old in Europe, but also in view of the widespread currency of the white-nescient missionary position exemplified by Father Jos Bischofs (1908: 37): 'After many years of experience it seems that the following statement may be made about the aborigines. A black woman will not, as a rule, give birth to a full-blooded child after she has once given birth to a half-caste child. In other words, even though she lives in a continuous and unbroken union with her black husband under the most favourable conditions, she will thereafter only give birth to half caste children, even if she has only on one occasion had intercourse previously with a white or coloured (Chinese or Malay) man'.

218 Without emphasizing nescience, therefore, the primary point could be made about the Coronation Hill case of 1991, in which the issue of the Jawoyn people's entitlement hinged not on demonstrably immemorial occupation but on a theogonic disagreement between anthropologists (Brunton 1991, Merlan 1991) to the extent that the doctrinal credentials of a sacred ancestor named Bula became a popular tabloid topic. For this controversy see also, e.g. Keen and Merlan 1990, Keen 1992, Maddock 1987; 1988.

ment that *terra nullius* expressed and sustained. To keep sight of the long-run continuities in Australian cultural logic, we should avoid being diverted by the tortuous unfolding of land-rights pleading through the 1980s. We should also avoid conspicuous developments that did not actually change anything, such as the Hawke Labor government's 1986 post-election abandonment of a pre-election pledge to introduce national (as opposed to just Northern Territory) land-rights legislation, or the much-publicized Coronation Hill case of 1991 (which was anyway not decided on the basis of the 1976 Act). The first change of an order comparable to the introduction of the 1976 Act began in June 1992 with the full bench of the High Court of Australia's judgement in the Mabo case and culminated in the passing, in December 1993, of the national legislation to which that judgement gave rise. The formal significance of these developments, which have almost universally been heralded as a turning-point in the history of the nation, was that they officially revoked the doctrine of *terra nullius* (or, more strictly, denied its application, which is not the same thing as undoing actions historically premised upon it). To maintain our focus on the relevant cultural logic, therefore, we should compare the provisions of the Native Title legislation with those of the 1976 Act in order to assess the significance of the changes that were introduced. To what extent can we conclude that they were more than formal? – which is to say, regardless of their perceived significance at the time, to what extent can they be said to have affected the elementary structures of settler-colonization?

In this regard, the key provision of the Native Title legislation is that, to qualify for native title, Aborigines have to prove 'traditional connection' with the claimed land,[219] a requirement that displaces the burden of history from the fact of expropriation to the character of the expropriated. Indeed, to the extent that the empirical details of the Mabo case itself were to constitute any form of precedent, the legislation would restrict land-rights entitlement to an even narrower category. This is because the colonial formation in the Torres Strait, which was the subject of the court case, is quite different from that prevailing elsewhere in Australia. Colonization of the Torres Strait islands was based on the exploitation of native labour, which, rather than being applied to the land, was employed offshore, principally for the purpose of pearl-lugging. Accordingly, the land functioned primarily as a condition of the reproduction of labour, a factor that has enabled the subsistence-generating components of Torres Strait societies to evince a considerably higher degree of continuity and equilibrium than those on the mainland (Beckett 1977). Whether or not the full implications of this distinction come to govern legal understandings of traditional connection, there is nothing to suggest that traditional connection will be interpreted more widely on a national level than traditional

---

[219] 'The expression "native title" or "native title rights and interests" means the communal, group or individual rights and interests of Aboriginal peoples or Torres Strait Islanders in relation to land or waters, where: (a) the rights and interests are possessed under the traditional laws acknowledged, and the traditional customs observed, by the Aboriginal peoples or Torres Strait Islanders; and (b) the Aboriginal peoples or Torres Strait Islanders, by those laws of customs, have a connection with the land or waters; and (c) the rights and interests are recognized by the common laws of Australia' (*Native Title Act* 1993, S.208, i). Claimants also have to demonstrate 'continuing association' with the land in question.

ownership has been interpreted in the Northern Territory.[220] Indeed, there is nothing to suggest that the territorial beneficiaries of Native Title will not be so narrowly defined that, rather than removing *terra nullius*, the legislation will come to be seen as its fulfilment, as marking the point where *terra nullius* had completed its historical task.

Though it is still (in 1998) hard to say just what traditional connection will comprise, we can at least see that it is unlikely to stray far from – and might well offer less than – the basic character of the 1976 Act's 'traditional owner'. For this, we do not need a crystal ball. The question is not what we can see in the future but what we do not see in the present. Since the structures sustaining the logic of elimination have not been unequivocally dismantled, we can be confident that they will not go away. On this basis, it behoves us to look more carefully at the acknowledgement of native title, especially when it is borne in mind that, in denying native title, *terra nullius* had also precluded its extinguishment – *you can't extinguish something that isn't already there*. As a formula for extinguishment, the *Native Title Act* refurbished and reinvigorated the logic of elimination for a new (republican?) century.

It is highly significant that, as the twentieth century draws to a close and the Australian government licences the public advocacy of policies and sentiments that would have been rejected as racist until very recently, no one – not even the most emboldened opponents of Aboriginal interests – has argued for the reinstatement of *terra nullius*. It is not hard to see why this should be so. In the context of contemporary world politics, *terra nullius* would be patently indefensible. Indeed, it is astonishing that we had to wait until the 1990s before such a flimsy rationalization for violent dispossession underwent any significant modification. When it was finally modified, though, it was greatly refurbished and updated. Ideologically speaking, the difference between a *terra nullius* that is flagrantly untenable and a native title that people are held to have had but lost is the difference between invasion and assimilation – or, perhaps, between the nineteenth century and the twenty-first. From a political point of view, this makes the situation complex. On the one hand, it is clearly imperative that the issue of Indigenous rights, including Indigenous sovereignty, not be reduced to a defence of native title. On the other hand, even though native title legislation principally functions to provide grounds for extinguishment, any acknowledgement of a violated Indigenous entitlement is fraught with hazards for a state that, in keeping with *terra nullius*, never saw the need for treaties. As such, it has never accommodated the Indigenous sovereignty underlying native title.

Apart from anything else (and there seems to be no need to doubt that some of its framers regarded it as a historical breakthrough for Aboriginal people), the *Native Title Act* was a response to a constitutional crisis. In removing *terra nullius*, the Mabo judgement had removed the ideological

---

220 It should, however, be acknowledged that, in the explanatory memorandum (part B) appended to the Act, it is stated that 'In accordance with the High Court's decision, the use of the word "traditional" in reference to laws and customs in this definition, is not to be interpreted as meaning that the land and customs must be the same as those that were in existence at the time of European settlement'. Again, the full application of this condition remains to be determined. In this regard, the outcome of the Yorta claim to Barmah State Forest will be interesting, since part of the claim involves the assertion that confinement on a reserve sustained traditional connection when the reserve was on confinees' traditional country.

basis to settler-colonization. Thus the ideologically charged interval between the High Court judgement of June 1992 and the passing of the legislation in December 1993 marked a legitimation crisis whose containment consisted in a declaration that some native title would be recognized but most would be extinguished through being made an object of compensation.[221] On this basis, the legislation represents an altogether internal symptom of contradiction that does not necessitate a resort to liberal philanthropy for its explanation.[222] Moreover, its primary narrative feature – a structural bifurcation separating a category to be accorded territorial entitlement from a category to be compensated by a range of depoliticized welfare measures generally glossed as 'social justice' – reproduces the primary ideological binarism that has historically characterized settler-colonial discourse. To situate the post-Mabo order in the cultural context of the long run, therefore – which is to extend the analysis into the present – we need to situate this structural bifurcation in relation to the logic of elimination. We now have enough material to do this and, in the process, to move towards some analytical, theoretical and political conclusions.

Inclusion, Exclusion and the Nation-State

Analytically, to recap, it can be seen how the logic of elimination, most crudely manifest in the initial massacres, has persisted into the present by way of a number of strategic transformations. This continuity proceeds from Australian society's primary determination as a settler-colonial state, founded on what I have termed a negative articulation. So far as the present is concerned, over the key question of land, Australian policy continues to be exclusive rather than inclusive in that, at the price of a minimal enfranchisement, the bulk of the Indigenous population is eliminated from the reckoning. This is achieved by means of a culturalist version of the descending opposition which, earlier in the century, conceded the minimal constituency in the idiom of genetics. The culturalist analogue to 'full-bloodedness' is a fragile Edenic trap from which the only way out is down. In either case, authentic Aboriginality is constructed as a frozen precontact essence, a quantity of such radical historical instability that its primary effect is to provide a formula for disqualification.

It remains, therefore, to relate this discourse of exclusion to the discourse of inclusion whose interplay with it has already been noted. For, as observed, where territory is not involved, the Australian state has shown itself willing to devote not only large amounts of money and bureaucratic energy to Aboriginal welfare but also to devolve significant control over expenditure on Aboriginal affairs to Indigenous people. In areas such as health, penal reform, education, housing, employment and related welfare issues, the establishment in the 1980s of a bureaucratic triptych made up of the Aboriginal and Torres Strait Islanders Commission, the Royal Commission

---

221 As Woodward observed, in his second (1974: 10) report to the Government, 'Cash compensation in the pockets of this generation of Aborigines is no answer to the legitimate land claims of a people with a distinct past who want to maintain their separate identity in the future.'

222 A point which is ruled out of debate by pre-emptive 'questions' such as Rowse's (1993b: 24) 'How did a liberal tradition of respect for indigenous rights survive at all in twentieth-century Australia?'

into Aboriginal Deaths in Custody and the Committee for National Reconciliation marked the emergence of a striking level of official concern in relation to Aboriginal issues. This concern resulted in large measure from Indigenous political mobilization – the campaign leading up to the 1967 Referendum, the Yirrkala bark petition, the Gurindjis' walk-off from Wave Hill Station, the establishment of community-controlled health and legal aid centres, the Tent Embassy, the campaigns against the Brisbane Games and the Bicentenary, the solitary resistances of those who have died in custody – to mention just some of the more conspicuous activities of the last quarter-century or so.[223] In relation to organized Indigenous resistance, especially since this has been mobilized in an increasingly supportive decolonized international context, it is easy enough to see the discourses of exclusion and inclusion (or land rights and welfare) as a twin-track strategy that seeks to protect the territorial basis of the settler-colonial state by limiting concessions to the welfare area. In many instances, this strategy is belied by palpable contradictions in the rhetoric in which it is publicly framed. For instance, when they were in office, Labor Party ministers responsible for Aboriginal affairs were in the habit of characterizing government welfare initiatives as being 'Aboriginal community-based'. Needless to state, these ministers did not refer to police stations as being 'Aboriginal community-based', though they would have been equally justified in doing so. The tactic was not, of course, demographic but political, intended to instal 'community-based' (as opposed to the 'community-controlled' that Indigenous people invariably demanded) as an electorally viable signifier for racial democracy. The 'community-based' formula betrays a desire, common to both sides of Australian parliamentary politics, that welfare might substitute for territory as a solution to 'the Aboriginal problem'. Correspondingly, the demand for community control aims for official acknowledgement of a separately constituted – which is to say, an extranational – sovereignty.

In response, governments have conceded an increased measure of 'community' control. But the operative construction of 'community' could hardly differ further from that current in the domain of federal land-rights legislation. For, in order to exercise the control that has been conceded, it is necessary for Aboriginal office-bearers to be elected by Aborigines whose names appear on the electoral roll, an acknowledgement of the settler-colonial state's legitimacy that the great majority of Indigenous people avoided until registration became automatic.[224] In other words, the criteria for Aboriginality that determine community membership for the purposes of exercising control in the welfare domain significantly include ratification of the settler-colonial Constitution. As opposed to a ritual continuity which is by definition external to Australian society, the inclusive discourse of the welfare domain is an assimilatory strategy of citizen-construction ('Aboriginal Australians'). This

---

223 For some examples and overviews from a vast literature on the modern Indigenous political movement, see, e.g., Anderson 1988, Attwood and Markus 1997, Bandler 1989, Bennett 1989, M. Burgmann 1983, V. Burgmann 1993: 24–74, Duncan 1989, Goodall 1996, Hardy 1968, Howard 1982b, Langton 1982, McGinness 1991, Middleton 1977, Miller 1985: 192–226, Nathan 1980, Rowley 1986, Sykes 1989, Tatz 1979, Wanganeen 1986.

224 Whilst I am not sure as to quite how one might demonstrate this avoidance by means of official documents, I have frequently heard it asserted both publicly and privately by Indigenous speakers. Moreover, it is consistent with the discreditingly low level of participation in ATSIC voting.

distinction can be seen with particular clarity in the area of service-delivery, where, as Tim Rowse (1993a) has described, Indigenous people are assimilated into all levels of welfare bureaucracy, with the result that, neither at the point of local service delivery nor at that of central administration, is it possible to distinguish (phenomenally, in terms of personnel) an Aboriginal 'side' from an official white one. This situation should be contrasted with land rights, where members of applicant communities are clearly plaintiffs, to the extent that any comparable participation in decision-making would be held to constitute a conflict of interests.

Thus it is easy enough to distinguish an inclusive welfare discourse from the exclusive one of native-title legislation. As stated, however, the main point is not to distinguish the two but to assess their interplay, to appreciate how they constitute alternative aspects of the one process.

It is significant that inclusive discourses on Aboriginality have proliferated in Australian state practice in concert with the development of pluralist or multiculturalist strategies for assimilating the (in Anglo-Celtic terms) heterogeneous waves of migrants who have succeeded each other since World War Two. Just as the nation-state which assimilated Aborigines was a different society from the settled colony which had introduced reservations (which was different again from the invading parties that had prepared the way for settlement), so did the ethnically diverse society in which the policy of Aboriginal self-determination was introduced differ from the overwhelmingly Anglo-Celtic fragment which had first resorted to assimilationism.[225] In constructing new Aboriginalities, white Australia has reconstructed itself. But the question remains as to whether these shifts are of a comparable order. Should we see the shift to multiculturalism as being commensurate with that to nation-statehood? So far as Aboriginal policy is concerned, it is clear that we should not. For, given a differentiated polity, to differentiate is to assimilate. In other words, what has changed is not the assimilationism but the ethnic profile of that whose mimicry constitutes assimilation – assimilation just looks different. As argued above, colour (to which can be added ethnicity, language, religion, etc.) constitute second-order differentiators which are categorically subordinate to the primary historical relationship of invasion that distinguishes Indigenous from settler.

Despite arguing that an empirical or prediscursive binarism (the relation of invasion) should be recuperated, I have critiqued the binary structure (excluded middle) of repressive authenticity. Thus the issue of binarism needs to be clarified.

The difference is ultimately one of scope. The Australian state acknowledged the binary relation of invasion in its native-title legislation. It sought to restrict the beneficiaries of this acknowledgement. To effect this restriction, it limited the category of native-title beneficiaries to those who could meet certain criteria for *un*invadedness. Rather than a change of heart, therefore, this formula entailed a ratification – even a redoubling – of the history of oppression, since it provided that *the more you have lost, the less you stand to*

---

[225] For overviews and examples of changing attitudes to immigration and assimilation, on which a vast amount has been written, see, e.g., Castles 1992, Easson 1990, Goot 1988, Lyng 1927, McAllister 1993, Yarwood 1964; 1968. For a useful bibliography on assimilation and integration up to 1979, see Price 1979: 38–43.

gain. To fall within native-title criteria, it is necessary to fall outside history. In this light, the welfare 'track' of the twin-track strategy of inclusion/ exclusion signifies the state's refusal to recognize invasion as a structure rather than an event. Correspondingly, native title legislation represented an agreement to relent rather than to compensate – which is to say, an agreement (however qualified) to allow history not to start.

The realm thus excused history is categorically external. This has a number of implications. Firstly, the complementarity between the discourses of inclusion and exclusion recalls that which was seen to obtain between the anthropological modes of autography and xenography. In both cases, projection and reimportation constitute alternate aspects of the same ideological movement. So far, we have only dealt with one half of this movement in relation to Australian state discourse – that projection outwards, or onto the margins, of an authentic Aboriginality whose separation from history de-authenticates empirical Indigenous people within, converting the historical structures of their invadedness into secular welfare problems. How, then, does the other half of this movement operate? How does the ethnographically constructed authentic Aboriginality of the margins become reimported into domestic discourse? Again, the answer relates to the construction of the nation-state.

It should, by now, be no surprise that the precontact stereotypes of repressive authenticity should figure on the money, postage stamps and related imprints of the settler-colonial state, even though that state is predicated on the elimination of those stereotypes' empirical counterparts. This is because, as Andrew Lattas (1990, 1991, 1992) and others have pointed out, in order to produce a narrative that can bind it transcendentally to its territorial base – to make it, as it were, spring organically from the local soil – the settler state is obliged to appropriate the symbolism of the very Aboriginality that it has historically effaced.[226] Hence, as in Michael Taussig's (1987) Putumayo grotesque, internal contradictions reduce the invader to seeking salvation from the dispossessed. In the Australian case, the dilemma of state-formation can be simply expressed, in local terms, as the problem of how to be a Clayton's Britain, a Britain under erasure that is simultaneously not-Britain.[227] It is the problem of the fragment: how to be British for the purpose of expropriating Australians and Australian for the purpose of independence from Britain? Solutions to this conundrum included symbolic juxtapositions whose absurdity pre-empted surrealism – regal insignia in which emus and kangaroos stood in for lions and unicorns, for example. The

---

226 In a different theoretical idiom, Nic Peterson (1990: 16) expressed much of this as follows: 'The success of the [assimilation] policy would end once and for all the chance to secure the insights Aboriginal societies and cultures could provide. With the [1960s] prosperity also went an increasing interest in Australian history and culture and a loosening of the ties with Britain which was to climax in the cultural and economic nationalism of the early 1970s . . . Aboriginal people and their cultures were a crucial icon of an independent Australian identity. But there was a firm preference for the schematic authority of normative accounts to the reality of the disorder and the poverty of many Aboriginal people's lives which gave the lie to the success, or even the possibility, of an assimilation policy.'

227 Without disagreeing with Stuart Macintyre's summary observation (1986: 122) that 'The strength of the new nationalism was therefore undeniable but its meaning remained ambiguous', I would be inclined to exchange the 'but' for an 'and' – it was a positive, constitutive ambiguity, albeit demographically manifest as a spectrum of opinion.

serious underside to this symbolism is, however, that it suppresses the historical process of replacement. A human analogue to the heraldic kangaroo and emu is provided by the conspicuous inclusion in the architecture of Canberra's national parliament house of a Warlpiri totemic design, drawn up by a Western Desert artist, sanctioned by the ritual owners of the design and turned into a mosaic by Italian ceramicists.[228] Reportedly, the design's representation of serpents converging on a waterhole denotes a meeting place at the centre of things. Yet the Western Desert locale from which the design originates is some three thousand kilometres from Canberra, whilst those to whom such events are really central – the dispossessed Ngunawal[229] on whose country the national capital has been planted – go symbolically unregistered and can only manage a physical presence about the national capital (cf. Jackson-Nakano 1994). Thus the continuing dispossession (cum welfare-dependency) of historical Indigenous subjects is effaced by the valorization of an authenticated extrahistorical Aboriginality which, for its part, seals an eternal bond between the settler-colonial state and the land of the Ngunawal. Hence the romanticized indigenous stereotype simultaneously performs two vital ideological services – positively, it grounds the national narrative in the local soil; negatively, it effaces the disruptive counter-narrative embodied by the dispossessed.

This discussion clearly overlaps with Renato Rosaldo's influential analysis of what he termed 'imperialist nostalgia', that curious phenomenon whereby colonizing agencies often celebrate native society as it was before they came and destroyed it: 'Imperialist nostalgia revolves around a paradox: A person kills somebody, and then mourns the victim' (Rosaldo 1989: 69). Whether or not such behaviour is paradoxical, Rosaldo unaccountably leaves its analysis at that, frustrating us with the descriptiveness of his exposition. What the colonial nation-state nostalgicizes (solicits, appropriates, etc.) is *not*, of course, the precolonial indigene as this subject 'really was' – that would only conflict with the business of subjugating empirical natives. It is, rather, an imaginary precolonial subject who is no more than a fantasy that the colonizer entertains about himself, in which the colonized are discursively recruited to fulfil the colonizer's own ancestral wishes. This phylogenetic narrative, in which the colonized first figured as the colonizer's precursor but more recently came to share in a universal ancestry, constructs the colonizer as the legitimate heir and successor to the colonized. Colonialism does not appropriate a historical indigeneity; it replaces it with a conveniently mythical one of its own construction.[230] The condition of this replacement is precisely the elimination, or *dis*placement, of the empirical indigene within civilization.[231] For all his

---

228 For details and critiques, see, e.g. Lattas 1990, Weirick 1989.

229 I use Ngunawal rather than Indigenous here because of the need to specify a precise local affiliation in contradistinction to the Warlpiri/Western Desert one.

230 For a comparable analysis of the role played by archaeology and museology in constructing a Bolivian state which, though depending upon indigenous symbols, practically excludes empirical Indigenous people from the urban centres, see Condori 1989.

231 Or even, to take up a perceptive line of analysis being developed by Denise Cuthbert and Michele Grossman, *re*placing (Cuthbert and Grossman's term is 'trading places' with) the indigene, whereby the colonizer usurps 'the subject position of a mythically constructed, universalised "indigene", ejecting indigenous people themselves from modernity and from history – both their own and that of colonialism – twice over' (Cuthbert and Grossman 1996: 20).

descriptive insight, Rosaldo missed how the displacement of empirical natives is simultaneously the production of colonial citizen-subjects (during the official era of assimilation, for example, it is not the case that abducted Indigenous people were not produced as subjects, merely that they were not produced as *Aboriginal* subjects). It is, therefore, necessary to go beyond description, which, in this case, involves attending to the material social effects of settler-colonial nostalgia.

When authentic Aboriginality is imported back into domestic discourse, it loses not only its history but its territorial specificity as well, surrendering both to the homogeneous space/time continuum of the nation-state (cf. Beckett 1988). In the process, it yields a distinctive national narrative that is simultaneously both European and autochthonous, both invasive and native (the Australian Natives Association is definitely not an Indigenous club). In this light, the concession to Aboriginality contained in repressive authenticity makes further sense, since the discourse yields the state its specific residue. Authentic Aborigines and the Australian state construct each other.

This concession provides a key to the binarisms. As a *concession*, there is nothing specifically binary about it. It simply represents a cut-off point, a strategic resolution as to the limit within which heteronomy will be tolerated. Thus there is no point in attacking the binarism *per se*, since this cannot affect the primary issue of the scope of the concession (i.e. its narrowness). If, on the other hand, ignoring the binarism, we attack the *scope* of state discourses on Aboriginality – if, in particular, we insist on history – then a whole range of *specifically Aboriginal* determinations (e.g. child abduction on racial grounds) springs into discourse. To do this, we have to demonstrate that invasion is a structure rather than an event; that expropriation continues as a foundational characteristic of settler-colonial society.

Thus the reason for what might otherwise seem an incoherent insistence on both critiquing an ideological binarism and recuperating an empirical one is that the ideological binarism misrepresents not the structure but the scope of the empirical (which is to say, historical) one. At this point, the theoretical inadequacy of the term 'empirical' becomes inescapable. This is because, precisely by being binarily structured, the state ideology derives much of its force from its resonance with historical reality. This resonance makes it much more potent than a groundless illusion. Thus it could be misleading to counterpose ideological and empirical binarisms since, to this extent, both are empirical. Again, therefore, 'the battleground of repressive authenticity is that of Indigenous "post"colonial identities, which strive to historicise the mythical duality that the discourse proclaims' – historicize, rather than subvert, narrow or pluralize, which would simply be to fall for multiculturalism.

Since the discourses of inclusion and exclusion are mutually supplementary aspects of Australian state strategy, contestation of the Aboriginalities that they construct and promulgate goes on within the arena of state discourse. It concerns the imagery, domain and scope of state-conceded Aboriginalities. Indigenous people can exploit the contradictions of assimilationism by contesting within this arena (succeeding, for instance, in having an element of cultural sensitivity inserted into police procedures). My counterposing of an 'empirical/welfare' Aboriginality to an 'ideal/authentic' one is also staged within this public arena, being intended to contest a set of subject-positions that are discursively produced and given practical social form through the routine material workings of certain state bureaucratic and other institutional apparatuses. This proviso is important because it means that the analysis does not claim to encompass an Indigenous residue. Contestation of state-constructed Aboriginalities ('traditional owner', 'welfare case', etc.) goes on *within* state discourse and does *not* address an opposition between 'public' and 'private' Aboriginalities (cf. Weaver 1984). On the contrary, both state constructions are categorically public and produced by specific apparatuses (particular ministries, departments, commissions, etc.). Whatever may be the nature(s) of the specific residue(s) that provide Indigenous people with bases for resistance (a matter on which I have nothing to say), these bases should be distinguished from resources (in the form, say, of discursive contradictions) that Indigenous people may or may not exploit in the realm of Australian state discourse.

The importance of the above proviso is that, given the analysis of the central role that imposed definitions of Aboriginality have played in the Australian state's attempts to eliminate Indigenous people, it would discredit – indeed, invalidate – my position if my own analysis were itself to dispense a definition of Aboriginality, yet another normative subject-position for Indigenous people to be contained in. To this it may be objected that, in replacing one external or essential determination of Aboriginality (colour, genetic status, etc.) with another (invadedness) this analysis has fallen into the same trap. But I am not stipulating that Indigenous people's collective sense of identity is contingent on their sharing a sense of invadedness (and, presumably, acting on it). To repeat, I have nothing to say about what makes people Indigenous to themselves or to other Indigenous people. What I have tried to do is foreground the historical fact that Australian state discourse is principally structured to repress. As a critique of state discourse, the analysis only deals with Aboriginal people as constructed and/or appropriated (as in the case of the Western Desert artist) by that discourse. It makes no attempt to pursue them into areas of their lives that exceed such constructions. This procedure is altogether different from the invasive practice of prescribing proxy Aboriginalities, however gratifyingly oppositional these may seem.[232]

This is not to say that repressive authenticity is a one-way street. As Foucault taught us, modalities of power generate their own resistance. Thus Indigenous people can strategically acquiesce in repressive authenticity to achieve local goals. As functionalist anthropology taught us, though, the obvious danger with this is that, in generating its own resistance, settler-colonial power also contains it. The symptoms of this containment are plain to see in Indigenous communities that are being divided into groups whom white anthropologists and lawyers have chosen as likely candidates for native

---

[232] Though our politics otherwise differ substantially, I endorse Adam Kuper's (1994) denunciation of the inconsistency (hypocrisy?) of those who argue that ethnographers should not appropriate native voices unless they are saying what the ethnographer feels they should be saying.

title and those whom they have excluded from this reckoning. At first sight, it might seem reasonable to distinguish between the two groups along lines akin to Lyotard's (1988) distinction between the plaintiff and the victim, according to which the plaintiff's grievance is formally prescribed whilst that of the victim is discursively inexpressible. For our purposes, however, it would be a mistake to see plaintiffs and victims as different people. The set of victims includes that of plaintiffs – as members of Indigenous communities, they are commonly subject to a single divisive strategy.

Native title does not inhere in Indigenous people because the Australian government deigned to concede it to them. On the contrary, their title predates and is independent of the institutions that Europeans brought to Australia. Thus native title is not a national but an international issue, one whose dispensation exceeds the authority of an Australian government.[233] To resist the attenuation of native title that the Australian government's *Native Title Act* seeks to effect, therefore, it is necessary (amongst other things) to situate Australian institutions in the globalized international context rather than accepting them as providing the boundaries of dispute. This is a broadly ideological as much as a formally legal undertaking. Indigenous people constitute a small demographic minority. As indicated at the outset, the anticolonial resources at their disposal are exclusively ideological, since, even if they wished to adopt them, neither violence nor the wholesale withdrawal of their labour would be promising options. The most potent ideological force available to Indigenous people is international opinion, to which Australian governments have consistently shown themselves to be acutely sensitive – as well they might, given their geographical location as a European colonial enclave deep in the postcolonial Pacific.[234] In the current context, this vulnerability obtains at a particularly enabling moment, since the next Olympic Games are to be held in Sydney. If the past few decades are anything to go by, the ideological uses to which Indigenous people put the Games and other international forums could prove transformative.

My intention is not, however, to comment on current affairs, for which it would be hard to find poorer means than a book. It is, rather, to establish the deep historical framework within which the ongoing contest over Australian settler-colonialism continues to be conducted. Since I first ventured the general perspective that I am developing here (Wolfe 1994), many superficial changes have taken place, in particular the election of the Howard government and its campaign against the Wik judgement. Yet such developments make it easier for my argument, which is most pressed to accommodate the subtler manifestations of the logic of elimination. As an attempt to convert pastoral leases, which account for more than 40 per cent of the Australian land mass, into something equivalent to freehold ownership

---

233 The Australian High Court would seem to have acknowledged this in its 1978 ruling in *Coe v. The Commonwealth*, in which it held that it was beyond its powers to consider the constitutional basis from which it derived its own authority. This, at least, is how I read Mr Justice Mason's statement that 'In so far as the plaintiff's case as pleaded rests on a claim of continuing sovereignty in the aboriginal people it is plainly unarguable. It is inconsistent with the accepted legal foundations of Australia deriving from British occupation and settlement . . . Whatever that Advisory Opinion [of the International Court of Justice] may say it has no relevance to the domestic or municipal law of Australia based on *the Constitution which this Court is bound to apply*' (Mason 1978: 336, my emphasis).

234 This is not, of course, to overlook the fact that Tonga has never been formally colonized.

of what is currently classified as Crown land, for instance, the Howard government's campaign against Wik represents a land-grab whose speed and comprehensiveness would have flabbergasted the most rapacious of nineteenth-century squatters. Clearly, my analysis encounters no difficulty in accommodating such returns to the cruder policies of the past. More controversially, though, it does not hold out native title as unproblematic.[235] Thus it looks beyond the return of a Labor government or some change of heart (or leader) on the part of the current government to a fundamental renegotiation of the Indigenous/settler relationship, one that will start from a recognition of the historical continuity of the logic of elimination. For it is only on the basis of such a recognition that the two issues that dominate relations between Indigenous people and the Australian state – the issues of native title and of the so-called 'stolen children' – can be properly addressed, not as separate issues but as related aspects of a historical programme that has consistently sought to eliminate actual Indigenous people (as opposed to symbolic stereotypes) from the settler-colonial polity. To start anywhere else would be to misrepresent history – and, accordingly, to condemn future generations to the continuing national curse of the Aboriginal (which is to say, the Australian) problem.

None of this means that the retaining of native title, where this occurs, cannot represent a significant Indigenous gain. It does, however, mean that legislating for native title constitutes a state strategy for containing Indigenous resistance. It is important to keep the two perspectives separate. As stated, my purpose is to categorize colonizing strategies employed in Australia. It is not to categorize Indigenous strategies of resistance, survival or anything else. The failure to distinguish between the two perspectives recapitulates assimilationism. Accordingly, though it is no doubt the case that, over the past thirty or so years, new modes of Indigenous renewal have set in, this does not warrant a shift of focus from Australian state discourse to Indigenous discourses. To do so would be to deny the fact that Indigenous resistance has been a constant feature of the entire settler-colonial era. It would also be to promulgate a *de facto* assimilation which, by ratifying the deceptive philanthropy of official rhetoric, obscures the underlying continuity of the logic of elimination. In the absence of a credible treaty, Indigenous and settler-colonial discourses remain distinct. This means that, just as Indigenous 'renewal' should be traced backwards through a continuous history of Indigenous resistance, so should the assimilation policy be traced forwards through the continuing history of Australian settler colonialism.

— * —

[235] Whilst this book was in press, the Australian parliament passed the Native Title Amendment Act, which further tightens the criteria for Native Title that, as observed, makes it easier for my argument. Moreover, in stark contrast to the Australian Labor Party's co-option of selected Aborigines into the process that produced the original Native Title Act, the Howard government excluded Aborigines from the consultations that led up to the Native Title Amendment Act. Tactically, this seems astonishingly inept, since it means that Aboriginal people cannot be held to have acquiesced in the alienation of their rights, a consideration that has clear implications for international law. To this extent, the Labor Party's subtler policy was much more insidious and potentially disabling.

So far as nescience is concerned, the shift from its negative to its positive readings encompasses the twentieth century. Negatively, as a primal ignorance that was more fragile than any other item in the salvage inventory, nescience signified a savagery which, in being both abased and vanishing, perfectly harmonized with the conquering epistemology of the expanding colonial frontier. Read positively, in the impeccable ambience of late twentieth-century liberal correctness, spirit-conception hallmarks an official romance that effaces the empirical presence of the dispossessed.

However much we may dislike evolutionary anthropology's account of how it came to be that Europeans should be the ones who practised anthropology, at least evolutionary anthropology offered such an account. It was not blind to the conditions of its own possibility. To return to where we started, settler colonialism makes positionality inescapable. Even if we set aside the closure of the anthropological soliloquy whose fabrication we have been examining, the very relationship between academic and Indigenous knowledges is structured by a political version of the uncertainty principle. Writing two buildings down from where Baldwin Spencer wrote (though anywhere within the Australian academy would do), I have no grounds for claiming a personal exemption from the effects of an invasive discourse which, not satisfied with territory, hurries on into the inner being. Academic knowledge about Aboriginal knowledge can never be innocent. It is too deeply enmeshed in a historical relationship through which one's power is the other's disempowerment. From the outset, authoritative pronouncements on Aboriginal mentalities have been central to the expropriation of Indigenous people – *terra nullius* was, after all, a discourse on rationality. Good intentions cannot absolve me from this legacy. The road to oppression has consistently been paved with good intentions (read, for instance, Spencer's fateful statement [1913: 21] advocating the Australian state's abduction of Indigenous children, which evinces a clear concern for the children's welfare). Nor could I seek amnesty on methodological grounds (e.g. that mine is an interpretivist – as opposed to a positivist or evolutionist – approach) since the issue is a relationship rather than its modes. A refusal to acknowledge this relationship underlies a blossoming academic industry devoted to the analysis of Aboriginal cultural production. The fluidity of the category 'cultural production' is particularly insidious in this regard since, by means of the self-righteous posture of not privileging literary discourse, it enables the academy to claim the deepest recesses of Aboriginal life for its unblinking gaze. In this way, the linguistic turn becomes a key invasive strategy. This is not to rehearse the old charge of idealism. The point is, rather, the panopticism whereby nothing can escape being turned into a text for the analyst to appropriate, interrogate and reconstruct. In this hegemonic communicational economy, all use-values become exchange-values. Silence constitutes consent. The outcome is an ethnographic ventriloquism whereby invaded subjects are made to speak unawares, in contexts in which they could reasonably believe they were doing something else. A cigar is never just a cigar for the model of the text.

My position has clear implications for the current liberal preoccupation with writing in the agency of the subaltern. A question that generally goes resoundingly unasked in this connection is, Writing into what? In the settler-colonial context, the question answers itself: the ideal of writing in agency is a contradiction in terms. To write in is to contain within discourse. This is a function of the relationships involved and obtains irrespective of content. It follows, therefore, that what needs to be written in is not the agency of the colonized but the total context of inscription. This, it seems to me, is an anthropological agenda.

References

Ackerman, R. (1987) *J.G. Frazer: His Life and Work* (Cambridge: Cambridge University Press).

Albritton, C.C., Jr (1980) *The Abyss of Time: Changing Conceptions of the Earth's Antiquity after the Sixteenth Century* (San Francisco: Freeman, Cooper).

Allen, D.E. (1976) *The Naturalist in Britain: A Social History* (London: Allen Lane).

Allen, D.E. (1979) 'The lost limb: geology and natural history', in L.J. Jordanova and R.S. Porter (eds), *Images of the Earth: Essays in the History of the Environmental Sciences* (Chalfont St Giles: British Society for the History of Science), pp. 200–12.

Allen, L. (1975) *Time Before Morning: Art and Myth of the Australian Aborigines* (New York: Crowell).

Anderson, B. (1983) *Imagined Communities: The Origin and Spread of Nationalism* (London: Verso).

Anderson, I. (1988) *Koorie Health in Koorie Hands* (Melbourne: Koorie Health Unit).

Anderson, P. (1987) 'The figures of descent', *New Left Review*, 61, 20–77.

Asad, T. (ed.) (1973) *Anthropology and the Colonial Encounter* (London: Ithaca Press).

Asad, T. (1979) 'Anthropology and the analysis of ideology', *Man* (n.s.), 14, 607–27.

Asad, T. (1991) 'Afterword: from the history of colonial anthropology to the anthropology of Western hegemony', in Stocking (1991), pp. 314–24.

Ashley-Montagu, A.M.F. (1937) *Coming Into Being Among the Australian Aborigines: A Study of the Procreative Beliefs of the Native Tribes of Australia* (London: Routledge).

Atkinson, J.J. (1903) *Primal Law* (incorporated in Lang 1903, pp. 209–93).

Attwood, B. (1989) *The Making of the Aborigines* (Sydney: Allen & Unwin).

Attwood, B. and Markus, A. (1997) *The 1967 Referendum, or When Aborigines Didn't Get the Vote* (Canberra: Australian Institute of Aboriginal and Torres Strait Islander Studies).

Bachelard, G. (1934) [1984] *Le nouvel Ésprit scientifique* (Paris: Presses Universitaires de France), *The New Scientific Spirit* (H. Goldhammer tr.) (Boston: Beacon).

Bachofen, J.J. (1861) [1969] *Das Mutterrecht: Eine Unterschung über die Gynaikokratie der alten Welt nach ihrer religiösen und rechlichen Natur* (Brussels: Culture and Civilisation).

Bachofen, J.J. (1967a) *Myth, Religion and Mother Right: Selected Writings of J.J. Bachofen* (R. Manheim tr., R. Marx ed.) (Princeton: Princeton University Press).

Bachofen, J.J. (1967b) 'Mother Right: an investigation of the religious and juridical character of matriarchy in the ancient world', in Bachofen (1967a), pp. 67–207.

Banaji, J. (1970) 'The crisis of British anthropology', *New Left Review*, 64, 71–85.

Bandler, F. (1989) *Turning the Tide: A Personal History of the Federal Council for the Advancement of Aborigines and Torres Strait Islanders* (Canberra: Aboriginal Studies Press).

Banta, M. and Hinsley, C.M. (1986) *From Site to Sight: Anthropology, Photography and the Power of Images* (Cambridge, MA: Peabody Museum Press, distributed by Harvard University Press).

Barbosa, D. (1563) [1921] *The Book of Duarte Barbosa: An Account of the Countries Bordering on the Indian Ocean and their Inhabitants, written by Duarte Barbosa, and completed about the year 1518 A.D.* (tr. from 1812 Portuguese text by M.L. Dames) (vol. 1, 1918) (London: The Hakluyt Society).

Barnes, B. and Shapin, S. (1979) *Natural Order: Historical Studies of Scientific Culture* (London: Sage).

Barnes, J.A. (1973) 'Genetrix:Genitor:Nature:Culture?' in J. Goody (ed.), *The Character of Kinship* (Cambridge: Cambridge University Press), pp. 61–74.

Barnett, H.G. (1956) *Anthropology in Administration* (New York: Row, Peterson).

Barnett, S.A. (ed.) (1962) *A Century of Darwin* (London: Mercury).

Barraclough, G. (1967) *An Introduction to Contemporary History* (Harmondsworth: Penguin).

Barraclough, G. (1979) *Turning Points in World History* (London: Thames & Hudson).

Barthes, R. (1977) 'Rhetoric of the image' in his *Image-Music-Text* (S. Heath, tr.) (Glasgow: Fontana/Collins, pp. 32–51).

Bartholomew, M. (1979) 'The singularity of Lyell', *History of Science*, 17, 276–93.

Bartra, R. (1992) *The Cage of Melancholy: Identity and Metamorphosis in the Mexican Character* (New Brunswick, NJ: Rutgers University Press).

Barwick, D.E. (1962) 'Economic absorption without assimilation? the case of some Melbourne Part-Aboriginal families', *Oceania*, 33, 18–23.

Barwick, D.E. (1972) 'Coranderrk and Coomooragunja: Pioneers and Policy', in T.S. Epstein and D. Penny (eds), *Opportunity and Response* (London: Hurst), pp. 11–68.

Basedow, H. (1925) *The Australian Aboriginal* (Adelaide: F.W. Preece).

Bastian, A. (1868) *Beiträge zur Vergleichenden Psychologie: Die Seele und ihre Erscheinungsweisen in der Ethnographie* (Berlin: Ferd. Dümmler).

Bates, D. (1906) 'The marriage laws and some customs of the West Australian Aborigines', *Victorian Geographical Journal*, 23–4, 36–60.

Bates, D. (1938) [1966] *The Passing of the Aborigines: A Lifetime Spent among the Natives of Australia* (London: John Murray).

Bates, D. (1985) *The Native Tribes of Western Australia* (I. White, ed.) (Canberra: National Library of Australia).

Bradford, P.V. and H. Blume (1992) *Ota: The Pygmy in the Zoo* (New York: St Martin's Press).

Baumgarten, W. (1980) *Imperialism: The Idea and Reality of British and French Colonial Expansion, 1880–1914* (Oxford: Oxford University Press).

Beaglehole, J.C. (ed.) (1955) *The Journals of Captain James Cook*, vol. 1 (London: Cambridge University Press).

Beaglehole, J.C. (1961) *The Journals of Captain James Cook*, vol. 2 (London: Cambridge University Press).

Beale, H. (1962) '"After the Dreaming Time": the story of the economic development of Australia' (pamphlet) (New York: Newcomer Society).

Beattie, J. (1964) *Other Cultures: Aims, Methods and Achievements in Social Anthropology* (London: Cohen & West).

Beatty, B. (1962) *Early Australia: With Shame Remembered* (Melbourne: Cassell).

Beckett, J. (1958) 'Marginal men: a study of two half caste Aborigines', in *Oceania*, 29, 91–108.

Beckett, J. (1977) 'The Torres Strait Islanders and the pearling industry: a case of internal colonialism', *Aboriginal History*, 1, 77–104.

Beckett, J. (1987) *Torres Strait Islanders: Custom and Colonialism* (Sydney: Cambridge University Press).

Beckett, J. (1988) 'The past in the present: the present in the past: constructing a national Aboriginality', in his (ed.) *Past and Present: The Construction of Aboriginality* (Canberra: Aboriginal Studies Press), pp. 191–217.

Beckett, J. (1989) 'Aboriginality in a nation-state: the Australian case', in M.C. Howard (ed.), *Ethnicity and Nation – Building in the Pacific* (Tokyo: United Nations University), pp. 118–35.

Beidelmann, T.O. (1974) *W. Robertson Smith and the Sociological Study of Religion* (Chicago: University of Chicago Press).

Bell, J.H. (1956) 'The economic life of mixed-blood Aborigines on the South Coast of New South Wales', *Oceania*, 26, 181–99.

Ben-David, J. and Collins, R. (1966) 'Social fathers in the origins of a new science: the case of psychology', *American Sociological Review*, 31, 451–65.

Bennett, S. (1989) *Aborigines and Political Power* (Sydney: Allen & Unwin).

Bentley, M. (1984) *Politics Without Democracy, 1815–1914: Perception and Preoccupation in British Government* (London: Fontana).

Benyon, J. (1991) 'Overlords of Empire? British 'proconsular imperialism' in comparative perspective', *Journal of Imperial and Commonwealth History*, 19, 164–202.

Berdahl, R.O. (1959) *British Universities and the State* (Berkeley: University of California Press).

Berkhofer, R.J., Jr (1978) *The White Man's Indian: Images of the American Indian from Columbus to the Present* (New York: Knopf).

Berndt, R.M. (1951) *Kunapipi* (Melbourne: Chesire).

Berndt, R.M. (1974) *Australian Aboriginal Religion* (Leiden: Brill).

Berndt, R.M. (1979) 'Obituary: T.G.H. Strehlow, 1908–1978', *Oceania*, 49, 230–3.

Berndt, R.M. (1987) 'The Dreaming', *Encyclopedia of Religion* (M. Eliade, ed.), vol. 4: 479–81 (New York: Macmillan).

Berndt, R.M. and Berndt, C.H. (1946) 'Review' of G. Roheim, *Eternal Ones of the Dream*. *Oceania*, 17, 67–8.

Berndt, R.M. and Berndt, C.H. (1987) *End of an Era: Aboriginal Labour in the Northern Territory* (Canberra: Australian Institute of Aboriginal Studies).

Berreman, G.D. (1968) 'Is anthropology alive? social responsibility in anthropology', *Current Anthropology*, 9, 391–8.

Berzins, B. (1988) *The Coming of the Strangers: Life in Australia 1788–1922* (Sydney: Collins Australia).

Bhabha, H. (1986) 'Of mimicry and man: the ambivalence of colonial discourse', in J. Donald and S. Hall (eds), *Politics and Ideology* (Milton Keynes: Open University Press), pp. 198–205.

Birdsell, J.B. (1953) 'Some environmental and cultural factors influencing the structuring of Australian Aboriginal populations', *American Naturalist*, 87, 171–207.

Birdsell, J.B. (1969) 'Ecology, spacing mechanisms and adaptive behaviour in Australian Aboriginal land tenure', in R. Crocombe (ed.), *Land Tenure in the South Pacific* (Oxford: Oxford University Press).

Birdsell, J.B. (1970) 'Local group composition among the Australian Aborigines: a critique of the evidence from fieldwork conducted since 1930', *Current Anthropology*, 2, 115–42.

Bischofs, J. (1908) 'Die Niol-Niol, ein eingeborenstamm in Nordwest-Australien', *Anthropos*, 3, 32–40.

Biskup, P. (1982) 'Aboriginal history', in G. Osborne and W.F. Mandle (eds), *New History: Studying History Today* (Sydney: Allen & Unwin), pp. 11–31.

Blackburn, J. (1971) *Milirrpum and Others vs. Nabalco Pty Ltd. and the Commonwealth of Australia*, *Australian Federal Law Reports*, 17, 141–294.

Blackstone, W. (1783) [1978] *Commentaries on the Law of England* (9th edn) (Facsimile) (New York: Garland Publishing).

Blainey, G. (1975) *Triumph of the Nomads: A History of Ancient Australia* (South Melbourne: Macmillan).

Bleakley, J.W. (1929) *The Aboriginals and Half-Castes of Central Australia and North Australia. Report (1928). Commonwealth of Australia Parliamentary Papers*, 1929, vol. 2, pt. 1: 1159–1225.

Bleakley, J.W. (1961) *The Aboriginals of Australia: Their History, Their Habits, Their Assimilation* (Brisbane: Jacaranda).

Bloch, M. (1974) 'Symbols, song, dance and features of articulation', *Archives Européennes de Sociologie*, 15, 55–81.

Bloch, M. (1975) 'Introduction' to his *Political Language and Oratory in Traditional Society* (New York: Academic Press).

Bloch, M. (1977) 'The past and the present in the present', *Man* (n.s.), 12, 278–92.

Blumenbach, J.F. (1865) *The Anthropological Treatises of Johann Friedrich Blumenbach, with memoirs of him by Marx and Flourens, and an account of his anthropological museum by Professor R. Wagner, and the inaugural Dissertation of John Hunter, M.D., on the Varieties of Man* (tr. & ed. T. Bendyshe) (London: Longman, Green, Longman, Roberts & Green).

Boas, F. (1897) 'The social organization and the secret societies of the Kwakiutl Indians', *Report of the U.S. National Museum for 1895* (Washington, DC).

Boas, G. (1948) *Essays on Primitivism and Related Ideas in the Middle Ages* (Baltimore: Johns Hopkins University Press).

Boime, A. (1990) *The Art of Exclusion: Representing Blacks in the Nineteenth Century* (New York: Thames & Hudson).

Boorse, H.A., Motz, L. and Weaver, J.H. (1989) *The Atomic Scientists: A Biographical History* (New York: Wiley Science).

Boorstin, D.J. (1984) *The Discoverers* (London: Dent).

Bourdieu, P. (1963) 'The attitude of the Algerian peasant towards time', *Mediterranean Countryman*, 6, 55–72.

Bourdieu, P. (1986) *Distinction: A Social Critique of the Judgement of Taste* (R. Nice tr.) (London: Routledge & Kegan Paul).

Boyce, D.G. (1988) *The Irish Question and British Politics, 1868–1986* (London: Macmillan).

Brewer, A. (1990) *Marxist Theories of Imperialism: A Critical Survey* (London: Routledge and Kegan Paul).

Bridges, B. (1970) 'The Aborigines and the land question: New South Wales in the period of imperial responsibility', *Journal of the Royal Australian Historical Society*, 56: 2, 92–110.

Briffault, R. (1927) *The Mothers: A Study of the Origins of Sentiments and Institutions* (3 vols), vol. 1 (London: Allen & Unwin).

Brock, P. and Kartinyeri, D. (1989) *Poonindie: The Rise and Destruction of an Aboriginal Agricultural Community* (Adelaide: Government Printer).

Brook, J. and Kohen, J.L. (1991) *The Parramatta Native Institution and the Black Town: A History* (Kensington, NSW: University of New South Wales Press).

Broome, R. (1982) *Aboriginal Australians: Black Responses to White Dominance, 1788–1980* (Sydney: Allen & Unwin).

Brown, H.P. (1983) *The Origins of Trade Union Power* (Oxford: Clarendon).

Brown, K.D. (1982) *The English Labour Movement, 1700–1951* (Dublin: Gill & MacMillan).

Bruce, C., Comstock, E. and McDonald, F. (1982) *Eugen von Guerard, 1811–1901: A German Romantic in the Antipodes* (Martinborough, NZ: Alister Taylor).

Brunton, R. (1991) 'Aborigines and environmental myths: apocalypse in Kakadu' (Canberra: Institute of Public Affairs).

Buchanan, F. (1807) *A Journey from Madras through the Countries of Mysore, Canara and Malabar, performed under the orders of the Most Noble the Marquis Wellesley, Governor General of India, for the express purpose of investigating the state of Agriculture, Arts and Commerce; the Religion, Manners and Customs; the History, Natural and Civil, and Antiquities, in the Dominion of the Rajah of Mysore, and the Countries Acquired by the Honourable East India Company, in the Late and Former Wars, from Tipoo Sultaun.* (3 vols) (London: Cadell & Davies; Black, Parry and Kingsbury).

Buffon, Comte de (1812) *Natural History, General and Particular. Vol. 3: The History of Man and Quadrupeds* (W. Smellie tr., W. Wood ed.) (London: Cadell & Davies).

Burchfield, J.D. (1975) *Lord Kelvin and the Age of the Earth* (London: Macmillan/Science History Publications).

Burgmann, M. (1983) 'Aborigines: the struggle continues', in R. Lucy (ed.) *The Pieces of Politics* (Melbourne: Macmillan), pp. 299–310.

Burgmann, V. (1993) *Power and Protest: Movements for Change in Australian Society* (Sydney: Allen & Unwin).

Burke, J.G. (1972) 'The wild man's pedigree: scientific method and racial anthropology', in E. Dudley and M.E. Novak (eds), *The Wild Man Within: An Image in Western Thought from the Renaissance to Romanticism* (Pittsburgh: University of Pittsburgh Press), pp. 259–80.

Burrow, J.W. (1966) *Evolution and Society: A Study in Victorian Social Theory* (Cambridge: Cambridge University Press).

Burrow, J.W. (1981) *A Liberal Descent: Victorian Historians and the English Past* (Cambridge: Cambridge University Press).

Butler, S. (1872) *Erewhon or Over the Range* (London: Trübner).

Butlin, N.G. (1983) *Our Original Aggression: Aboriginal Populations of Southeastern Australia, 1788–1850* (Sydney: Allen & Unwin).

Butlin, N.G. (1985) 'Macassans and Aboriginal smallpox: the '1788' and '1829' epidemics', *Historical Studies* (Melbourne), 21: 84, 315–35.

Butlin, N.G. (1993) *Economics and the Dreamtime: A Hypothetical History* (New York: Cambridge University Press).

Bynum, W.F. (1975) 'The great chain of being after 400 years: an appraisal', *History of Science* 13, 1–28.

Cabral, A. (1973) *Return to the Source: Selected Writings of Amil Cabral* (New York: Monthly Review Press).

Caine, B. (1992) *Victorian Feminists* (Oxford: Oxford University Press).

Calley, M. (1956) 'Economic life of mixed-blood communities in Northern New South Wales', *Oceania*, 26, 200–13.

Calley, M. (1957) 'Race relations on the North Coast of New South Wales', *Oceania*, 27, 190–209.

Cameron, A.L.P. (1885) 'Notes on some tribes of New South Wales', *Journal of the Anthropological Institute*, 14, 344–70.

Campbell, J. (1983) 'Smallpox in Aboriginal Australia 1829–31', *Historical Studies* (Melbourne), 20, 536–56.

Campbell, J. (1985) 'Smallpox in Aboriginal Australia: the early 1830s', *Historical Studies* (Melbourne), 21, 336–57.

Canny, N.P. and Pagden, A. (eds) (1987) *Colonial Identity in the Atlantic World, 1500–1800* (Princeton, NJ: Institute for Advanced Study).

Carrère d'Encausse, H. and Schram, S. (1969) *Marxism and Asia: An Introduction with Readings* (London: Allen Lane).

Carter, P. (1987) *The Road to Botany Bay: An Essay in Spatial History* (London: Faber & Faber).

Castles, S. (1992) 'Australian multiculturalism: social policy and identity in a changing society', in G.P. Freeman and J. Jupp (eds), *Nations of Immigrants: Australia, The United States and International Migration* (Melbourne: Oxford University Press), pp. 184–201.

Cell, John (1979) 'The imperial conscience', in P. Marsh (ed.), *The Conscience of the Victorian State* (New York: Syracuse University Press), pp. 173–213.

Chambers, R. (anon.) (1844) [1969] *Vestiges of the Natural History of Creation* (Leicester: Leicester University Press).

Chant, C. and Fauvel, J. (eds) (1980) *Darwin to Einstein: Historical Studies on Science and Belief* (London: Longman and The Open University Press).

Chesterman, J. and Galligan, B. (1997) *Citizens Without Rights: Aborigines and Australian Citizenship* (Melbourne: Cambridge University Press).

Christie, M.F. (1979) *Aborigines in Colonial Victoria, 1835–86* (Sydney: Sydney University Press).

Clanchy, M.T. (1979) *From Memory to Written Record* (London: Edward Arnold).

Clarke, T. and Galligan, B. (1995) '"Aboriginal Native" and the institutional construction of the Australian citizen, 1901–48', *Australian Historical Studies*, 26: 105, 523–43.

Clastres, P. (1988) 'On ethnocide' (J. Pefanis and B. Maher, tr.), *Art and Text*, 28, 50–8.

Clifford, J. (1987) 'Of other peoples: beyond the "salvage" paradigm', in M. Foster (ed.), *Discussions in Contemporary Culture* (no. 1) (Seattle: Bay Press), pp. 121–30.

Clifford, J. (1988) *The Predicament of Culture: Twentieth-Century Ethnography, Literature, and Art* (Cambridge, MA: Harvard University Press).

Clifford J. and Marcus, G.E. (1986) *Writing Culture: The Poetics and Politics of Ethnography* (Berkeley: University of California Press).

Clodd, E. (1885) *Myths and Dreams* (London: Chatto & Windus).

Cocks, P. (1995) 'The rhetoric of science and critique of imperialism in British social anthropology, c. 1870–1940', *History and Anthropology*, 9, 93–119.

Cole, C.W. (1933) 'The relativity of history', *Political Science Quarterly*, 8, 161–71.

Coleman, W. (1971) *Biology in the Nineteenth Century: Problems of Form, Function and Translation* (New York: Wiley).

Collins, S., Winch, D. and Burrow, J. (1983) *That Noble Science of Politics: A Study in*

Nineteenth-Century Intellectual History (Cambridge: Cambridge University Press).
Commonwealth of Australia (1937) *Aboriginal Welfare: Initial Conference of Commonwealth and State Aboriginal Authorities held at Canberra, 21st to 23rd April, 1937* (Canberra: Government Printer).
Commonwealth of Australia (1997) *Bringing Them Home* (Report of the National Inquiry into the Separation of Aboriginal and Torres Strait Islander Children from their Families) (Canberra: Commonwealth of Australia).
Comte, A. (1853) *The Positive Philosophy of Auguste Comte*. (H. Martineau, tr.) (2 vols) (London: John Chapman).
Condorcet, A.-N. de (1795) [1955] *Sketch for a Historical Picture of the Progress of the Human Mind* (London: Weidenfeld & Nicolson).
Condori, C.M. (1989) 'History and prehistory in Bolivia: what about the Indians?', in R. Layton (ed.), *Conflict in the Archaeology of Living Traditions* (London: Unwin Hayman), pp. 46–59.
Cook, S. (1974) 'Structural substantivism: a critical review of Sahlins' *Stone Age Economics*', *Comparative Studies in Society and History*, 16, 355–79.
Cooter, R. (1984) *The Cultural Meaning of Popular Science: Phrenology and the Organization of Consent in Nineteenth-century Britain* (Cambridge: Cambridge University Press).
Cope, E.D. (1887) *The Origin of the Fittest: Essays on Evolution* (New York: Appleton).
Coward, R. (1983) *Patriarchal Precedents: Sexuality and Social Relations* (London: Routledge & Kegan Paul).
Cowles, T. (1936) 'Malthus, Darwin and Bagehot: a study in the transference of a concept', *Isis*, 26, 341–8.
Cowlishaw, G. (1986a) 'Aborigines and anthropologists', *Australian Aboriginal Studies*, 1, 2–12.
Cowlishaw, G. (1986b) 'Colour, culture and the Aboriginalists', *Man*, (n.s.) 22, 221–37.
Cowlishaw, G. (1990) 'Helping anthropologists', *Canberra Anthropology*, 13: 2, 1–28.
Cowlishaw, G. (1992) 'Studying Aborigines: changing canons in anthropology and history', in B. Attwood and J. Arnold (eds), *Power, Knowledge and Aborigines* (special edn of the *Journal of Australian Studies*, no. 35), pp. 20–31.
Cox, M.R. (1893) *Cinderella: Three Hundred and Forty-five Variants of Cinderella, Catskin, and Cap O'Rushes, Abstracted and Tabulated, with a Discussion of Mediæval Analogues and Notes* (London: David Nutt).
Crawford, O.G.S. (1932) 'The dialectical process in the history of science', *Sociological Review*, 24, 165–73.
Creamer, H. (1988) 'Aboriginality in New South Wales: beyond the image of cultureless outcasts', in J. Beckett (ed.), *Past and Present: The Construction of Aboriginality* (Canberra: Aboriginal Studies Press), pp. 45–62.
Crease, R.P. and Mann, C.C. (1986) *The Second Creation: Makers of the Revolution in Twentieth-Century Physics* (New York: Macmillan).
Critchett, J. (1980) *Our Land Till We Die: A History of the Framlingham Aborigines* (Warrnambool: Warrnambool Institute Press).
Critchett, J. (1990) *A Distant Field of Murder: Western District Frontiers, 1834–1848* (Melbourne: Melbourne University Press).
Crosby, A.W. (1986) *Ecological Imperialism: The Biological Expansion of Europe, 900–1900* (Cambridge: Cambridge University Press).
Crow, W.B. (1968) *A History of Magic, Witchcraft and Occultism* (London: Aquarian Press).
Crowe, S.E. (1970) *The Berlin West African Conference, 1884–1885* (Westport, CT: Negro Universities Press).
Cummings, B. (1990) *Take This Child . . . From Kahlin Compound to the Retta Dixon Children's Home* (Canberra: Aboriginal Studies Press).
Cunow, H. (1897–98) *Die oekonomischen Grundlagen der Mutterherrschaft*. (*Die Neue Zeit*, 16, nos 4–8).
Cunow, H. (1912) *Zur Urgeschichte der Ehe und der Familie* (Ergänzungs heft zur *Neuen Zeit*, 14): Stuttgart.
Curr, E.M. (1886) *The Australian Race* (4 vols) (Melbourne: John Ferres, Government Printer).
Curthoys, A. (1982) 'Good Christians and useful workers: Aborigines, church and state in N.S.W., 1870–1883', in Sydney Labour History Group (ed.), *What Rough Beast?: The State and Social Order in Australian History* (Sydney: Allen & Unwin).
Cuthbert, D. and Grossman, M. (1996) 'Trading places: locating the indigenous in the new age', *Thamyris*, 3: 1, 18–36.
D'Ambrosio, U. (1992) 'For a new historiographical approach of [sic] the so-called "traditional knowledge"', in P. Petitjean, C. Jami and A.M. Moulin (eds), *Science and Empires: Historical Studies About Scientific Development and European Expansion* (Dordrecht: Kluwer).
Daniel, G. (1962) *The Idea of Prehistory* (London: Watts).
Daniel, G. (1976a) *A Hundred Years of Archaeology* (rev. edn) (London: Duckworth).
Daniel, G. (1976b) *Cambridge and the Back-Looking Curiosity* (Cambridge: Cambridge University Press).
Darwin, C. (1871) *The Descent of Man, and Selection in Relation to Sex* (2 vols) (London: John Murray).

Darwin, C. (1896) *The Descent of Man, and Selection in Relation to Sex* (2nd rev. edn) (London: John Murray).
Davies, N. (1996) *Europe: A History* (Oxford: Oxford University Press).
Davis, F.J. (1991) *Who Is Black? One Nation's Definition* (University Park: Pennsylvania State University Press).
de Brosses, C. (1760 [1989]) *Du Culte des Dieux fétiches, ou Parallèle de l'ancienne Religion d'Égypte avec la Religion actuelle de Nigritie* (Paris: Fayard).
Delaney, C. (1986) 'The meaning of paternity and the virgin birth debate', *Man*, (n.s.) 21, 494–513.
Descartes, R. (1642) [1954] *Philosophical Writings* (E. Anscombe and P.T. Geach, eds and trans.) (London: Nelson).
Desmond, A. (1982) *Archetypes and Ancestors: Palaeontology in Victorian London, 1850–1875* (Chicago: University of Chicago Press).
Desmond, A. and Moore, J. (1991) *Darwin* (London: Michael Joseph).
Dixon, R.M.W., Ramson, W.S. and Thomas, M. (1990) *Australian Aboriginal Words in English: Their Origin and Meaning* (Oxford: Oxford University Press).
Dominguez, V. (1994) *White By Definition: Social Classification in Creole Louisiana* (New Brunswick, NJ: Rutgers University Press).
Donnelly, M. (1983) *Managing the Mind: A Study of Medical Psychology in Early Nineteenth Century Britain* (London: Tavistock).
Drakakis-Smith, D. (1984) 'Advance Australia Fair: internal colonialism in the Antipodes', in D. Drakakis-Smith and S. Wyn Williams (eds), *Internal Colonialism: Essays Around a Theme* (London: Institute of British Geographers), pp. 81–103.
Dudley, E. and Novak, M.E. (eds) (1972) *The Wild Man Within: An Image in Western Thought from the Renaissance to Romanticism* (Pittsburgh: University of Pittsburgh Press).
Duerr, H.P. (1985) *Dreamtime: Concerning the Boundary Between Wilderness and Civilization* (F. Goodman, trans.) (Oxford: Blackwell).
Duncan, G. (1989) *Dying Inside* (Sydney: Allen & Unwin).
Durkheim, E. (1897) [1898] 'La prohibition de l'inceste et ses origines', *L'Année Sociologique*, 1, 1–70.
Durkheim, E. (1898) 'Revue' of Cunow (1897–1898), *Année Sociologique*, 2, 315–18.
Durkheim, E. (1900–01) 'Sur le totémisme', *L'Année Sociologique*, 5, 82–121.
Durkheim, E. (1912) *Les Formes Elémentaires de la Vie Religieuse: Le système totémique en Australie* (Paris: Alcan).
Easson, M. (ed.) (1990) *Australia and Immigration: Able to Grow?* (Lloyd Ross Forum Series no. 4) (Leichhardt, NSW: Pluto Press).

Eddington, A. (1920) *Space, Time and Gravitation: An Outline of the General Relativity Theory* (Cambridge: Cambridge University Press).
Eddy, J. and Schreuder, D. (eds) (1988) *The Rise of Colonial Nationalism: Australia, New Zealand, Canada and South Africa first assert their nationalities, 1880–1914* (Sydney: Allen & Unwin).
Eder, J.M. (1945) *History of Photography* (E. Epstean, tr.) (New York: Columbia University Press).
Edwards, C. and Read, P. (eds) (1989) *The Lost Children* (Sydney: Doubleday).
Eicher, D.L. (1968) *Geologic Time* (Englewood Cliffs, NJ: Prentice-Hall).
Elder, B. (1988) *Blood on the Wattle: Massacres and Maltreatment of Australian Aborigines since 1788* (Sydney: Child).
Eldridge, C. (1978) *Victorian Imperialism* (London: Hodder & Stoughton).
Eldridge, C. (ed.) (1984) *British Imperialism in the Nineteenth Century* (London: Macmillan).
Elkin, A.P. (1932) 'The secret life of the Australian Aborigines', *Oceania*, 3, 119–38.
Elkin, A.P. (1933) *Studies in Australian Totemism* (*Oceania* monograph no. 2) (Sydney: Oceania).
Elkin, A.P. (1937) 'Notes on the psychic life of the Australian Aborigines', *Mankind*, 2: 3, 49–56.
Elkin, A.P. (1944) *Citizenship for the Aborigines: A National Aboriginal Policy* (Sydney: Australasian Publishing).
Elkin, A.P. (1947) 'Introduction' in A.O. Neville, *Australia's Coloured Minority: Its Place in the Community* (Sydney: Currawong Publishing).
Elkin, A.P. (1951) 'Reaction and interaction: a food gathering people and European settlement in Australia', *American Anthropologist*, 53, 164–86.
Elkin, A.P. (1952) 'Review' of C. Simpson, *Adam in Ochre*. *Oceania*, 23, 243–44.
Elkin, A.P. (1956) 'A.R. Radcliffe-Brown, 1880–1955', *Oceania*, 26, 239–51.
Elkin, A.P. (1961) 'The Yabuduruwa', *Oceania*, 31, 166–209.
Elkin, A.P. (1964) *The Australian Aborigines: How to Understand Them* (4th edn) (Sydney: Angus & Robertson).
Elkin, A.P. (1975) 'R.H. Mathews: his contribution to Aboriginal studies', *Oceania*, 46, 1–24, 126–52, 206–34.
Elliott Smith, G., Malinowski, B., Spinden, H.J. and Goldenweiser, A. (1928) *Culture: The Diffusion Controversy* (London: Psyche Miniatures).
Engel, A.J. (1983) *From Clergyman to Don: The Rise of the Academic Profession in Nineteenth Century Oxford* (Oxford: Clarendon Press).
Engels, F. (1954) *Dialectics of Nature* (Moscow: Progress).

Ensor, R.C.K. (1936) *England 1870–1914* (Oxford: Clarendon Press).
Evans, I.B.N. (1939) *Man of Power: The Life Story of Baron Rutherford of Nelson, O.M., F.R.S.* (London: Stanley Paul).
Evans, R. (1984) '"Kings in brass crescents": defining Aboriginal labour patterns in Colonial Queensland', in K. Saunders (ed.), *Indentured Labour in the British Empire* (London: Croom Helm), pp. 183–212.
Evans-Pritchard, E.E. (1940) *The Nuer* (Oxford: Oxford University Press).
Eve, A.S. (1939) *Rutherford, Being the Life and Letters of the Rt. Hon. Lord Rutherford, O.M.* (Cambridge: Cambridge University Press).
Eyre, E.J. (1845) *Journals of Expeditions of Discovery into Central Australia, and Overland from Adelaide to King George's Sound, in the years 1840–1; sent by the Colonists to South Australia, with the Sanction and Support of the Government: Including an Account of the Manners and Customs of the Aborigines and the State of their Relations with Europeans* (2 vols) (London: T. & W. Boone).
Fabian, J. (1983) *Time and the Other: How Anthropology Makes Its Object* (New York: Columbia University Press).
Fanon, F. (1967) *The Wretched of the Earth* (Harmondsworth: Penguin).
Faris, J. (1973) 'Pax Britannica and the Sudan: S.F. Nadel', in Asad (1973), pp. 153–72.
Farrar, F.W. (1864) 'On the universality of belief in God, and in a future state', *Anthropological Review and Journal of the Anthropological Institute*, 2, ccxvii–ccxxii.
Feather, N. (1940) *Lord Rutherford* (London: Blackie).
Fee, E. (1974) 'The sexual politics of Victorian social anthropology', in M. Hartman and L. Banner (eds), *Clio's Consciousness Raised: New Perspectives on the History of Women* (New York: Harper & Row), pp. 86–102.
Feest, F.C. (ed.) (1987) *Indians and Europe* (Aachen: Edition Herodot, Rader Verlag).
Fels, M. (1988) *Good Men and True: The Aboriginal Police of the Port Phillip District 1837–1853* (Melbourne: Melbourne University Press).
Feuchtwang, S. (1973) 'The discipline and its sponsors', in Asad (1973), pp. 71–102.
Fink, R.A. (1957) 'The caste barrier: an obstacle to the assimilation of Part-Aborigines in North-West New South Wales', *Oceania*, 28, 100–10.
Firth, R. (1931) 'Anthropology and native administration', *Oceania*, 2, 1–8.
Fisher, J. (1968) *The Australians: From 1788 to Modern Times* (Adelaide: Rigby).
Fison, L. and Howitt, A. (1880) *Kamilaroi and Kurnai: Group-Marriage and Relationship, and Marriage by Elopement, Drawn directly from the Usage of the Australian Aborigines, also the Kurnai Tribe, their customs in Peace and War* (Melbourne: Geo. Robertson).

Fitzgerald, R. (1982) *From the Dreaming to 1915: A History of Queensland* (St. Lucia: University of Queensland Press).
Flewelling, R.T. (1934) 'A quantum view of history', *Personalist*, 15, 199–208.
Flood, J. (1983) *Archaeology of the Dreamtime* (Sydney: Collins).
Flugel, J.C. (1964) *A Hundred Years of Psychology, 1833–1933* (London: Duckworth).
Fontenelle, B. le B. de (1758) 'De l'origine des fables', in his *Oeuvres de M. de Fontenelle* (Paris: Brunet, 10 vols), 3, 270–96.
Forbes, J.D. (1988) *Black Africans and Native Americans: Color, Race and Caste in the Evolution of Red-Black Peoples* (Oxford: Blackwell).
Foster, M. and Lankester, E.R. (1898–1902) *The Scientific Memoirs of Thomas Henry Huxley* (4 vols) (London: Macmillan).
Foucault, M. (1967) *Madness and Civilization* (R. Howard, tr.) (London: Tavistock).
Foucault, M. (1970) *The Order of Things: An Archaeology of the Human Sciences* (London: Tavistock).
Foucault, M. (1977) *Discipline and Punish* (A. Sheridan, tr.) (Harmondsworth: Penguin).
Foucault, M. (1979) *The History of Sexuality* (vol. 1) (London: Allen Lane).
Fowler, O.S. (1848) *Hereditary Descent* (New York: Fowlers and Wells).
Frazer, J.G. (1885) 'Totemism', in *Encyclopædia Britannica*, 9th edn, 23, 467–76.
Frazer, J.G. (1890) *The Golden Bough: Studies in Magic and Religion* (2 vols) (London: Macmillan).
Frazer, J.G. (1898) 'Observations on Central Australian Totemism', *Journal of the Anthropological Institute*, 28, 281–6.
Frazer, J.G. (1899) 'The origin of totemism', *The Fortnightly Review*, (n.s.) 65, 647–65, 835–52.
Frazer, J.G. (1901) 'On some ceremonies of the Central Australian Tribes', *Report of the Eighth Meeting of the Australasian Association for the Advancement of Science*, Section F, 312–21.
Frazer, J.G. (1905) 'The beginnings of religion and totemism among the Australian Aborigines', *Fortnightly Review*, July to December 1905, (n.s.) 78; (o.s.) 84, 162–72, 452–66.
Frazer, J.G. (1908) 'The Australian marriage laws', *Man* (o.s.), 8, 21–2.
Frazer, J.G. (1909) 'Beliefs and customs of the Australian Aborigines', *Man* (o.s.), 9, 145–7 (no. 86).
Frazer, J.G. (1910) *Totemism and Exogamy: A Treatise on Certain Early Forms of Superstition and Society* (4 vols) (London: Macmillan).
Frazer, J.G. (1931) 'Baldwin Spencer as anthropologist', Introduction to R.R. Marett and T.K. Penniman (eds), *Spencer's Last Journey: Being the Journal of an Expedition to Tierra del Fuego by the Late Sir*

Baldwin Spencer, with a Memoir (Oxford: Clarendon), pp. 1–13.

Frazer, J.G. (1938) 'Preface' to 1938 reprint of W.B. Spencer and F.J. Gillen (1899) *The Native Tribes of Central Australia* (London: Macmillan), pp. vii–x.

Freud, S. (1900) [1976] *The Interpretation of Dreams* (Penguin Freud Library, vol. 4) (Harmondsworth: Penguin).

Freud, S. (1901) [1976] *The Psychopathology of Everyday Life* (Pelican Freud Library vol. 5) (Harmondsworth: Penguin).

Freud, S. (1912) [1960] *Totem and Taboo: Some points of agreement between the mental lives of savages and neurotics* (J. Strachey, tr.) (London: Routledge and Kegan Paul).

Freud, S. (1917) [1957] 'Mourning and melancholia', *Standard Edition of the Complete Psychological Works of Sigmund Freud* (J. Strachey, ed.) (London: The Hogarth Press/The Institute of Psycho-Analysis), 14, 243–58.

Freud, S. (1925) [1974] 'A note on "The Mystic Writing Pad"', *Standard Edition of the Complete Psychological Works of Sigmund Freud* (J. Strachey, ed.) (London: The Hogarth Press/The Institute of Psycho-Analysis), 19, 227–32.

Friedman, J.B. (1981) *The Monstrous Races in Mediaeval Art and Thought* (Cambridge, MA: Harvard University Press).

Frost, A. (1990) 'New South Wales as *terra nullius*: The British denial of Aboriginal land rights', in S. Janson and S. Macintyre (eds), *Through White Eyes* (Sydney: Allen & Unwin), pp. 65–76.

Fulford, R. (1957) *Votes for Women: The Story of a Struggle* (London: Faber & Faber).

Fuller, C.J. (1976) *The Nayars Today* (Cambridge: Cambridge University Press).

Gale, F. (1990) 'Aboriginal Australia: survival by separation', in M. Chisolm and D.M. Smith (eds), *Shared Space: Divided Space. Essays on Conflict and Territorial Organization* (London: Unwin Hyman), pp. 217–34.

Galtung, J. (1967) 'Scientific colonialism: the lessons of Project Camelot', *Transition*, 6: 30, 11–15.

Gamow, G. (1966) *Thirty Years that Shook Physics: The Story of Quantum Theory* (New York: Doubleday).

Garcilaso de la Vega, E. (1609) [1966] *Royal Commentaries of the Incas, and General History of Peru* (Part 1) (H. Livermore, tr.) (Austin: University of Texas Press).

Gasman, D. (1971) *The Scientific Origins of National Socialism: Social Darwinism in Ernst Haeckel and the German Marxist League* (London: MacDonald).

Geertz, C. (1973) *The Interpretation of Cultures: Selected Essays* (New York: Basic Books).

Geikie, A. (1905) *The Founders of Geology* (London: Macmillan).

Genovese, E. (1974) *Roll, Jordan, Roll: The World the Slaves Made* (New York: Pantheon).

Gernsheim, H. with Gernsheim, A. (1955) *The History of Photography: From the Earliest Use of the Camera Obscura in the Eleventh Century up to 1914* (London: Geoffrey Cumbedege, Oxford University Press).

Ghiselin, M.T. (1969) *The Triumph of the Darwinian Method* (Berkeley: University of California Press).

Gillen, F.J. (1899) 'Evidence', in 'Select Committee of the Legislative Council on the Aborigines Bill, 1899. Minutes of Evidence and Appendices', *Proceedings of the Parliament of South Australia*, 1899, vol. 2, Item no. 77, 94–101.

Gillen, F.J. (1901) 'Magic amongst the natives of Central Australia', in *Report of the 8th Meeting of the Australasian Association for the Advancement of Science* (Melbourne: AAAS), pp. 107–23.

Giraud-Telon, A. (1884) *Les Origines du Mariage et de la Famille* (Geneva: A. Cherbuliez).

Gjessing, G. (1968) 'The social responsibility of the social scientist', *Current Anthropology*, 9, 397–402.

Glass, B., Temkin, O. and Strauss, W.L., Jr. (eds) (1968) *Forerunners of Darwin: 1745–1859* (Baltimore: Johns Hopkins University Press).

Goetzmann, W.H. and Porter, J.C. (1981) *The West as Romantic Horizon: Selections from the Collection of the International Art Foundation* (Omaha: International Art Foundation).

Goldstein, D.S. (1983) 'The professionalisation of history in Britain in the later nineteenth and early twentieth century', *Storia della Storiografia*, 3, 3–26.

Goodall, H. (1996) *Invasion to Embassy: Land in Aboriginal Politics in New South Wales, 1770–1972* (Sydney: Allen & Unwin).

Goody, J. (1977) *The Domestication of the Savage Mind* (Cambridge: Cambridge University Press).

Goody, J. (1987) *The Interface Between the Written and the Oral* (Cambridge: Cambridge University Press).

Goody, J. and Watt, I. (1968) 'The consequences of literacy', in J. Goody (ed.), *Literacy in Traditional Societies* (Cambridge, Cambridge University Press).

Goot, M. (1988) 'Immigrants and immigration: evidence and argument from the polls, 1943–1987', in Commonwealth of Australia, *Immigration: A Commitment to Australia. Consultants' Reports* (Canberra: Australian Government Publishing Service), pp. 1–31.

Gordon, L.A. (1974) *Bengal: The Nationalist Movement 1876–1940* (New York: Columbia University Press).

Gosse, P.H. (1857) *Omphalos: An Attempt to Untie the Geological Knot* (London: John Van Voorst).

Gough, K. (1968) 'New proposals for anthropologists', *Current Anthropology*, 9, 403–7.

Gould, S.J. (1977a) *Ever Since Darwin: Reflections in Natural History* (New York: Norton).

Gould, S.J. (1977b) *Ontogeny and Phylogeny* (Cambridge, MA: Belknap/Harvard University Press).

Gould, S.J. (1981) *The Mismeasure of Man* (Harmondsworth: Penguin).

Gould, S.J. (1987) *Time's Arrow, Time's Cycle: Myth and Metaphor in the Discovery of Geological Time* (Cambridge, MA: Harvard University Press).

Grant Watson, E.L. (1946) *But To What Purpose: The Autobiography of a Contemporary* (London: Cresset).

Grant Watson, E.L. (1968) *Journey Under the Southern Stars* (London: Abelard-Schurman).

Gray, A. (1908) *Lord Kelvin: An Account of his Scientific Life and Work* (London: Dent).

Green, N. (1984) *Broken Spears: Aborigines and Europeans in the Southwest of Australia* (Perth: Focus Education Services).

Greene, M.T. (1982) *Geology in the Nineteenth Century: Changing Views of a Changing World* (Ithaca: Cornell University Press).

Greenwood, D.J. (1984) *The Taming of Evolution: The Persistence of Nonevolutionary Views in the Study of Humans* (Ithaca: Cornell University Press).

Gregg, D. and Williams, E. (1948) 'The dismal science of functionalism', *American Anthropologist*, 50, 594–611.

Gregor, A.J. and Chang, M.H. (1982) 'Marxism, Sun Yat-sen and the concept of imperialism', *Pacific Affairs*, 55, 54–79.

Grey, G. (1841) *Journals of Two Expeditions of Discovery in North-West and Western Australia, during the years 1837, 38, and 39* (2 vols) (London: T. and W. Boone).

Griffiths, T. (1996) *Hunters and Collectors: The Antiquarian Imagination in Australia* (Cambridge: Cambridge University Press).

Grotius, H. (1609) [1916] *Mare Liberum (The Freedom of the Seas; or, the right which belongs to the Dutch to take part in the East Indian trade)* (New York: Oxford University Press).

Grotius, H. (1625) [1925] *De Jure Belli ac Pacis Libri Tres* (reproduction and translation of 1642 edn) (London: H. Milford).

Gruber, J. (1965) 'Brixham Cave and the antiquity of man', in M.E. Spiro (ed.), *Context and Meaning in Cultural Anthropology: In Honor of A. Irving Hallowell* (New York: Free Press), pp. 393–402.

Gruber, J. (1970) 'Ethnographic salvage and the shaping of anthropology', *American Anthropologist*, 72, 1289–99.

Guillaumin, C. (1988) 'Race and nature: the system of marks: the idea of a natural group and social relationships', *Feminist Issues*, 8: 2, 25–43.

Gumbert, M. (1981) 'Paradigm lost: an analysis of anthropological models and their effect on Aboriginal land rights', *Oceania*, 52: 2, 103–23.

Gumbert, M. (1984) *Neither Justice Nor Reason: A Legal and Anthropological Analysis of Aboriginal Land Rights* (St. Lucia: University of Queensland Press).

Gunson, N. (ed.) (1974) *The Australian Reminiscences and Papers of L.E. Threlkeld* (Canberra: Australian Institute of Aboriginal Studies).

Haebich, A. (1989) *For Their Own Good: Aborigines and Government in the South West of Western Australia, 1900–1940* (Nedlands: University of Western Australia Press).

Haithcox, J.P. (1971) *Communism and Nationalism in India: M.N. Roy and Comintern Policy 1920–1979* (Princeton: Princeton University Press).

Hamilton, A. (1739) *A New Account of the East-Indies: Being the Observations and Remarks of Capt. Alexander Hamilton, who Resided in Those Parts, From the Year 1688, to 1723. Trading and Travelling, by Sea and Land, to most of the Countries and Islands of COMMERCE and NAVIGATION, between the Cape of Good Hope and the Island of Japan* (2nd edn, vol. 1) (London: Bettesworth & Hitch).

Hamilton, A. (1982) 'Anthropology in Australia: some notes and a few queries', in G. McCall (ed.), *Anthropology in Australia: Essays to Honour 80 Years of Mankind* (Sydney South: Anthropological Society of New South Wales), pp. 91–106.

Handler, R. (1994) 'Is "identity" a useful cross-cultural concept?', in J.R. Gillis (ed.), *Commemorations: The Politics of National Identity* (Princeton: Princeton University Press), pp. 27–40.

Haney Lopez, I.F. (1996) *White By Law: The Legal Construction of Race* (New York: New York University Press).

Hardy, F. (1968) *The Unlucky Australians* (Sydney: Nelson).

Harris, J. (1990) *One Blood: 200 Years of Aboriginal Encounter with Christianity: A Story of Hope* (Sutherland, NSW: Albatross Books).

Harris, M. (1967) 'Introduction', in M. Harris and A. Forbes, *The Land That Waited* (Melbourne: Lansdowne), pp. 1–2.

Harrison, R. and Mort, F. (1980) 'Patriarchal aspects of 19th century state formation: property relations, marriage and divorce, and sexuality', in P. Corrigan (ed.), *Capitalism, State Formation and Marxist Theory* (London: Quartet).

Harte, N. (1986) *The University of London 1836–1986: An Illustrated History* (London: Athlone Press).
Hartland, E.S. (1891) *The Science of Fairy Tales: An Inquiry Into Fairy Mythology* (London: Walter Scott).
Hartland, E.S. (1893) 'Pin-wells and rag-bushes', *Folk-Lore*, 4, 451–70.
Hartland, E.S. (1894–96) *The Legend of Perseus: A Study of Tradition in Story, Custom and Belief* (3 vols) (London: David Nutt).
Hartland, E.S. (1894) *The Supernatural Birth* (Vol. 1 of Hartland, 1894–5–6) (Grimm Library no. 2).
Hartland, E.S. (1895) *The Life-Token* (Vol. 2 of Hartland 1894–5–6) (Grimm Library no. 3).
Hartland, E.S. (1899) *Review* of Spencer and Gillen, *Folk-Lore*, 10, 233–9.
Hartland, E.S. (1900) 'Presidential Address' [to the Folk-Lore Society], *Folk-Lore*, 9, 52–80.
Hartland, E.S. (1904) 'Review' of Spencer and Gillen (1904) in *Folk-Lore*, 15, 465–74.
Hartland, E.S. (1909–10) *Primitive Paternity* (2 vols) (London: Folk-Lore Society).
Hartland, E.S. (1917) 'Matrilineal kinship and the question of its priority', *Memoirs of the American Anthropological Association*, 4, 1–87.
Hartog, F. (1988) *The Mirror of Herodotus* (J. Lloyd, tr.) (Berkeley: University of California Press).
Hartwig, M. (1972) 'Aborigines and racism: an historical perspective', in F.S. Stevens (ed.), *Racism: The Australian Experience* (Sydney: Australia and New Zealand Book Co.), pp. 9–24.
Hasluck, P. (1988) *Shades of Darkness. Aboriginal Affairs 1925–1965* (Melbourne: Melbourne University Press).
Hassard, J. (ed.) (1990) *The Sociology of Time* (London: Macmillan).
Hastings, J. (ed.) (1908) *Encyclopædia of Religion and Ethics*, vol. 1 (Edinburgh: T. & T. Clark).
Hawkins, M. (1997) *Social Darwinism in European and American Thought, 1860–1945: Nature as Model and Nature as Threat* (Cambridge: Cambridge University Press).
Healy, C. (1997) *From the Ruins of Colonialism: History as Social Memory* (Cambridge: Cambridge University Press).
Hearnshaw, L. (1964) *A Short History of British Psychology, 1840–1940* (New York: Barnes & Noble).
Hearnshaw, L.S. (1987) *The Shaping of Modern Psychology* (New York: Routledge & Kegan Paul).
Hechter, M. (1978) *Internal Colonialism: The Celtic Fringe in British National Development, 1536–1966* (London: Routledge and Kegan Paul).
Hergenhahn, B.R. (1992) *An Introduction to the History of Psychology* (2nd edn) (Belmont, CA: Wadsworth).

Hiatt, L.R. (1962) 'Local organization among the Australian Aborigines', *Oceania*, 32, 267–86.
Hiatt, L.R. (1966) 'The lost horde', *Oceania*, 37, 81–92.
Hiatt, L.R. (1982) Letter to the editor, *Oceania*, 53, 261–5.
Hiatt, L.R. (1984) 'Traditional land tenure and contemporary land claims', in L.R. Hiatt (ed.), *Aboriginal Landowners* (Sydney, (*Oceania* monograph no. 27)), pp. 11–23.
Hiatt, L.R. (1996) *Arguments About Aborigines: Australia and the Evolution of Social Anthropology* (Cambridge: Cambridge University Press).
Higginbotham, A.L., Jr (1978) *In the Matter of Color: Race and the American Legal Process* (New York: Oxford University Press).
Hillner, K.P. (1984) *History and Systems of Modern Psychology: A Conceptual Approach* (New York: Gardner Press).
Hinsley, F.H. (1959) 'Great Britain and the Powers, 1904–1914', in *Cambridge History of the British Empire*, vol. 3, *The Empire-Commonwealth 1870–1919* (Cambridge: Cambridge University Press).
Hobbes, T. (1651) [1909] *Leviathan* (Oxford: Clarendon).
Hobsbawm, E.J. (1987) *The Age of Empire, 1875–1914* (London: Weidenfeld & Nicolson).
Hocart, A.M. (1933) 'Arunta language: Strehlow vs. Spencer and Gillen' (Letter), *Man* (o.s.), 33, 92 (no. 96).
Hodge, B. and Mishra, V. (1991) *Dark Side of the Dream: Australian Literature and the Postcolonial Mind* (Sydney: Allen & Unwin).
Hodgen, M.T. (1936) *The Doctrine of Survivals: A Chapter in the History of Scientific Method in the Study of Man* (London: Allenson).
Hodgen, M.T. (1964) *Early Anthropology in the Sixteenth and Seventeenth Centuries* (Philadelphia: University of Pennsylvania Press).
Hoetink, H. (1970) 'The Dominican Republic in the nineteenth century: some notes on stratification, immigration and race', in M. Mörner (ed.), *Race and Class in Latin America* (New York: Columbia University Press), pp. 96–121.
Holcombe, L. (1977) 'Victorian wives and property: reform of the Married Women's Property Law, 1857–1882', in M. Vicinus (ed.) *A Widening Sphere. Changing Roles of Victorian Women* (Bloomington: Indiana University Press), pp. 3–28.
Holcombe, L. (1983) *Wives and Property: Reform of the Married Women's Property Law in Nineteenth-Century England* (Toronto: University of Toronto Press).
Hole, C. (1945) *Witchcraft in England* (London: Batsford).
Hollinsworth, D. (1992) 'Discourses on Aboriginality and the politics of identity in urban Australia', *Oceania*, 63, 137–55.

Holton, G. (1991) 'Quanta, relativity, and rhetoric', in M. Pera and W. R. Shea (eds), *Persuading Science: The Art of Scientific Rhetoric* (Canton, MD: Science History Publications), pp. 173–203.

Honour, H. (1975) *The New Golden Land: European Images of America from the Discoveries to the Present Time* (New York: Pantheon).

Hooker, J.R. (1963) 'The anthropological frontier: the last phase of African exploitation', *Journal of Modern African Studies*, 1, 455–9.

Hothersall, D. (1984) *History of Psychology* (Philadelphia: Temple University Press).

Howard, M.C. (ed.) (1982a) *Aboriginal Power in Australian Society* (Honolulu: University of Hawaii Press).

Howard, M.C. (1982b) 'Aboriginal brokerage and political development in South-Western Australia', in Howard (1982a), pp. 159–83.

Howitt, A.W. (1884) 'On some Australian beliefs', *Journal of the Anthropological Institute*, 13, 185–98.

Howitt, A.W. (1885) 'Australian group relations', in *Annual Report of the Board of Regents of the Smithsonian Institution showing the operations, expenditures and condition of the Institution for the year 1883* (Washington: Government Printing Office), pp. 797–824.

Howitt, A.W. (1889) 'Further notes on the Australian class system', *Journal of the Anthropological Institute*, 18, 31–68.

Howitt, A.W. (1904) *The Native Tribes of South-East Australia* (London: Macmillan).

Howitt, A.W. (1908) 'A message to anthropologists', *Revue des Études Ethnographiques et Sociologiques*, 1, 481–2.

Howitt, A.W. and Fison, L. (1882) 'From Mother-right to Father-right', *Journal of the Anthropological Institute*, 12, 30–43.

Howitt, W.E. (1855) *Land, Labour and Gold, or Two Years in Victoria* (2 vols) (London: Longman, Green, Longman, Roberts & Green).

Howorth, M. (1958) *Pioneer Research on the Atom: The Life Story of Frederick Soddy* (London: New World).

Hubert, H. and Mauss, M. (1898) 'Essai sur la nature et la fonction du sacrifice', *Anneé Sociologique*, 2, 29–138.

Hubert, H. and Mauss, M. (1899) 'Analyse' of Spencer and Gillen (1899), *Anneé Sociologique*, 3, 1898–9: 205–15.

Huggins, J. (1988) '"Firing on in the mind": Aboriginal domestic servants', *Hecate*, 13: 2, 5–23.

Huizer, G. and Mannheim, B. (eds) (1979) *The Politics of Anthropology: From Colonialism and Sexism toward a View from Below* (The Hague: Mouton).

Hulme, P. (1986) 'Columbus and the cannibals', in his *Colonial Encounters: Europe and the Native Caribbean, 1492–1797* (London: Methuen), pp. 13–43.

Hulme, P. (1990) 'The spontaneous hand of nature: savagery, colonialism and the enlightenment', in P. Hulme and L. Jordanova (eds), *The Enlightenment and Its Shadows* (London: Routledge).

Hume, D. (1757) [1978] *The Natural History of Religion* (A.W. Cohen, ed.) (published together with his *Dialogues Concerning Natural Religion*. [J.V. Price, ed.]) (Oxford: Clarendon).

Husband, T. (1980) *The Wild Man: Medieval Myth and Symbolism* (New York: Metropolitan Museum of Art).

Hutton, J. (1788) 'Theory of the earth: or an investigation of the laws observable in the composition, dissolution and restoration of land upon the globe', *Transactions of the Royal Society of Edinburgh*, 1, 209–304.

Hutton, J. (1795) *Theory of the Earth, with Proofs and Illustrations* (2 vols) (Edinburgh: W. Creech).

Hutton, J. (1973) *James Hutton's 'System of the Earth', 1785. 'Theory of the Earth', 1788. 'Observations on Granite', 1794: Together with Playfair's Biography of Hutton* (facsimiles) (New York: Hafner).

Hyam, R. (1976) *Britain's Imperial Century, 1815–1914: A Study of Empire and Expansion* (London: Batsford).

Ivins, W.M., Jr (1953) [1980] 'New reports and new vision: the nineteenth century', in A. Tracktenberg (ed.), *Classic Essays on Photography* (New Haven, CT: Leete's Island Books), pp. 217–36.

Jackson-Nakano, A. (1994) The death and resurrection of the Ngunnawal: a living history (Unpublished M Litt thesis, Australian National University).

Jacobs, J.M. (1988) 'The construction of identity', in J. Beckett (ed.), *Past and Present: The Construction of Aboriginality* (Canberra: Aboriginal Studies Press), pp. 31–44.

Jacobs, P. (1986) 'Science and veiled assumptions: miscegenation in Western Australia 1930–1937', *Australian Aboriginal Studies*, 2, 15–23.

Jacobs, P. (1990) *Mister Neville: A Biography* (Fremantle: Fremantle Arts Centre Press).

Jaimes, M.A. (1992) 'Federal Indian identification policy: a usurpation of indigenous sovereignty in North America', in F.J. Lyden and L.H. Legters (eds), *Native Americans and Public Policy* (Pittsburgh: University of Pittsburgh Press), pp. 113–35.

Jebb, R. (1905) *Studies in Colonial Nationalism* (London: Edward Arnold).

Jeffreys, S. (1985) *The Spinster and Her Enemies: Feminism and Sexuality 1880–1930* (London: Pandora).

Jenkin, G. (1979) *Conquest of the Ngarrindjeri* (Adelaide: Rigby).

Jones, D.J. and Hill-Burnett, J. (1982) 'The political context of ethnogenesis: an Australian example', in M.C. Howard (ed.), *Aboriginal Power in Australian Society* (Honolulu: University of Hawaii Press), pp. 214–46.

Jones, E. (1925) 'Mother-right and the sexual ignorance of savages', *International Journal of Psycho-analysis*, 6: part 2, 109–30.

Jones, F. L. (1970) *The Structure and Growth of Australia's Aboriginal Population* (Canberra: ANU Press).

Jones, G. (1980) *Social Darwinism and English Thought: The Interaction Between Biological and Social Theory* (Brighton: Harvester).

Jones, P. (1987) 'South Australian anthropological history: the Board for Anthropological Research and its early expeditions', *Records of the South Australian Museum*, 20, 71–92.

Jones, P. (1988) 'Perceptions of Aboriginal art: a history', in P. Sutton (ed.), *Dreamings: The Art of Aboriginal Australia* (London: Viking), pp. 143–79.

Jones, R.A. (1984) 'Robertson Smith and James Frazer on religion: two traditions in British social anthropology', in Stocking (1984), pp. 31–58.

Jordanova, L.J. and Porter, R.S. (eds) (1979) *Images of the Earth: Essays in the History of the Environmental Sciences* (Chalfont St. Giles: British Society for the History of Science).

Kaberry, P. (1936) 'Spirit-children and spirit-centres of the North Kimberley Division, West Australia', *Oceania*, 6, 392–400.

Kaberry, P. (1939) *Aboriginal Woman: Sacred and Profane* (London: Routledge).

Kaberry, P. (1968) 'Virgin birth' (letter), *Man* (n.s.), 3, 311–13.

Kant, I. (1798) [1978] *Anthropology from a Pragmatic Point of View (Anthropologie in pragmatischer Hinsicht*, V.W. Dowdell, tr.) (Carbondale: Southern Illinois University Press).

Keeffe, K. (1988) 'Aboriginality: resistance and persistence', *Australian Aboriginal Studies*, 1, 67–81.

Keen, I. (1992) 'Undermining credibility: advocacy and objectivity in the Coronation Hill debate', *Anthropology Today*, 8: 2, 6–9.

Keen, I. and Merlan, F. (1990) 'The significance of the conservation zone to Aboriginal people' (Canberra: Australian Government Publishing Service for the Resource Assessment Commission (Kakadu Conservation Zone Enquiry)).

Kelly, C. T. (1935) 'Tribes of Cherburg [sic] Settlement, Queensland', *Oceania* 5, 461–73.

Kemp, T. (1967) *Theories of Imperialism* (London: Dobson).

Kempe, H. (1883) 'Zur Sittenkunde der Centralaustralischen Schwarzen', *Mittheilungen des Vereins für Erdkunde zu Halle*, pp. 52–6.

Kendler, H.H. (1987) *Historical Foundations of Modern Psychology* (Philadelphia: Temple University Press).

Kennedy, P. (1983) 'Why did the British Empire last so long?', in his *Strategy and Diplomacy 1870–1945, Eight Studies* (London: ?????), pp. 199–218.

Ker, J.C. (1918) [1973] *Political Trouble in India 1907–1917* (Calcutta: Editions India (reprint)).

Kiernan, V.G. (1974) *Marxism and Imperialism* (London: Edward Arnold).

Kiernan, V.G. (1982) *From Conquest to Collapse: European Empires from 1815 to 1960* (New York: Pantheon).

Kimball, B.A. (1986) *Orators and Philosophers: A History of the Idea of Liberal Education* (New York: Teachers College Press).

Kindleberger, C.P. (1984) 'International propagation of financial crisis: the experience of 1888–1893', in W. Engels (*et al.*) (eds), *International Capital Movements, Debt and Monetary Systems* (Maintz: Hase & Köhler).

Krichauff, F.E.H. (1887) [1890] 'Further Notes on the "Aldolinga" or "Mbenderinga" Tribe of Aborigines', *Proceedings of the Royal Geographical Society of Australasia, South Australian Branch*, vol. 2 (1886–88), 77–80.

Kruger, S.F. (1992) *Dreaming in the Middle Ages* (Cambridge: Cambridge University Press).

Kuklick, H. (1991) *The Savage Within: The Social History of British Anthropology, 1885–1945* (Cambridge: Cambridge University Press).

Kuper, A. (ed.) (1977) *The Social Anthropology of Radcliffe-Brown* (London: Routledge and Kegan Paul).

Kuper, A. (1983) *Anthropology and Anthropologists: The Modern British School* (rev. edn) (London: Routledge & Kegan Paul).

Kuper, A. (1988) *The Invention of Primitive Society: Transformations of an Illusion* (London: Routledge).

Kuper, A. (1994) 'Culture, identity and the project of a cosmopolitan anthropology', *Man* (n.s.), 29, 537–54.

LaCapra, D. (1983) *Rethinking Intellectual History: Texts, Contexts, Language* (Ithaca: Cornell University Press).

Lackner, H. (1973) 'Colonial administration and social anthropology: Eastern Nigeria, 1920–1940', in Asad (1973), pp. 123–52.

Lafitau, J.-F. (1724) *Moeurs des Sauvages ameriquains comparées aux Moeurs des premiers temps* (Paris: Sangrain et Hochereau).

Lancaster Jones, F. (1970) *The Structure and Growth of Australia's Aboriginal Population* (Canberra: ANU Press).

Lang, A. (1883) 'The early history of the family', *Contemporary Review*, 44 (July–December), 406–22.

Lang, A. (1884a) *Custom and Myth* (London: Longman, Green).
Lang, A. (1884b) 'Mythology', *Encyclopædia Britannica*, 9th edn, 17, 135–58.
Lang, A. (1887) *Myth, Ritual and Religion* (2 vols) (London: Longman, Green).
Lang, A. (1887) [1899c] *Myth, Ritual and Religion* (2 vols) (London: Longman, Green).
Lang, A. (1890) 'Presidential Address to the Folk-Lore Society. Session 1889–90', *Folk-Lore*, 1, 4–15.
Lang, A. (1893) 'Introduction' to Cox 1893, pp. vii–xxiii.
Lang, A. (1896) 'Introduction' to Parker 1896, pp. xiii–xvi.
Lang, A. (1897) *The Book of Dreams and Ghosts* (London: Longmans, Green).
Lang, A. (1898a) 'Introduction' to Parker 1898, pp. xvii–xxiii.
Lang, A. (1898b) *The Making of Religion* (London: Longman, Green).
Lang, A. (1899a) 'Australian gods: a reply', *Folk-Lore*, 10, 1–46.
Lang, A. (1899b) 'Are savage gods borrowed from missionaries?', *Nineteenth Century*, 45, January-June, 132–44.
Lang, A. (1903) *Social Origins* (incorporating Atkinson 1903) (London: Longman, Green).
Lang, A. (1904) 'A theory of Arunta totemism', *Man*, (o.s.) 44, 67–9.
Lang, A. (1905a) *The Secret of the Totem* (London: Longman, Green).
Lang, A. (1905b) 'Introduction' to Parker 1905, pp. ix–xxvii.
Lang, A. (1905c) 'The primitive and the advanced in totemism', *Journal of the Anthropological Institute*, 25, 315–36.
Lang, A. (1907a) 'Australian problems', in N.W. Thomas, R.R. Marett and W.H.R. Rivers (eds), *Anthropological Essays Presented to Edward Burnett Tylor in Honour of his 75th Birthday, October 2nd, 1907* (Oxford: Clarendon Press), pp. 203–18.
Lang, A. (1907b) 'Conceptional totemism and exogamy', *Man*, (o.s.) 55, 88–90.
Lang, A. (1908a) *The Origins of Religion and Other Essays* (London: Watts & Co. for the Rationalist Press Association).
Lang, A. (1908b) 'The origin of terms of human relationship' (pamphlet) (London: Oxford University Press for the British Academy).
Lang, A. (1908c) 'Homer and anthropology', in R.R. Marett (ed.), *Anthropology and the Classics: Six Lectures Delivered Before the University of Oxford* (Oxford: Clarendon Press), pp. 42–65.
Lang, A. (1909) 'The Alcheringa and the All Father', *Revue des Études Ethnographiques et Sociologiques*, 2, 141–54.
Lang, A. (1910) 'J.G. Frazer's Totemism and Exogamy', *Anthropos*, 5, 1092–1108.
Lang, A. (1911) 'Totemism', in *Encyclopædia Britannica* 11th edn, vol. 27, 79–91.
Lang, J.D. (1861) *Queensland, Australia* (London: Edward Stanford).
Langham, I. (1981) *The Building of British Social Anthropology* (Dordrecht: Reidel).
Langton, M. (1981) 'Urbanizing Aborigines: the social scientists' great deception', *Social Alternatives*, 2: 2, 16–22.
Langton, M. (1982) *After the Tent Embassy: Images of Aboriginal History in Black and White Photographs* (Sydney: Valadon Publishing).
Langton, M. (1993) '*Well, I heard it on the radio and I saw it on the television . . .*'. *An Essay for the Australian Film Commission on the Politics and Aesthetics of Filmmaking By and About Aboriginal People and Things* (North Sydney: Australian Film Commission).
Lattas, A. (1990) 'Aborigines and contemporary Australian nationalism: primordiality and the cultural politics of otherness', in J. Marcus (ed.), *Writing Australian Culture (Social Analysis* special issue no. 27), 50–69.
Lattas, A. (1991) 'Nationalism, aesthetic redemption and Aboriginality', *Australian Journal of Anthropology*, 2, 307–24.
Lattas, A. (1992) 'Primitivism, nationalism, and popular culture: true Aboriginality and contemporary Australian culture', in B. Attwood and J. Arnold (eds), *Power, Knowledge and Aborigines (Journal of Australian Studies* special issue no. 35), pp. 45–58.
Leach, E.R. (1954) *Political Systems of Highland Burma: A Study of Kachin Social Structure* (London: Bell).
Leach, E.R. (1969) 'Virgin birth', in his *Genesis as Myth and Other Essays* (London: Jonathan Cape).
Leahey, T.H. (1980) *A History of Psychology: Main Currents in Psychological Thought* (1st edn) (Englewood Cliffs, NJ: Prentice Hall).
Leahey, T.H. (1991) *A History of Modern Psychology* (New York: Prentice Hall).
Leahey, T.H. (1992) *A History of Psychology: Main Currents in Psychological Thought* (3rd edn) (Englewood Cliffs, NJ: Prentice Hall).
Leahey, T.H. and Leahey, G.E. (1983) *Psychology's Occult Doubles: Psychology and the Problem of Pseudoscience* (Chicago: Nelson Hall).
Leclerc, G. (1971) *Anthropologie et Colonialisme: Essai sur l'histoire de l'Africanisme* (Paris: Fayard).
Le Gay Brereton, J. (1962) 'An estimate of assimilation rate of Mixed-Blood Aborigines in New South Wales', *Oceania*, 32, 187–90.
Legters, L.H. (1988) 'The American genocide', *Policy Studies Journal*, 16, 768–77.
Leiris, M. (1950) 'L'ethnographie devant le colonialisme', *Les Temps Modernes*, 6: 58, 357–74.

Lenin, N. (V.I.) (1916) [1970] *Imperialism, The Highest Stage of Capitalism* (Moscow: Progress).
Leonhardi, von M. Freiherr v. (1907) 'Über einige religiöse und totemistische Vorstellungen der Aranda und Loritja in Zentralaustralien', *Globus*, 91, 285–90.
Leopold, J. (1980) *Culture in Comparative and Evolutionary Perspective: E.B. Tylor and the Making of 'Primitive Culture'* (Berlin: Dietrich Reimer).
Lerner, G. (1986) *The Creation of Patriarchy* (Oxford: Oxford University Press).
Letourneau, C.H. (1892) *Property: Its Origin and Development* (London: Walter Scott).
Letourneau, C.H. (1893) *Sociology: Based Upon Ethnography* (H.M. Trollope, tr.) (London: Chapman & Hall).
Levine, P. (1986) *The Amateur and the Professional: Antiquarians, Historians and Archaeologists in Victorian England, 1838–1886* (Cambridge: Cambridge University Press).
Lévi-Strauss, C. (1947) [1969] *The Elementary Structures of Kinship (Les Structures élémentaires de la Parenté)* (R. Needham, tr.) (Boston: Beacon).
Lévi-Strauss, C. (1963) *Totemism* (R. Needham, tr.) (Boston: Beacon).
Lévi-Strauss, C. (1966) *The Savage Mind (La Pensée Sauvage)* (London: Weidenfeld and Nicolson).
Lévi-Strauss, C. (1973) *Tristes Tropiques* (London: Jonathan Cape).
Lévi-Strauss, C. (1973) [1978] 'Reflections on the atom of kinship', in his *Structural Anthropology 2*. (M. Layton, tr.) (Harmondsworth: Penguin), pp. 82–112.
Lévy-Bruhl, L. (1910) *Les Fonctions Mentales dans les Sociétés Inférieures* (Paris: Librairie Félix Alcan) (Travaux de l'Année Sociologique).
Lévy-Bruhl, L. (1923) *Primitive Mentality* (L.A. Clare, tr.) (London: Allen & Unwin).
Lippert, J. (1887) [1931] *The Evolution of Culture* (G.P. Murdock, tr. and ed.) (London: Allen & Unwin).
Lippmann, L. (1981) *Generations of Resistance: The Aboriginal Struggle for Justice* (Melbourne: Longman Cheshire).
Lips, J.E. (1937) *The Savage Hits Back, or The White Man Through Native Eyes* (London: Lovat Dickson).
Lloyd, D. (1990) 'Analogies of the aesthetic: the politics of culture and the limits of materialist aesthetics', *New Formations*, 10 (Spring 1990), 109–26.
Lloyd, D. (1991) 'Race under representation', *Oxford Literary Review*, 13, 62–94.
Lloyd, T.O. (1970) *Empire to Welfare State: English History 1906–1967* (London: Oxford University Press).
Locke (1690) [1970] *Two Treatises of Government* (P. Laslett, ed.) (Cambridge: Cambridge University Press).

Long, J.K. (1791) [1922] *Voyages and Travels of an Indian Interpreter and Trader* (Chicago: University of Chicago Press).
Loos, N. (1982) *Invasion and Resistance: Aboriginal-European Relations on the North Queensland Frontier, 1861–1897* (Canberra: ANU Press).
Lorimer, D. (1978) *Colour, Class and the Victorians* (Leicester: Leicester University Press).
Loughlin, J. (1986) *Gladstone, Home Rule and the Irish Question 1882–93* (Dublin: Gill & MacMillan).
Lovejoy, A.O. (1960) *The Great Chain of Being: A Study in the History of an Idea* (New York: Harper).
Lovejoy, A.O. (1968) 'Recent criticism of the Darwinian theory of recapitulation: its grounds and its initiator', in B. Glass, O. Temkin and W.L. Straus, Jr (eds), *Forerunners of Darwin: 1745–1859* (Baltimore: Johns Hopkins University Press), pp. 438–58.
Lovejoy, A.O. and Boas, G. (1935) *Primitivism and Related Ideas in Antiquity* (Baltimore: Johns Hopkins University Press).
Lovell, J. (1982) 'Trade unions and the development of independent labour politics 1889–1906', in B. Pimlott and C. Cook (eds), *Trade Unions in British Politics* (New York: Longman), pp. 38–57.
Lowry, R. (1982) *The Evolution of Psychological Theory: A Critical History of Concepts and Presuppositions* (New York: Aldine).
Lubbock, J. (1865) *Prehistoric Times: As Illustrated by Ancient Remains, and the Manners and Customs of Modern Savages* (London: Williams & Norgate).
Lubbock, J. (1870) *The Origin of Civilisation and the Primitive Condition of Man: Mental and Social Condition of Savages* (London: Longman, Green).
Lubbock, J. (1885) 'On the customs of marriage and systems of relationship among the Australians', *Journal of the Anthropological Institute*, 14, 292–300.
Lubbock, J. (Lord Avebury) (1911) *Marriage, Totemism and Religion: An Answer to Critics* (London: Longman, Green).
Lucretius (1886) *De Rerum Natura: Libri Sex* (H.A.J. Munro, tr.) 4th edn (Cambridge: Deighton, Bell).
Lyell, C. (1830) *Principles of Geology: being an attempt to explain the former changes of the earth's surface, by references to causes now in operation* (London: J. Murray).
Lyell, C. (1863) *The Geological Evidences of the Antiquity of Man with Remarks on the Origin of Species by Variation* (London: Murray).
Lynd, H. (1945) *England in the 1880s* (London: Frank Cass).
Lyng, J. (1927) *Non-Britishers in Australia: Influence on Population and Progress* (Melbourne: Macmillan).

Lyons, F.S.L. (1977) *Charles Stewart Parnell* (London: Collins).

Macintyre, S. (1986) *The Oxford History of Australia. Vol. 4. 1901–1942: The Succeeding Age* (Melbourne: Oxford University Press).

Mackenzie, D. (1978) 'Statistical theory and social interests: a case study', *Social Studies of Science*, 8, 35–83.

Madden, A.F. (1959) 'Changing attitudes and widening responsibilities, 1895–1914', c.10, *Cambridge History of the British Empire*, vol. 3, *The Empire-Commonwealth 1870–1919* (Cambridge: Cambridge University Press), pp. 339–405.

Maddock, K. (1980) *Anthropology, Law and the Definition of Australian Aboriginal Rights to Land* (Nijmegen: Institute of Folk Law [sic], Catholic University.

Maddock, K. (1987) 'Yet another "sacred site": the Bula controversy', in B. Wright, G. Fry and L. Petchkovsky (eds), *Contemporary Issues in Aboriginal Studies* (Sydney: Firebird Press), pp. 119–40.

Maddock, K. (1988) 'God, Caesar and Mammon at Coronation Hill', *Oceania*, 58, 305–10.

Mafeje, A. (1971) 'The ideology of tribalism', *Journal of Modern African Studies*, 9, 253–61.

Maine, H.S. (1861) [1866] *Ancient Law: Its Connection with the Early History of Society, and Its Relation to Modern Ideas* (London: John Murray).

Maine, H.S. (1883) *Dissertations on Early Law and Custom, Chiefly Selected from Lectures Delivered at Oxford* (London: John Murray).

Malik, K. (1996) *The Meaning of Race: Race, History and Culture in Western Society* (London: MacMillan).

Malinowski, B. (1913) *The Family Among the Australian Aborigines: A Sociological Study* (London: Hodder & Stoughton for the University of London Press).

Malinowski, B. (1916) 'Baloma: the spirits of the dead in the Trobriand Islands', *Journal of the Royal Anthropological Institute*, 46, 353–430.

Malinowski, B. (1922) *Argonauts of the Western Pacific: an account of native enterprise and adventure in the archipelagoes of Melanesian New Guinea* (London: Routledge & Kegan Paul).

Malinowski, B. (1924) 'Mutterrechtliche Familie und Ödipus-Komplex', *Imago zeitschrift für Anwendung der psychoanalyse auf die Geisteswissenschaften* (X Band) (Leipzig: Internationaler Psychoanalytischer Verlag), pp. 228–77.

Malinowski, B. (1927) [1966] *The Father in Primitive Psychology* (New York: Norton).

Malinowski, B. (1929) *The Sexual Life of Savages in North-Western Melanesia* (London: Routledge & Kegan Paul).

Malinowski, B. (1944) *A Scientific Theory of Culture and Other Essays* (Chapel Hill: University of North Carolina Press).

Malthus, T.R. (1798) *An Essay on the Principle of Population, as it Affects the Future Improvement of Society, with remarks on the speculations of Mr. Godwin, M. Condorcet, and other writers* (London: J. Johnson).

Malthus, T.R. (1806) *An Essay on the Principle of Population: Or a view of its past and present effects on human happiness with an inquiry into our prospects respecting the future removal or mitigation of the evils which it occasions* (3rd edn of Malthus 1798) (London).

Mandelbaum, M. (1969) 'Functionalism in social anthropology', in S. Morgenbesser, P. Suppes and M. White (eds), *Philosophy, Science, and Method: Essays in Honor of Ernest Nagel* (New York: St. Martin's Press), pp. 306–32.

Mangum, C.S., Jr (1940) *The Legal Status of the Negro* (Chapel Hill: University of North Carolina Press).

Mansergh, N. (1965) *The Irish Question 1840–1921: A Commentary on Anglo-Irish Relations and on Social and Political Forces in Ireland in the Age of Reform and Revolution* (London: Allen & Unwin).

Mansergh, N. (1991) *The Unresolved Question: The Anglo-Irish Settlement and its Undoing 1912–72* (New Haven, CT: Yale University Press).

Marcus, J. (1988) 'Journey to the centre: the cultural appropriation of Ayers Rock', in A. Rutherford (ed.), *Aboriginal Culture Today* (Sydney: Dangaroo Press), pp. 254–74.

Marcuse, H. (1965) 'Repressive tolerance', in R.P. Wolff, B. Moore and H. Marcuse, *A Critique of Pure Tolerance* (London: Jonathan Cape), pp. 95–137.

Marett, R.R. (1941) *A Jerseyman at Oxford* (Oxford: Oxford University Press).

Marett, R.R. and Penniman, T.K. (eds) (1931) *Spencer's Last Journey. Being the Journal of an Expedition to Tierra del Fuego by the Late Sir Baldwin Spencer, with a Memoir* (Oxford: Clarendon).

Marett, R.R. and Penniman, T.K. (eds) (1932) *Spencer's Scientific Correspondence with Sir J.G. Frazer and Others* (Oxford: Clarendon).

Markus, A. (1974) *From the Barrel of a Gun: The Oppression of the Aborigines. 1860–1900* (West Melbourne: Victorian Historical Association).

Markus, A. (1990) *Governing Savages* (Sydney: Allen & Unwin).

Marx, K. (1973) *Grundrisse: Foundations of the Critique of Political Economy* (M. Nicolaus, tr.) (Harmondsworth: Penguin).

Mason, J. (1978) *Coe v. The Commonwealth of Australia and the Government of the United Kingdom of Great Britain and Northern Ireland. Australian Law Journal Reports*, vol. 52, 334–7.

Mauss, M. (1903–04) 'Revue' of Roth (1903). *Année Sociologique*, 8, 252–5.

Mauss, M. (1904–05) 'Essai sur les Variations Saissonières Des Sociétés Eskimos. Etude de morphologie sociale', *Année Sociologique*, 9, 39–130.
Mauss, M. (1905–1906) Revue of A. van Gennep, *Mythes et Legendes d'Australie* (van Gennep 1906b), *Année Sociologique*, 10, 226–9.
Mauss, M. (1925) [1970] *The Gift* (I Cunnison, tr.) (London: Routledge & Kegan Paul).
Mauss, M. (1938) [1985] 'A category of the human mind: the notion of person: the notion of self' (W.D. Halls, tr.) in M. Carrithers, S. Collins and S. Lukes (eds), *The Category of the Person: Anthropology, Philosophy, History* (Cambridge: Cambridge University Press), pp. 1–25.
May, D. (1983) 'The articulation of the Aboriginal and capitalist modes on the North Queensland frontier', *Journal of Australian Studies*, 12, 34–44.
May, D. (1986) *From Bush to Station: Aboriginal Labour in the North Queensland Pastoral Industry, 1861–1897* (Townsville: History Department, James Cook University).
McAllister, I. (1993) 'Immigration, bipartisanship and public opinion', in J. Jupp and M. Kabala (eds), *The Politics of Australian Immigration* (Canberra: Australian Government Publishing Service), pp. 161–78.
McCall, G. (ed.) (1982) *Anthropology in Australia: Essays to Honour 50 Years of Mankind* (Sydney South: Anthropological Society of New South Wales).
McClintock, A. (1995) *Imperial Leather: Race, Gender and Sexuality in the Colonial Contest* (New York: Routledge).
McGinness, J. (1991) *Son of Alyandabu: My Fight for Aboriginal Rights* (St. Lucia: University of Queensland Press).
McGrath, A. (1978) 'Aboriginal women workers in the N.T., 1911–1939', *Hecate*, 4: 2, 5–25.
McGrath, A. (1987) *Born in the Cattle: Aborigines in Cattle Country* (Sydney: Allen & Unwin).
McGrath, A. (1990) 'The white man's looking glass: Aboriginal-colonial gender relations at Port Jackson', *Australian Historical Studies*, 24, 189–206.
McGrath, A. (1995) (ed.) *Contested Ground: Australian Aborigines Under the British Crown* (Sydney: Allen & Unwin).
McHugh, P. (1980) *Prostitution and Victorian Social Reform* (London: Croom Helm).
McLachlan, J.O. (1947) 'The origin and early development of the Cambridge History Tripos', *Cambridge Historical Journal*, 9, 78–105.
McLennan, D. (1885) 'Preface' to his (ed. and completed) *The Patriarchal Theory: Based on the Papers of the Late John Ferguson McLennan* (London: Macmillan).

McLennan, J.F. (1859) 'Law', in *Encyclopædia Britannica*, 8th edn, vol. 13, 253–79.
McLennan, J.F. (1865) *Primitive Marriage: An Inquiry into the Origin of the Form of Capture in Marriage Ceremonies* (Edinburgh: Adam & Charles Black).
McLennan, J.F. (1867) *Memoir of Thomas Drummond, R.E., F.R.A.S., Under Secretary to the Lord Lieutenant of Ireland, 1835 to 1840* (Edinburgh: Edmonston & Douglas).
McLennan, J.F. (1868) 'Totem', in *Chamber's Encyclopædia*, 1st edn, 'Supplement' (London: W. & R. Chambers), pp. 753–4.
McLennan, J.F. [?] (1869) 'The early history of man' (anon.; Rivière 1970: l/*Wellesley Index*, attrib.), *North British Review*, o.s., 50, 516–49 (see n. 106, p. 98).
McLennan, J.F. (1869–70) 'The Worship of Animals and Plants', *Fortnightly Review*, 6, 407–27 (pt. 1), 6, 562–82 (pt. 2), 7, 194–216 (pt. 3).
McLennan, J.F. (1876) [1886a] *Studies in Ancient History, Comprising a Reprint of Primitive Marriage: An Inquiry into the Origin of the Form of Capture in Marriage Ceremonies* (2nd edn) (London: Macmillan).
McLennan, J.F. (1885) *The Patriarchal Theory Based on the Papers of the Late John Ferguson McLennan* (D. McLennan, ed. and completed) (London: Macmillan).
McLennan, J.F. (1886b) 'Primitive marriage' (reprint), in McLennan 1886a.
McLennan, J.F. (1896) *Studies in Ancient History. The Second Series. Comprising an Enquiry into the Origin of Exogamy* (D. McLennan, A. Eleanor and A. Platt, eds) (London: Macmillan).
McNally, W. (1981) *Aborigines, Artefacts and Anguish* (Adelaide: Lutheran Publishing House).
Meek, R. (1976) *Social Science and the Ignoble Savage* (Cambridge: Cambridge University Press).
Meggitt, M.J. (1962) *Desert People: A Study of the Walbiri Aborigines of Central Australia* (Sydney: Angus & Robertson).
Meggitt, M.J. (1963) 'Social organization: morphology and typology', in W.E.H. Stanner and H. Shiels (eds), *Australian Aboriginal Studies: A Symposium of Papers Presented to the 1961 Research Conference* (Melbourne: Oxford University Press).
Meillassoux, C. (1967) 'Recherche d'un niveau de détermination dans la société cynégétique', *L'Homme et la Société*, 6, 95–106.
Merlan, F. (1986) 'Australian Aboriginal conception beliefs revisited', *Man*, (n.s.) 21, 474–93.
Merlan, F. (1991) 'The limits of cultural constructionism: the case of Coronation Hill', *Oceania*, 61, 341–52.
Micha, F.J. (1970) 'Trade and change in Aboriginal Australian cultures: Australian Aboriginal trade as an expression of close

culture contact and as a mediator of culture change', in A.R. Pilling and R.A. Waterman (eds), *Diptrodon to Detribalization: Studies of Change Among Australian Aborigines* (East Lansing: Michigan State University Press), pp. 285–313.

Middleton, H. (1977) *But Now We Want the Land Back* (Sydney: New Age Publishers).

Millar, J. (1771) *Observations Concerning the Distinction of Ranks in Society* (London: John Murray).

Miller, J. (1985) *Koori: A Will to Win* (Sydney: Angus & Robertson).

Milliss, R. (1992) *Waterloo Creek: The Australia Day Massacre of 1838, George Gipps and the British Conquest of New South Wales* (Ringwood: McPhee Gribble/Penguin).

Moi, T. (1985) *Sexual, Textual Politics: Feminist Literary Theory* (London: Routledge).

Montrose, L. (1991) 'The work of gender in the discourse of discovery', *Representations*, 33, 1–41.

Morgan, A. and Bostock, G. (prod.) (1984) *Lousy Little Sixpence* (video) (Sydney: New South Wales Department of Education).

Morgan, L.H. (1851) *League of the Ho-d-eno-sau-nee, Iroquois* (Rochester: Sage & Brothers).

Morgan, L.H. (1866) 'A conjectural solution of the origin of the classificatory system of relationship', in *Proceedings of the American Academy of Arts and Sciences*, Vol. 8, 11 February 1866, meeting no. 591, 436–77, reprinted 1868 (Cambridge, MA: Welch, Bigelow).

Morgan, L.H. (1871) *Systems of Consanguinity and Affinity of the Human Family* (Smithsonian Contributions to Knowledge, vol. 17, no. 218) (Washington: Smithsonian Institution).

Morgan, L.H. (1872) 'Paper on Australian kinship', in *Proceedings of the American Academy of Arts and Sciences*, Vol. 8, 12 March 1872, meeting no. 642, 412–28.

Morgan, L.H. (1877) *Ancient Society, or Researches in the Lines of Human Progress from Savagery through Barbarism to Civilization* (1963 reprint, E.B. Leacock, ed.) (New York: Meridian).

Morgan, L.H. (1880) 'Prefatory Note' to Fison and Howitt (1880), pp. 1–20.

Mörner, M. (1967) *Race Mixture in the History of Latin America* (Boston: Little, Brown).

Mörner, M., (ed.) (1970) *Race and Class in Latin America* (New York: Columbia University Press).

Morphy, H. (1990) 'Myth, totemism and the creation of clans', *Oceania*, 60, 312–28.

Morphy, H. (1996) 'More than mere facts: repositioning Spencer and Gillen in the history of anthropology', in S.R. Morton and D.J. Mulvaney (eds), *Exploring Central Australia: Society, the Environment and the 1894 Horn Expedition* (Chipping Norton, NSW: Surrey Beatty and Sons), pp. 135–48.

Morphy, H. (1997) 'Gillen: man of science', in J. Mulvaney, H. Morphy and A. Petch (eds), *My Dear Spencer: The Letters of F.J. Gillen to Baldwin Spencer* (Melbourne: Hyland House), pp. 23–50.

Morris, B. (1988) 'Dhan-gadi resistance to assimilation', in I. Keen (ed.), *Being Black: Aboriginal Cultures in 'Settled' Australia* (Canberra: Aboriginal Studies Press), pp. 33–63.

Morris, B. (1989) *Domesticating Resistance: The Dhan-gadi Aborigines and the Australian State* (New York: Berg).

Mosse, G.L. (1985) *Toward the Final Solution: A History of European Racism* (Madison: Wisconsin University Press).

Motz, L. and Weaver, J.H. (1988) *The Concepts of Science: From Newton to Einstein* (New York: Plenum Press).

Motz, L. and Weaver, J.H. (1989) *The Story of Physics* (New York: Plenum Press).

Mountford, C.P. (1976) *Nomads of the Australian Desert* (Adelaide: Rigby).

Mountford, C.P. (1981) *Aboriginal Conception Beliefs* (Melbourne: Hyland House).

Mowbray, M. (1986) 'State control or self-regulation? on the political economy of local government in remote Aboriginal townships', *Australian Aboriginal Studies*, 2, 31–9.

Müller, F.M. (1861) *Lectures on the Science of Language* (London: Trubner).

Müller, F.M. (1864) *Lectures on the Science of Language* (2nd series) (London: Longman, Green, Longman, Roberts & Green).

Müller, F.M. (1872) 'On the results of comparative philology' (Inaugural Lecture, Strassburg, 23 May 1872) in F.M. Müller, *Selected Essays on Language, Mythology and Religion* (London: Longman, Green), pp. 174–227.

Müller, F.M. (1877) *The Science of Language*, 9th edn (London: Longman, Green).

Müller, F.M. (1897) *Contributions to the Science of Mythology* (2 vols) (London: Longman, Green).

Mulvaney, D.J. (1987) 'Walter Baldwin Spencer', Introduction to R. Vanderwal (ed.), *The Aboriginal Photographs of Baldwin Spencer* (Melbourne: Viking O'Neil), pp. vii–x.

Mulvaney, D.J. (1989) *Encounters in Place: Outsiders and Aboriginal Australians, 1606–1985* (St. Lucia: University of Queensland Press).

Mulvaney, D.J. (1996) '"A splendid lot of fellows": achievements and consequences of the Horn Expedition', in S.R. Morton and D.J. Mulvaney (eds), *Exploring Central Australia: Society, the Environment and the 1894 Horn Expedition* (Chipping Norton, NSW: Surrey Beatty and Sons), pp. 3–12.

Mulvaney, D.J. and Calaby, J.H. (1985) *'So Much That Is New': Baldwin Spencer,*

1860–1929: A Biography (Melbourne: Melbourne University Press).
Murray, D.J. (1988) *A History of Western Psychology* (2nd edn) (Englewood Cliffs, NJ: Prentice Hall).
Murray, L.A. (1977) 'The Human-Hair Thread', *Meanjin*, 36, 550–71.
Nance, B. (1981) 'The level of violence: Europeans and Aborigines in Port Phillip, 1835–1850', *Historical Studies* (Melbourne), 19: 77, 532–52.
Nathan, P. (1980) *A Home Away from Home: A Study of the Aboriginal Health Service in Fitzroy* (Bundoora, Victoria: Preston Institute of Technology Press).
Native American Consultants, Inc. (1980) *Indian Definition Study* (Contracted pursuant to PL 95–561, Title IV, s. 1147. Submitted to the Office of the Assistant Secretary of Education, Department of Education, Washington, DC, January 1980).
Neate, G. (1989) *Aboriginal Land Rights Law in the Northern Territory* (vol. 1) (Chippendale, NSW: Alternative Publishing Co-op).
Neville, A.O. [n.d.] (1947) *Australia's Coloured Minority: Its Place in the Community* (Sydney: Currawong Publishing).
Nilsson, S. (1834) [1868] *The Primitive Inhabitants of Scandinavia: an essay on comparative ethnography, and a contribution to the history of the development of mankind: containing a description of the implements, dwellings, tombs and mode of living of the savages in the North of Europe during the Stone Age* (J. Lubbock, tr.) (London: Longmans Green).
Nordenskiöld, E. (1928) *The History of Biology: A Survey* (New York: Tudor Publishing).
Obeyesekere, G. (1992) *The Apotheosis of Captain Cook: European Mythmaking in the Pacific* (Princeton: Princeton University Press).
O'Brien, C.C. (1968) *Parnell and His Party 1880–90* (Oxford: Oxford University Press).
O'Brien, M. (1981) *The Politics of Reproduction* (London: Routledge & Kegan Paul).
Oldroyd, D.R. (1980) *Darwinian Impacts: An Introduction to the Darwinian Revolution* (Kensington, NSW: New South Wales University Press).
Oldroyd, D. and Langham, I. (eds) (1983) *The Wider Domain of Evolutionary Thought* (Dordrecht: Reidel).
Olender, M. (1992) *The Languages of Paradise: Race, Religion and Philology in the Nineteenth Century* (A. Goldhammer, tr.) (Cambridge, MA: Harvard University Press).
Olsen, J., Durack, M., Dutton, G., Serventy, V. and Bortignon, A. (1984) *The Land Beyond Time: A Modern Exploration of Australia's North-West Frontier* (South Melbourne: Macmillan Australia).
Oppenheimer, J. (1968) 'An embryological enigma in *The Origin of Species*', in Glass, Temkin and Straus (1968), pp. 292–322.

Ortner, S.B. (1974) 'Is female to male as nature is to culture?', in M.Z. Rosaldo and L. Lamphere (eds), *Woman, Culture and Society* (Stanford: Stanford University Press), pp. 67–87.
Owen, R. and Sutcliffe, B. (eds) (1972) *Studies in the Theory of Imperialism* (London: Longman).
Paley, W. (1802) *Natural Theology: or, evidence of the existence & attributes of the Deity: Collected from the appearances of nature* (London: R. Faulder).
Pares, R. (1961) *The Historian's Business, and Other Essays* (R. Humphreys and E. Humphreys, eds) (Oxford: Clarendon).
Parker, K.L. (1896) *Australian Legendary Tales: Folk-Lore of the Noorgahburrahs as told to the Piccaninnies* (Melbourne: Melville, Mullen & Slade).
Parker, K.L. (1898) *More Australian Legendary Tales* (London: David Nutt).
Parker, K.L. (1905) *The Euahlayi Tribe: A Study of Aboriginal Life in Australia* (London: Constable).
Pateman, C. (1988) *The Sexual Contract* (Oxford: Polity).
Patterson, O. (1982) *Slavery and Social Death: A Comparative Study* (Cambridge, MA: Harvard University Press).
Pearson, N. (1993) '204 years of invisible title', in M.A. Stephenson and S. Ratnapala (eds), <u>Mabo</u>: *A Judicial Revolution: The Aboriginal Land Rights Decision and Its Impact on Australian Law* (St. Lucia: University of Queensland Press), pp. 75–95.
Pedersen, H. (1962) *The Discovery of Language: Linguistic Science in the Nineteenth Century* (J.W. Spargo, tr.) (Bloomington: Indiana University Press).
Pels, P. and Salemink, O. (eds) (1994) *Colonial Ethnographies* (History and Anthropology, vol. 8, nos. 1–4).
Penniman, T.K. (1935) [1965] *A Hundred Years of Anthropology* (rev. edn) (London: Duckworth).
Pepper, P. with de Araugo, T. (1985) *The Kurnai of Gippsland: What Did Happen to the Aborigines of Victoria*. vol. 1 (Melbourne: Hyland House).
Perry, W.J. (1923) *The Children of the Sun: A Study in the Early History of Civilization* (London: Methuen).
Pescott, R.T.M. (1954) *Collections of a Century: The History of the First Hundred Years of the National Museum of Victoria* (Melbourne: National Museum of Victoria).
Peterson, N. (1983) 'Donald Thomson: a biographical sketch', in his (ed.), *Donald Thomson in Arnhem Land* (South Yarra, Victoria: Currey O'Neil), pp. 1–18.
Peterson, N. (1990) '"Studying man and man's nature": the history of the institutionalisation of Aboriginal

anthropology', *Australian Aboriginal Studies*, 2, 3–19.

Peterson, N. and Langton, M. (eds) (1983) *Aborigines, Land and Land Rights* (Canberra: Australian Institute of Aboriginal Studies).

Petitjean, P., Jami, C. and Moulin, A.M. (eds) (1992) *Science and Empires: Historical Studies About Scientific Development and European Expansion* (Dordrecht: Kluwer Academic Publishers).

Piddington, R. (1932) 'Totemic system of the Karadjeri tribe', *Oceania*, 2, 373–400.

Playfair, J. (1802) *Illustrations of the Huttonian Theory of the Earth* (Edinburgh: Cadell & Davies).

Playfair, J. (1805) 'Biographical account of the late James Hutton, F.R.S. Edinburgh', *Trans. Royal Society Edinburgh*, vol. 5: pt. 3, 39–99.

Plomley, N.J.B. (ed.) (1991) *Jorgen Jorgensen and the Aborigines of Van Diemen's Land, being a reconstruction of his 'lost' book on their customs and habits and his role in the Roving Parties and the Black Line* (Hobart: Blubber Head Press).

Pope, A. (1988) 'Aboriginal adaptation to early colonial labour markets: the South Australian experience', *Labour History*, 54, 1–15.

Porter, B. (1968) *Critics of Empire: British Radical Attitudes to Colonialism in Africa 1895–1914* (London: Macmillan).

Porter, B. (1987) *Britain, Europe and the World, 1830–1986: Delusions of Grandeur* (Boston: Allen & Unwin).

Porter, R. (1973) 'The Industrial Revolution and the rise of the science of geology', in M. Teich and R. Young (eds), *Changing Perspectives in the History of Science* (London: Heinemann).

Porter, R. (1976) 'Charles Lyell and the principles of the history of geology', *British Journal of the History of Science*, 9, 91–103.

Porteus, S.D. (1931) *The Psychology of a Primitive People: A Study of the Australian Aborigine* (London: Arnold).

Potter, M.A. (1902) *Sohrab and Rustem: The Epic Theme of a Combat Between Father and Son. A Study of its Genesis and Use in Literature and Popular Tradition* (London: David Nutt).

Powell, J.P. (1965) 'Some nineteenth-century views on the university curriculum', *History of Education Quarterly*, 5, 102–5.

Price, C.A. (ed.) (1979) *Australian Immigration: A Bibliography and Digest (no. 4)* (Canberra: Australian National University, Department of Demography).

Pufendorf, S. (1688) [1934] *De Jure Naturae Et Gentium* (facsimile) (Oxford: Clarendon Press).

Purcell, B.H. (1893) 'Rites and customs of Australian Aborigines', *Verhandlungen der Berliner Gesellschaft für Anthropologie, Ethnologie und Urgeschichte* (Berlin: Verlag von A. Asher), pp. 286–9.

Pyenson, L. (1990) 'Science and imperialism', in R.C. Olby, G.N. Cantor, J.R.R. Christie and M.J.S. Hodge (eds), *Companion to the History of Modern Science* (London: Routledge), pp. 920–33.

Radcliffe-Brown, A.R. [Brown, A.R.] (1910) 'Marriage and Descent in North Australia', *Man* (o.s.), 10, 55–9.

Radcliffe-Brown, A.R. [Brown, A.R.] (1912a) 'Marriage and descent in North and Central Australia', *Man* (o.s.), 12, 123–4.

Radcliffe-Brown, A.R. [Brown, A.R.] (1912b) 'Beliefs concerning childbirth in some Australian tribes', *Man* (o.s.), 12, 180–2 (no. 96).

Radcliffe-Brown, A.R. [Brown, A.R.] (1913) 'Three tribes of Western Australia', *Journal of the Royal Anthropological Institute*, 43, 143–95.

Radcliffe-Brown, A.R. [not Brown, A.R.] (1922) *The Andaman Islanders: A Study in Social Anthropology* (Cambridge: Cambridge University Press).

Radcliffe-Brown, A.R. [not Brown, A.R.] (1929) 'A further note on Ambryn', *Man*, 29, 50–3 (no. 35).

Radcliffe-Brown, A.R. [not Brown, A.R.] (1930) 'Editorial', *Oceania*, 1, 1–4.

Radcliffe-Brown, A.R. [not Brown, A.R.] (1930–31) 'The social organization of Australian tribes', *Oceania*, 1: 34–63, 206–56, 322–41, 426–56.

Radcliffe-Brown, A.R. [not Brown, A.R.] (1952) *Structure and Function in Primitive Society* (London: Routledge & Kegan Paul).

Rappaport, R. (1982) 'Borrowed words: problems of vocabulary in eighteenth-century geology', *British Journal of the History of Science*, 15, 27–44.

Read, C. (1918) 'No paternity', *Journal of the Royal Anthropological Institute*, 48, 146–54.

Read, P. (1983a) 'The stolen generations' (NSW Ministry of Aboriginal Affairs Occasional Paper No. 1) (Sydney).

Read, P. (1983b) '"A rape of the soul so profound": some reflections on the dispersal policy in NSW', *Aboriginal History*, 7: 1, 23–33.

Read, P. (1984) '"Breaking up these camps entirely": the dispersal policy in Wiradjuri Country, 1909–1929', *Aboriginal History*, 8: 1, 45–62.

Read, P. (1988) *A Hundred Years War: The Wiradjuri People and the State* (Canberra: Australian National University Press).

Reay, M. (1945) 'A Half-Caste Aboriginal community in North-Western New South Wales', *Oceania*, 15, 296–323.

Reay, M. (1951) 'Mixed-blood marriage in North-Western New South Wales: a survey of the marital conditions of 264 Aboriginal and Mixed-Blood women', *Oceania*, 22, 116–29.

Reay, M. and Sitlington, G. (1948) 'Class and status in a Mixed-Blood community (Mooree, NSW)', *Oceania*, 18, 179–207.

Reece, R.H.W. (1974) *Aborigines and Colonists: Aborigines in Colonial Society in NSW in the 1830s and 1840s* (Sydney: Sydney University Press).

Reichenbach, H. (1938) *Experience and Prediction* (Chicago: University of Chicago Press).

Reid, G. (1982) *A Nest of Hornets: The Massacre of the Fraser family at Hornet Bank Station, Central Queensland 1857 and Related Events* (Melbourne: Oxford University Press).

Reid, G. (1990) *A Picnic with the Natives: Aboriginal-European Relations in the Northern Territory to 1910* (Melbourne: Melbourne University Press).

Reinach, S. (1909) *Orpheus: A General History of Religions* (F. Simmonds, tr.) (London: Heinemann).

Rendall, J. (1985) *The Origins of Modern Feminism: Women in Britain, France and the United States, 1780–1860* (London: Macmillan).

Resek, C. (1960) *Lewis Henry Morgan: American Scholar* (Chicago: University of Chicago Press).

Reynolds, H. (1981) *The Other Side of the Frontier: Aboriginal Resistance to the European Invasion of Australia* (Townsville: James Cook University History Department).

Reynolds, H. (1987) *Frontier: Aborigines, Settlers and Land* (Sydney: Allen & Unwin).

Reynolds, H. (comp.) (1989) *Dispossession: Black Australians and White Invaders* (Australian Experience Series) (Sydney: Allen & Unwin).

Reynolds, H. (1990) *With the White People* (Melbourne: Penguin).

Reynolds, H. (1991) *With the White People: The Crucial Role of Aborigines in the Exploration and Development of Australia* (Melbourne: Penguin).

Reynolds, H. (1992) *The Law of the Land* (2nd edn) (Melbourne: Penguin).

Richards, S. (1983) *Philosophy and Sociology of Science: An Introduction* (Oxford: Blackwell).

Ricoeur, P. (1981) 'The model of the text: meaningful action considered as a text', in his *Hermeneutics and the Human Sciences* (Cambridge: Cambridge University Press), pp. 197–221.

Rivers, W.H.R. (1913) 'Survival in sociology', *Sociological Review*, 6: 4 (October 1913), 291–305.

Rivers, W.H.R. (1915) 'Mother-right', in *Encyclopædia of Religion and Ethics* (J. Hastings, ed.), 8, 851–9.

Rivière, P. (1970) 'Introduction' to his (ed.) McLennan (1865) (London: University of Chicago Press), pp. vii–li.

Roberts, A. and Mountford, C.P. (1969) *The Dawn of Time: Australian Aboriginal Myths in Paintings* (Adelaide: Rigby).

Roberts, J.M. (1989) *Europe, 1880–1945* (New York: Longman).

Roberts, M.J.D. (1995) 'Feminism and the state in later Victorian England', *Historical Journal*, 38, 85–110.

Robinson, F. and York, B. (1977) *The Black Resistance: An Introduction to the History of the Aborigines' Struggle against British Colonialism* (Victoria: Widescope Press).

Robinson, K. (1965) *The Dilemmas of Trusteeship: Aspects of British Colonial Policy Between the Wars* (London: Oxford University Press).

Roheim, G. (1925) *Australian Totemism: A Psycho-analytic Study in Anthropology* (London: Allen & Unwin).

Romer, A. (1982) *The Restless Atom* (New York: Dover).

Rosaldo, R. (1989) 'Imperialist nostalgia', in his *Culture and Truth: The Remaking of Social Analysis* (Boston: Beacon), pp. 68–87.

Rose, D.B. (1991) *Hidden Histories: Black Stories from Victoria River Downs, Humbert River and Wave Hill Stations* (Canberra: Aboriginal Studies Press).

Rosen, A. (1974) *Rise Up Women! The Militant Campaign of the Women's Social and Political Union 1903–1914* (Boston: Routledge & Kegan Paul).

Rosser, B. (1978) *This is Palm Island* (Canberra: Australian Institute of Aboriginal Studies).

Rosser, B. (1985) *Dreamtime Nightmares: Biographies of Aborigines under the Queensland Aborigines Act* (Canberra: Australian Institute of Aboriginal Studies).

Rosser, B. (1991) *Up Rode the Troopers: The Black Police in Queensland* (St. Lucia: University of Queensland Press).

Rossi, P. (1984) *The Dark Abyss of Time: The History of the Earth and the History of Nations from Hooke to Vico* (L.G. Cochrane, tr.) (Chicago: University of Chicago Press).

Roth, W.E. (1897) *Ethnological Studies among the North-West-Central Queensland Aborigines* (Brisbane: Government Printer).

Roth, W.E. (1903) 'Superstition, magic and medicine', *North Queensland Ethnography Bulletin* No. 5 (Brisbane: Government Printer (Home Secretary's Department)).

Rothblatt, S. (1976) *Tradition and Change in English Liberal Education: An Essay in History and Culture* (London: Faber & Faber).

Rothblatt, S. (1981) *The Revolution of the Dons: Cambridge and Society in Victorian England* (Cambridge: Cambridge University Press).

Rousseau, G.S. and Porter, R. (eds) (1980) *The Ferment of Knowledge: Studies in the Historiography of Eighteenth-century Science* (Cambridge: Cambridge University Press).

Rover, C. (1967) *Women's Suffrage and Party Politics in Britain 1866–1914* (London: Routledge & Kegan Paul).

Rowland, J. (1955) *Ernest Rutherford: Atom Pioneer* (London: Werner Laurie).

Rowley, C.D. (1970) *The Destruction of Aboriginal Society* (Canberra: Australian National University Press).

Rowley, C.D. (1978) *A Matter of Justice* (Canberra: Australian National University Press).

Rowley, C.D. (1986) *Recovery: The Politics of Aboriginal Reform* (Melbourne: Penguin).

Rowse, T. (1992) 'Top-down tensions: can ATSIC really contribute to Aboriginal self-determination?', *Modern Times* (Australia), June, 22–3.

Rowse, T. (1993a) 'Aboriginal resistance: the example of the Community Employment Development Projects (CDEP) Program', *Oceania*, 63, 268–86.

Rowse, T. (1993b) *After Mabo: Interpreting Indigenous Traditions* (Melbourne: Melbourne University Press).

Rubinstein, D. (1986) *Before the Suffragettes: Women's Emancipation in the 1890s* (Brighton: Harvester).

Rudwick, M.J.S. (1970) 'The strategy of Lyell's *Principles of Geology*', *Isis*, 61, 5–33.

Rudwick, M.J.S. (1979) 'Transposed concepts from the human sciences in the early work of Charles Lyell', in L.J. Jordanova and R.S. Porter (eds), *Images of the Earth: Essays in the History of the Environmental Sciences* (Chalfont St. Giles: British Society for the History of Science), pp. 66–83.

Rueff, J. (1929) *From the Physical to the Social Sciences: Introduction to a Study of Economic and Ethical Theory* (H. Green, tr.) (Baltimore: Johns Hopkins University Press).

Rumsey, A. (1989) 'Language groups in Australian Aboriginal land claims', *Anthropological Forum*, 6, 69–80.

Rupke, N.A. (1983) *The Great Chain of History: William Buckland and the English School of Geology, 1814–1849* (Oxford: Clarendon Press).

Russell, B. (1910) [1973] *The Theory of Logical Types*, in B. Russell, *Essays in Analysis* (D. Lackey, ed.) (London: Allen & Unwin), pp. 215–52.

Russell, B. (1959) 'My philosophical development', *Encounter*, 12: 2, 18–29.

Ryan, L. (1981) *The Aboriginal Tasmanians* (St. Lucia: University of Queensland Press).

Saha, M.D. (1973) 'Foreword' to Ker 1973, v-vii.

Sahlins, M. (1974) *Stone Age Economics* (London: Tavistock).

Sahlins, M. (1977) *The Use and Abuse of Biology: An Anthropological Critique of Sociobiology* (London: Tavistock).

Said, E.W. (1978) *Orientalism* (New York: Routledge).

Sanderson, M. (1975) *The Universities in the Nineteenth Century* (London: Routledge & Kegan Paul).

Sansom, B. (1980) *The Camp at Wallaby Cross* (Canberra: Australian Institute of Aboriginal Studies).

Saul, S.B. (1969) *The Myth of the Great Depression, 1873–1896* (London: Macmillan).

Schaffer, K. (1988) *Women and the Bush: Forces of Desire in the Australian Cultural Tradition* (Melbourne: Cambridge University Press).

Scheffler, H. (1976) Review of 1974 edn of Ashley-Montagu (1937), *American Anthropologist*, 78, 922–3.

Scheick, W.J. (1979) *The Half-Blood: A Cultural Symbol in Nineteenth-Century American Fiction* (Lexington: University of Kentucky Press).

Schmidt, W. (1912–54) *Der Ursprung der Gottesidee: eine historisch-kritische und positive Studie* (11 vols) (Munster: Aschendorftsche Verlagsbuchandlung).

Schmidt, W. (1931) *The Origin and Growth of Religion. Facts and Theories* (H.J. Rose, tr.) (London: Methuen).

Schulze, L. (Rev.) (1891) 'The Aborigines of the Upper and Middle Finke River: their habits and customs with introductory notes on the physical and natural-history features of the country' (J.G.O. Tepper, tr.), *Transactions and Proceedings and Report of the Royal Society of South Australia*, 14: 2, 210–46.

Scott, J.W. (1988) 'Gender: a useful category of historical analysis', in her *Gender and the Politics of History* (New York: Columbia University Press), pp. 28–52.

Secord, J.A. (1986) *Controversy in Victorian Geology: The Cambrian-Silurian Dispute* (Princeton: Princeton University Press).

Semmel, B. (1966) *Imperialism and Social reform: English Social-imperial Thought, 1895–1914* (London: Allen and Unwin).

Shamos, M. (1959) *Great Experiments in Physics* (New York: Dryden).

Shannon, C.B. (1988) *Arthur J. Balfour and Ireland 1874–1922* (Washington DC: Catholic University of America).

Shannon, R. (1974) *The Crisis of Imperialism, 1865–1915* (London: Hart-Davis, MacGibbon).

Shapin, S. (1982) 'History of Science and Its Sociological Reconstructions', *History of Science*, 20, 157–211.

Sharp, L.R. (1952) 'Steel Axes for Stone Age Australians', in E.H. Spicer (ed.), *Human Problems in Technological Change* (New York: Sage), pp. 69–81.

Shaw, G.B. (1898) [1905] *Mrs. Warren's Profession: An Unpleasant Play* (New York: Brentano).

Sidgwick, E. (1992) *Epistemologies of the Closet* (Berkeley: University of California Press).

Singer, C. (1950) *A History of Biology: A General Introduction to the Study of Living Things* (rev. edn) (New York: Henry Schuman).

Smart, C. (1984) *The Ties that Bind: Law, Marriage and the Reproduction of Patriarchal Relations* (London: Routledge & Kegan Paul).

Smith, B. (1985) *European Vision and the South Pacific* (2nd edn) (Sydney: Harper & Row).

Smith, D. (1984) '"That register business": the role of the Land Councils in determining traditional Aboriginal owners', in L.R. Hiatt (ed.), *Aboriginal Landowners*. Sydney (*Oceania* monograph no. 27), pp. 84–103.

Smith, F.B. (1971) 'Ethics and disease in the later nineteenth century: the Contagious Diseases Acts', *Historical Studies* (Melbourne), 15: 57, 118–35.

Smith, H.Q. (1879) 'The "Nimbalda" Tribe (Far North)', in G. Taplin, *The Folklore, Manners, Customs, and Languages of the South Australian Aborigines: gathered from enquiries made by authority of South Australian Government* (Adelaide: Government Printer), pp. 87–9.

Smith, W. Robertson (1880) 'Animal worship and animal tribes among the Arabs and in the Old Testament', *Journal of Philology*, 9, 75–100.

Smith, W. Robertson (1884) 'Sacrifice', in *Encyclopædia Britannica*, 9th edn, vol. 21, 132–8.

Smith, W. Robertson (1885) *Kinship and Marriage in Early Arabia* (Cambridge: Cambridge University Press).

Smith, W. Robertson (1894) [1st edn. 1889] *Lectures on the Religion of the Semites First Series: The Fundamental Institutions* (The Burnett Lectures, 1888–89) (London: Adam & Charles Black).

Smith, W. Robertson (1907) *Kinship and Marriage in Early Arabia* (2nd edn) (London: Adam and Charles Black).

Spencer, H. (1852) 'A theory of population deduced from the general law of animal fertility', *Westminster Review* (n.s.) 1: 2, 468–501.

Spencer, H. (1854) 'Manners and fashions', *Westminster Review*, April, 357–92.

Spencer, H. (1864) *The Principles of Biology* (2 vols) (London: Williams & Norgate).

Spencer, H. (1870a) 'The origin of animal worship, etc.', in *Fortnightly Review*, n.s. vol. 2 (o.s. vol. 13), 535–50.

Spencer, H. (1870b) 'The right to the use of the earth' (Land Reform League Tract No. 1) (Melbourne: Robert Bell).

Spencer, H. (1871) *The Principles of Sociology*, vol. 1 (vol. 6 of *A System of Synthetic Philosophy*) (London: Williams and Norgate).

Spencer, [W.] B. (ed.) (1896a) *Report on the Work of the Horn Scientific Expedition to Central Australia* (London: Dulan).

Spencer, [W.] B. (1896b) *Through Larapinta Land: A Narrative of the Horn Expedition to Central Australia* (Pt. 1 of Spencer 1896a), pp. 1–136.

Spencer, W.B. (1901) *Guide to the Australian Ethnographical Collection in the National Museum of Victoria* (Melbourne: R.S. Brain (Govt. Printer)).

Spencer, W. B. (1904) 'Totemism in Australia', in *Report of the Tenth Meeting of the AAAS* (Dunedin: New Zealand), pp. 376–423.

Spencer, W.B. (1913) *Preliminary Report on the Aboriginals of the Northern Territory* (Northern Territory Bulletin, no. 7) (Melbourne: Australian Ministry of External Affairs (Mullett, Government Printer)).

Spencer, W.B. (1914) *The Native Tribes of the Northern Territory of Australia* (London: Macmillan).

Spencer, W.B. (1921) 'Presidential address' to the 15th (Hobart-Melbourne) Meeting of ANZAAS, 10/1/21 (Melbourne: Mullett (Government Printer)).

Spencer, W.B. (1928) *Wanderings in Wild Australia* (2 vols) (London: Macmillan).

Spencer, W.B. and Gillen, F.J. (1897a) 'An account of the Engwurra or Fire Ceremony of Certain Central Australian Tribes', (Abstract) [read 8 April 1897], *Proceedings of the Royal Society of Victoria*, n.s., vol. 10, pt. 1: 17–28.

Spencer, [W.] B. and Gillen, F.J. (1897b) 'The Engwurra, or Fire Ceremony of Certain Central Australian Tribes', *Nature*, no. 1441, vol. 56, 136–9.

Spencer, [W.] B. and Gillen, F.J. (1898) 'Some remarks on totemism as applied to Australian tribes', in *Journal of the Anthropological Institute*, 28, 275–80.

Spencer, [W.] B. and Gillen, F.J. (1899) *The Native Tribes of Central Australia* (London: Macmillan).

Spencer, [W.] B. and Gillen, F.J. (1904) *The Northern Tribes of Central Australia* (London: Macmillan).

Spencer, [W.] B. and Gillen, F.J. (1912) *Across Australia* (vol. 1) (London: Macmillan).

Spencer, [W.] B. and Gillen, F.J. (1927) *The Arunta* (2 vols) (London: Macmillan).

Spiro, M.E. (1968) 'Virgin birth, parthenogenesis and physiological paternity: an essay in cultural interpretation', *Man* (n.s.) 3, 242–61.

Spivak, G.C. (1988) 'Can the subaltern speak?', in C. Nelson and L. Grossberg (eds), *Marxism and the Interpretation of Culture* (Basingstoke: Macmillan Education), pp. 271–313.

Stanner, W.E.H. (1956) 'The Dreaming', in T.A.G. Hungerford (ed.), *Australian Signpost: An Anthology* (Melbourne: Cheshire), pp. 51–65.

Stanner, W.E.H. (1965) 'Religion, totemism and symbolism', in R.M. Berndt and C.H.

Berndt (eds), *Aboriginal Man in Australia: Essays in Honour of Emeritus Professor A.P. Elkin* (Sydney: Angus & Robertson), pp. 207–37.

Stanner, W.E.H. (1965a) 'Aboriginal territorial organization: estate, range, domain and regime', *Oceania*, 36, 1–26.

Stanner, W.E.H. (1967) 'Reflections on Durkheim and Aboriginal religion', in M. Freedman (ed.), *Social Organization: Essays Presented to Raymond Firth* (London: Cass), pp. 217–40.

Stanner, W.E.H. (1968) [1991] 'The great Australian silence', in his *After the Dreaming* (Crow's Nest, NSW: Australian Broadcasting Corporation), pp. 18–29.

Stanner, W.E.H. (1977) 'The history of indifference thus begins', *Aboriginal History*, 1, 2–26.

Stanner, W.E.H. (1979) *White Man Got No Dreaming* (Canberra: Australian National University Press).

Stanner, W.E.H. and Sheils, H. (eds) (1963) *Australian Aboriginal Studies: A Symposium of Papers Presented at the 1961 Research Conference* (Melbourne: Oxford University Press).

Starcke, C.N. (1889) *The Primitive Family in Its Origin and Development* (The International Scientific Series, vol. 66) (London: Kegan Paul, Trench).

Stern, B.J. (ed.) (1930) 'Selections from the letters of Lorimer Fison and A.W. Howitt to Lewis Henry Morgan', *American Anthropologist*, 32, 257–79, 419–53.

Stirling, E.C. (1896) 'Anthropology', Pt 4 of Spencer (1896a), pp. 1–158.

Stirling, E.C. (1913) 'Called and examined', in 'Progress Report of the Royal Commission on the Aborigines', *Proceedings of the Parliament of South Australia*, 1913, vol. 2, item no. 26, 123–5.

Stocking, G.W., Jr (1968a) *Race, Culture, and Evolution: Essays in the History of Anthropology* (London: Collier-Macmillan).

Stocking, G.W., Jr (1968b) 'On the limits of "presentism" and "historicism" in the historiography of the behavioral sciences', in Stocking (1968a), pp. 1–12.

Stocking, G.W., Jr (1968c) 'The persistence of polygenist thought in post-Darwinian anthropology', in Stocking (1968a), pp. 42–68.

Stocking, G.W., Jr (1968d) 'From physics to ethnology', in Stocking (1968a), pp. 133–60.

Stocking, G.W., Jr (1968e) 'The critique of racial formalism', in Stocking (1968a), pp. 161–94.

Stocking, G.W., Jr (1968f) 'Lamarckianism in American social science, 1810–1915', in Stocking (1968a), pp. 234–69.

Stocking, G.W., Jr (1971) 'Animism in theory and practice: E.B. Tylor's unpublished "Notes on Spiritualism"', *Man* (n.s.) 6, 88–104.

Stocking, G.W., Jr (1983) 'The ethnographer's magic: fieldwork in British anthropology from Tylor to Malinowski', in his *Observers Observed: Essays on Ethnographic Fieldwork* (History of Anthropology, vol. 1) (Madison: University of Wisconsin Press).

Stocking, G.W., Jr (ed.) (1984) *Functionalism Historicized: Essays on British Social Anthropology* (History of Anthropology, vol. 2) (Madison: University of Wisconsin Press).

Stocking, G.W., Jr (1987) *Victorian Anthropology* (New York: Macmillan Free Press).

Stocking, G.W., Jr (ed.) (1991) *Colonial Situations: Essays on the Contextualization of Ethnographic Knowledge* (History of Anthropology, vol. 7) (Madison: University of Wisconsin Press).

Stocking, G.W., Jr (1992) 'Paradigmatic traditions in the history of anthropology', in his *The Ethnographer's Magic and Other Essays in the History of Anthropology* (Madison: University of Wisconsin Press), pp. 342–61.

Stocking, G.W., Jr (1995) *After Tylor: British Social Anthropology 1888–1951* (Madison: University of Wisconsin Press).

Stoler, A.L. (1989) 'Making Empire respectable: the politics of race and sexual morality in 20th-century colonial cultures', *American Ethnologist*, 16: 4, 634–60.

Stoler, A.L. (1995) *Race and the Education of Desire: Foucault's History of Sexuality and the Colonial Order of Things* (Durham, NC: Duke University Press).

Stoler, A.L. (1997) 'Sexual affronts and racial frontiers: European identities and the cultural politics of exclusion in Colonial Southeast Asia', in F. Cooper and A.L. Stoler (eds), *Tensions of Empire: Colonial Cultures in a Bourgeois World* (Berkeley: California University Press), pp. 198–237.

Strachey, R. (1928) *'The Cause': A Short History of the Women's Movement in Great Britain* (London: G. Bell & Sons).

Strehlow, C. (1907) *Die Aranda- und Loritja-Stämme in Zentral-Australien* (Teil 1. *Mythen, sagen und Märchen Des Aranda-Stammes in Zentral Australien*) (Frankfurt: Joseph Baer).

Strehlow, T.G.H. (1947) 'Anthropology and the study of languages' (Presidential Address read before Section F [Anthropology] of ANZAAS, at its Perth Meeting, August).

Strehlow, T.G.H. (1969) *Journey to Horseshoe Bend* (Sydney: Angus & Robertson).

Strehlow, T.G.H. (1978) *Central Australian Religion: Personal Monototemism in a Polytotemic Community* (Australian Association for the Study of Religions, Special Studies in Religions Series, vol. 2) (Adelaide: AASR).

Strehlow, T.G.H. (1991) *Songs of Central Australia* (Sydney: Angus & Robertson).
Sutton, P. (1988) 'Dreamings', in his (ed.), *Dreamings: The Art of Aboriginal Australia* (London: Viking), pp. 13–32.
Swain, T. (1985) 'Interpreting Aboriginal religion: an historical account' (Special Studies in Religions, no. 5) (Adelaide: Australian Association for the Study of Religions).
Swain, T. (1988) 'The ghost of space: reflections on Warlpiri Christian iconography and ritual', in T. Swain and D.B. Rose (eds), *Aboriginal Australians and Christian Missions: Ethnographic and Historical Studies* (Adelaide: Australian Association for the Study of Religions), pp. 452–69.
Swain, T. (1989) 'Dreaming, whites and the Australian landscape: some popular misconceptions', *Journal of Religious History*, 15: 3, 345–50.
Swain, T. (1993) *A Place for Strangers: Towards a History of Australian Aboriginal Being* (Sydney: Cambridge University Press).
Sykes, R. (1989) *Black Majority: An Analysis of 21 Years of Black Australian Experience as Emancipated Australian Citizens* (Melbourne: Hudson).
Tatz, C. (1977) 'Aborigines: political options and strategies', in R. Berndt (ed.), *Aborigines and Change: Australia in the '70s* (Canberra: Australian Institute of Aboriginal Studies), pp. 384–401.
Tatz, C. (1979) *Race Politics in Australia: Aborigines, Politics and the Law* (Armidale, NSW: University of New England Publishing Unit).
Tatz, C. (1982) *Aborigines and Uranium and Other Essays* (Melbourne: Heinemann).
Taussig, M. (1986) *Shamanism, Colonialism and the Wild Man: A study in Terror and Healing* (Chicago: University of Chicago Press).
Teich, M. and Young, R.M. (eds) (1973) *Changing Perspectives in the History of Science: Essays in Honour of Joseph Needham* (London: Heinemann).
Terray, E. (1975) 'Classes and class consciousness in the Abron Kingdom of Gyaman' (A. Bailey, tr.) in M. Bloch (ed.), *Marxist Analyses and Social Anthropology* (London: Malaby Press), pp. 85–136.
Thomas, N. (1994) *Colonialism's Culture: Anthropology, Travel and Government* (Cambridge: Polity).
Thomas, N.W. (1905) 'The religious ideas of the Arunta', *Folk-Lore*, 16, 428–33.
Thomas, N.W. (1908) 'Alcheringa', in J. Hastings (ed.), *Encyclopædia of Religion and Ethics*, vol. 1 (Edinburgh: T. & T. Clark), p. 298.
Thomas, S. (prod.) (1992) *Black Man's Houses* (video) (Melbourne: Open Channel Co-operative).

Thompson, E.P. (1967) 'Time, work-discipline, and industrial capitalism', *Past and Present*, 38, 56–97.
Thompson, S.P. (1910) *The Life of William Thomson, Baron Kelvin of Largs* (2 vols) (London: Macmillan).
Thomson, D.F. (1933) 'The hero-cult, initiation and totemism on Cape York', *Journal of the Royal Anthropological Institute*, 63, 453–537.
Thomson, D.F. (1936) 'Fatherhood in the Wik Monkan Tribe', *American Anthropologist*, 38, 374–93.
Thomson, G.P. (1964) *J.J. Thomson and the Cavendish Laboratory in his Day* (London: Nelson).
Thomson, W. (later Lord Kelvin) (1864) 'On the secular cooling of the earth', *Trans. Edinburgh Royal Society*, 23, 157–70.
Thornton, A.P. (1965) *Doctrines of Imperialism* (New York: Wiley).
Thornton, A.P. (1966) *The Imperial Idea and Its Enemies: A Study in British Power* (New York: Macmillan).
Thornton, R. (1981) 'Evolution, salvation and history in the rise of the ethnographic monograph in Southern Africa, 1860–1920', *Social Dynamics*, 6, 14–23.
Thornton, R. (1983) 'Narrative ethnography in Africa, 1850–1920: the creation and capture of an appropriate domain for anthropology', *Man* (n.s.), 18, 502–20.
Thrift, N. (1990) 'The making of a capitalist time consciousness', in Hassard (1990), pp. 105–29.
Tonkinson, M. (1988) 'Sisterhood or Aboriginal servitude? black women and white women on the Australian frontier', *Aboriginal History*, 12, 27–40.
Tonkinson, R. (1978) 'Semen versus spirit-child in a Western Desert culture', in L.R. Hiatt (ed.), *Australian Aboriginal Concepts* (Canberra: Australian Institute of Aboriginal Studies), pp. 81–92.
Toohey, J. (1978a) [1979] *Borroloola Land Claim* (Canberra: Australian Government Publishing Service).
Toohey, J. (1978b) [1979] *Land Claim by Warlpiri and Kartangarurru-Kurintji* (Canberra: Australian Government Publishing Service).
Toohey, J. (1979a) *Land Claim by Alyawarra and Kaititja* (Canberra: Australian Government Publishing Service).
Toohey, J. (1979b) [1980] *Uluru (Ayers Rock) National Park and Lake Amadeus/Luritja Land Claim* (Canberra: Australian Government Publishing Service).
Torres, G. and Milun, K. (1990) 'Translating Yonnondio by precedent and evidence: the Mashpee Indian case', *Duke Law Journal*, 625–59.
Trachtenberg, A. (1980) 'Introduction' to his (ed.) *Classic Essays on Photography* (New Haven: Leete's Island Books), pp. vii–xiii.

Trautmann, T.R. (1984) 'Decoding Dravidian kinship: Morgan and McIlvaine', *Man* (n.s.), 19, 421–31.

Trautmann, T.R. (1987) *Lewis Henry Morgan and the Invention of Kinship* (Berkeley: California University Press).

Trigger, B.G. (1984) 'Alternative archaeologies: nationalist, colonialist, imperialist', *Man* (n.s.), 19, 355–70.

Trigger, D.S. (1993) 'No place for vague radicalism in cultural studies', *The Australian, Higher Education Supplement*, 20 January.

Tucker, M. (1977) *If Everyone Cared: Autobiography of Margaret Tucker, M.B.E.* (Sydney: Ure Smith).

Turley, D. (1991) *The Culture of English Antislavery, 1780–1860* (London: Routledge).

Turnbull, C. et al. (1949) *Black War: The Extermination of the Tasmanian Aborigines* (Melbourne: Cheshire).

Turnbull, D. (1982) *Phrenology: The First Science of Man* (Waurn Ponds, Victoria, Australia).

Turner, F.M. (1974) *Between Science and Religion: The Reaction to Scientific Naturalism in Late Victorian England* (New Haven: Yale University Press).

Tylor, E.B. (1861) *Anahuac: Or Mexico and the Mexicans, Ancient and Modern* (London: Longman, Green, Longman & Roberts).

Tylor, E.B. (1865) *Researches Into the Early History of Mankind and the Development of Civilization* (London: John Murray).

Tylor, E.B. (1866a) 'The religion of savages', *Fortnightly Review* (o.s.) 4, 71–86.

Tylor, E.B. (1866b) 'On the origin of language', *Fortnightly Review*, (o.s.) 4, 544–59.

Tylor, E.B. (1866c) 'On phenomena of the higher civilization traceable to a rudimental origin among savage tribes', *British Association, Nottingham meeting (1866). Geography and Ethnology Section* (W.T. Robertson, ed.), pp. 97–115.

Tylor, E.B. (1867) 'On traces of the early mental condition of man', in *Notices of the Proceedings at the Meetings of the Members of the Royal Institution of Great Britain with Abstracts of the Discourses Delivered at the Evening Meetings*, vol. 5 (1866–69), pp. 83–93.

Tylor, E.B. (1869) 'On the survival of savage thought in modern civilization', in *Notices of the Proceedings at the Meetings of the Members of the Royal Institution of Great Britain with Abstracts of the Discourses Delivered at the Evening Meetings*, vol. 5 (1866–69), pp. 522–35.

Tylor, E.B. (1871) *Primitive Culture: Researches Into the Development of Mythology, Philosophy, Religion, Art and Custom* (2 vols) (London: John Murray).

Tylor, E.B. (1881) 'Obituary' for J.F. McLennan, *Academy*, 20 (2 July), 9–10.

Tylor, E.B. (1885) 'The patriarchal theory' (Review of McLennan 1885), *Academy*, 28, 67–8.

Tylor, E.B. (1889) 'On a method of investigating the development of institutions: applied to laws of marriage and descent', *Journal of the Anthropological Institute*, 18, 245–72.

Tylor, E.B. (1892) 'On the limits of savage religion', *Journal of the Anthropological Institute*, 21, 283–99.

Tylor, E.B. (1896) 'The matriarchal family system', *The Nineteenth Century*, 40, 81–96.

Tylor, E.B. (1898) 'Remarks on totemism, with especial reference to some modern theories respecting it', *Journal of the Anthropological Institute*, 28, 138–48.

Urry, J. (1979) 'Beyond the frontier: European influences, Aborigines and the concept of "traditional" culture', *Journal of Australian Studies*, 5, 1–16.

Urry, J. (1980) 'Aborigines, history and semantics: a reply', *Journal of Australian Studies*, 6, 68–72.

Urry, J. (1993) *Before Social Anthropology: Essays on the History of British Social Anthropology* (Chur (Switzerland): Harwood Academic Publishers).

van Gennep, A. (1904) *Tabou et Totémisme à Madagascar: Étude descriptive et théorique* (Paris: Ernest Leroux).

van Gennep, A. (1906a) 'Les idées des Australiens sur la conception et la reincarnation', *Mercure de France* (série moderne) 61 (May-June), 204–20.

van Gennep, A. (1906b) *Mythes et Légendes d'Australie: Études d'Ethnographie et de Sociologie* (Paris: Guilmoto, Librairie Orientale et Américaine).

van Gennep, A. (1908) *Totémisme et Méthode Comparative* (Paris: Ernest Leroux).

van Gennep, A. (1909) [1960] *The Rites of Passage* (London: Routledge and Kegan Paul).

van Krieken, R. (1992) *Children and the State: Social Control and the Formation of Australian Child Welfare* (Sydney: Allen & Unwin).

Vattel, E. (1758) [1916] *The Law of Nations.* (Facsimile) (Washington: Carnegie Institute).

Vaux, R. de (1965) *Ancient Israel: Its Life and Institutions* (2 vols) (New York: McGraw-Hill).

Verne, J. (1887) *A Voyage Around the World: Australia* (London: Geo. Routledge).

Verwey, G. (1985) *Psychiatry in an Anthropological and Biomedical Context: Philosophical Presuppositions and Implications of German Psychiatry, 1820–1870* (Boston: Reidel).

Voltaire, F.M.A. (1770) [1967] *Dictionnaire Philosophique* (Paris: Garnier Frères).

Waitz, T. (1863) *Introduction to Anthropology* (J.F. Collingwood, ed.) (London: Longman, Green, Longman & Roberts for the Anthropological Society).

Wake, C.S. (1889) [1967] *The Development of Marriage and Kinship* (R. Needham, ed.) (Chicago: University of Chicago Press).

Walkowitz, J. (1980) *Prostitution and Victorian Society* (Cambridge: Cambridge University Press).

Walsh, K. (1978) *Neuropsychology: A Clinical Approach* (Edinburgh: Churchill Livingstone).

Wanganeen, E. (1986) *Justice Without Prejudice: The Development of the Aboriginal Legal Rights Movement in South Australia* (Underdale, South Australia: S.A. College of Advanced Education).

Ward, W.R. (1965) *Victorian Oxford* (London: Frank Cass).

Warner, W.L. (1937) *A Black Civilization* (New York: Harper).

Warren, H.C. (1921) *A History of Association Psychology* (New York: Scribner).

Weaver, S. (1984) 'Struggles of the Nation-State to Define Ethnicity: Canada and Australia', in G.L. Gold (ed.), *Minorities and Mother-Country Imagery* (Social and Economic Papers, 13) (St. John's: Institute of Social and Economic Research).

Weeks, J. (1981) *Sex, Politics and Society: The Regulation of Sexuality Since 1800* (London: Longman).

Weirick, J. (1989) 'Don't you believe it: critical responses to the new Parliament House', *Transition*, Summer/Autumn, 5, 7–67.

Wells, H.G. (1895) [1931] *The Time Machine: An Invention* (New York: Random House).

Westermarck, E. (1891) *The History of Human Marriage* (London: Macmillan).

Whelan, F. (1991) 'Population and ideology in the Enlightenment', *History of Political Thought*, 12, 35–72.

White, H. (1972) 'The forms of wildness: archaeology of an idea', in E. Dudley and M.E. Novak (eds), *The Wild Man Within: An Image in Western Thought from the Renaissance to Romanticism* (Pittsburgh: University of Pittsburgh Press), pp. 3–38.

White, H. (1989) '"Figuring the nature of the times deceased": literary theory and historical writing', in R. Cohen (ed.), *The Future of Literary Theory* (New York: Routledge), pp. 19–43.

White, L. A. (1957) 'How Morgan came to write *Systems of Consanguinity and Affinity*', *Papers of the Michigan Academy of Science, Arts and Letters*, no. 42.

White, R. (1981) *Inventing Australia: Images and Identity 1688–1980* (Sydney: Allen & Unwin).

Whitney, W.D. (1875) *The Life and Growth of Language* (London: Henry S. King).

Wilken, G.A. (1883) 'Over de Verwantschap en het Huwelijks – en Erfrecht bij de Volken van het Maleische Ras', (*De Indische Gids*, Deel I), *Ve Jaargang*, vol. 4. Leiden, pp. 656–764.

Wilken, G.A. (1884) [1912] 'Het matriarchaat bij de oude Arabieren', in *De Verspreide Geschriften van Prof. Dr. G.A. Wilken*, Deel II: *Geschriften op het gebied van vergelijkende rechtswetenschap* (Ossenbruggen, F.D.E. van ed.) (Soerabaja: G.C.T. Van Dorp), pp. 1–55.

Wilken, G.A. (1921) *The Sociology of Malayan Peoples, Being Three Essays on Kinship, Marriage and Inheritance in Indonesia* (G.A. Hunt, tr.) (Kuala Lumpur: Committee for Malay Studies).

Wilkes, K. (1988) '"External" factors in the development of psychology in the West', in I. Hronszky, M.Fehér and B. Dajka (eds), *Scientific Knowledge Socialized* (Dordrecht: Kluwer Academic Publishers), pp. 265–86.

Wilkinson, L. (1987) 'Fractured families, squatting and poverty: the impact of the 1886 "Half-Caste" Act on the Framlingham Aboriginal Community', in D.D. Kirkby (ed.), *Law and History in Australia*, vol. 4, pp. 1–25.

Willard, M. (1974) *History of the White Australia Policy to 1920* (Melbourne: Melbourne University Press).

Williams, L. (1993) 'The architecture of reform: Richard Dunn's "Surveillance and Punishment" 1988' (catalogue essay) (Melbourne: Faculty of Art and Design, Royal Melbourne Institute of Technology).

Williams, R. (1977) *Marxism and Literature* (Oxford: Oxford University Press).

Williams, R. (1980) *Problems in Materialism and Culture: Selected Essays* (London: Verso).

Williamson, J. (1984) *The Crucible of Race: Black-White Relations in the American South Since Emancipation* (New York: Oxford University Press).

Willshire, W.H. (1888) *The Aborigines of Central Australia, with a vocabulary of the dialect of the Alice Springs natives* (Port Augusta: Dugsdale).

Willshire, W.H. (1896) *The Land of the Dawning: Being Facts Cleaned from Cannibals in the Australian Stone Age* (Adelaide: W.K. Thomas).

Wilson, D. (1851) *The Archaeology and Prehistoric Annals of Scotland, with two hundred illustrations, including six steel engravings, chiefly from drawings by the author* (Edinburgh: Sutherland and Knox).

Wilson, L.G. (1972) *Charles Lyell: The Years to 1841: The Revolution in Geology* (New Haven: Yale University Press).

Wilson, L.G. (1980) 'Geology on the eve of Charles Lyell's First Visit to America', *Proceedings of the American Philosophical Society*, 124, 168–202.

Winstanley, D.A. (1947) *Later Victorian Cambridge* (Cambridge: Cambridge University Press).

Wise, T. (1985) *The Self-Made Anthropologist: A Life of A.P. Elkin* (Sydney: Geo. Allen & Unwin).

Wittgenstein, L. (1955) [1922] *Tractatus Logico-Philosophicus* (London: Routledge & Kegan Paul).

Wittkower, R. (1942) 'Marvels of the East: a study in the history of monsters', *Journal of the Warburg and Courtauld Institutes*, 5, 159–97.

Wolfe, P. (1991) 'On being woken up: the Dreamtime in anthropology and in Australian settler culture', *Comparative Studies in Society and History*, 33, 197–224.

Wolfe, P. (1994) 'Nation and MiscegeNation: discursive continuity in the post-Mabo era', *Social Analysis*, 34, 93–152.

Wolfe, P. (1997a) 'History and imperialism: a century of theory, from Marx to postcolonialism', *American Historical Review*, 102, 388–420.

Wolfe, P. (1997b) 'Should the subaltern dream? "Australian Aborigines" and the problem of ethnographic ventriloquism', in S. Humphreys (ed.), *Cultures of Scholarship* (Ann Arbor: University of Michigan Press), pp. 57–96.

Wolff, C. (1764) [1934] *Jus Gentium* (Oxford: Clarendon).

Woodward, A.E. (1974) *Aboriginal Land Rights Commission: Second Report* (Canberra: Australian Government Publishing Services).

Woolmington, J. (1986) 'The civilisation/Christianisation debate and the Australian Aborigines', *Aboriginal History*, 10: 2, 90–8.

Worsley, P. (1966) 'The end of anthropology?' (mimeo) Sociology and Social Anthropology Working Group, Sixth World Congress of Sociology.

Wright, H.M. (ed.) (1961) *The 'New Imperialism': Analysis of Late Nineteenth-Century Expansion* (Boston: Heath).

Wright, L. (1994) 'One drop of blood', *New Yorker*, 25 July, 46–55.

Wundt, W. (1900) [1916] *Elements of Folk Psychology: Outlines of a Psychological History of the Development of Mankind* (E.L. Schaub, tr.) (London: Geo. Allen & Unwin).

Yarwood, A.T. (1964) *Asian Migration to Australia: The Background to Exclusion, 1896–1923* (Melbourne: Melbourne University Press).

Yarwood, A.T. (ed.) (1968) *Attitudes to Non-European Immigration* (Melbourne: Cassell Australia).

Yengoyan, A. (1970) 'Demographic factors in Pitjandjara social organization', in R.M. Berndt (ed.), *Australian Aboriginal Anthropology: Modern Studies in the Social Anthropology of the Australian Aborigines* (Nedlands: University of Western Australia Press), pp. 70–91.

Yengoyan, A. (1978) 'Copulation, conception and deception in Aboriginal Australia' (review of 1974 edn of Ashley-Montagu 1937), *Annual Review of Anthropology*, 108–15.

Young, R.M. (1965) 'The development of Herbert Spencer's Concept of Evolution', *Congrès International d'Histoire des Sciences*, 11: 1, 273–8.

Young, R.M. (1967) 'Animal soul', in P. Edwards (ed.), *The Encyclopædia of Philosophy*, vol. 1 (New York: Macmillan), pp. 122–7.

Young, R.M. (1971) 'Evolutionary biology and ideology: then and now', *Science Studies*, 1, 177–206.

Young, R.M. (1972) 'The anthropology of science', *New Humanist*, 88, 102–5.

Young, R.M. (1973a) 'The historiographic and ideological contexts of the nineteenth-century debate on man's place in nature', in Teich and Young (1973), 344–438

Young, R.M. (1973b) 'The role of psychology in the nineteenth-century evolutionary debate', in M. Henle, J. Jaynes and J.J. Sullivan (eds), *Historical Conceptions of Psychology* (New York: Springer), pp. 180–204.

Young, R.M. (1985) *Darwin's Metaphor: Nature's Place in Victorian Culture* (Cambridge: Cambridge University Press).

Zika, C. (1994) 'Fashioning new worlds from old fathers: reflections on Saturn, Amerindians and witches in a sixteenth-century print', in D. Merwick (ed.), *Dangerous Liaisons: Essays in Honour of Greg Dening* (Parkville: University of Melbourne History Department) (monograph no. 19), pp. 249–81.

Zika, C. (1997) 'Cannibalism and witchcraft in early modern Europe: reading the visual images', *History Workshop Journal*, 44, 77–105.

Index

Numbers in italics indicate illustrations

Aboriginal and Torres Strait Islanders Commission 204
Aboriginal Land Commission 200
Aboriginal Tent Embassy 199, 205
Aboriginality 176, 178–81, 183, 184, 185, 188, 190, 204–10
Aborigines
  abduction of Indigenous children 11, 176, 177, 180, 183, 188, 209, 213
  assimilation policy *see* assimilationism
  'cultural production' 213
  as a flaw in Australian nationhood 33–4
  matrilineality 84
  Spencer's report 10–11
  Victorian Act 175
abstraction 85
adhesions method 138, 139
aetherialization 121
Africa
  division of 50
  scramble for 53
African Americans 1–2
agnatic system 97, 98
Alcheringa ('dream-times') 20, 127
Alice Springs 22, 23
Alyawarra claim 200
Amazonism 86–7
Amerindians 45
Andean folk cults 109
Anderson, Benedict, *Imagined Communities* 33
androcentrism 192, 200
animal worship 112
animism 12, 15–19, 25, 67, 73, 105, 107, 111, 115, 116, 121, 122, 128, 131, 138, 146, 151
Année Sociologique school 137
anthropology
  Australian history 7
  colonialism 43, 57
  disciplinary context 133–8
  discipline in crisis 197
  politicization 43
  social 83, 106, 114, 137

sociocultural 66, 105, 135, 138, 150
soft science 65
synchronic 190
twentieth-century threat to 155
archaeology 132, 143, 147, 148, 153
Arnhem Land 158
Arunta of Central Australia 24, 34, 35, 103, 161
  conception 6, 9, 10, 21, 23, 109, 123–4, 125
  dispossessed and slaughtered 127–8
  ethnogenetics 9–10
  initiation 38
  myths 126–7
  nescience 10, 19, 20, 23, 25, 102, 104, 110
  patriliny 102–3
  photography 154
  spirit children 21, 102
  totemism 109–10
Asad, Talal 51
Ashley-Montagu, A.M.F. 102
assimilationism 6, 11, 30–36, 39, 40, 168, 169, 175–6, 180, 181, 184, 185, 186, 188–9, 190, 206, 210, 212
'association of ideas' 16, 146
astrology 131, 139, 145–50, 161
atavism 131, 185
Atkinson, Jasper 97
Australia
  Bicentenary 205
  constitutional coup d'état (1975) 199
  emerging nation-state 33, 34
  government policy 167, 177, 184, 202, 205
  independence 50
  land rights 42, 105, 159, 162, 177, 183, 190, 198–200, 202, 205
  landing of the First Fleet 26, 27, 163, 164, 165
  Referendum (1967) 205
  settler-colonial Constitution 205
  settler-colonization first phase (confrontation) 27–8, 29, 168, 175, 181, 184

  second phase (carceration) 28–9, 168
  third phase (assimilation) 31, 168
  see also repressive authenticity
state discourse 209–10
autography 46, 47, 48, 53, 54, 84, 93, 130, 151, 154, 207
Ayers Rock (Uluru) claim 200

Bachelard, Gaston 64
Bachofen, Johann Jakob 12–13, 35, 73, 84–7, 95, 98, 101, 120, 135, 140, 149
  Das Mutterrecht 96
Banks, Sir Joseph 26
Bates, D. 189
Becquerel, Henri 59, 60, 62
behavioural patterns 135
Benedict, Ruth 58
Bentley, Michael 49
Berlin Conference (1885) 50
Berndt, Professor Ronald 158, 177, 178, 190, 199
binarism 206, 209
biology 57, 58, 188
Biskup, P. 166
Blackburn, Justice 177, 199
blood-brotherhood 119, 121, 122
blood-feud 112–13, 117, 118, 119
Boas, Franz 41, 58, 100, 101
Boers 50
Bopp, Franz 133
Borroloola claim 200
Boucher de Perthes, Jacques 131
Bourdieu, P. 129
bourgeois liberalism 48, 49
bourgeoisie 48, 49, 51, 69, 134
Brisbane Games 205
Britain
  domestic adversity 49, 50–51
Brixham caves 131
brotherhood 77, 79, 82, 113
Brougham, Lord 71
Brown, Ambrose Golden 159
Buffon, Comte de 62
Butler, Josephine 70
Butler, Samuel, *Erewhon* 55

Cabral, Amil 1
cannibalism 45, 117, 119, 120, 122, 127, 135

INDEX

'Cape Kaffirs' 170
capitalism 54, 55, 167, 178
Carrodus, J.A. 31
categorical imperative 87
Chamberlain, Joseph 49, 50, 51
children
 abduction of 11, 176, 177, 180, 183, 188, 209, 213
 spirit 21, 102
Christianity 125
circumstantial and cognitive explanations 12, 15, 18, 25, 73, 111, 116, 128
clan, the 191–3, 194
 membership 200, 201
classificatory system 88
Cleland, Professor 176
Clifford, J. and Marcus, G.E.
 Writing Culture 4
Cobbe, Frances 71
Cocks, Paul 64
collective identity 101
colonialism
 and anthropology 43, 57
 and patriarchy 87
colonization
 capitalist 54
 global 25–6
 Torres Strait islands 202
Columbus, Christopher 45, 89–90
Committee for National Reconciliation 205
Commonwealth of Australia 30, 168
'community' control 205
Comte, Auguste 41
Conference on Aboriginal Welfare (Australia 1937) 176, 189
Consanguine Family 90, 94
consanguinity 13, 74–8, 80, 82, 87, 89, 91, 97, 102, 104
 maternal 99, 113
 matrilineal 112
 territoriality 82
Contagious Diseases Acts 14, 70, 72
contiguity 74
contraception 23, 24
convicts 26, 29, 45
Cook, Captain James 12, 26
copartnery 74–7, 79, 80
Coronation Hill case (1991) 202
couvade 138–9, 140, 150
craniometry 46
Critchett, Jan 165
cultural relativism 44, 52
Cunow, Heinrich 100
Curie, Marie 59–60
Curie, Pierre 59, 60
Curr, Edward 28
 The Australian Race 30
Cyclopean family 96, 99, 196
Cyclopean tradition 97

Darwin, Charles 32, 62, 96, 97, 98, 128, 132
 The Origin of Species 96
Darwinism 7, 57, 58, 132, 133
debating-effects 67, 75, 81, 83, 84, 105, 118, 122, 130, 195

descent 100, 138
descriptive system 88
diffusionism 56–7
disease 27, 28
'diseases of language' theory 134
divination 146
divorce 14
Dravidian kinship system *see* Turanian kinship system
Dream-time 20, 55, 127
Du Ponceau, Stephen 89
dual mandates 51
Duerr, Hans Peter 55
Durkheim, Emile 16, 41, 106, 115, 125, 128, 137, 188
dying race 2, 29, 30

earth, age of 61–3
Eastman, George 152
Eddington, Sir Arthur 59
Einstein, Albert 58, 59
Elkin, A.P. 39, 158, 177, 190–91
 The Australian Aborigines: How To Understand Them 158
Elliott-Smith, G. 56
Encyclopædia Britannica 97, 117, 119
endogamy 13
endophagy 120
Engels, Friedrich 83, 87, 88
Engwura ceremonial ground 22
Enlightenment 44, 45, 47, 128
Ensor, R.C.K. 72
Ensor, Robert 51
epistemological slack 55, 66, 103, 111, 124
epistemology 16
ethnocide 11
ethnogenetics 9–10, 161
ethnographic museology 153
ethnography 23, 36, 37, 39, 40, 54, 56, 143, 147, 155, 161
 Arunta 126
 Australian 20
 and imperialism 10, 11
 and photography 152, 158, 159, 160
 and politics 25
 and prehistoric record 35
Eurocentrism 1, 25, 151
European self 46
Evans-Pritchard, Sir Edward 58
evolution 88, 89
evolutionary anthropology 6–7, 10–14, 25, 35, 46, 66, 67, 73, 75, 85, 87, 96, 105, 125, 129, 135, 139, 144, 150, 175
evolutionism 41, 44–5, 47, 48–9, 51, 53, 55–8, 64, 66, 67, 105, 106, 123, 124, 130, 137, 141, 142, 143, 150, 151, 158, 160, 161, 162, 175, 178, 183
evolutionist ethnography 10, 34, 35, 36, 55
Exeter Hall group 170
exogamy 13, 14, 73, 74, 76, 78, 81, 98, 114, 116, 186, 192

Fabian, Johannes 47
family
 and the horde 194–5

and marriage 99–100
 nuclear 196
 patriarchal 12, 97
 site of material production 191, 194, 195
 Victorian bourgeois 69, 83, 136
Fanon, Frantz 1, 3
father-right 85, 91, 100, 101–2, 116, 118, 138
fatherhood
 divine 125
 social 105, 162, 196, 200–201
federation 30, 31
female principle 12, 83, 84, 86
feminism 69, 70
Fernyhough, W.H. 170, 172
fetishism 16, 46, 115, 116, 150
fictional ancestor 114, 115, 116
field photography 151–4
First Fleet 26, 27, 163, 164, 165
Fison, Lorimer 15, 94, 95, 103
folklore 17, 35, 47, 143
Foucault, Michel 64, 210
Frazer, Sir James 21–5, 40, 94, 95, 102–4, 106, 108, 110, 112, 124–7, 158
 The Golden Bough 18, 107, 109, 155
Freud, Sigmund 41
 Totem and Taboo 97
'fringe-camps' 31, 176, 188
'full bloods' 176, 180, 181, 183, 186

Gall, Franz 46, 47
Gallatin, Albert 89
Galton, Francis 138
Gamaraigal 26, 163
Ganowanian tribes 89, 90–91, 93
Garcilaso de la Vega 109
gender 7, 164–5, 200
genealogy 6
genetic arithmetic 185–6, 189
genetics 180
Gennep, Arnold van 21, 47, 102, 108, 141
genocide 1, 28, 39
geology 131, 133, 139
geopolitics 48–57
Germany 50, 57
'ghost theory' 17
Gillen, F.J. 32
 see also Spencer, W.B. and Gillen, F.J.
Gilruth, Administrator 153
Giraud-Telon, Alexis 95
Gnanji 103
Gove land rights case (1971) 177, 198, 199
Grey, George 14, 126
Grimm, Jacob and Wilhelm 133
Group Marriage 90, 94, 103
Guerard, Eugène von, *Natives Chasing Game* 174
Gulf of Carpentaria 22, 23
Gurindjis' walk-off, Wave Hill Station 205

Haeckel, Ernst 46
'half-breeds' 2
'half-caste menace' 30, 181

INDEX

'half-castes' 11, 31, 33, 37, 39, 40, 180, 185–6, *187*
Harkness, B.S. 189, 190
Hartland, E.S. 17–24, 35, 101, 102, 107, 110, 116, 117, 123, 127, 160, 161, 196, 201
The Legend of Perseus 19, 20, 21, 22
Hawke, Bob 202
Hegel, G.W.F. 63
Herodotus 12
hetaerism 86, 87
Hiatt, Les 190, 194, 195
Hindus, post-Vedic 98
Hobsbawm, Eric 49, 69
Holcombe, Lee 71
homicide 27, 32, 33, 34, 169–70, 173
hordes 73, 74, 75, 78, 79, 80, 82, 83, 96, 99–103, 112, 113, 114, 117, 190, 191–2, 194–5
Horn, William 22
Horn Expedition 22, 23, 24, 37, 40, 152–3
Howard, John 211
Howitt, A. 15, 94, 95, 103, 124, 126, 177
Hutton, James 61, 62

'illegitimacy' 14
imperialism 56
  American 53
  capitalist 41, 66
  and domestic adversity 49, 50
  and ethnography 10, 11
  global 10
  rivalries 50
  Western 6
incest 13, 73, 76, 78, 100, 135
India 50, 65
  South 88, 89
Indigenous people
  organized resistance 205, 212
  small demographic minority 211
  split into two groups 175
  and state discourse 209–10
Indirect Rule 49
individualism 85, 88, 97, 101, 151
infanticide, female 13, 73, 95, 99
inheritance 93
initiation *38*, 155, 159, 160
insemination 14, 15, 18
intellectualism 16, 109, 128, 138
Intichiuma ritual 9, 110
Irish Question 49
Iroquois 87–8

Jones, William 133

Kaberry, P. 158
Kakadu 179
Kamilaroi people of New South Wales 15
Kandinsky, Vasily 64
Kant, Immanuel 46, 47
kinship 13, 35, 54, 55, 58, 78, 135, 161, 162, 176, 188, 191
  bilineal 97
  comparative 89
  descriptive 91

female 95, 98
'indurated system' 90
lateral groupings 87
lineal descent groups 87
McLennan's twin criteria 79
male 76, 95, 114
maternal 74, 76, 79, 83
matrilineal 80, 81, 83, 84, 91, 115
patrilineal 97
rise of 75, 78, 79, 80, 112, 113, 114
kinship systems 12, 89, 90, 91, 136, 137, 139, 193, 196
kobong groups 115, 126
Kuklick, Henrika 64

La Capra, Dominick 5
labour
  Aboriginal 29
  African Americans 2
  black 2
  division of 107
  native 30, 163, 202
  red 2
  withdrawal of native 2
Lamarck, Jean 32
Lamarckism 57, 146
Lambroso, Cesar 46
land
  blood and 79, 80, 82, 83, 85, 91, 93, 96, 98, 101, 114, 128, 130, 138
  expropriated from Native (North) Americans 1
  settled in Australia 26, 27
land rights, Australia 42, 105, 159, 162, 177, 183, 190, 198–200, 202, 205
Land Rights (Northern Territory) Act (1976) 190
Lang, Andrew 21, 96–7, 103, 104, 106, 109, 125–6
Latin American *mestizaje* 30
Lattas, Andrew 207
Lefevre, George 71
Lévi-Strauss, Claude 58, 107, 108, 109, 127, 129, 137
  The Elementary Structures of Kinship 137
liberal rationalism 137
liberalism, bourgeois 48, 49
life-tokens 17
Lightfoot, John 61–2
Link-Up 33
Locke, John 45
Long, J.K. 115
Lorimer, Douglas 48
Lowe, Robert 71
Lubbock, J. 13, 96
Lugard, Baron 49
lycanthropy 117
Lyell, Charles 62
Lyotard, J.J. 211

Mabo judgement 26, 163, 202, 203–4
McGrath, Ann 164
McLennan, J.F. 12, 13, 16, 35, 73–85, 87, 88, 91–106, 111, 113, 115–16, 117, 120, 121, 128, 135–41, 149, 161, 192

Primitive Marriage 13, 14, 83, 95, 97, 98, 99, 112, 114, 115, 136, 137
'The Worship of Animals and Plants' 111–12
magic 124, 125
Maine, H.S. 96–9, 128
  Ancient Law 96
male principle 101
Malinowski, Bronislaw 56, 57, 58, 64, 105, 153, 154, 155, 158, 159
Malthus, Thomas 31–2, 46, 57
  An Essay on the Principle of Population 31
marriage 13, 17, 35, 86, 93, 99–100, 140, 192
  by capture 73–4, 78, 80, 81, 83, 99, 111–14, 136, 137, 141
  communal 96
  group *see* Group Marriage
Married Women's Property Act (1882) 14, 69, 94, 104
Marx, Karl 39, 46, 87
materialism 87
maternal principle 82, 114
maternity 84, 85, 89, 104
Mathews, R.H. 177
matriarchy 86
matrifiliation 95
matrilineal kinship systems 12
matrilineal moieties *157*
matrilineal organization 89
matrilineal societies 98
matrilineal tribes 124
matrilineality 13, 69, 77, 84
matriliny 84, 86, 92, 95, 115, 126
matrilocal societies 138
Maudsley, Henry 22, 24
Mauss, Marcel 3
  The Gift 41
Mead, Margaret 58
metaphysics 131–2
Mill, J.S., *The Subjection of Women* 70
Millar, John 14, 25
  Observations Concerning the Distinction of Ranks in Society 12
miscegenation 2, 30, 31, 32, 34, 36, 37, 39, 40–41, 180, 189, 196
missionaries 155, 158
missions 180, 181
monogamy 90, 91, 93
monogenesis 15, 130, 161
Montaigne, Michel de 45, 152
Morgan, L.H. 12, 13, 35, 73, 85, 87–96, 103, 115, 128, 135–9, 161
  Ancient Society 94
  The League of the Iroquois 87
  Systems of Consanguinity and Affinity of the Human Family 94
mother-right 7, 12–15, 19, 20, 25, 67–105, 130, 135, 149, 162
  abandoned 178
  communal family to private property 87–94
  from horde to house in McLennan 73–87

INDEX

married women's property 70–73
negation 101–4
under challenge 95–101
motherhood 83, 86, 101
Müller, Max 89, 133, 134, 135
multiculturalism 168, 209
myth/mythology 55, 126–7, 134, 135, 140, 141, 143, 149, 160, 161
mythography 161

Nairs (Nayars) 76, 77, 79, 80
nation-state 33, 34, 162, 168, 169, 206, 208, 209
National Museum of Victoria 153, 159
nationalism 31, 33, 41
Native Mounted Police 28, 29
Native (North) Americans 90
and African Americans 1–2
animal-named 115
kinship systems 89
source of 89, 90
native title 202–4, 206–7, 211
Native Title Act 163, 203, 211
'needs criterion' 199–200
nescience 11, 12, 14, 16, 34, 36, 37, 66, 79, 83, 159, 184, 196, 201
of agent (paternity uncertain) 15, 25, 102
Arunta 10, 19, 20, 23, 25
and assimilationism 40
dichotomy within 111
matrilineal 80, 89, 99
and 'miscegenation' 39
and primitive promiscuity 74
of principle (insemination unknown) 15, 19, 22, 24, 25, 104, 125
and repressive authenticity 190
and spirit-impregnation 123
and totem-sacrament 123, 125, 127, 161
and totemism 107–10, 127
Neville, A.O., *Australia's Coloured Minority* 187
New Zealand 30, 50
Ngunawal 208
Noble Savage 45, 48, 56, 87, 170
nomadism 45, 84, 120
Northern Territory, Australia
and assimilationist mentality 189
land rights 199
Spencer's report 10–11
Northern Territory (Land Rights) Act (1976) 200, 202
Northern Tribes expedition 153
nuclear physics 63–6

Occidocentrism 1
Oceania (journal) 158, 190
'octoroons' 185, *187*, 189
one-drop rule 2
ontogeny 17, 46
orphism 153–4, 184
Other, the 165
otherness 106, 154, 190

Palmer, Susannah 71
Palmer Gold Fields, Queensland *171*
Pankhurst, Richard 70
parenthood 82
social 102
Parkes, Bessie 71
'part-aboriginal' 32, 34, 35
pastoral settlement 27, 29
pastoralism 45
Pateman, Carol 84
paternal principle 84
paternity 92, 118, 201
certainty 40–41, 74–5
and couvade 138
father-right independent of 102
uncertain 14, 15, 19, 20, 36, 39, 75, 89, 108
Patria Potestas 97, 98, 99
patriarchalism 96, 99
patriarchy 67, 78, 84
and colonialism 87
patrilineal 13, 86
power 97
property-owning 81, 83
patrilineal moieties 157
patrilineal succession 114
patriliny 76, 78, 84, 96, 116
Arunta 102–3, 126
nescient 102
nomadic Semitic tribes 118
patrilocal patriline 91, 93
Pelsart (navigator) 189
People (weekly pictorial) 159
Perry, Sir Thomas Erskine 71
Perry, W.J. 57
Persians 120
Phillips, Captain Arthur 26
philology 89, 133–4, 136, 155, 161
philosophical associationism 140
photography 151–4, 155, 158–60
phrenology 46, 47
phylogeny 17, 89, 208
physics 58, 61, 63, 64, 65
physiology 105
Piddington 158
pidgin 37, 39, 40–41
pin-sticking 145, 147–50, 154, 160
Pitt Rivers Museum, Australia 22, 153
Planck, Max 59
plant worship 112
political organization 91
polyandry 76, 77, 79, 80, 99
adelphic (Tibetan) 76, 77, 80
polygenesis 15, 16, 47, 63, 130, 131
polygyny 98
Polynesia 90, 91, 145, 147
population growth 14, 32, 46, 109
positivism 132
prehistory 35, 46, 136, 138, 142, 143, 148, 149, 160, 161
primal parricide 97
promiscuity 95
male-imposed 86
primal 12, 14, 74, 84, 88, 90, 96, 99, 100, 137

property 91–2
common 77, 78
and consanguinity 78
emergence of 86
McLennan's concept 80, 93
married women's 14, 69, 70–73
matrilineal kinship 91
moveable 91
patriarchal 14, 73, 83, 84, 87, 98
patrilineal 80
women as 103, 104
prostitution 14, 70
psychic unity 15, 16, 130, 161
psychology 46, 47, 132, 150, 151

'quadroons' 11, 185, *187*

Radcliffe-Brown, A.R. 52, 54, 56, 57, 105, 154, 155, 158, 162, 177, 190–200
'The Social Organization of Australian Tribes' 157, 191, 195, 197
radiation 59–62
rain-making 145, 147, 148, 149
Reichenbach, Hans 58
reincarnation 20, 23
relativism 6, 9, 10, 41
anthropological 58
cultural 44, 52
synchronic 44, 45, 48, 52, 53, 55–8, 61, 63, 161, 162, 178, 179, 183
religion
beginning 17
and social improvement 85
as socially determined 106–7
repressive authenticity 163–214
another side of the frontier 166–8
frontier, history and miscegeNation 168–79
inclusion, exclusion and the nation-state 204–12
Radcliffe-Browne's horde 190–204
reserves 181, 199
'half-castes' expelled from 31
and the Victorian Act 180
residence 100, 138
Reynolds, Henry 166
ritual 54, 55, 135, 137, 141, 142, 145, 150, 155, 161, 162, 180
ritual time 198
Rivers, W.H.R. 56
Robertson Smith, William 16, 41, 73, 85, 87, 101, 106, 108–12, 114, 116–23, 125–8, 137
Rodius, Charles 170, *172*
Romans 97, 98, 161
Röntgen, Wilhelm 59
Rosaldo, Renato 208–9
Rose, Deborah Bird 1
Roth, Walter 24
Rowley, C.D. 166
Rowse, Tim 206
Roy, M.N. 49

INDEX

Royal Commission into Aboriginal Deaths in Custody 204–5
Russell, Bertrand 53, 64, 70
Rutherford, Ernest 60–61, 62–3
Rye, Susan 71

sacred principle 120, 122
sacrificial offering 120–21
Saracen camel saga 119, 120, 122
Saussure, Ferdinand de 41, 143
scientism 57
Scottish Enlightenment 45, 128
screening 129, 130, 134–5, 149–50, 156, 158
secession 113
Selborne, 1st Earl of 72
Semitic race 111, 118
Settled Land Act (1882) 72
settler-colonization
 Mabo judgement removes its ideological basis 203–4
 primary object of 163
 see also under Australia
settler-colonizing impulse 39
sexual abuse 27, 164
sexual exploitation 29–30, 32
sexual organization 94
sexual politics 14, 72, 93, 98, 101
sharing of food 118
siblingship 75–6, 79
signification 150
sister-exchange 76, 77
slavery 12, 15, 45–6, 130, 170
Social Darwinism 32, 48
social organization 16, 91, 94, 95, 98, 121, 157, 162
sociology 105
South African 'coloreds' 30
South Australian Museum 177
South Australian Royal Commission on Aborigines 40
Spencer, Herbert 16–17, 32, 41
Spencer, W.B. 177, 184, 201, 213
Spencer, W.B. and Gillen, F.J. 6, 9–11, 14, 15, 19–25, 33, 35, 36–7, 39, 40, 84, 102, 104, 105, 107, 109–10, 125, 126, 127, 130, 153–5, 158–61
 The Native Tribes of Central Australia 22, 23, 24, 37, 38, 94, 152, 156
 The Northern Tribes of Central Australia 22, 23, 24, 37, 152
spirit children 21, 102
spirit conception/impregnation 16, 123, 200, 201
spiritualism 131, 139, 146
Spivak, Gayatri 4
Spurzheim, Johann 46, 47
Stanner, W.E.H. 158, 177, 178, 190, 191, 194, 199
Starcke, C.N. 100
starvation 28
Stern magazine 159
Stirling, E.C. 22, 23, 24, 37, 40–41
Stocking, G.W. Jr 3, 16
stratigraphy 131

Strehlow, Carl 126, 154, 155, 158, 159, 177
 Die Aranda- und Loritja-Stämme in Zentral Australien 156
Strehlow, Frieda 159
Strehlow, Theodor 159, 160
Strehlow Research Foundation 159
structural-functionalism 44, 49, 51–2, 56, 57, 58, 155, 158, 198
structuralism 30, 44
substitution 17, 117, 148
supernatural births 18, 21, 127
superorganic culture 138
superstitious practices 135, 146
Supreme Intelligence 90
survivals concept 7, 35, 67, 128, 129–62
 anthropology in disciplinary context 133–8
 ethnography, texts and history 152–61
 rhetoric and method in Tylor 130–33
 ritual, text and epistemology 141–52
 theory and doctrine 138–41
Sydney Olympic Games 211
synchronic analysis 142–3, 150
synchronic relativism *see under* relativism

Taussig, Michael 207
teleology 87, 167
terra nullius doctrine 26–7, 84, 124, 178, 183, 190, 201–2, 203, 213
territoriality 81, 82, 83, 164, 194
theology 16
Thomson, Donald 158, 177
Thomson, William (Lord Kelvin) 61, 62, 63
Thornton, A.P. 50
Toohey, Justice 200
Torres Strait islands 202
totem centres 192, 193
totem-sacrament 122, 123, 125, 126, 127, 161, 191
totemism 7, 16, 17, 18, 24–5, 67, 100, 103, 105, 106–28, 193
 communion, cannibalism and transcendence 117–23
 conceptional 106, 107
 the concrete, the abstract and totemism 111–17
 matrilineal 100
 and nescience 107, 108, 109, 110, 127
 reclassification of 107
 totemism and/or nescience 123–8
trade unionism 41, 51
transcendence 85, 87, 96, 98, 99, 112, 118
transformationism 17, 18, 117, 123
transmigration 18, 19
tribe, the 193–4
trusteeship 49, 51
Tully River blacks 24
Turanian kinship system 89, 90–91

two-dollar coin 182, 183
Tylor, E.B. 7, 15, 16, 17, 22, 35, 73, 105, 107, 108, 111, 112, 116–17, 121, 128, 130–33, 135–41, 143, 153, 154, 155, 158, 159, 161
 Primitive Culture 16, 131, 155

Umbaia 103
uniformitarianism 62
universalism 47, 48, 140, 143
urethral subincision 22, 23, 24
Ussher, Archbishop 61, 62, 63

Van Diemen's Land 170
Victorian Act (1886) 175, 176, 180, 181
Victorian New Age 131, 137
Victorians
 bourgeois family 69, 83
 preoccupation with origins 133, 134
 sexual practice 14, 25
 sexual repression 15, 84
 Woman Question 68
virilocality, patrilineal 76

Waitz, Theodor 95
Wake, C.S. 99
Wallace, Alfred Russell 32
Warlpiri 191, 208
Warlpiri claim 200
Warner, W.L. 158
Wave Hill Station 205
Weber, Max 119
welfare issue 204, 205–6, 207
West, Cornel 66
Westermarck, Edvard 104
 The History of Human Marriage 99
Western Desert, Australia 208
Western imperialism 6
Western science 6
white convicts 2
'white man's flour' 28, 37, 40–41
Wik judgement 211–12
Wilken, G.A. 13, 99
Williams, Raymond 48
Willshire, W.H. 32–3
witchcraft 17, 45, 146, 148
women's rights 7, 14, 69
women's suffrage 69, 70
Woodward Commission 199, 200
Woodward, Edward 190, 199
World War One 31, 56

X-rays 59, 63
xenography 46, 47, 48, 53, 54, 84, 128, 131, 151, 152, 154, 160, 161, 207

Yirrkala 177, 198–9
Yirrkala bark petition 205
Young, Bob 132

Zadkiel's Almanac 145, 147, 148, 149
Zika, Charles 45
Zulus 145, 147, 148